三　分　一
SAMBUICHI
and the Inland Sea
瀬　戸　内

Hiroshi Sambuichi - Architecture of the Inland Sea

First published in Japan on March 18, 2016
Fourth published on April 20, 2022

Author: Hiroshi Sambuichi

Publisher: Takeshi Ito
                 TOTO Publishing (TOTO LTD.)
                 TOTO Nogizaka Bldg., 2F
                 1-24-3 Minami-Aoyama, Minato-ku
                 Tokyo 107-0062, Japan
                 [Sales] Telephone: +81-3-3402-7138
                         Facsimile : +81-3-3402-7187
                 [Editorial] Telephone: +81-3-3497-1010
                 URL: https://jp.toto.com/publishing

Story and layout: Alex Hummel Lee
Editor: Jens H. Jensen
Printer: Dai-Nippon Printing Co., Ltd.

Except as permitted under copyright law, this book may not be reproduced, in whole or in part, in any form or by any means, including photocopying, scanning, digitizing, or otherwise, without prior permission. Scanning or digitizing this book through a third party, even for personal or home use, is also strictly prohibited.
The list price is indicated on the cover.

ISBN978-4-88706-357-0

三 分 一
SAMBUICHI
and the Inland Sea
瀬 戸 内

風　水　太陽　月　地形
KAZE　MIZU　TAIYO　TSUKI　CHIKEI

ここに収められている写真やスケッチは、
三分一自らが行なった、
それぞれの地域や集落の風や水、太陽などの「動く素材」についての
発見・調査・研究の記録です。

三分一はプロジェクトが始まると、
敷地に赴き最低1年をかけて春夏秋冬の
「動く素材」と地形を観察します。
本書の写真は10万枚ほどのアーカイブから選んだ記録の一部です。

――――――――――

*The photos and sketches in this book are a record of
the rigorous research process Sambuichi undertakes
when working on a new site. At a minimum,
this research phase lasts one year.*

*The small selection of photos represented here
comes out of an archive of more than 100.000 images,
all taken by Sambuichi and his staff unless otherwise stated.*

プロジェクト

- 17　**宮島** / 宮島弥山展望台
- 65　**六甲** / 六甲枝垂れ
- 113　**犬島** / 犬島精錬所美術館
- 163　**直島** / 直島プラン / 直島の家またべえ / 直島ホール
- 253　**広島** / おりづるタワー

エッセイ

- 11　**地域固有種としての建築の種子** / アレックス・ホメル・リー
- 59　**大地を建てる** / ミニック・ロージング
- 107　**ウッツォンの後継者** / モーエンス・プリップ＝ブース
- 157　**在るものを活かし、無いものを創る** / 福武總一郎
- 245　**地球、あるいは瀬戸内海** / 千代章一郎

PROJECTS

Miyajima Misen Observatory / **Miyajima** 17

Rokko Observatory / **Rokko** 65

Inujima Seirensho Art Museum / **Inujima** 113

The Naoshima Plan / House in Naoshima - Matabe / Naoshima Hall / **Naoshima** 163

Hiroshima Orizuru Tower / **Hiroshima** 253

ESSAYS

Alex Hummel Lee / **Seeds of an endemic architecture** 13

Minik Rosing / **Building ground** 61

Mogens Prip-Buus / **Succeeding Utzon** 110

Soichiro Fukutake / **Use what exists to create what is to be** 159

Shoichiro Sendai / **The Earth, or the Seto Inland Sea** 248

私の建築の理想は、その姿形を見れば、
その地域や集落の風や水・太陽などの
動く素材が見えてくることです。
例えば嚴島神社の境内で瀬戸内海の
干潮や満潮の潮の動きを感じるような。
それが私の建築家としての挑戦です。

三分一博志

"In an ideal architecture, if one looks at its form,

the moving materials of the area or village, such as

the wind, water, and sun, will become visible.

For example, in the Itsukushima Shrine precinct,

the movement of the Seto Inland Sea

between low tide and high tide may be sensed.

This is the challenge for me as an architect."

Hiroshi Sambuichi

地域固有種としての建築の種子
アレックス・ホメル・リー／建築家

場所に固有な建築とは何か。かつてこんなことは、考えるまでもないナンセンスな問いとして片付けられてきたが、過去数世紀の間に技術的進歩が驚くほどに加速化するのに合わせ、建築言語もますます普遍化の一途を辿るようになると、この問題は改めて喫緊の関心事となったのである。こうして建築家たちは、さまざまな装いのもとに数えきれないほどの地域主義のコンセプトを考え出すことになる。それらは、時に道徳的なエートスをまとい、あるいは自然主義的なパトスを帯び、あるいは政治的議題に染まり、あるいは商業的誘因に主導されるという具合に、さまざまな相貌を見せる。だが、それらはどんな形にせよ、地域固有の伝統的工法だけで成り立っていた世界が崩壊しつつある時代にあって、場所との結び付きを何とか取り戻そうとする試みとして、明確に打ち出されたコンセプトであることに変わりはない。失われた特質を取り戻そうとする際の方法論には、ふたつの対照的なアプローチがあり得る。ひとつは、現実を計量可能なものと見て、技術的側面から最適化を図ろうとするやり方である。これは、有無を言わさぬ計算能力に物を言わせて建築をつくり出そうというものだ。もうひとつは、地霊（ゲニウス・ロキ）の概念に導かれて建築的直観を働かせるというやり方である。霊感的な才能に恵まれ、風土と一体化した建築家あれば、こうした直観によって土地の精霊という、捉えどころがなく、それでいて不変不滅とされる存在を捕まえることができるというわけである。

三分一博志の場合、そのどれとも異なり、場所とは、絶えず運動する物質がダイナミックにつくり出す形状のことである。物質は、さまざまな速度、密度、方向性をもって変異し、互いに関係を結ぶことで、立地の条件をつくり出す。場所が非時間的概念であるのに対し、立地とは、一点を時間と空間の両方から、しかもエネルギーの運動をも加味した上で、理解したものにほかならない。これは三分一の用語では、「エナジースケープ」と呼ばれ、この観点からすれば、場所とは複数の力が交錯するダイアグラムにほかならない。こうした諸力は、地球の物質を通じて、それも物質の三態（固体、液体、気体）すべてを通じて現れるのである。

三分一は自らの建築作品を地球のディテールであり、地球の現象のひとつであるとみなすことで、建築物と自然のランドスケープとの境界を曖昧にする。彼の考える建築素材には、空気、水、光をはじめとして、彼の言う無数の「動く素材」が含まれ、これに対比する形で相対的に動かない素材というものがある。両者は相互的に働きかけあい、動かない素材が動く素材を方向付けるとすれば、逆に動く素材は動かない素材の形をつくり変える。たとえば、河床が水流を方向付けるのに対し、川筋は水流によって削られ、形が変わっていくように。こうして、実際にすべての物質は運動しているが、環境を形成する決め手となるのは、物質それぞれの運動の違いなのである。

地球上のさまざまな運動にとって、太陽は生命を活動させる素材である。土や水のような素材と異なり、太陽の放射は大気の還流を生み出し、風を発生させる。同じく太陽の放射熱によって引き起こされる海水蒸発により、風は気体となった水を山頂にまで運ぶことができる。そこで再び水は、液体の形態に凝縮された後、地球の重力と大地の形状

に導かれて、ゆっくりと戻りの道筋を自ら形成しながら大洋へと戻ってゆく。その途上で、水は大地の生命に糧をもたらすのである。

速度、密度、方向性の異なるさまざまな要素の関連から無数の立地条件が生まれ、そうした条件同士の入り組んだ複雑な作用がエナジースケープの特徴を形づくる。こうした特徴を読むには霊的洞察力ではなく、物理学的知識に裏打ちされた鋭い直観に基づく厳格な感性的閃きが必要である。ということは、三分一にとって、ひとつのエナジースケープを初期調査するにしても、そのスケープの現象的相貌のすべてを観察してからでないと完了しないことになる。それは四季のすべてを通じての変化を見るということを意味するから、調査には少なくとも１年は掛かることになる。

建築はまた、用途、つまり人間と関わる要素、一般的には機能と呼ばれるものに常に奉仕するものである。機能の概念には、しばしば、フォルムと空間に関する確立した観念、あるいはこうであって欲しいという願望的観念に基づくタイポロジーを伴う。ところが、三分一がまず初めに行うのは、建物の外観を構想することでなく、機能に最適な条件を考えることなのである。無数にある条件のうちでもとりわけ、温度、光、湿度という感覚が空間それぞれの特質を決定し、それによってその空間はそれ自体において立地に固有のエナジースケープとなる。手近な素材からこうした条件をつくり出すことが、そのまま建物の内部へ、外へ、周囲へというように素材のフローを方向付ける作業となる。例えば、光に対しては、開口部を与える、反射させる、あるいは遮る。風には、入り口を与える、通り道をつくる、あるいはそらす。水には、そのまま引き込む、内部を貫流させる、あるいは堰き止める、といった具合だ。

エナジースケープをつくる動く素材を使ってそれを意図された機能に適合するように建築の構成条件にしてゆくやり方を、自然の応用と見ることもできよう。そして、三分一にとっては、そうした条件は、自然界の成長にも似たプロセスの中で生み出される。すなわち、それは恒常的な実験の反復の中で成長してゆき、最終的には自然界での解決法に近似したやり方で解決されるのである。本質的に、三分一は建築というものを植物とみなしており、それは厳格な実験を通して自らの素材と形状を発見してゆくものなのである。こうした発生論的な自然応用の方法は、三分一の建築の核を成す。素材のフローの構成こそが、作品のフォルムと空間を決めるのであり、その意味において建築が地球のディテールであるという概念はよく理解されるのである。その方法は自然の美学でも生物模倣的テクノロジーでもない。むしろ、地球の自然現象の一部なのだ。こうして、フォルムと空間は、それ自体が目的ではなく、ひとつの条件を獲得するための手段となるのである。

歴史的には、もちろんこれは特に目新しいアプローチとは言えない。いわゆる原始的な建築物、あるいは動物の構築物にとってさえ、場所の固有性や持続可能性は、建築の明確な質的特徴というより、むしろ、建物の欠くべからざる土台である。その場所の一部として全体の中に組み込まれたこうした建築物は、風土に特有な種として風土の構成条件と必然的に結ばれており、そうした構築物にとって装飾は本質的に贅沢なアクセサリーにすぎない。一見永遠に続くようにも見える安っぽいエネルギーの流れとともに、今や侵略的な生物種にも似た建築が繁殖しており、それらは東京でもコペンハーゲンでもほとんど同じような形をしている。こうした建築を支えるエネルギーは、途切れることなく都市の静脈へと廃棄され、建物とは離れた所にある供給源から新たな流れを補給する。今やこうした建築は、時に建物丸ご

と装飾的外観を呈することもあり得るが、そうなると持続可能性や場所特有の個性を追求する戦略といった、建築家にとって優先的に取り組むべきものが、任意の選択肢でしかなくなってしまう。

三分一博志は自らの建築を、建築の新たな地域固有種というコンセプトとして提示する。発想の出発点こそ、はるか過去の建築家たちと似通っているかもしれないが、その作品は反動的なものではない。むしろそれは、地域固有の工法を現代的に再解釈してみせた実例なのである。それが魅力的なのは、新たな美的マニフェストを信奉しているからではなく、植物のように、自ら生き延びるためにユーザーにとって魅力あるものにならなければならないからである。しかも、彼の作品は瀬戸内海とその周囲に位置していながら、作品そのものの重要性は個々の作品が置かれた政治的、気候的、あるいは地理学的な違いを超えている。なぜなら、植物の成長原理を応用するという出発点はどの場所においても変わらないからだ。作品はどれもがユニークだ。だが、ユニークなのは溢れんばかりの芸術的天才によって構想されたからと一義的に決めつけるわけにはいかない。むしろそれらは、与えられたエナジースケープとそれを構成する動く素材に対する三分一の読解から自然に成長したものなのである。作品が他に真似のできない独自なものであるのは、作品そのものが固有の立地条件と内的に深く一体化したものだからである。このようにして作品は地域性を獲得するのだが、その地域性はあらかじめ意図されたものでも、はっきり言明された目的でもなく、むしろ立地を自然の成長原理の応用によって地球のディテールへと発展させるというコンセプトから生まれた産物なのである。

そこで、筆者としては、まずは本書を楽しんで読んでいただきたいというのはもちろんであるが、それだけでなく本書を読むことで自ら外へ出て、こうした作品の数々を実地に体験したいと思っていただければと願うのである。というのも、読者は続くページを繰りながら楽しいひとときを過ごすだろうし、たぶんエキゾチックな別世界に感嘆の目を見張ることだろう。しかし、ここにある建築の目的をとことん感得するには、しばしのあいだ目を閉じ、盲目の状態でそれを感じ取る必要がある。感覚で把握しなければならないような建築を本にするぐらい紛らわしい、厄介な作業はないが、だからこそ、最後にどんな建築家にも勧めることのできる、常に適切なアドバイスで締めくくることにしよう。

旅に出よ！

SEEDS OF AN ENDEMIC ARCHITECTURE

Alex Hummel Lee, architect

What is an architecture of place? Once it was a nonsensical question, but with the staggering acceleration of advantageous developments in human technology during the latest centuries, it has become an urgent concern in the ever more universal language of architecture. Architects have devised countless concepts of regionalism in various guises, some imbued with moral ethos, naturalist pathos, political agendas or business incentives, but all explicitly proposed as attempts to regain an architectural connection to place in times when the tectonic integrity of situated architecture was dissolving. In the efforts at recovering this lost quality, two prominent methodologies can be contrasted: One, an approach of engineered optimization, based on a measurable reality, formulating architecture empowered by the unchallenged calculating prowess of machines. The other, an approach of the architectural intuition going by an idea of a genius loci, with which the spiritually gifted and attuned architect can grasp an elusive but immortal and presumably changeless spirit of a place.

Differently for Hiroshi Sambuichi, a place is a dynamic configuration of materials in unceasing motion. Their variations and relations in velocities, densities and directions define the conditions of a situation. Whereas a place is a timeless concept, a situation is an understanding of a point in both space and time, adding to the equation the movements of energies. This is in Sambuichi's terms the energyscape, and to this places are but diagrams of forces. These forces manifest themselves through the materials of Earth in all three states of matter.

Sambuichi considers his works of architecture as details of Earth and its phenomena, blurring the distinction between the built and the natural landscapes. His ideas of architectural materials include air, water, light, and a myriad other that he calls "moving materials", contrasting them with the comparatively inert materials that serve to direct their movements. Yet mutually, moving materials shape the inert materials, like a riverbed directs the flow of the water, yet its path is carved out by the current. Thus, in reality all materials move, but it is their differences in movement that shape the environment.

For the movements on Earth, the Sun is a vital actuating material. With the differences of materials such as soil and water, the radiation of the Sun creates convections of the air, giving birth to the winds. By evaporation of the oceans, also caused by the Sun, winds can carry water to the top of mountains. Condensing again to its liquid form, the water is then led by gravity and the formations of Earth, slowly shaping its returning path to the ocean, in its way giving nourishment to life on land.

From these relations of velocities, densities and directions spring an infinite number of situations, and their intricate workings are the characteristics of the energyscapes. Reading them does not require spiritual insight, but a rigorous sensible awareness empowered by a keen intuition grounded in physics. It follows, that for Sambuichi, the initial investigations of an energyscape are not concluded before all its phenomena have been observed. And so, it will take at least a year, as it means to observe the changes through all seasons.

Architecture also invariably serves a purpose, a relation to the human, generally described as a function. Concepts of functions often entail a typology with established notions or aspirations of form and space. Yet rather than envisioning an appearance, Sambuichi initially considers the conditions optimal to the function. Sensations of temperature, light and humidity among numerous others define the properties of the spaces that in themselves become situated energyscapes. Making such a condition from the materials at hand means to direct material flow, into, out of or around the architecture. To give openings for light, to reflect it or to block it. To give ingress for wind, to lead it or to evade it. To let water in, to let it through, or to shutter it out.

Such constructions of conditions, using the moving materials of the energyscape to accommodate the intended function, we may liken to the adaptations of nature. And for Sambuichi, they are worked out through a process that seems akin to natural growth, developed through constant iterations of experiments, eventually concluding with an approximation of a natural solution. In essence, Sambuichi considers architecture as a plant, and it is through the rigorous experimentation that it finds its materials and their shapes. These emerging adaptations are the core of Sambuichi's architecture. It is the composition of material flows that define the forms and spaces of his works, and it is in this sense that his concept of Earth details are to be understood. Not as natural aesthetics or biomimetic technologies, but as integral parts of the natural phenomena of Earth. Thus, form and space are not ends to themselves, but means to attain a condition.

Historically, of cours, this is not a novel approach. For the so-called primitive architecture or even animal architecture, place specificity or sustainability are not defined qualities of architecture, they are the indispensable fundament of building. Integral to its place, such architecture is of necessity bound to its situation as an endemic species, to which ornaments are essentially expendable accessory. However, human architecture has eventually been enabled to liberate itself from the shackles of its situation, relegating those once fundamental techniques of adaptation to those symbols of expendable accessory. With seemingly eternal streams of cheap energy, architecture similar to invasive species have proliferated, nearly identical whether in Tokyo or in Copenhagen. The energy on which they are predicated being delivered in continuous intravenous supplies flowing from remote sources. Such an architecture has in its entirety been able to attain the character of ornament, making sustainability and place specificity optional strategies for the architect to tackle preferentially.

Hiroshi Sambuichi formulates his work as the conception of new endemic species of architecture. Although his point of departure may be similar to builders of the distant past, his work is not reactionary, rather it is an embodiment of reconsidered situated tectonics. It is appealing, not because it adheres to an aesthetic manifesto, but because like a plant, in order to live it must be attractive to its users. And though his works are situated in the Setouchi area, they are relevant beyond their political, climatic or geologic denominations, for their point of departure concerning the principles of adaptation are the same anywhere. They are each unique, but they cannot be defined exclusively as products conceived by an overflowing artistic genius, rather they grow from Sambuichi's reading of a given energyscape and its moving materials. They are inimitable because they are intimately integrated with their situation. Thus they gain a regionality, not as an intended or stated purpose but as a result of their conception as situated adaptations into the details of Earth.

And though I hope that you may enjoy this book, I also hope that it will arouse you to go out and experience these works by yourself. For although you may be entertained by flipping through the following pages, perhaps marvelling at an exotic otherworldliness, in order to thoroughly appreciate the purpose of this architecture you must for a while close your eyes and sense it blindly. It is a nearly delusive challenge to make a book about architecture that must in reality be sensed, but it leaves me with the always relevant and urging advice to any architect:

Go travel!

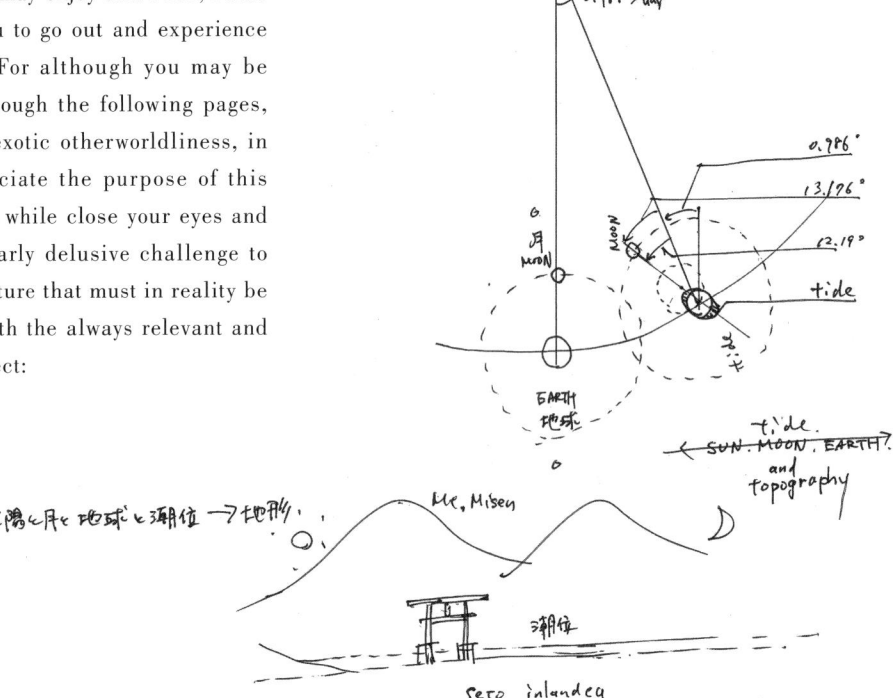

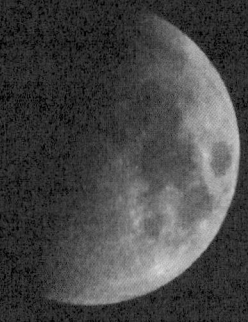

宮島

MIYAJIMA

月
MOON

嚴島神社の風景は、いにしえから月と共にある。

Unchanged for a thousand years, the landscape of the Itsukushima Shrine on Miyajima island has been defined by the Moon.

およそ6時間おきに訪れる水の変化は、嚴島神社を最も美しくみせる。

In the six hour interval of ebb and flow, the scenery changes dramatically.

21

社殿の床のラインが、自然の動きを美しくみせている。

The movements of the sea can be traced from the height of the shrine floors.

月と地球が創りだす海の干満を世界で最も美しく見せてくれているのが嚴島神社である。いにしえの人びとは、この自然の偉大さをよく理解していた。そして自然を味方にすることこそが人びとを引きつける力となり、さらに地がまとまることへとつながると考えていた。

The most beautiful display of the tides created by the Earth and the Moon can be experienced at the Itsukushima Shrine. Our ancestors had a thorough understanding of the greatness and movements of nature and used this knowledge to its full in the design of the shrine.

海抜0mから弥山山頂535mまで、水の変化が宮島そのものを創りだしている。弥山を登る時、標高によって植生が変化することに気が付くだろう。低い標高ではモミの林、中腹では原始林が最も豊かな表情を見せ、山頂付近に近付くにつれて乾燥したランドスケープになっていく。それらの変化は山の水の流れへの適応によってもたらされる。

From the ocean surface at zero metres to the peak at 535m, Miyajima is defined by the changes of water. Climbing Mount Misen on the island one may notice that vegetation changes with altitude. Fir forest at low altitudes and a more varied growth higher up. At the summit, the landscape turns completely dry. These differences are brought about due to the difference in water flow of the mountain.

石の門をくぐると、神が鎮座するといわれる山頂の磐座へと導かれる。

Passing through a natural stone gate one arrives at the *iwakura*, said to be the seat of the sacred spirits.

南側は神が鎮座する磐座。

From the summit, looking south - the *iwakura*.

南から東側は、瀬戸の海が広がる。南から西側は弥山原始林と大野の瀬戸の静かな水面が見える。

To the east, the Seto Inland Sea spreads out. To the west, the primeval forest of Miyajima and the calm waters of the Oono Seto strait.

北側の入江には厳島の社。自然の猛威から守られた、穏やかな水の美しさがみえる。人びとにとって、いにしえからこの山頂に「座」することは、自然なことであった。

In the cove to the north the Itsukushima Shrine can be seen. Sheltered from natural ravages, the wonders of water can be quietly observed, so it was natural that people would come to sit on the peak.

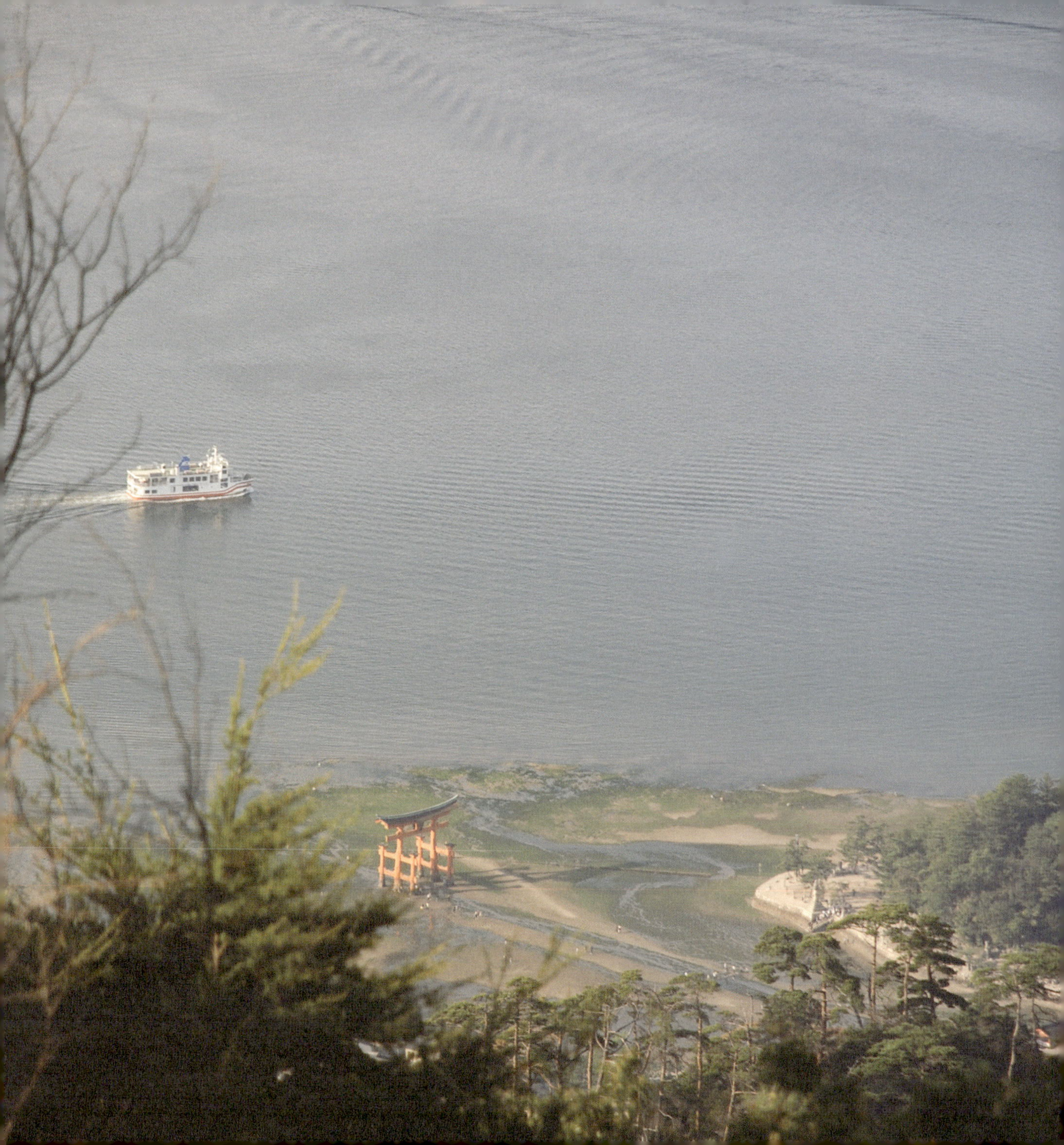

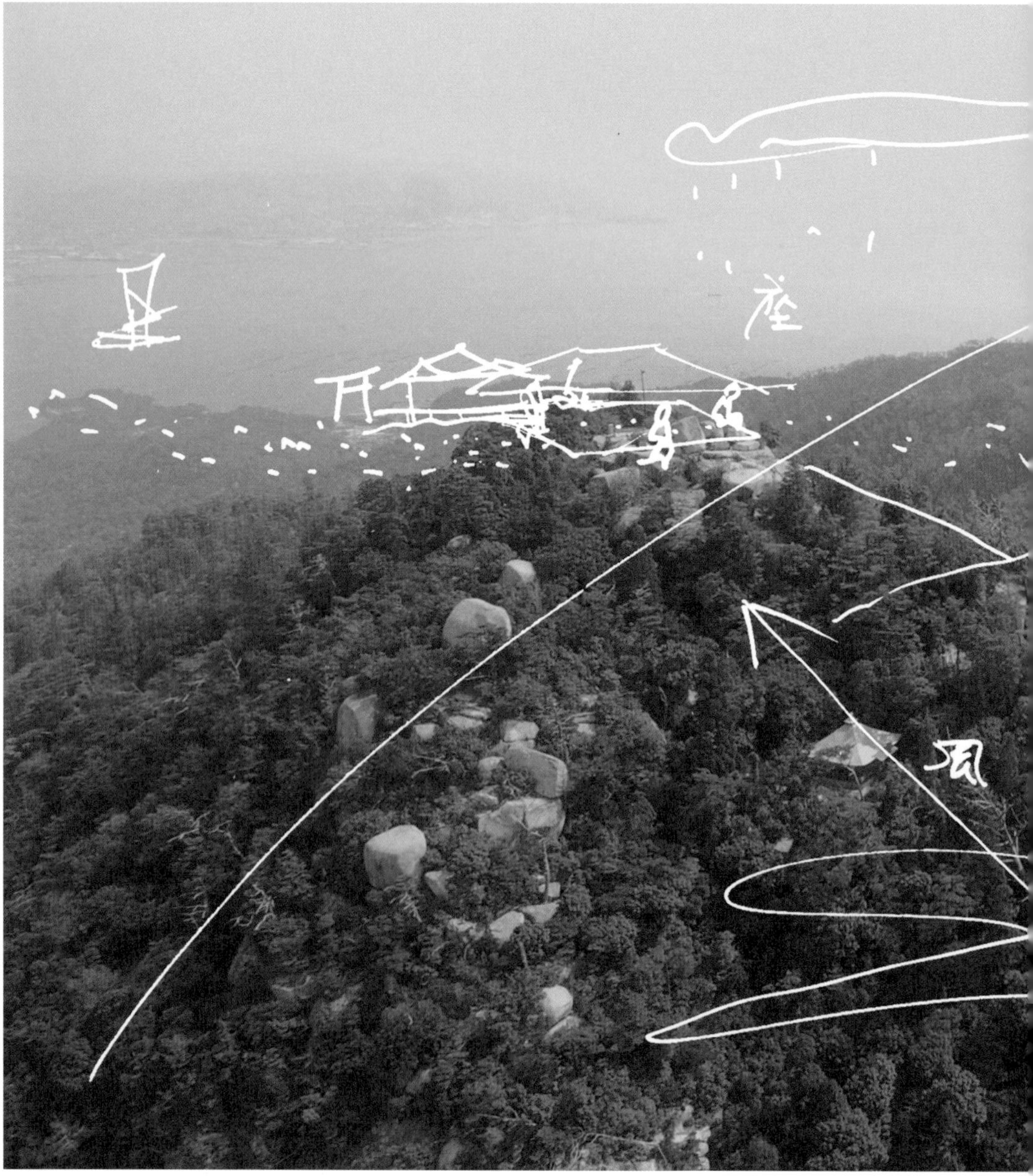
風

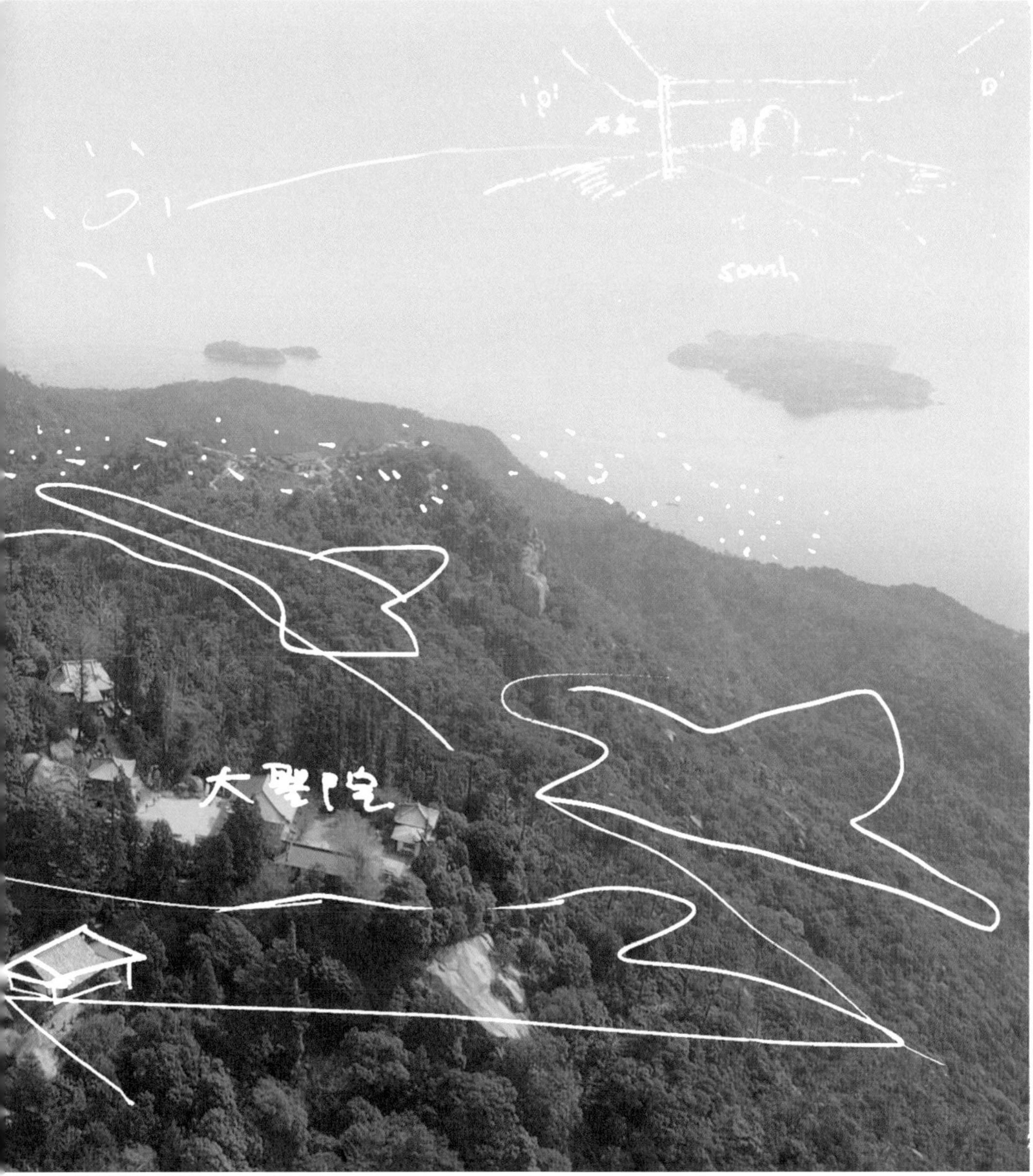
south
大聖院

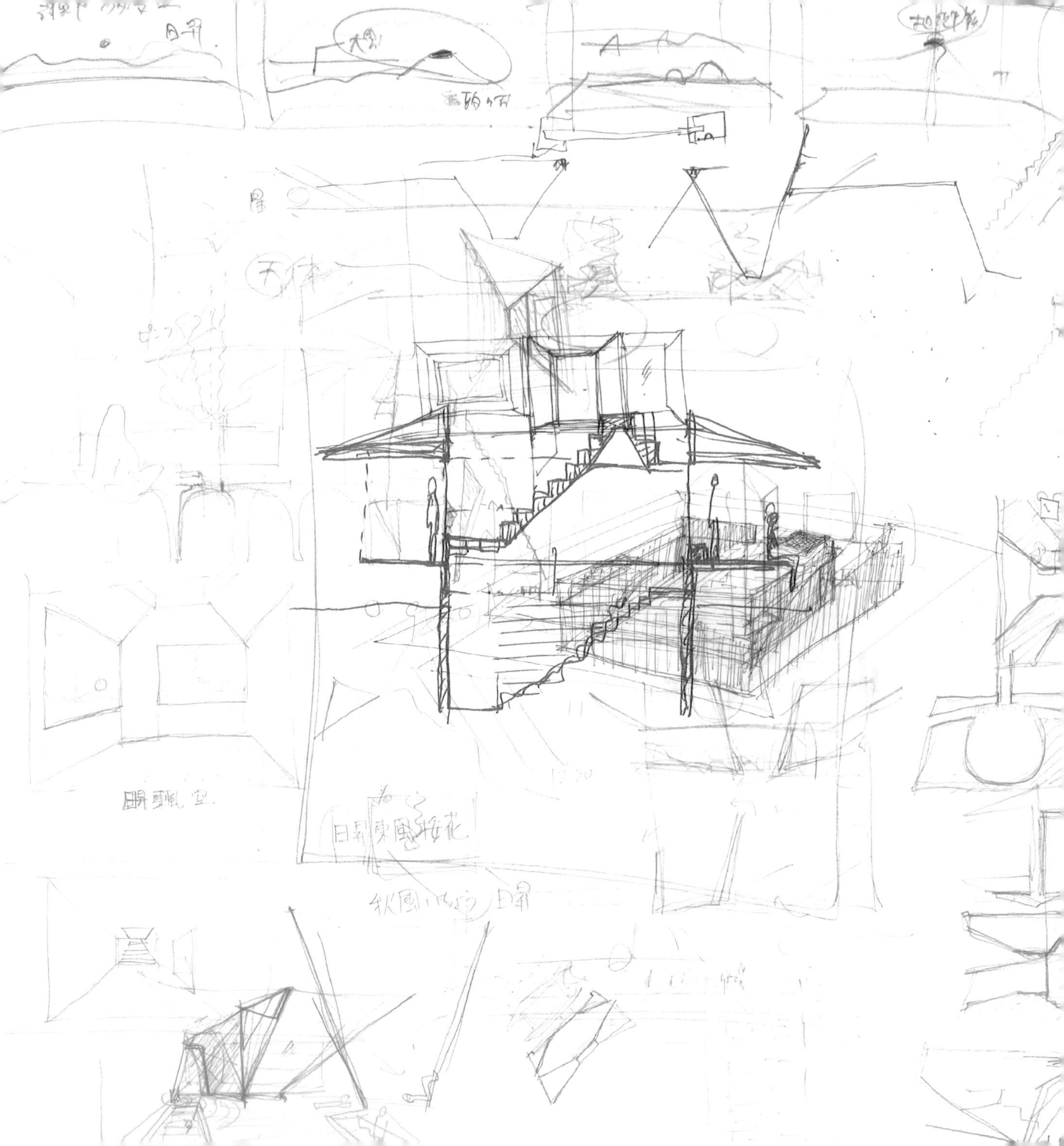

日昇東風桜花

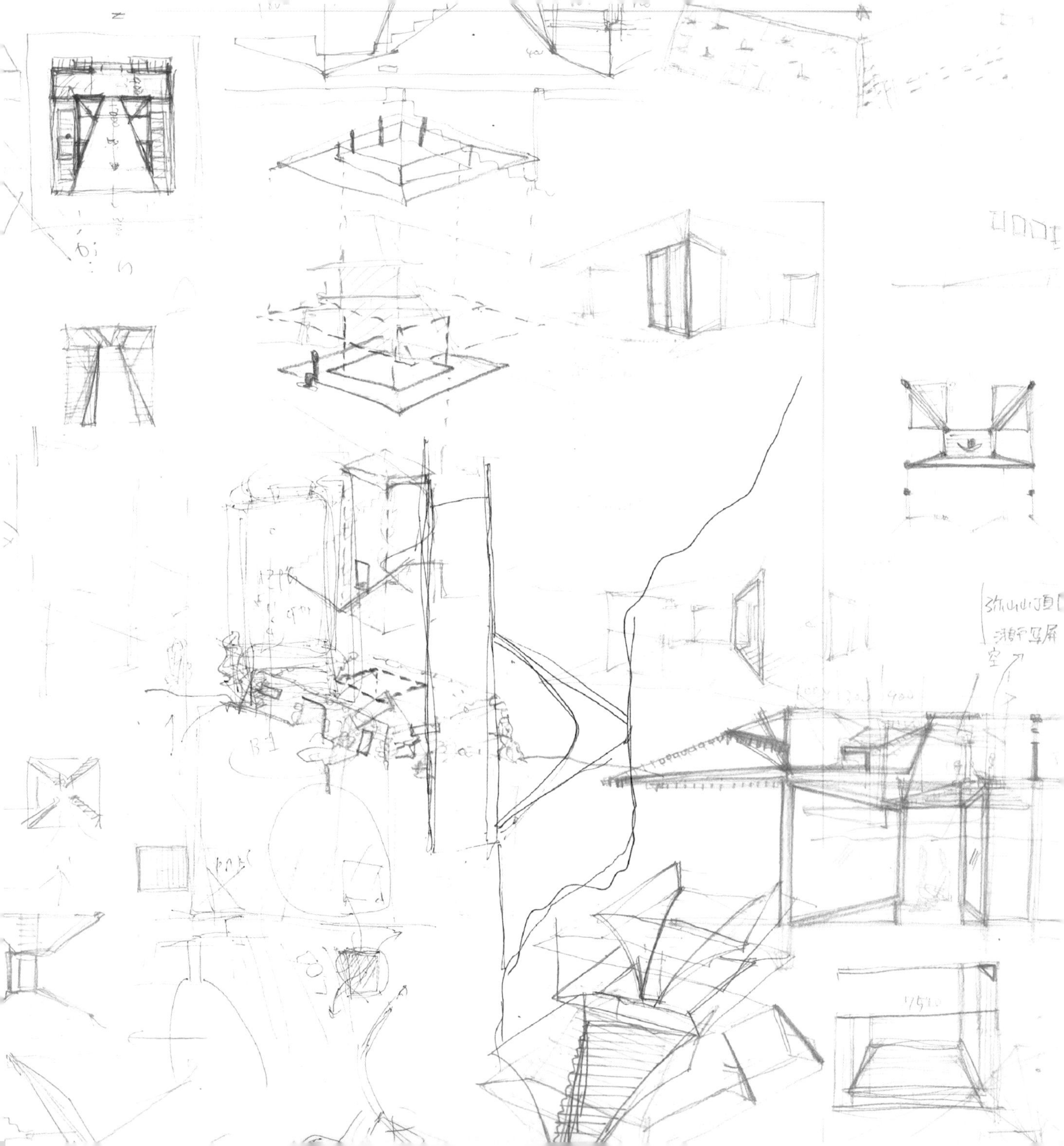
弥山山頂
空

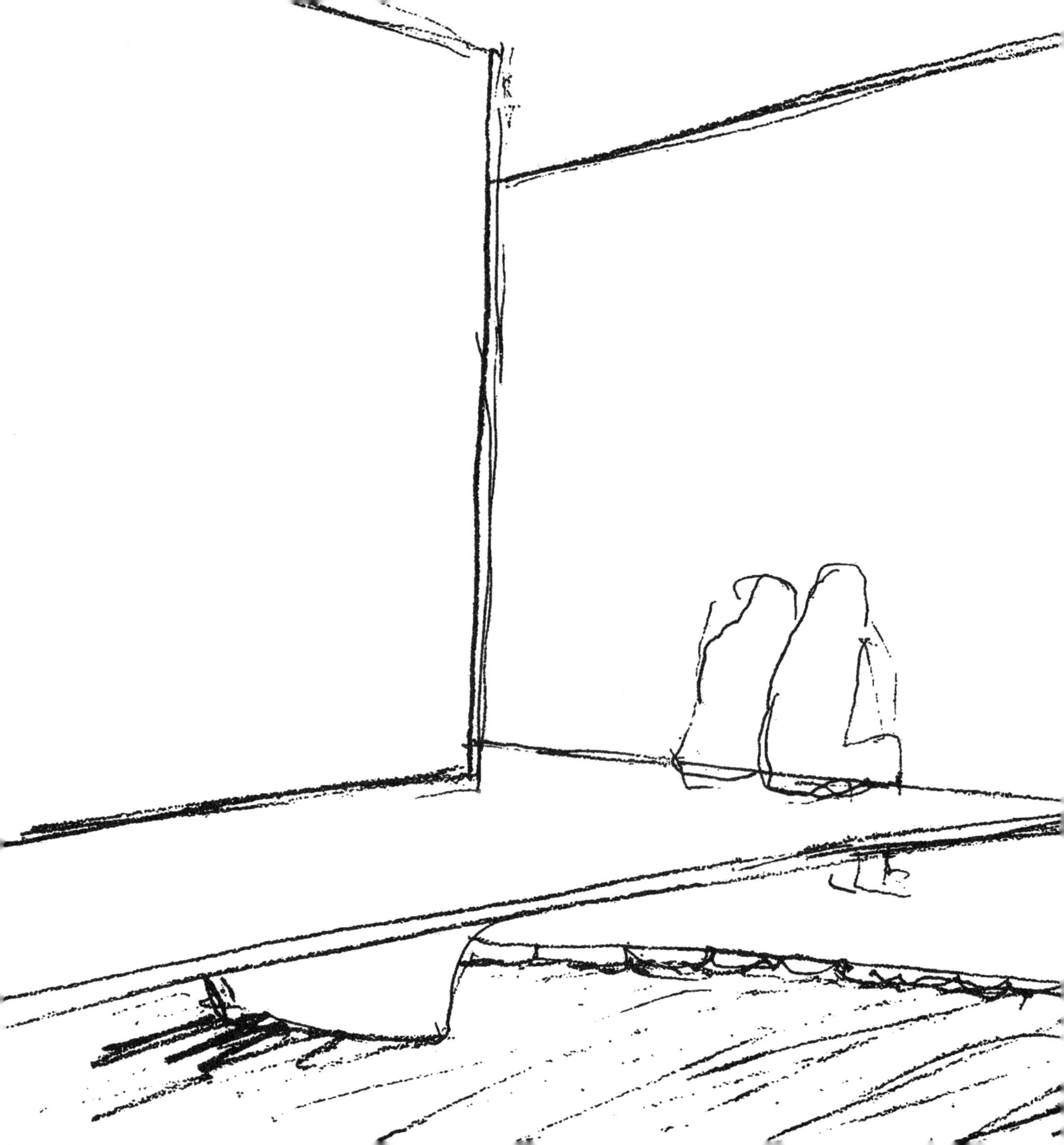

宮島弥山展望台

嚴島神社は世界で最も美しく、自然の営み「動く素材」を表現している建物だと考えている。それが天文的・地形的に美しく現れているのが干満と社殿との関係である。瀬戸内海の干満は約6時間おきに、およそ3mの水位の変化を繰り返し、社殿回廊の水平ラインがあることで初めてその動きが視覚化されていく。すなわち嚴島で感じてもらいたいことは、われわれ日本人が太古よりどのように自然と向き合ってきたか、自然を畏れ敬い尊び、自然を味方にすることがいかに人の心を引き付け、さらに民をまとめる力となってきたか。それを宮島弥山全体で感じることができる。

世界遺産弥山原始林の魅力は水と地形と太陽と月の関係によるさまざまな変化である。谷に沿った弥山参道には、水のせせらぎがある。標高の低い地域は樅の群生が見られ、それは太古より急激な水によって土砂の堆積が繰り返されてきた地域を示している。そのため神、自然の怒りを治める祠などが見られ、水と地形・信仰の関係が人びとの造形となって現れ始める。

水源は山の中腹辺りにあり、谷の水の流れに沿って登って行くといつの間にかせせらぎの音が消え、植生の豊かさも最大になる。さらに山頂に近付くと大聖院の弥山本堂や伽藍が点在し、井戸から人びとが水を得られる標高の限界であることが理解できる。

そして山頂に辿り着くと、展望台からは動く素材と宮島弥山の関係がすべて見て取れる。南を望むと、磐座とされる岩肌露わな巨石群。水の少ない乾燥した山頂は信仰修行の場であったことが想像される。北には嚴島神社が大野瀬戸の入り江にあり、動く素材すなわち「強い風雨」から守られた場所にあることに気付くだろう。西に広がる弥山原始林は、大野瀬戸から標高ごと、地形ごとに水と風が異なるように植生が異なっていることが見て取れる。眼下には瀬戸内海が広がり、多くの水を太陽が弥山原始林へと運んでくれる。われわれ人類の基本は常に水であり、海から山頂までの水のつながりと共生が文化芸術、信仰そして生活のすべてを司っていることがこの宮島弥山では深くかつ美しい形として読み取ることができる。

私は少年期から毎年正月に弥山へ登り、ご来光を拝んできた。最も美しく拝める、いつもの山頂に「座」して、と決まっていた。私が見て感じてきた宮島弥山は、何度登っても常に違う美しさを魅せてくれた。それを伝えるには変化し続ける自然、つまり動く素材を「座」してゆっくり感じてもらうことが弥山そのままを伝えることだと直感した。

ぜひ弥山と瀬戸内の地形、風・水・太陽・月・地形が織り成すエナジースケープを感じて欲しい。

MIYAJIMA MISEN OBSERVATORY

I think that Miyajima Shrine is of the world's most beautiful expressions of natural "moving materials". Its celestial and terrestrial beauty is manifest in the relationship between the shrine and the ebb and flow of the tides. Because the tides of the Seto Inland Sea regularly alter the water level by approximately three metres about every six hours, the first visualization of this movement is the horizontal line of the external corridors of the shrine. In other words, what I want to be felt at Itsukushima is how, since ancient times, we Japanese will confront nature, how we fear and worship nature, how we ally ourselves with nature, and how it has a power that appeals to the hearts of people and causes them to gather together. This can be sensed everywhere on Mount Misen in Miyajima.

The charm of the World Heritage designated virgin forest on Mount Misen lies in its water, terrain, and the way it changes in relation to the sun and moon. One hears the murmuring of water on the Mount Misen shrine approach path that runs along the valley. The low area is thick with fir trees, indicating an area where the sudden sedimentation of soil and sand due to water movement has been constantly repeated since ancient times. Small shrines to appease the anger of the gods and nature may be seen, and the relationships between water, terrain and religion are manifest in the character of the people.

There are water sources higher up, so when climbing along the water flows in the valley, the sound of small brooks disappears all too soon, and the richness of the vegetation becomes dominant. Furthermore, as one approaches the top of the moutain it is dotted with temple buildings and main hall of Misen Daishouin temple, allowing people to understand that this is the limit of the altitude at which water may be obtained from a well.

Finally arriving at the 535m-high summit, from the viewing platform one can perceive all the relationships between Mount Misen and the moving materials. Looking south, there is the bare face of the giant rock that looks like a dwelling place for the gods. I imagine that this arid mountaintop, with very little water, was a place for ascetic religious practices. To the north is Itsukushima Shrine in the inlet of Ono Seto, and I notice that it is in a place protected from moving materials, namely "strong wind and rain." Spreading to the west is the Mount Misen Virgin Forest, and one can perceive the differences in vegetation due to the differences in wind and water at each altitude and terrain from Ono Seto. The Seto Inland Sea spreads to the east, and the sun carries a great deal of water to the Mount Misen Virgin Forest. The eternal basis of we human beings is water, and the symbiosis and connection of water from the sea to the mountaintop is what governs our culture, art, religion, and ways of life, and here at Mount Misen it may be read as a deep and beautiful form.

Since I was a child, I have climbed Mount Misen annually for the New Year holidays, and worshipped the view of the sunrise from the high mountaintop. Seeing its extreme beauty, I always decided that the mountaintop was a *za* (seat). No matter how many times I climbed to the summit of Mount Misen, I had the sense of meditating, entranced by its varied beauty. In conveying the sense that the constantly changing nature – that is to say, moving materials – is a *za*, my instinct was to convey Mount Misen just as it is.

I want you to feel the energyscape that is woven throughout Mount Misen and the Seto region by the wind, water, sunlight, moon, and terrain.

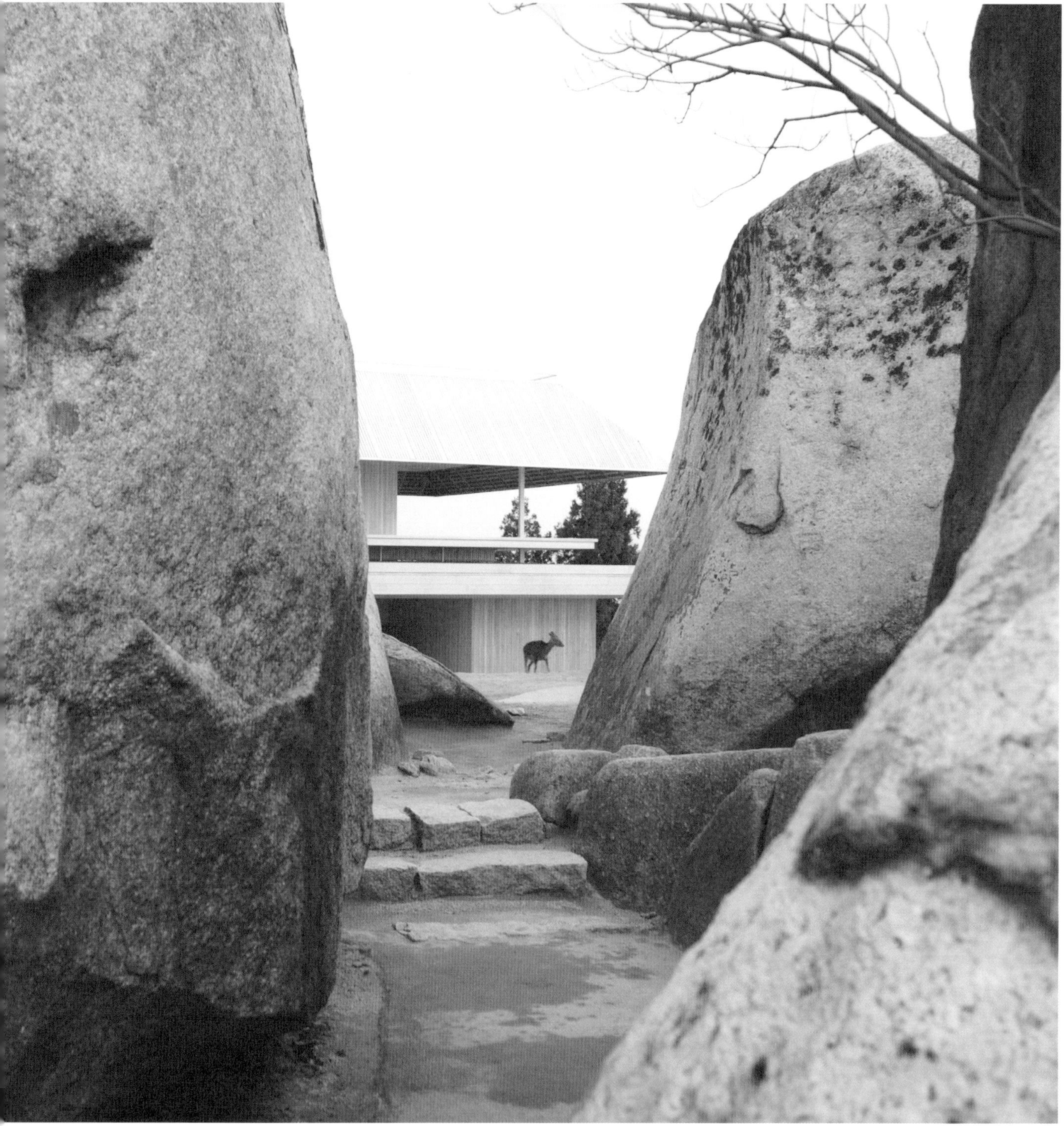

座の展望台。

An observatory for seated reflection.

| 1F | 2F | RF |

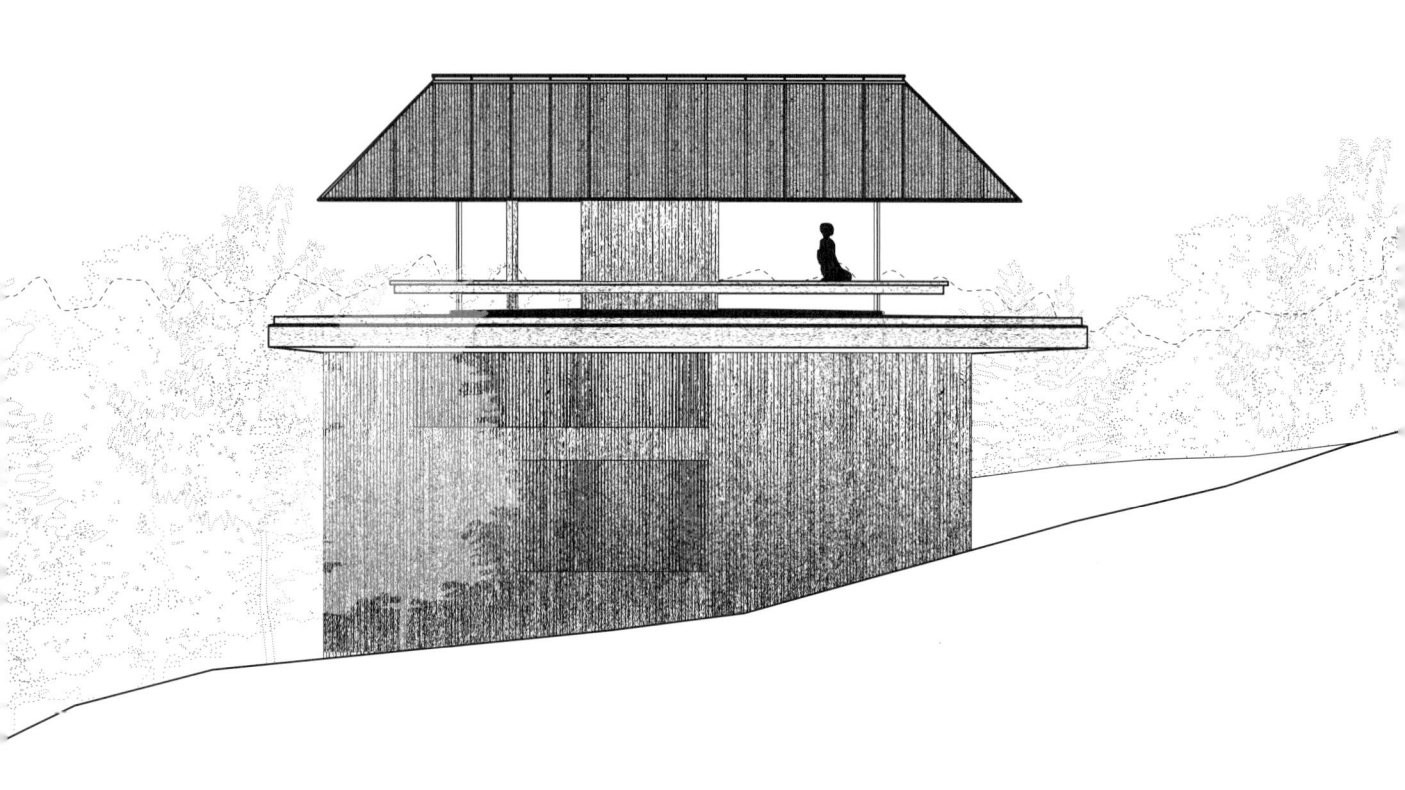

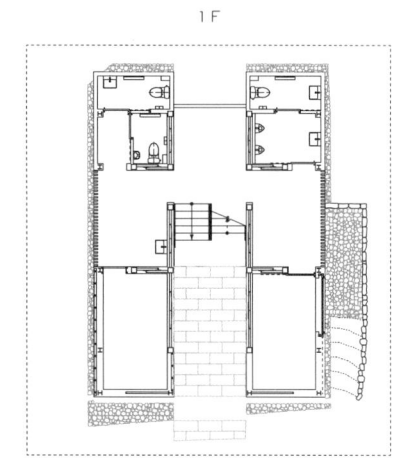

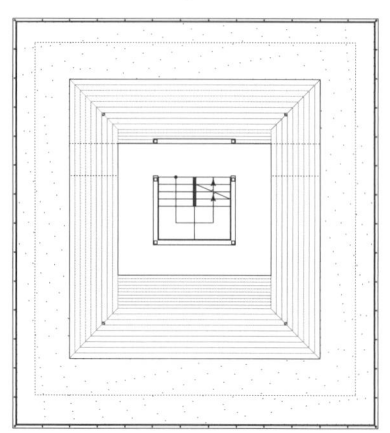

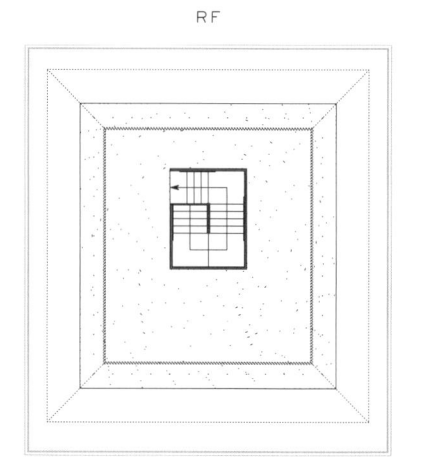

0 5 10M

「座」の空間は縁と庇が廻り、深く広がる庇は軒を下げ、縁に「座」することを促す断面形状としている。庇は格子とルーバーにより隙間をもった構成とし、強い風雨などの自然に逆らわないディテールとしている。これは嚴島神社の回廊の隙間の原理に倣った。また、庇のルーバーは、夏の強い太陽の日射しを和らげると共に軒先にいくほど角度を緩やかにし、雨水が流れ落ちる速度と風の力を緩めるディテールとなっている。すべて宮島弥山の風・水・太陽などの動く素材から姿形が決められている。

最高位の僧侶を座主、神が鎮座する磐座、座禅と言うように「座」は日本人にとって最も重要な所作のひとつであり、自然と向き合う姿勢が現れている。動く素材によってデザインされた座の空間に「座」して静態することで宮島弥山の動く素材が見えてくる。

The *za* (seat) space is ringed by an *engawa* (veranda) and *hisashi* (eaves), designed so that the ends of the eaves are lowered. This is to prompt the act of sitting. The eaves contain small gaps due to the use of lattices and louvres, details that naturally resist strong wind and rain. I had learned this from the gaps in the outer corridor floors of the Itsukushima Shrine adapted to the tides. In addition, the louvres of the eaves mitigate the strong summer sunlight, and the reduced angle toward the ends of the eaves is a detail that slows rainwater runoff and wind speed. The profile was determined in accordance with all the moving materials of Mount Misen, including wind, water, and sunlight.

The word *za* (seat) appears in the terms for senior Buddhist monk (*za-su*), the enshrinement of a god (*chin-za*), and meditation (*za-zen*), indicating that Japanese people consider sitting to be one of the most important acts – a posture oriented toward nature. Sitting still in a *za* space designed according to moving materials will allow one to see the moving materials of Miyajima's Mount Misen.

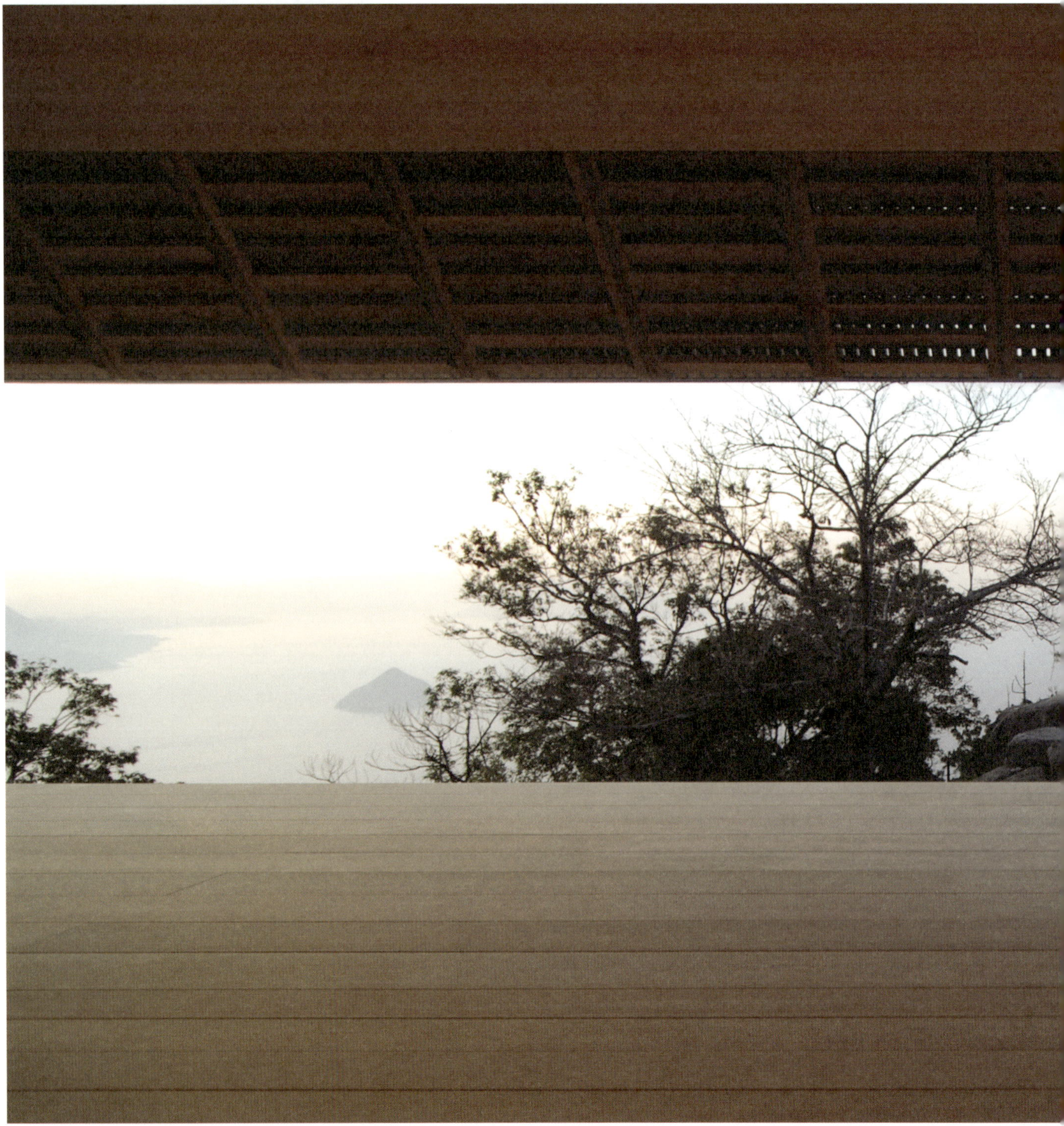

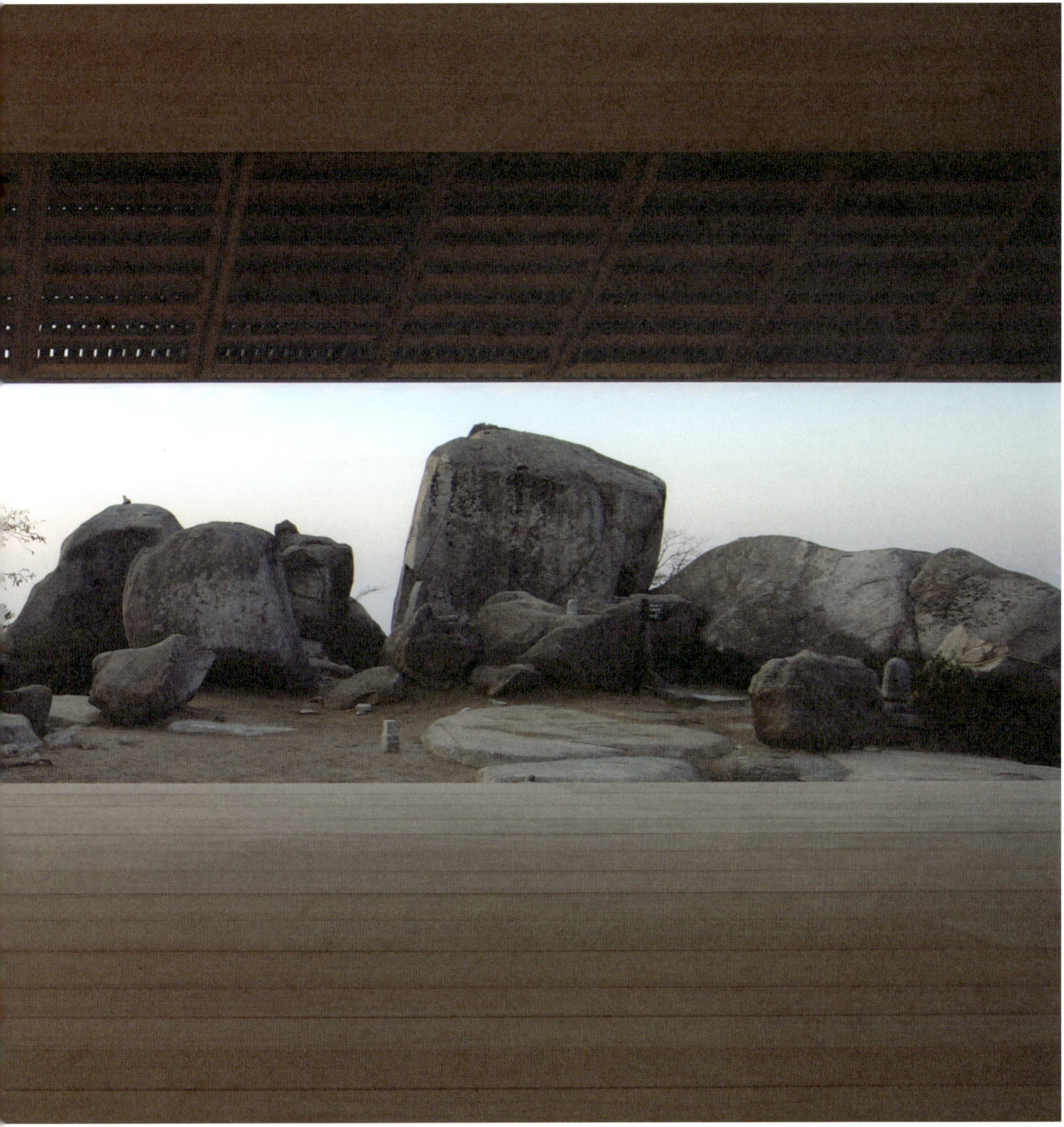

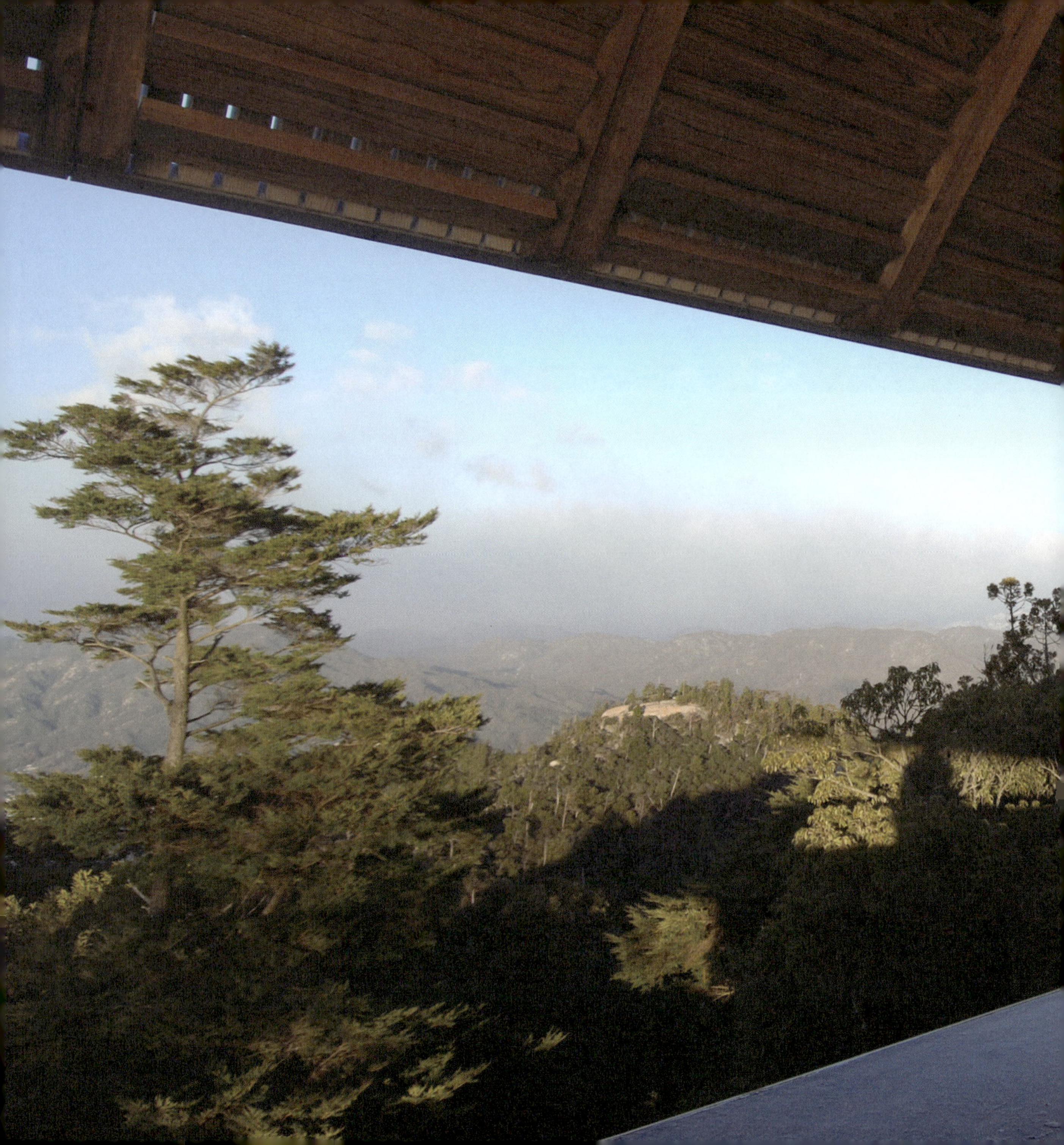

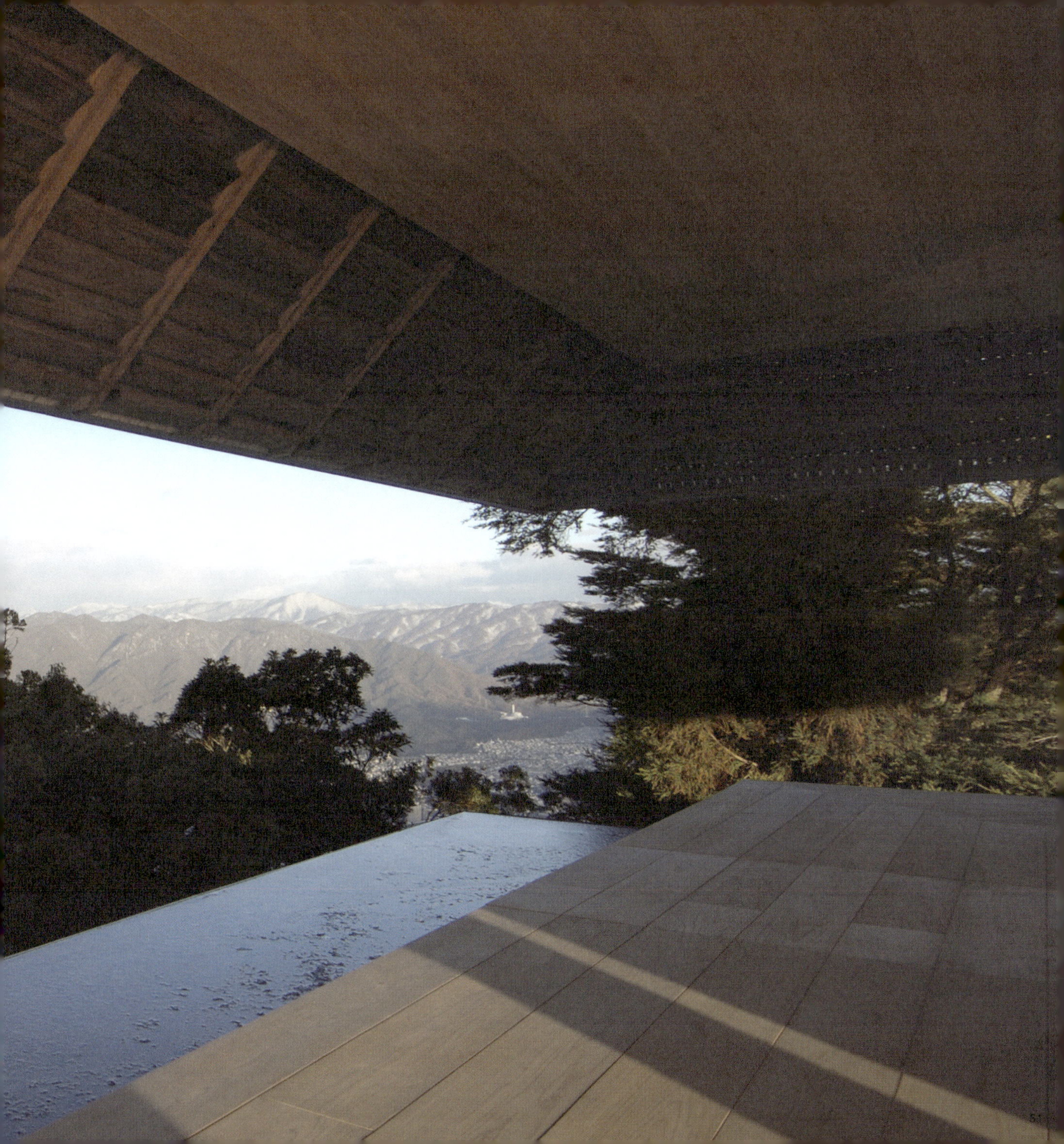

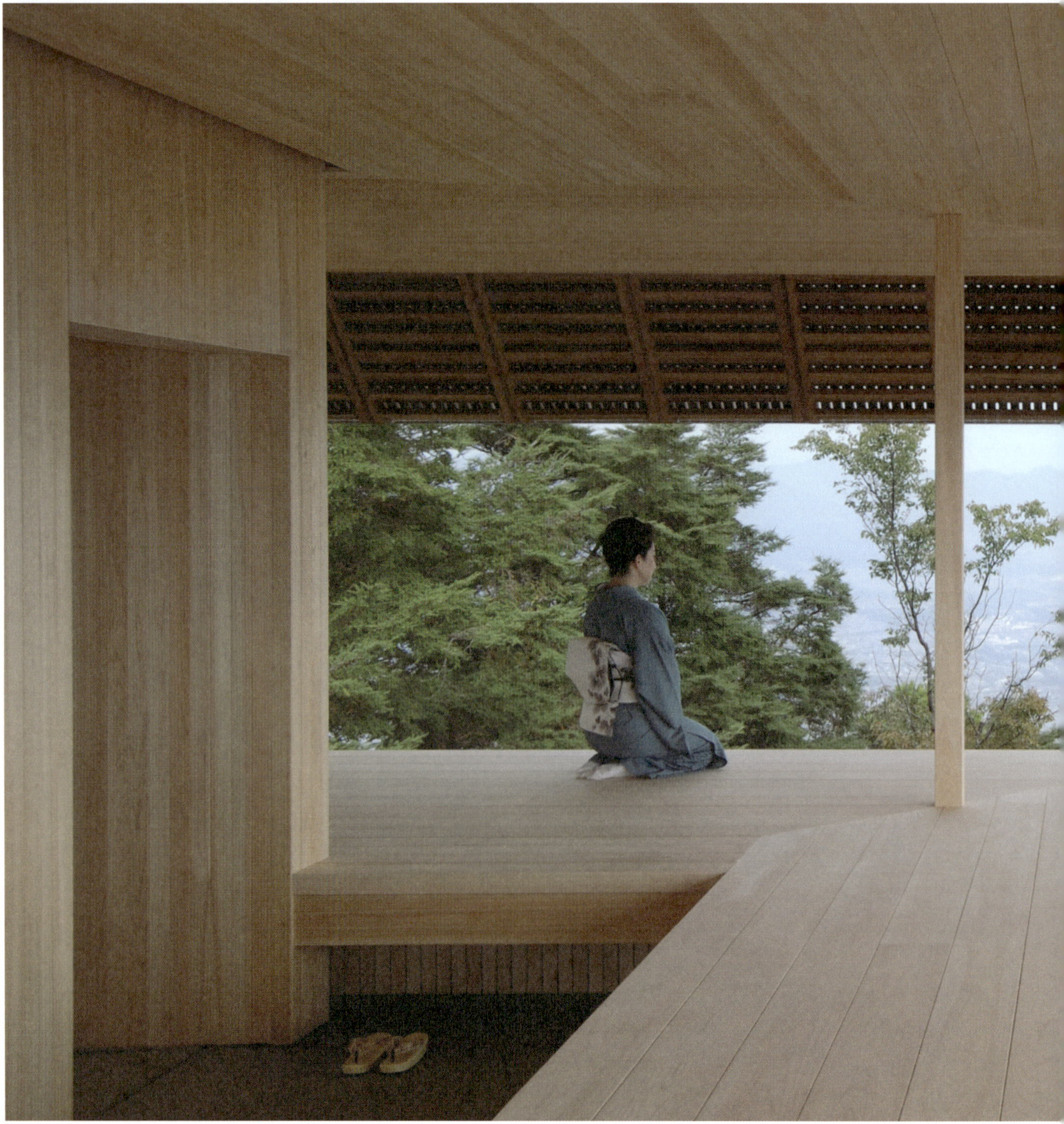

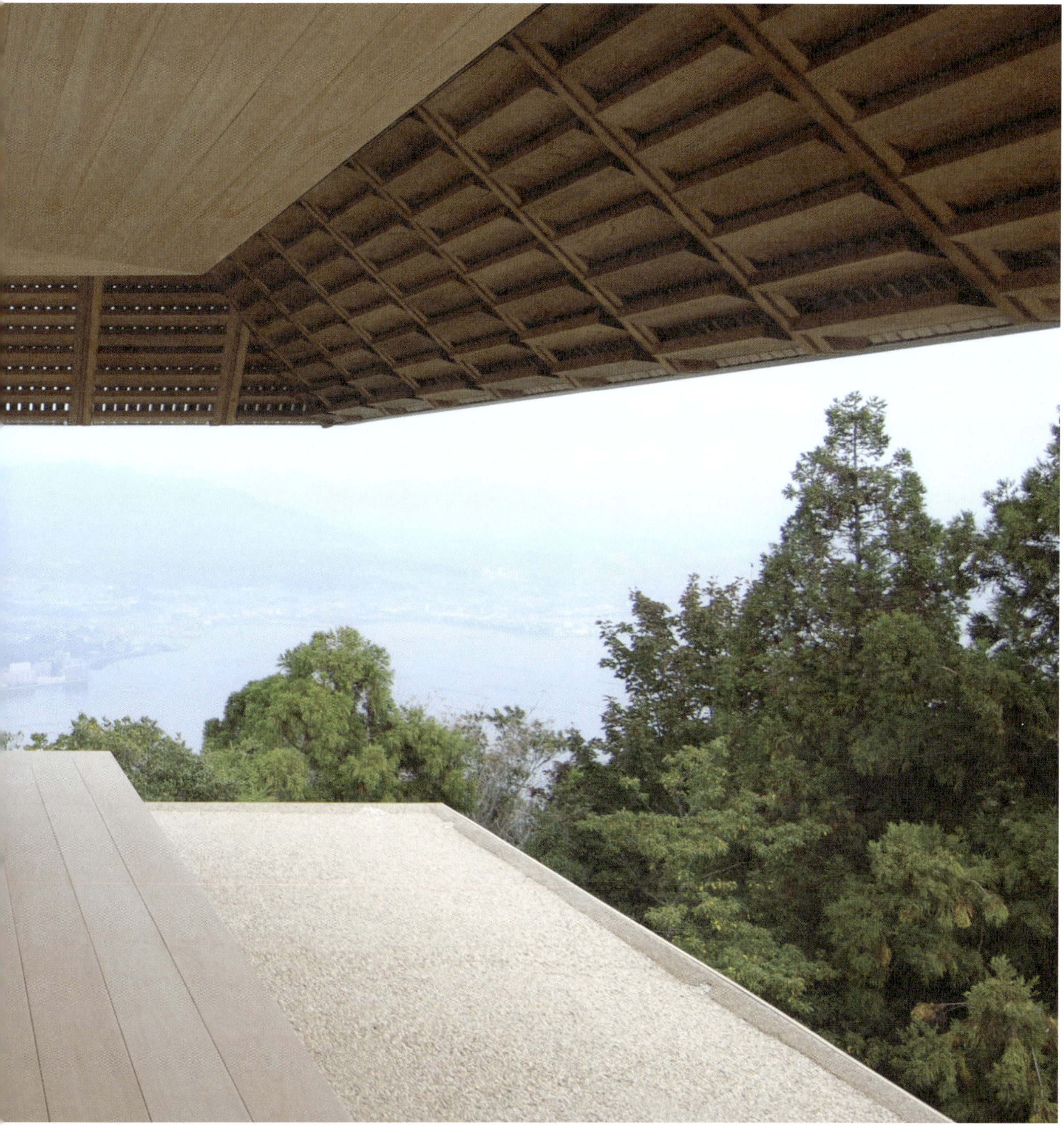

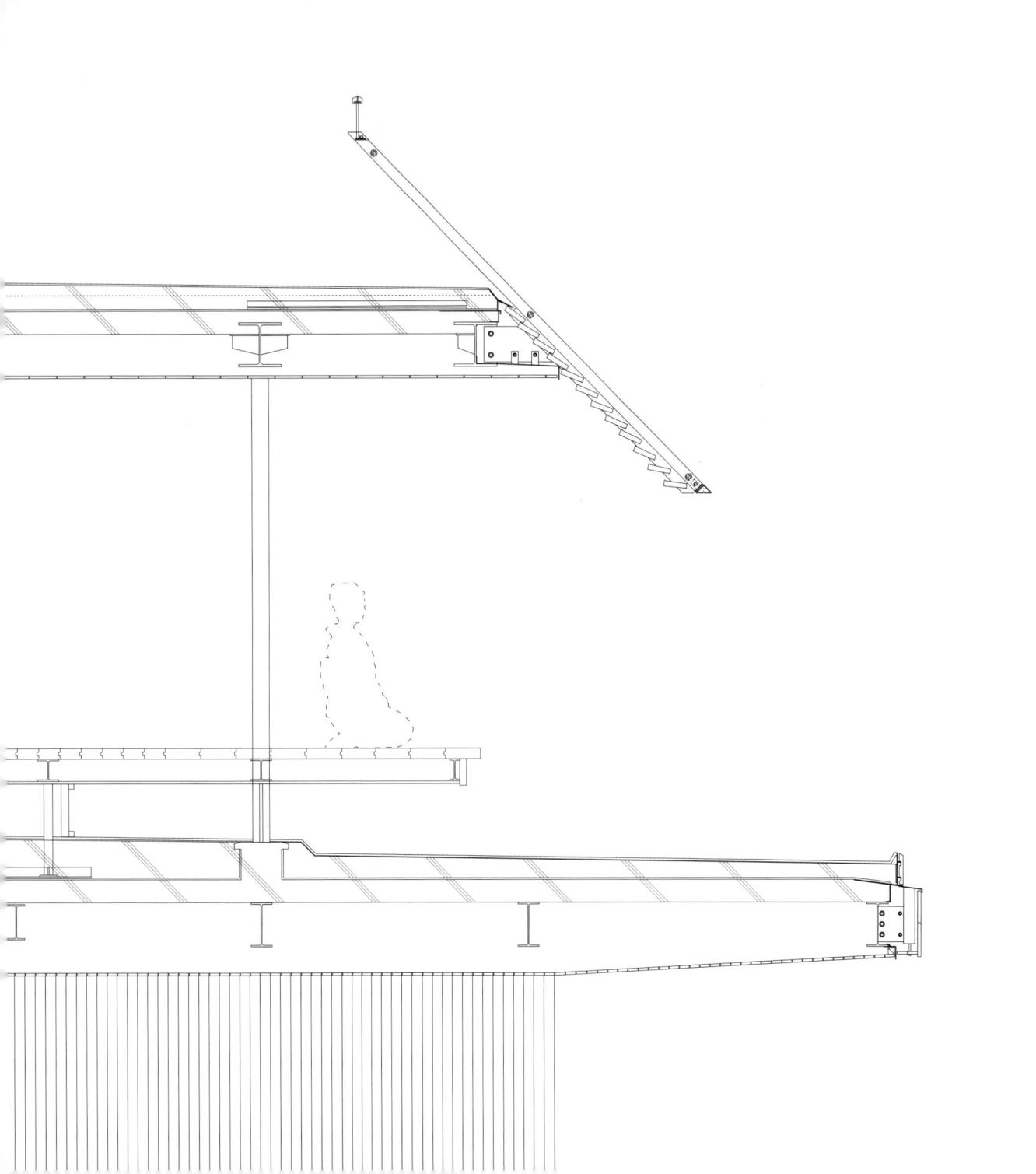

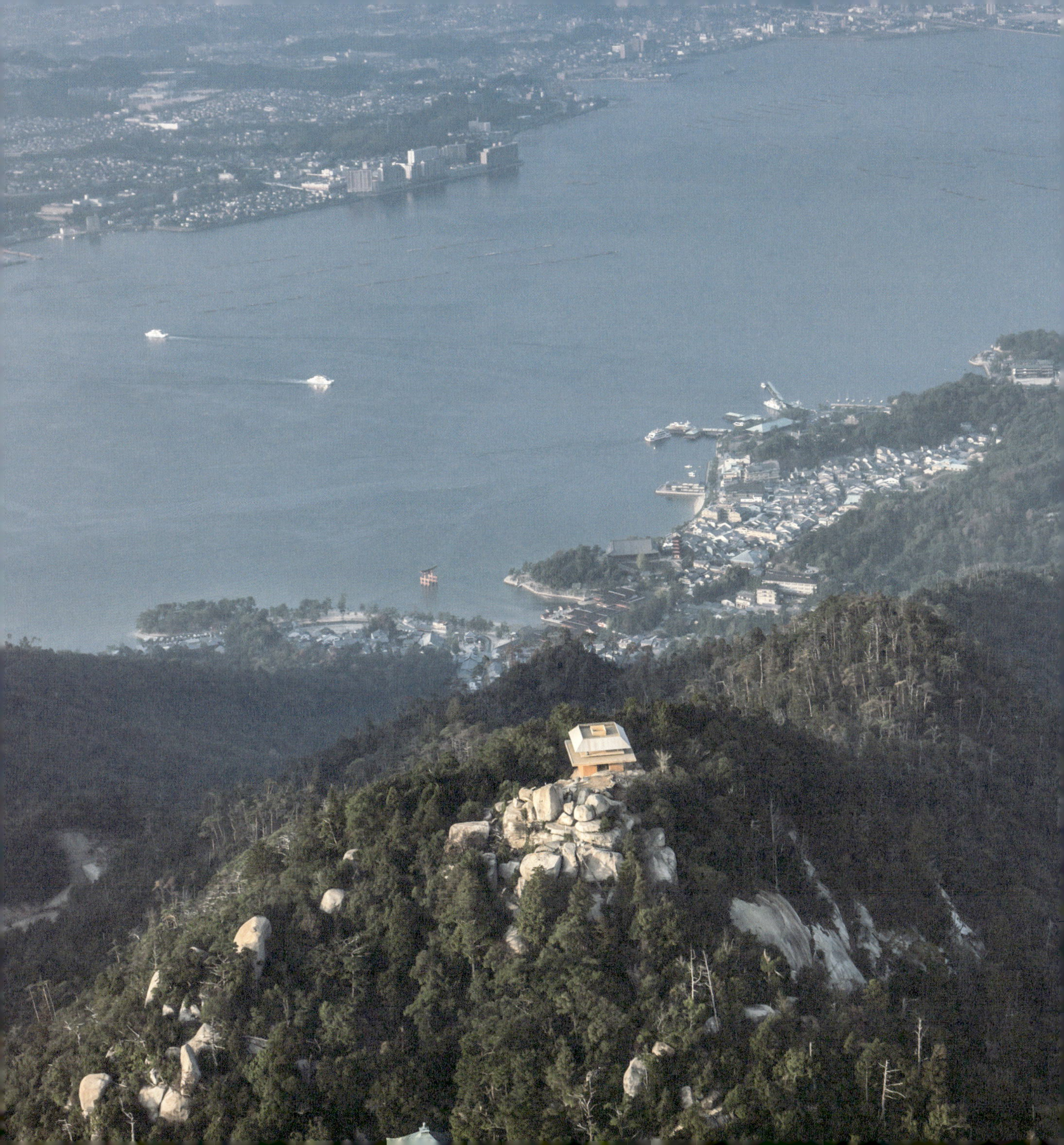

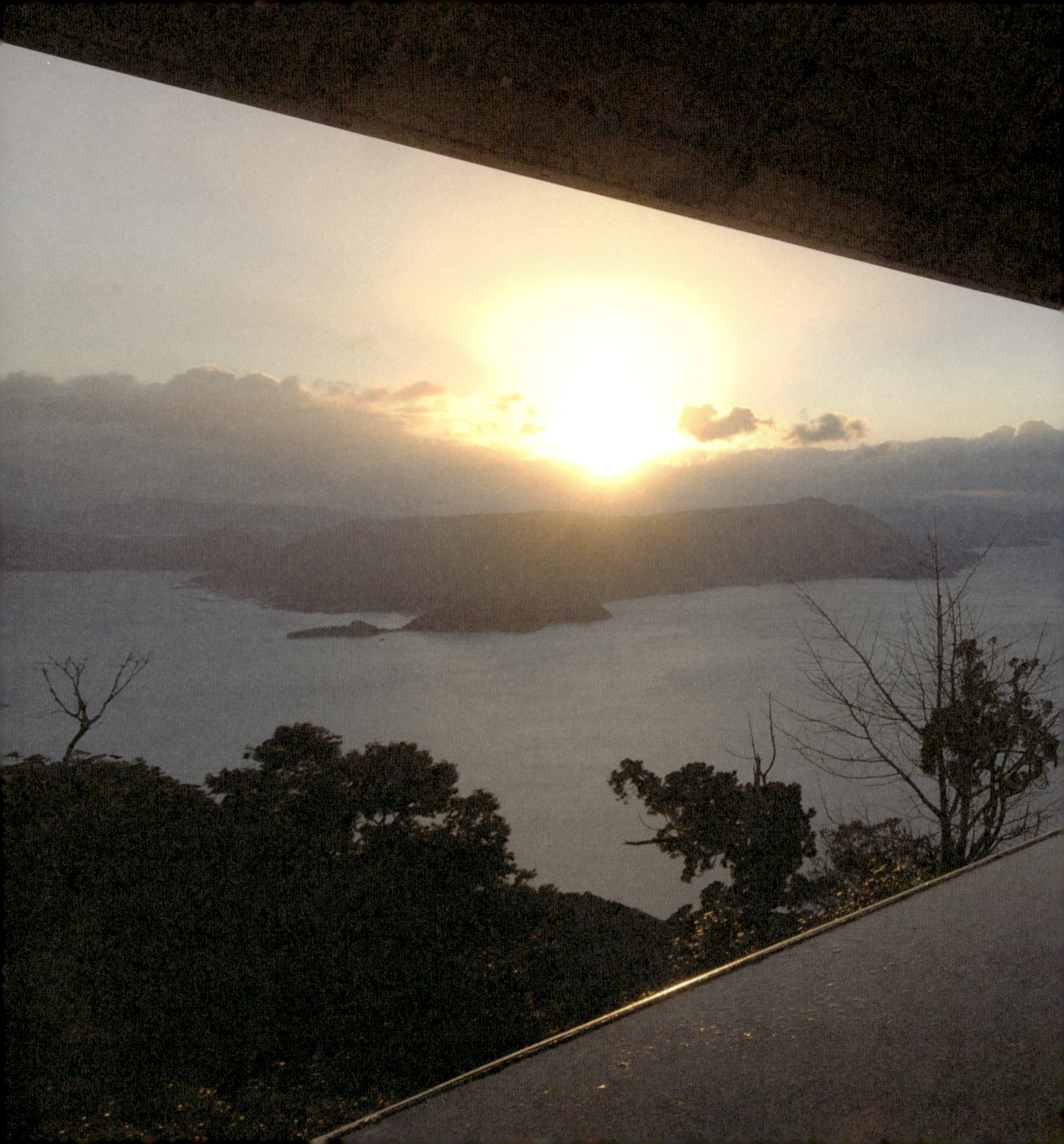

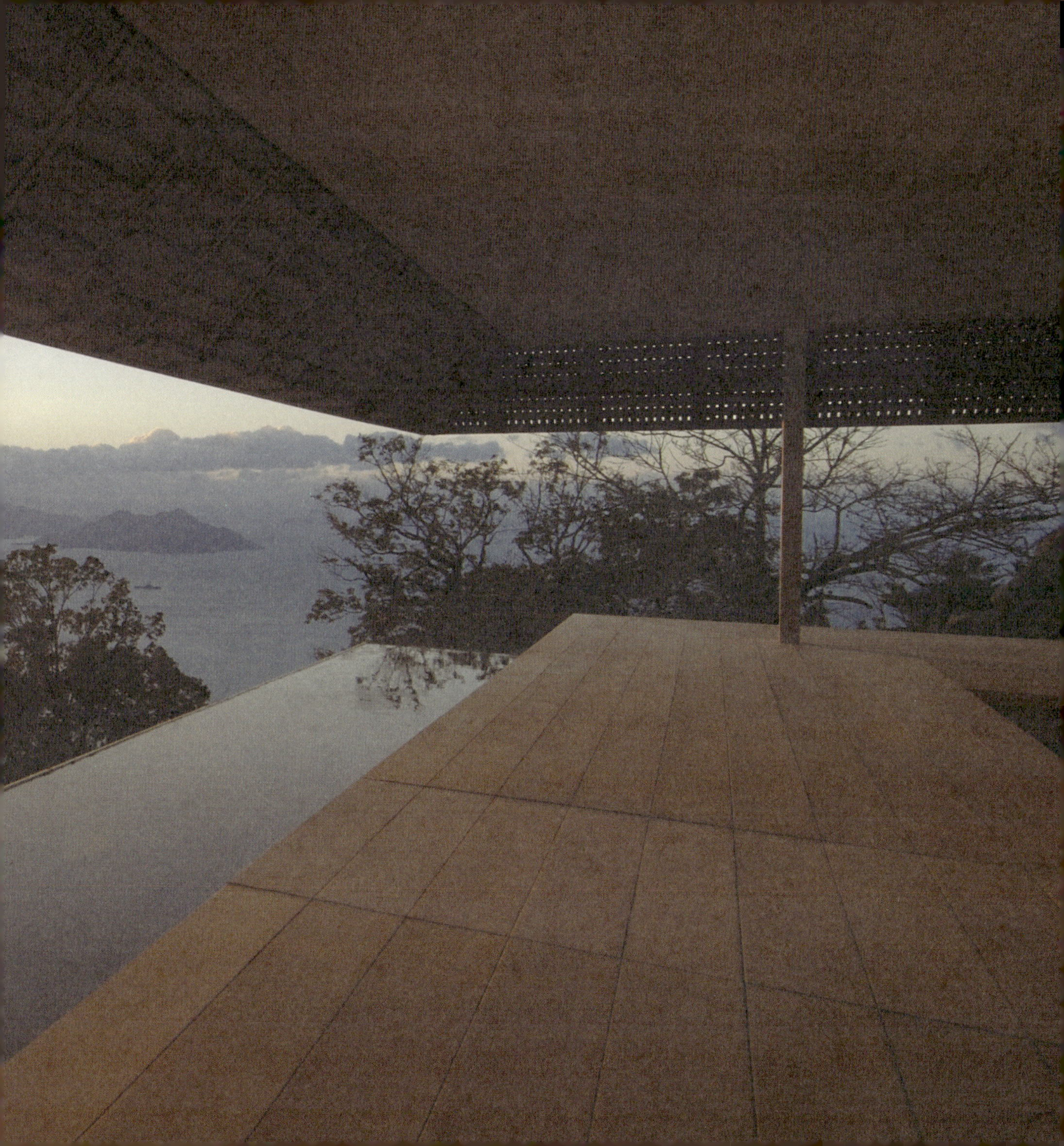

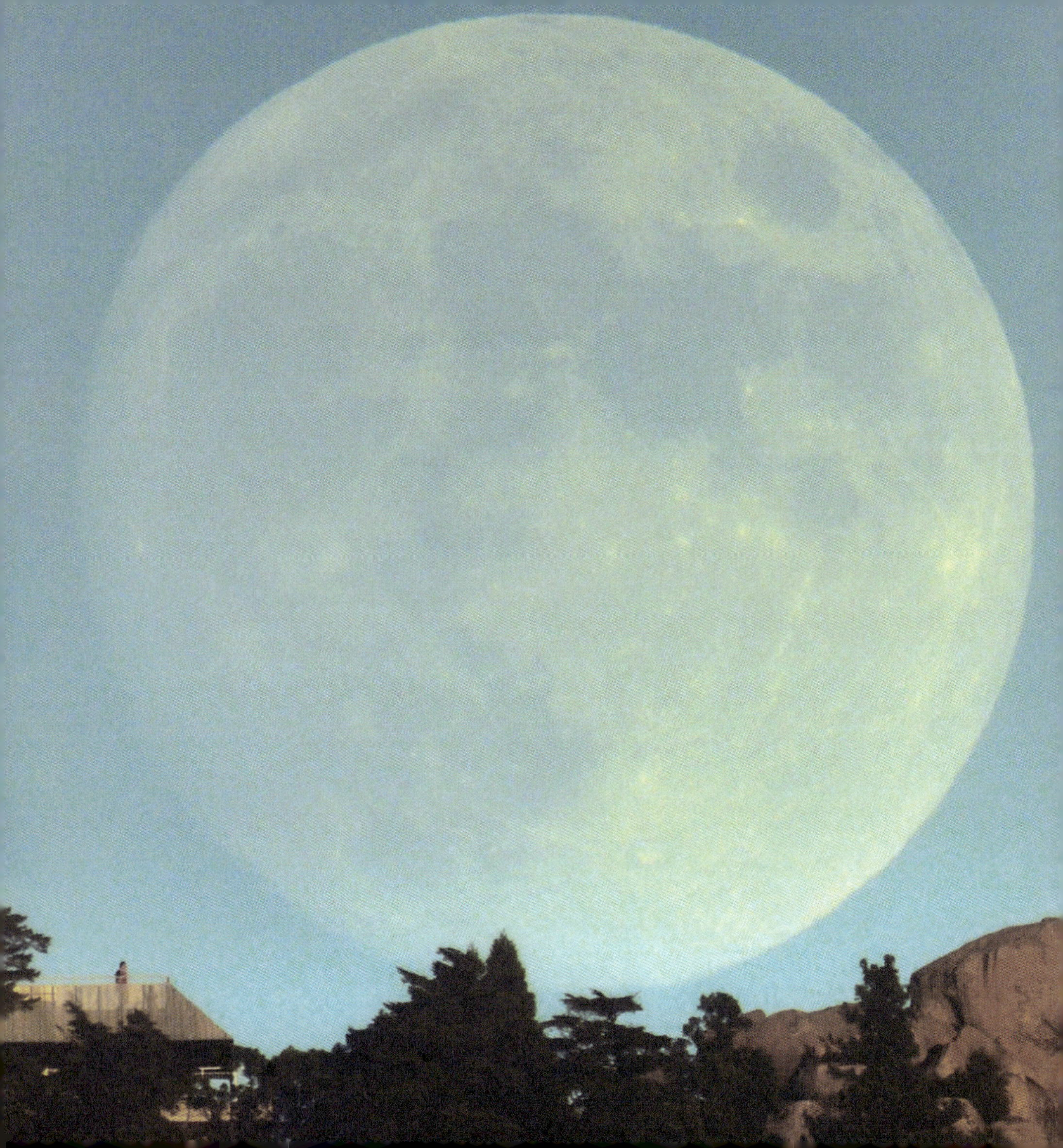

大地を建てる
ミニック・ロージング／地質学者

チャールズ・ダーウィンは初めてわれわれの世界に、自然選択（自然淘汰）の概念を導入した。それはしばしば、最適者の生存として定式化され、生物学的進化を単刀直入に説明する道具となってきた。すなわち、地球が提供する環境に適合しないものは絶滅の運命にある！　というわけだ。ところが、有機体は、地球が提供する環境内に生息するようには定められていない。逆に、有機体は自らの必要と欲求に適合した独自の環境を創り出すことができるのである。

生命を支える根本原理のひとつは新陳代謝(メタボリズム)である。これは、環境資源を利用してエネルギーを獲得し、生体構造をつくり出す能力のことである。莫大なエネルギーを使って、有機体は自身の利益になるように、または競争相手にダメージを与えられるように環境をつくり変えるのである。

環境をコントロールするにしても、地球全体を扱うよりは、小さな空間を扱う方がやりやすい。そのため、有機体は構築された構造という形を使って自らを表現することが多い。だから住処を建てるのであり、それを太古より孜孜として行ってきた。

建物に暮らすということは、すべての有機体をひとつのジレンマに直面させる。すなわち、建物はわれわれを外界から効率よく遮断する一方、遮断された当の環境との間でのエネルギーと情報のやり取りを許容しつつ、周囲から得られる有用な物貨へのアクセスをも提供しなければならないからである。このジレンマを調整するために、すべての有機体は良くできた建築構造に頼るのである。このことは、細菌粘液、蟻塚、蜂の巣についても、人間やその住居の場合と同様にあてはまる。

優れた建築構造や効果的な新陳代謝戦略をもつ有機体は、成功し、繁栄する。ところが、そんな優れた能力のおかげで、有機体はかえって資源環境を枯渇させ、ゴミで汚し、結局は自らの成功を産んだ環境適応力を失うことになる。優れた建築物や新陳代謝を特徴付けるものは、エネルギー獲得効率の良さである。地球上で最も豊富なエネルギー源は太陽光である。太陽は、火山活動、地震、造山活動といった形で地球内部から発せられるエネルギーの全放出量の4千倍ものエネルギーを地表にもたらす。地球上に現れた最初の生命はおそらく、地球内部のかすかなエネルギーに頼って生存していた確率が高いが、その程度のエネルギーではほとんどまともな活動を賄うことはできなかったろう。従って、原初の生命は環境にほとんど、またはまったく影響を与えなかった。地球の歴史のうち、最初の5億年間、地球環境をコントロールしたのは地質要素だけだったのである。

およそ38億年前、生命は光合成を手に入れた。これは、太陽からの豊かなエネルギーの恵みを採り入れる能力である。下から細々と栄養を摂取するだけの窮乏生活はこうして終わりを告げた。やがて生命は増え、勤勉な活動を行うようになり、地球環境に影響を与え始める。生命のコントロール下に入る領域もますます拡大してゆく。対流圏は、地球の大気圏の中でも最下層かつ最も容積の小さい部分で、それだけに最も下からの影響を受けやすい。われわれが毎朝、鏡の中で顔を合わせる生物種とまさに一緒で、最初の微生物たちも、大気や海洋はまるで無限であるかのように、自

分の出したゴミをどんどん海や空気中に捨てていた。

光合成によってできるゴミのひとつは酸素である。酸素は、たいていの微生物にとって有毒、もしくは危険なガスである。従って、地球の表面環境を酸素で充満させることは、この世界がそれまで経験した中でも最悪の環境的災厄であった。これで、地球という惑星とその積荷であるすべての生命の運命がすっかり変わってしまった。新たに生まれた種は、酸素に対する耐性を身に付け、それどころか呼吸で体内に取り込むことさえ可能にするのに対して、別の種は離れた、孤立した環境に避難場所を見いだすか、自分の身の回りに防御的構造を構築するかしなければならなくなったのである。

酸素の標的は生きた有機体だけではない。酸素は海水中や大気中に露出した岩石にも作用する。風化作用は、赤熱するマグマが結晶化して生まれた光沢のある堅い鉱物を、鈍い色の柔らかく湿った粘土に変質させてしまう。こうして、光合成を行う有機体が獲得したエネルギーは、部分的には地球のゴミを別の物質に変容させるのに使われる。実際には、光合成が地質に与えた影響は、地球の全内部活動が与えた影響の3倍に上ることが判明している。光合成を獲得した生命は、地球に対する、より上位の地質的影響力となったのである。

すべての岩石惑星、さらには月やいくつかの小惑星でさえも、玄武岩でできた地殻をもつ。これは一般的な惑星表面を構成する物質である。数百万年以上の時間をかけて、地球の海洋の下にある分厚い玄武岩層の地殻は、その下の高温の地層であるマントルへと沈み込んでゆく。このプロセスによって絶えず玄武岩はリサイクルされ、海底の玄武岩層は新鮮でまっさらな状態に保たれる。

風化作用を受けた玄武岩のうち、粘土化したものや新しく

形成された玄武岩以外の鉱物のあるものは、地球内部に沈み込む間に熱の影響で部分的に溶解する。溶けた鉱物はやがて地表へと上昇し、冷え固まって花崗岩となる。この浮揚性の物質は、過去40億年にわたり地表面に堆積しながら、次第に大陸を形成してゆく。こうして、玄武岩の風化は花崗岩形成にとって、さらには地球の大陸形成にとっての決定的な一歩となった。風化作用そのものは、光合成を行なう有機体が海洋と大気のあり方に変化をもたらした結果生じたものであり、乾燥した陸地は、生命が地球環境を支配したことによって生じた結果である。つまり、われわれ生物が暮らす陸地は、生命が自らの環境の形をつくり出そうと望んだ結果生じたものなのである。

われわれが小さな島に自分の建物を建てる時、自分たちはこの処女地に定住する最初の人間なのだと思うかもしれない。しかし、海に浮かぶどんなに小さな島に至るまで、構築された構造物としての性格はあまねく行き渡っていて、その構造物は何十億もの微生物の、何百万もの昆虫の、何千もの脊椎動物の、そして無数のその他生物にとっての住処となっている。その島からして1個の建造物であり、内的に協調し合う地球規模の生物圏が太陽からのエネルギーを得ながら、何百万年、何十億年にわたって新陳代謝の過程を繰り返して徐々に徐々に建造してきたものなのである。われわれ自身がつくる建物というのは、豊かな多様性を見せる自然の構築物に付加される一過性の構造物に過ぎない。自然の構築物の大半はわれわれよりずっと長く残るだろう。あるいは、三分一の言葉を借りてこう言うこともできよう。「われわれの建築とは、地球のディテールにほかならない」と。

あらゆる建物は、われわれが自分の生きる環境をつくり変え、コントロールしようとする時に用いる技術と能力の表現なのである。上手に、そして賢くそれを行なえば、われわれは本質的なバランスを維持することができる。さらには、われわれ人間の必要と欲求に見合う、その土地固有の空間領域を創造し、文明としての、かつ種としてのわれわれの存続の基盤となる地球環境を保護することができるだろう。

BUILDING GROUND
Minik Rosing, professor of geology

Charles Darwin introduced us to the idea of natural selection, often formulated as the survival of the fittest, the blunt instrument of biologic evolution: species unfit for the environments offered by Earth are subject to extinction! But organisms are not doomed to live within the environments offered by Earth. They can create their own environments to accommodate their needs and desires.

One of the pillars of life is metabolism, the capacity to appropriate resources from the environment, acquire energy and manufacture biologic structures. Large amounts of energy are spent on changing the environment to the benefit of the organism or the detriment of its competitors. Controlling the environment is the key to survival.

It is much easier to control a small parcel of space rather than the whole Earth. For that reason, life often expresses itself in built structures. Life builds homes, and has done so since the dawn of time.

Living in buildings confronts all organisms with a dilemma. On one hand, a building must efficiently separate us from the outer environment. On the other, it must provide access to commodities from the surroundings and allow an exchange of energy and information with that same environment from which the building was intended to isolate us. To balance this dilemma all organisms are dependent on good architecture. That is as true for microbial slime mounds, anthills and beehives as it is for humans and their houses.

Organisms that have successful architecture and efficient metabolic strategies thrive and proliferate. But they also deplete the environment of resources, pollute it with waste and, in the end, undermine the environmental adaptations that defined their success. Successful architectures and metabolisms are characterized by their efficiency to harvest energy. By far the most abundant source of energy on Earth is sunlight. The sun sheds 4000 times more energy on Earth's surface than the sum of all the energy released from Earth's interior and which is expressed in volcanism, earthquakes and mountain building. The first life on Earth, most likely, depended on the sparse energy from Earth's interior, which could hardly fuel any work at all. Consequently early life had little or no environmental impact. During the first half billion years of Earth's history, Earth environments were controlled by geology alone.

About 3800 million years ago life developed photosynthesis, the ability to harvest the generous energy from the Sun. Starving on the humble diet from below was over. Life became plentiful and industrious and immediately began to influence the global environment. Greater and greater domains of Earth came under biological control. The ethereal atmosphere is the smallest of Earth's spheres and the easiest to influence. Just like the species we meet in the mirror every morning, the first microbes behaved as though the atmosphere and oceans were infinite, and dumped their wastes into the sea and the air.

One of the waste products from photosynthesis is oxygen, a gas that is poisonous or lethal to most microbes. The oxygenation of Earth's surface environments was by far the worst environmental disaster that this world has ever seen. It completely changed the fate of the planet and all her living cargo. New species learned to tolerate oxygen and even exploit it for respiration, while others had to seek asylum in remote and isolated environments or build protective structures around them.

Oxygen does not only attack living organisms. It also reacts with rocks exposed to the oceans and the atmosphere. Weathering transforms the shiny, hard minerals originally crystallized out of glowing magma to dull, soft and wet clays. The energy harvested by photosynthetic organisms is thus partly responsible for transforming Earth's crust. It turns out, that the geological impact from photosynthesis is in fact three times greater than the impact from all of Earth's inner machinery. With photosynthesis, life became a superior geologic force on Earth.

All the rocky planets, and even the moon and some asteroids have crusts made of basalt. This is the generic planetary surface material. Over millions of years the dense black basalt crust under Earth's oceans sink back into the hot mantle below. This process perpetually recycles basalt and maintains a fresh and pristine basalt bottom under the oceans.

In weathered basalt, some of the clay and other newly-formed minerals partially melt as they are heated during descend into Earth's interior . The melt ascends towards the surface and solidifies as granite. This is the buoyant material that has accumulated on Earth's surface during the past four billion years and has gradually built the continents. The weathering of basalt is a crucial step in the production of granite, and thus in the construction of Earth's continents. Weathering is a consequence of the tampering with the oceans and atmosphere by photosynthetic organisms - and dry land is a consequence of life's dominion over Earth's environments. The land we live on is one of the more impressive consequences of life's aspiration to shape its environment. Land is a building.

When we erect a building of our own on a small island, we might think we are the first settlers on virgin land. However, every little island that sticks out of the sea is permeated by built structures which are home to billions of microbes, millions of insects, thousands of vertebrates and myriads of other beings. Even the island itself is a construct, slowly erected by the global biosphere in concert, through metabolic processes over millions or billions of years, and powered by energy from the sun. Our own buildings are just transient additions to a rich diversity of other constructions, most of which will outlast us. Or, in the words of Sambuichi: Our buildings are just details of the Earth.

Every building is an expression of our skill and capacity to change and control the environment in which we live. Done well and done wisely, we can uphold an essential balance. We can create localized domains of space sympathetic to our human needs and aspirations, and preserve the global environment that is the foundation for our survival, as civilizations and as a species.

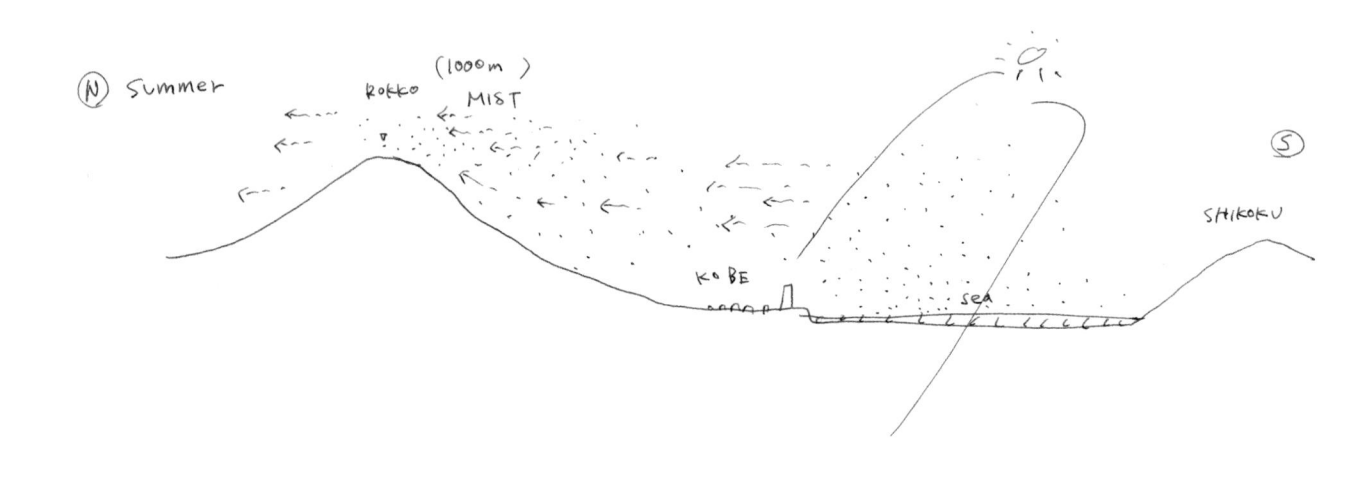

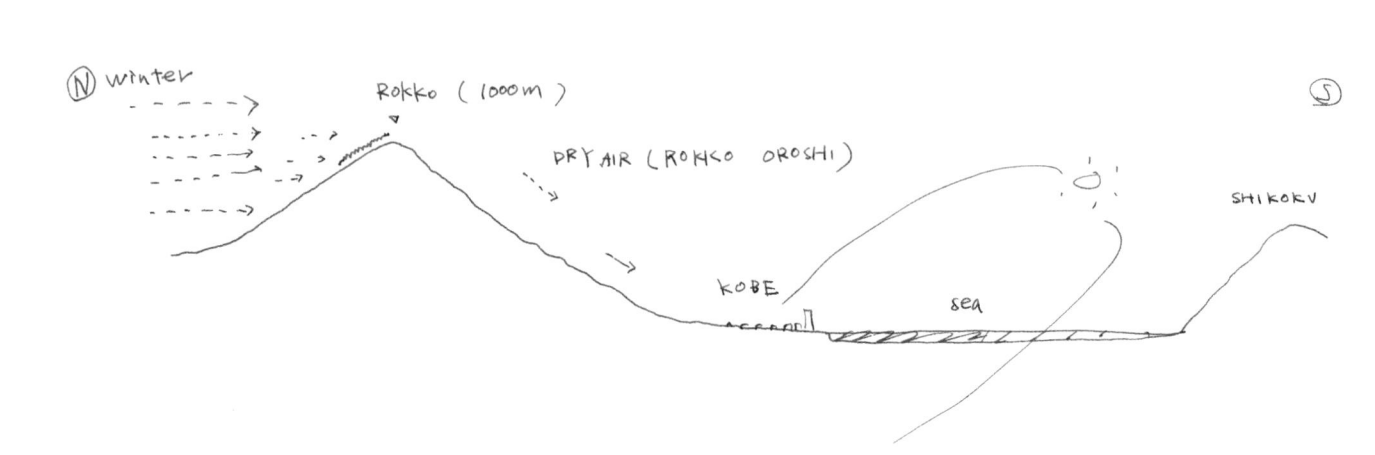

六甲

ROKKO

水
WATER

標高1000mの六甲山から見る瀬戸内海。温暖な気候と1000万人の暮らし。

Seen from the frequently snowcapped peak of Mount Rokko, the warm Seto Inland Sea and the 10 million people of Osaka Bay.

太陽の力によって海の水は水蒸気に変わる。真の六甲山の魅力は数分置きに変化する水の姿形にある。

By the energy of the sun, the sea turns to vapour. Constantly changing expressions of water in the air is one of the unique charms of Mount Rokko.

眼下に雲海が広がる時、太陽は水を山頂まで運ぶことはできない。

By the energy of the Sun, water is carried as vapour to the peak, often forming a veritable sea of clouds.

標高1,000mの六甲山頂。夜明けのミーティング。

本当に面白いのは水によってもたらされる変化である。同じ山頂から水の三態変化——気体、液体、固体の違いによるさまざまな景色を見ることができる。それらは、速度、湿度、温度などの条件の違いによって変わる。その魅力を建築で表現したいと考えた。

A meeting at sunrise on the summit of Mount Rokko.

In a single unique perspective from this mist enveloped peak at an altitude 1000 metres, the metropolis of 10 million people and the warm Inland Sea. However, the true marvel of this view is the changes of its skies, phenomena dominated by water. One can in that same perspective observe the three states of water – liquid, gas and solid and within each of these one may even observe several variations, such as various kinds of ice.

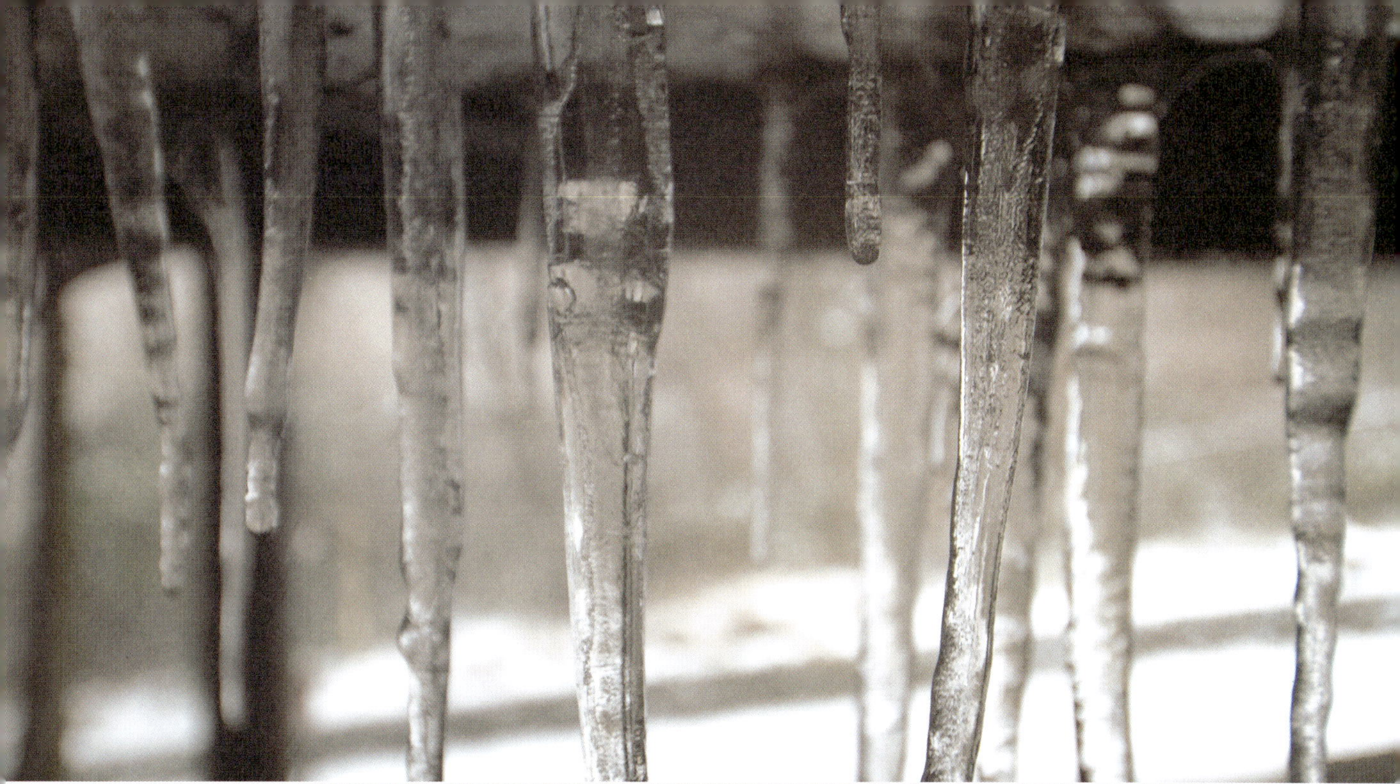

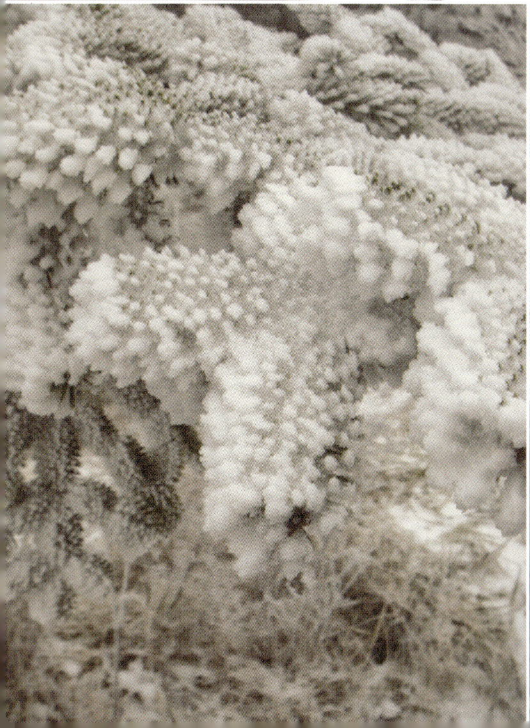

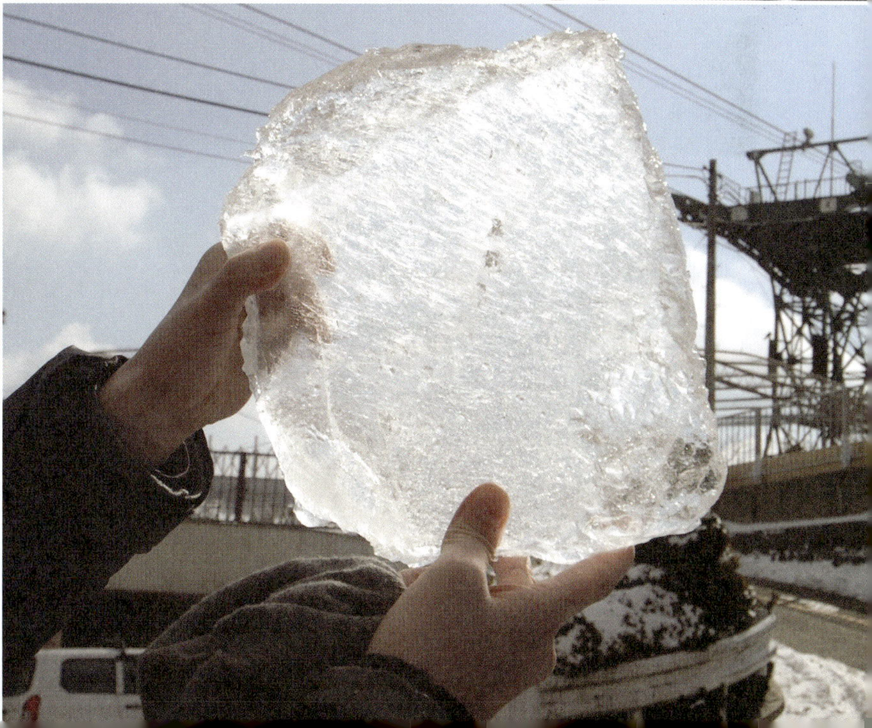

六甲山の特に美しく、珍しい現象は冬の樹氷である。動く素材にある特定の気象条件がそろった時のみ、その特別な景色が現れる。その動く素材を受け止める側にも条件があることが分かってきた。それは振動であり、わずかな衝撃による振動と風を受け流す形状が重要である。受け止める物体の大きさや性質と動く素材の気象条件など、調査は、あらゆる素材におよんだ。樹氷は風向に従って成長する。ゆえに樹氷の姿形は空気の流れを示している。

Soft rime. An otherwise rare phenomenon, yet often observed on Mount Rokko in the winter. Under specific atmospheric conditions water vapour transforms directly into ice upon meeting objects of certain sizes and properties. As soft rime grows against the direction of wind, every branch becomes a testimony to the movements of air.

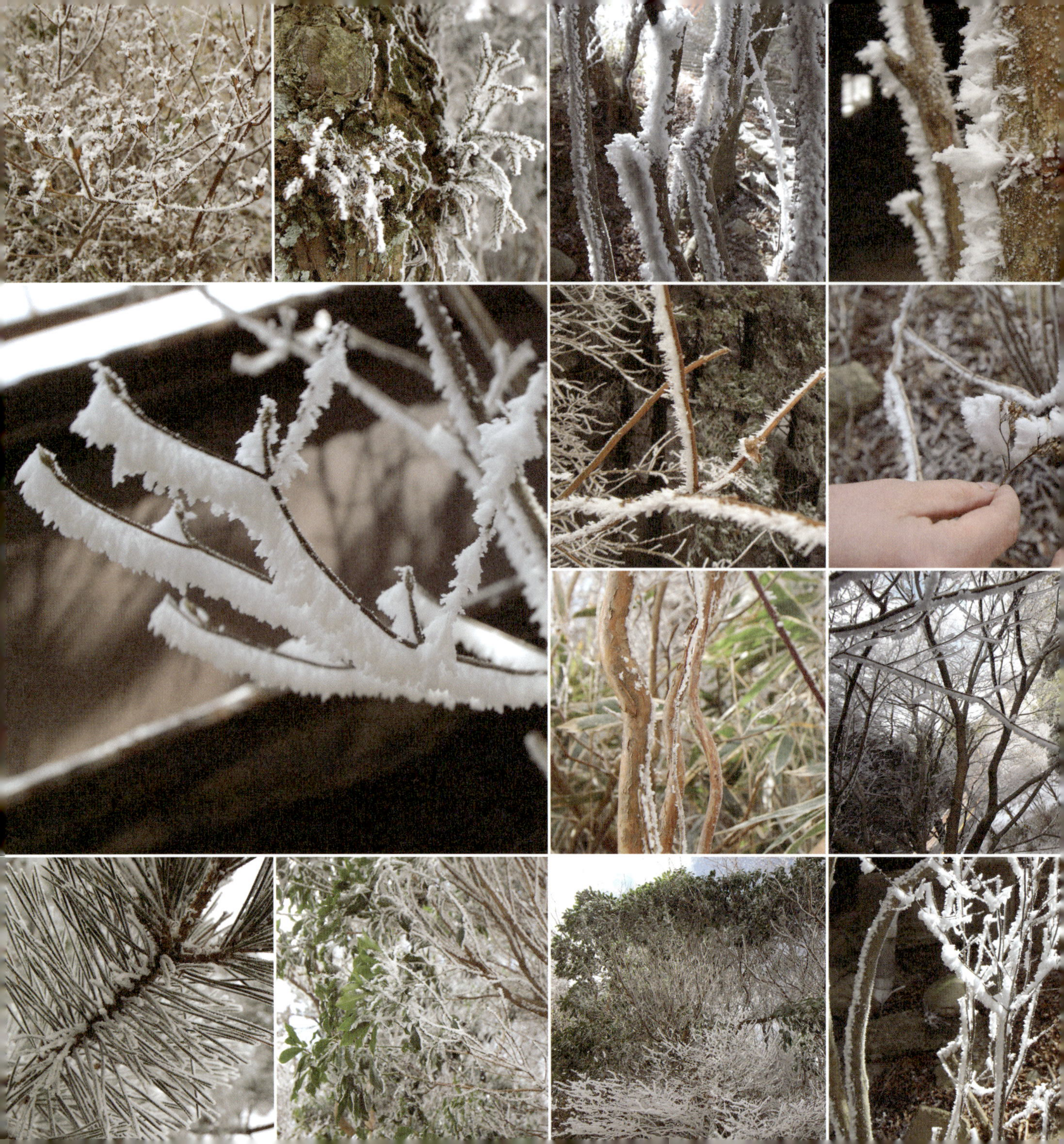

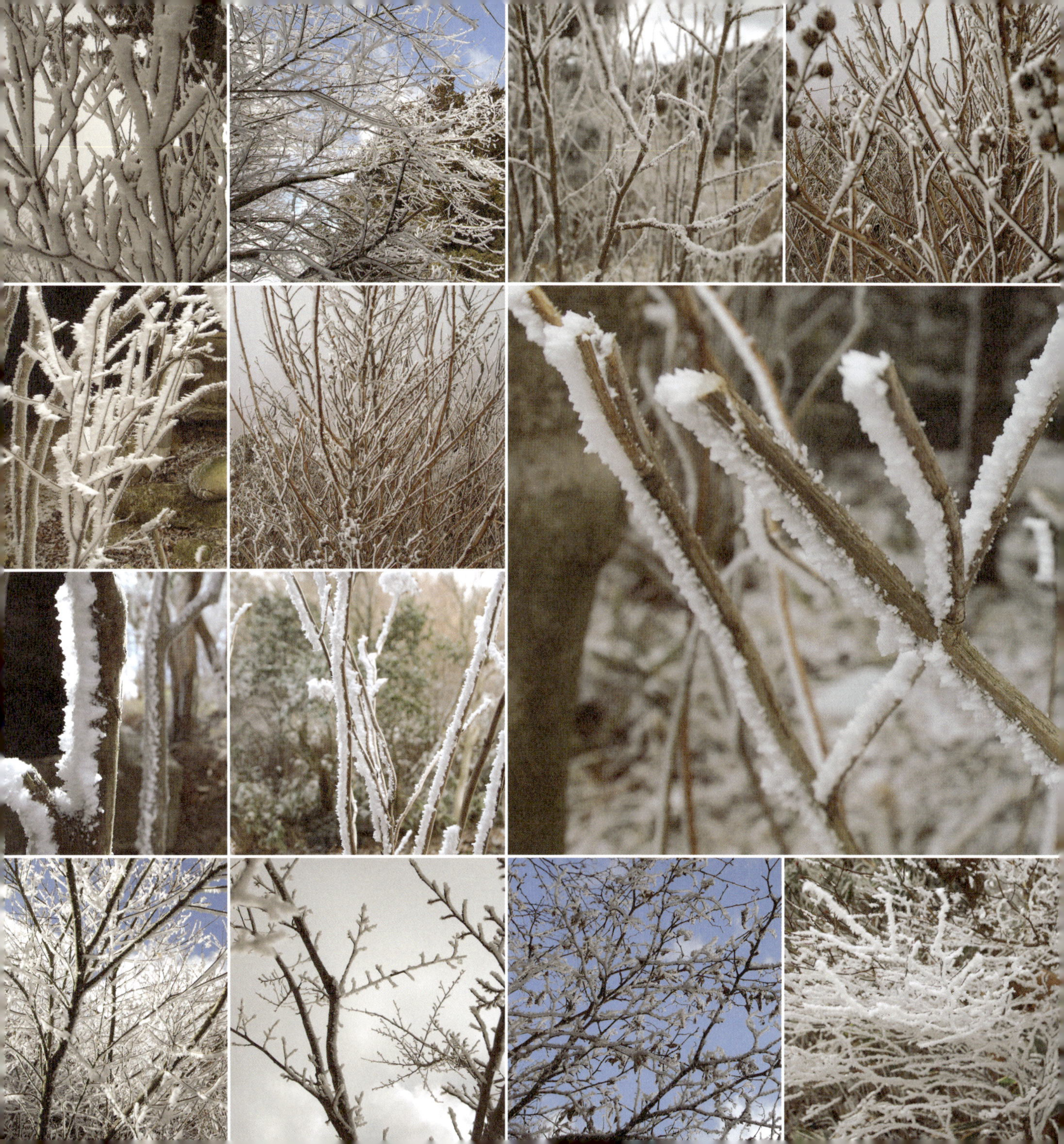

動く素材を受け止める素材は、その太さの違いで振動と表面を流れる風の速度が異なることが分かった。

Attentive research of soft rime reveals criteria for material thickness, surface wind speeds and vibration.

できるだけ長く美しく樹氷を見せるための建築を求めて山頂にモックアップを設置した。水を含みやすい木などが優れていた。水は接着剤であることが確認できた。夜明けには、周りの木々と同様に着氷が見られた。

An experiment to facilitate the most extensive soft rime was carried out on the mountain peak. The investigations of branch dimensions were put to use and wood that was particularly permeable by water was chosen. After a night of the right conditions, the mock-up was covered with soft rime similarly to the trees around it.

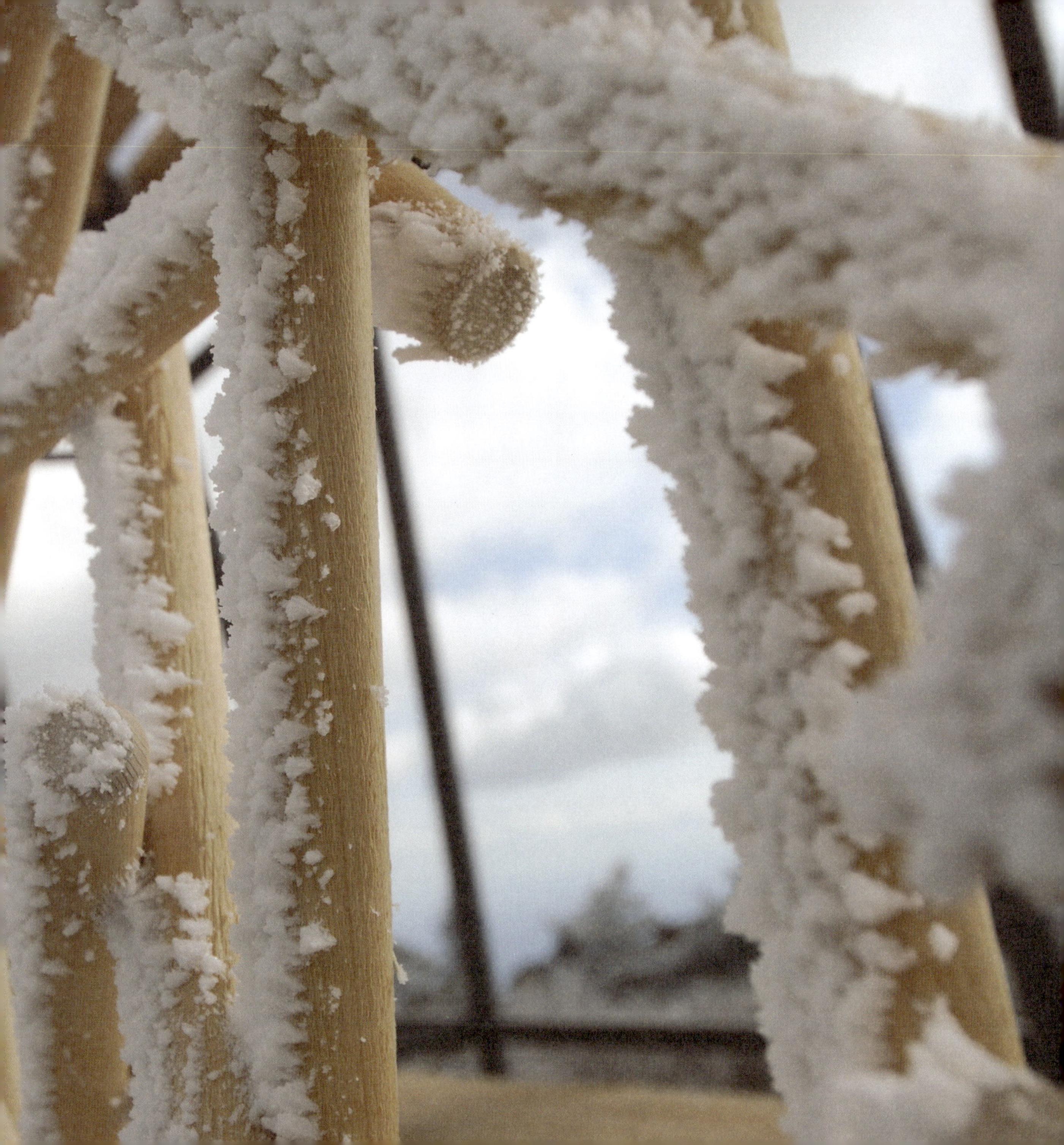

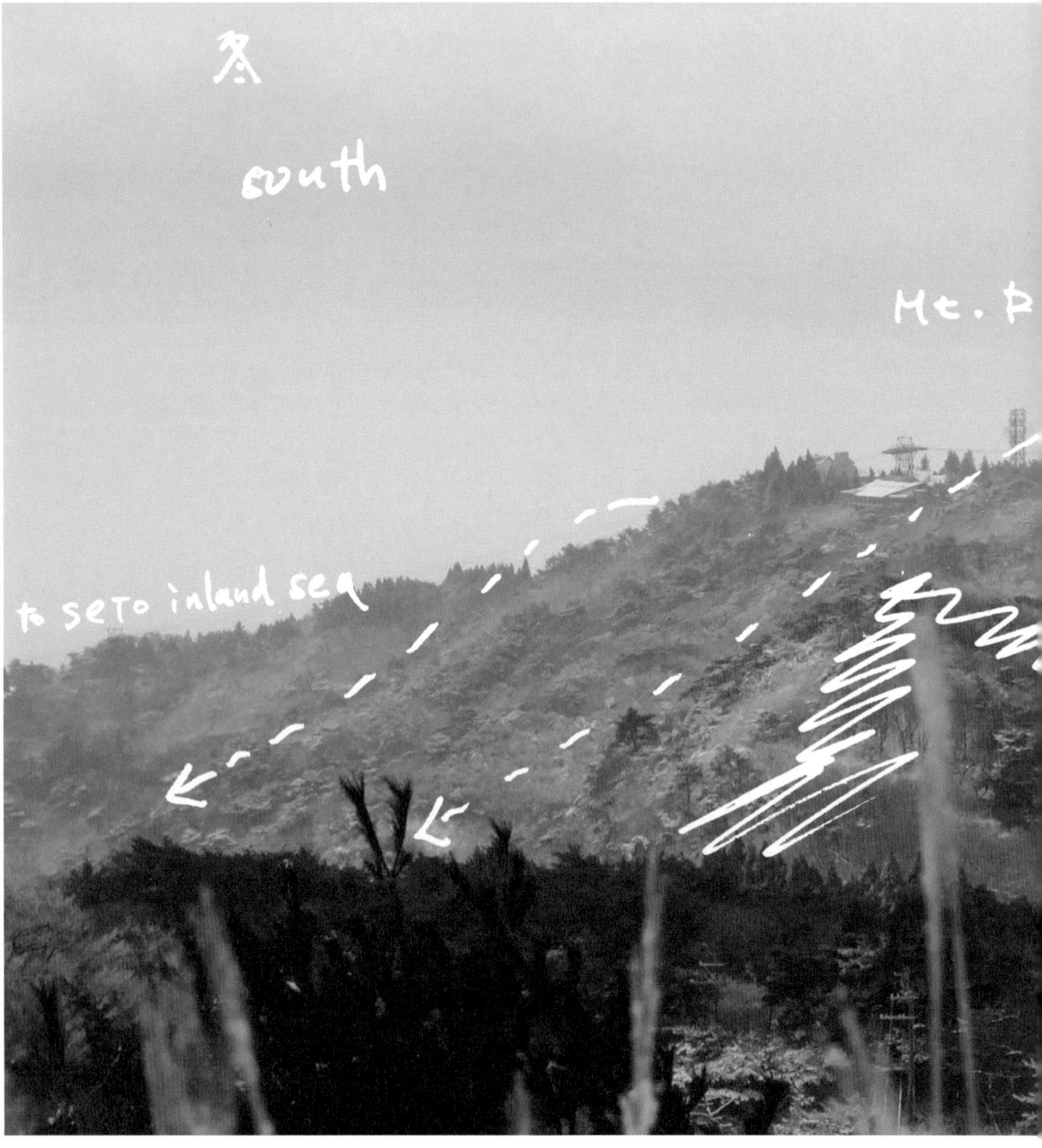
冬
south
Mt.
to seto inland sea

North

from JAPAN SEA 日本海から

樹木

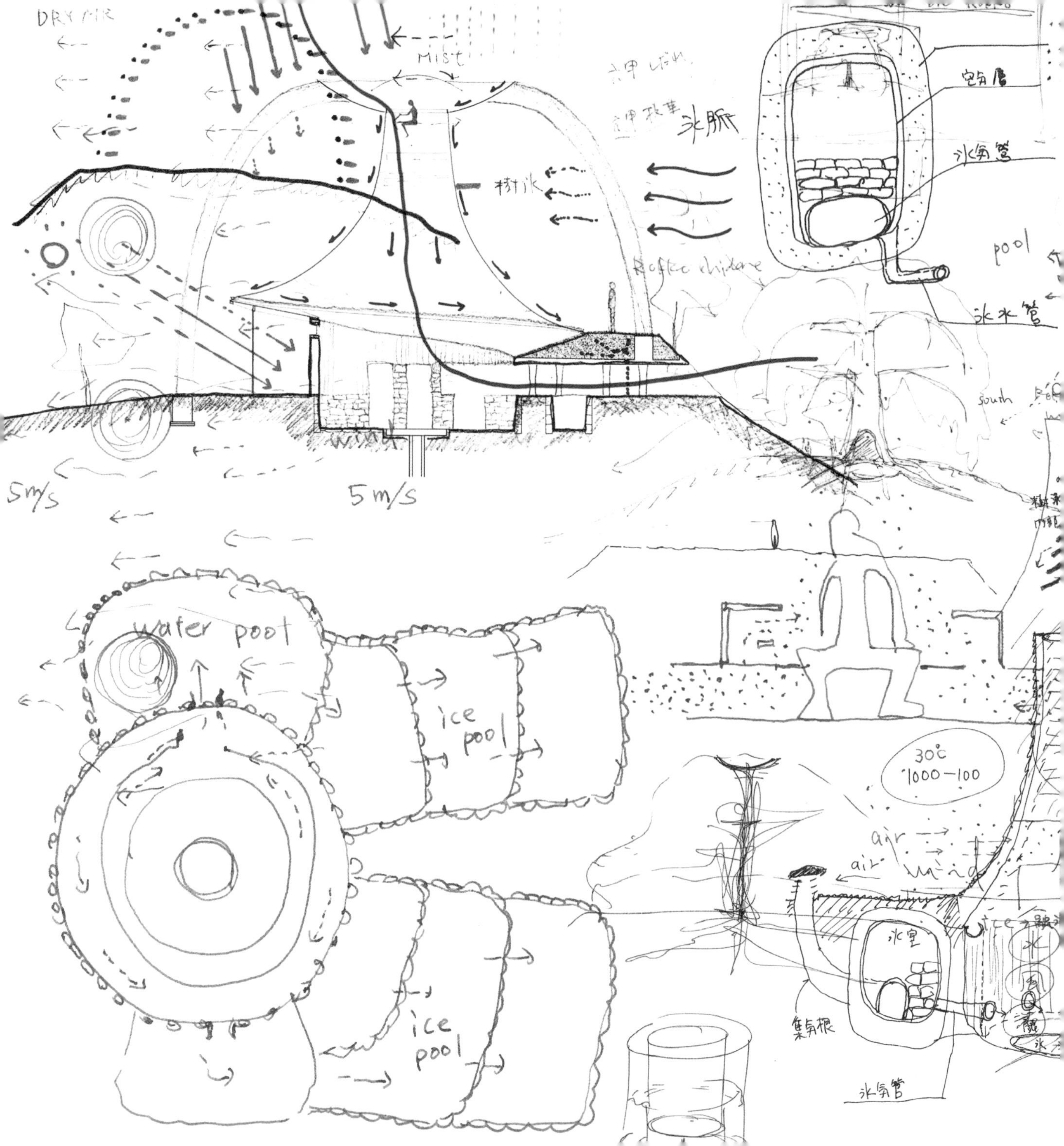
DRY AIR
Mist
樹氷
氷脈
空気層
氷気管
pool
氷水管
south
5m/s
5 m/s
water pool
ice pool
ice pool
30°C
1000−100
air
air
氷室
集気根
氷気管

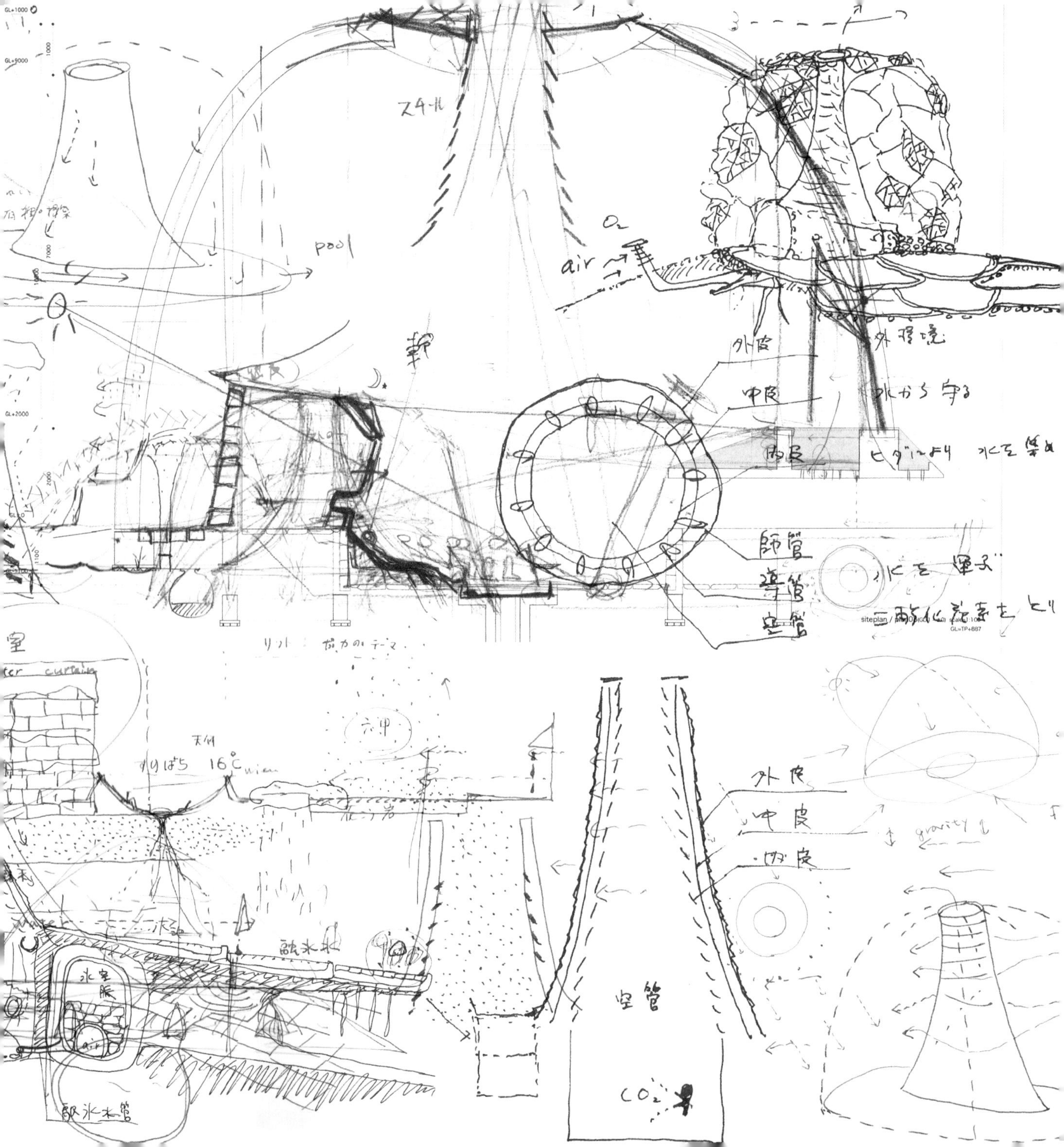

GL+1000
GL+9000
GL+2000
pool
air
O_2
外皮
中皮
内皮
外環境
水から守る
ヒダにより 水を集め
師管
導管
空管
siteplan / plan
GL=TP+887
16°C
外皮
中皮
内皮
空管
CO_2
gravity
air

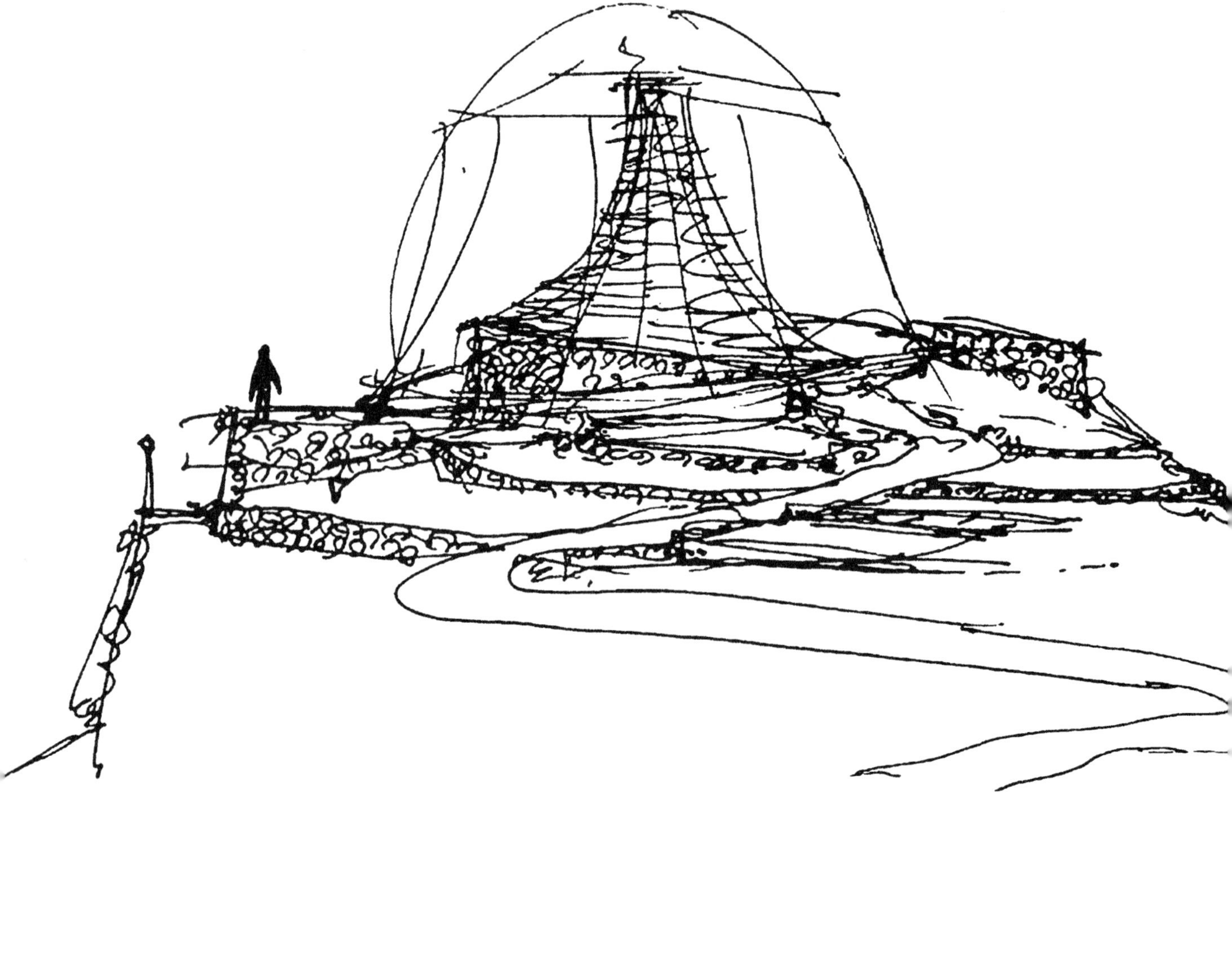

六甲枝垂れ

1,000mの山頂には、川もなければ水源もない。では、水は誰がどこから運んでくるのか。

六甲山の頂きからは日本海と瀬戸内海、ふたつの海が望める。私の建築家としてのキャリアの中で最も標高が高く最も過酷な気象条件でのチャレンジは、私を引き付けた。この山頂に最もふさわしい固有の姿とはどのようなものか。

地球上で最も美しく、かつ知的な営みのひとつは、「水は太陽によって運ばれる」ということである。夏は南の瀬戸内海に注がれた太陽によって水は雲・霧となり、山肌を上がって頂上付近まで運ばれると雨へと変わり山頂に水をもたらす。霧の六甲、雲海の六甲と呼ばれる風景である。また冬になると逆に北の日本海から運ばれてくる湿った空気によって山頂へ雪や氷として水をもたらす。山上では水が気体・液体・固体とさまざまに変化し、六甲山固有の「水」の循環がこの場所の美しさを引き立てている。中でも最も美しいのは樹氷と呼ばれる現象である。温度、湿度、風速、風向のすべての条件がそろった時にのみ特異な姿形を見せる。

標高1,000m、極寒の冬の六甲の孤独なリサーチが始まった。温度、湿度、風速、風向の、すべての気象条件を読み、樹氷着氷を予測し、前日から六甲山の登山が始まる。そして朝を迎えると六甲山は一面が白い光の世界に包まれた、とても美しい景色だった。

私はこの場所で水が織り成すエナジースケープが体感できる建築を六甲山につくりたいと考えた。周りの木々と同じように着氷しこの自然の美しさを見せることができる建築は六甲山を展望するにふさわしいものになると確信した。

紅葉や雪景色、雲海、そして樹氷といった、美しいと感じる地球の景色。それは自然のエネルギーの循環がもたらす変化の景色である。建築も、その場所の風・水・太陽・月・地形に合わせて素材やディテール・サイズを整理していくと、その場所ならではの姿形が現れてくる。結果、すべてのディテールは地球に通じ、その場所のもつ最も個性的かつ固有の文化を導くものではないかと考えている。

感じ取って欲しいのは、水に導かれた六甲山固有の姿形を示すことで地球の真の美しさを再認識してもらい、われわれ人類や植物等の生命もその水の循環の中に宿っているということである。

あなたが六甲山を訪れ、街の美しい景色が見下ろせなかったとしても、むしろそれはとても幸運なことなのかもしれない。なぜなら今あなたは、六甲山の水を見ている。そして六甲山の本来あるべき姿、エナジースケープの中にいるのだから。

ROKKO OBSERVATORY

On a 1000m-high mountaintop, if there are no rivers, there are no river sources. So who carries the water, and from where?

From the top of Mount Rokko, I can see two seas: the Sea of Japan and the Seto Inland Sea. During my career as an architect, I have been attracted by the challenge of high altitudes and severe climatic conditions. What is the inherent form appropriate to this mountaintop?

One of the most beautiful, intellectual actions on the Earth is "water carried by the sun." In summer, due to the sunlight pouring onto the Seto Inland Sea, the water becomes clouds or mist, climbs the mountain faces toward their summits, changes into rain, and brings water to the mountain peaks. This scene is known as Rokko in fog, or Rokko in a sea of clouds. In winter, water is brought as snow and ice by the wet air carried from the Sea of Japan to the mountaintop. On the mountain, water changes between gas, liquid, and solid, and a circulation of "water" unique to Mount Rokko enhances the beauty of this place. Above all, the most beautiful phenomenon is called soft rime, the ice that forms on trees. This particular form is only shown when all the necessary conditions of temperature, humidity, wind velocity, and wind direction coincide.

I began my solitary research on Mount Rokko at an altitude of 1000m, in the severe cold of winter. I read all the climatic conditions of temperature, humidity, wind velocity, wind direction, estimated when rime would form on the trees, and began climbing Mount Rokko the day before. When Mount Rokko greeted the morning, one side was enveloped in a world of white light – an extremely beautiful scene.

I wanted to place on Mount Rokko a building that would enable a bodily sensation of the energyscape woven by water in this place. I was convinced that architecture showing the beauty of nature by icing up in the same way as the surrounding trees would be appropriate for viewing Mount Rokko.

Scenes that give a sense of the Earth's beauty: autumn leaves, snowscapes, a sea of fog, frost-covered trees. These are scenes of the changes brought about by the circulation of natural energy. In architecture too, by adjusting the sizes of details and materials, including the wind, water, Sun, Moon, and terrain of the place, a form unique to this place will appear. As a result, all the details are connected to the Earth, and I think that this may lead toward the most individual and characteristic culture of a place.

What I want you to perceive is that, by manifesting a form derived from water that is unique to Mount Rokko, you again realize anew the true beauty of the Earth, and that the lives of plants and we humans are also part of the water cycle.
Even if you visit Mount Rokko, it may be a very lucky thing that you are not able to look down at the beautiful scenery of the town. That is because now you are watching the water of Mount Rokko. And that is because you are in the energyscape that comprises the original form of Mount Rokko.

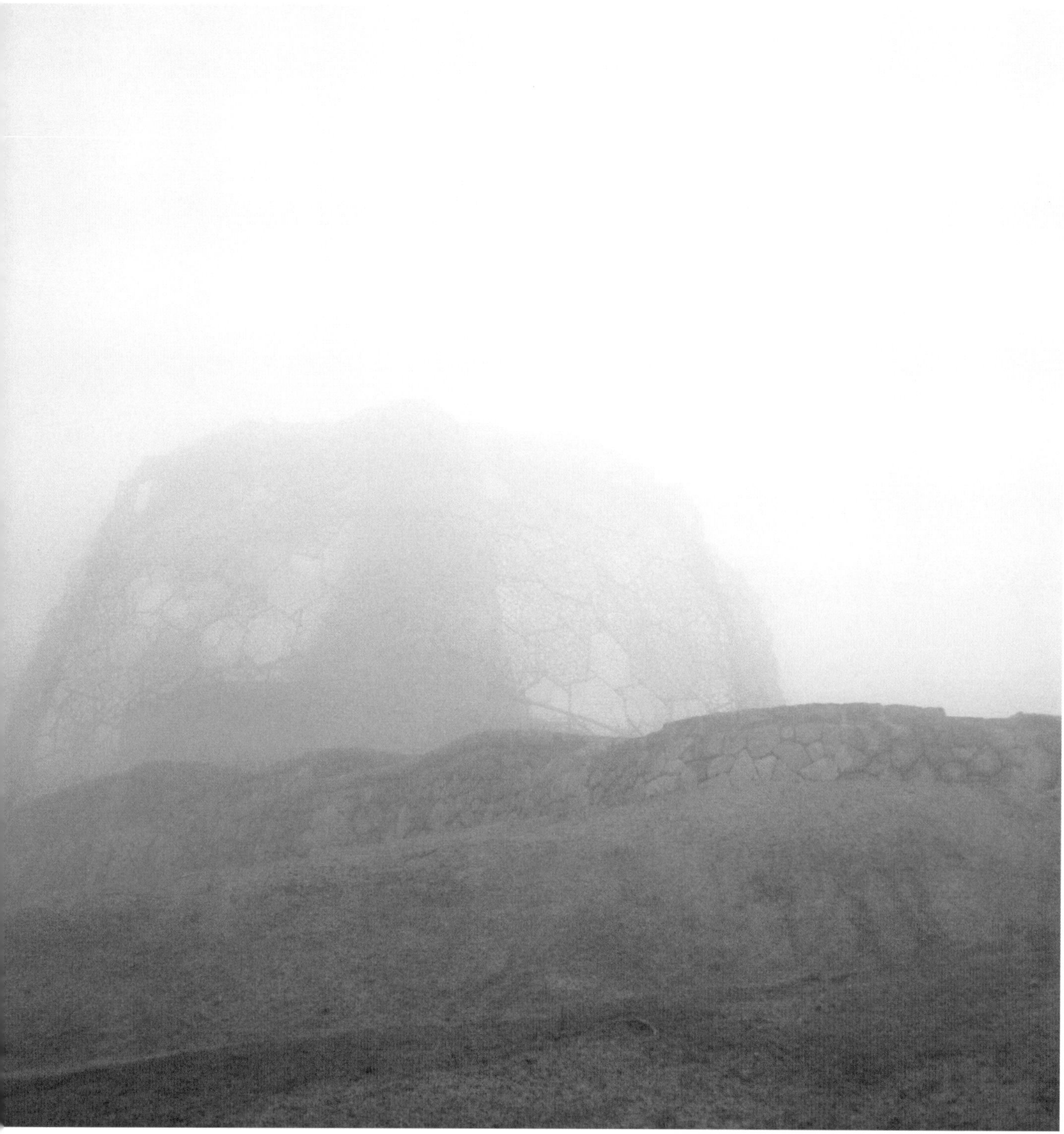

展望デッキは枝葉や、葉脈のような空間に包まれ、中央の幹は風を吸い上げるために筒状になっている。

The observation deck is wrapped in a skin of branches and sits on an interior space protruding its conical opening through the center of the deck.

頂上には水を溜めるための棚状の石積みがある。夏に溜まった水は冬にここで氷となる。

The approach twists through terraces of water that is filled in the summer and cut in the winter.

水は1000m下の瀬戸内海から太陽によって水蒸気となって運ばれてくる。水源のない山頂に豊かな水をもたらす。

Water is carried by the energy of the Sun as vapour from the Inland Sea a thousand metres below to the peak where there is no other water source.

夏から冬へ。水は、液体から固体へと変化する。水は固体の状態で液体に浮かぶ、地球上で唯一の特別な素材である。そのため人類は氷をさまざまなかたちで利用することができた。ここでは氷室に溜めて、夏の冷却エネルギーに利用する。

From summer to winter, water changes from liquid to solid. It is the only material on our planet that floats solid on liquid. Because of this humans have been able to conveniently access and utilize it. Here it is cut and stored in ice rooms, becoming a cooling energy in summer.

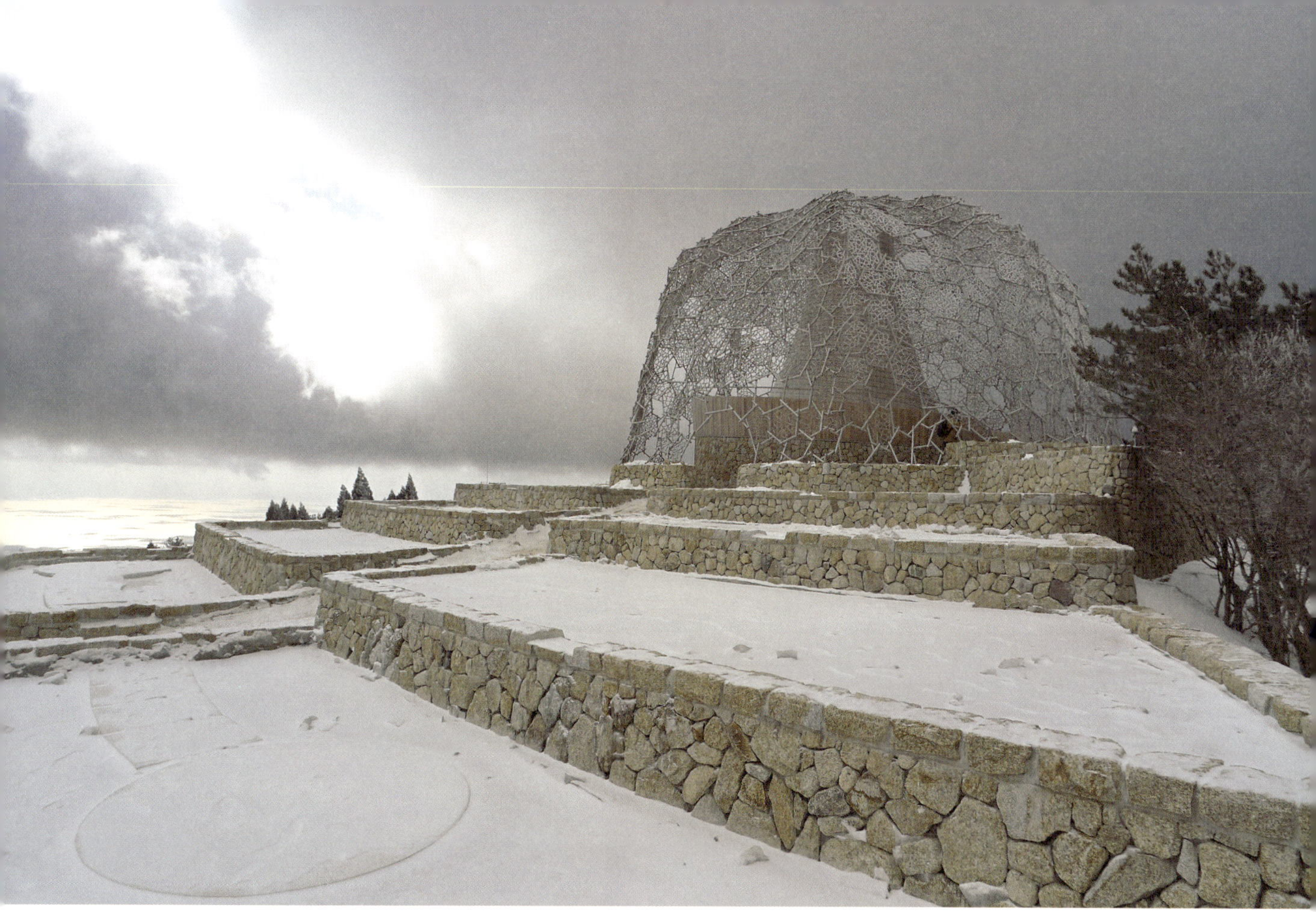

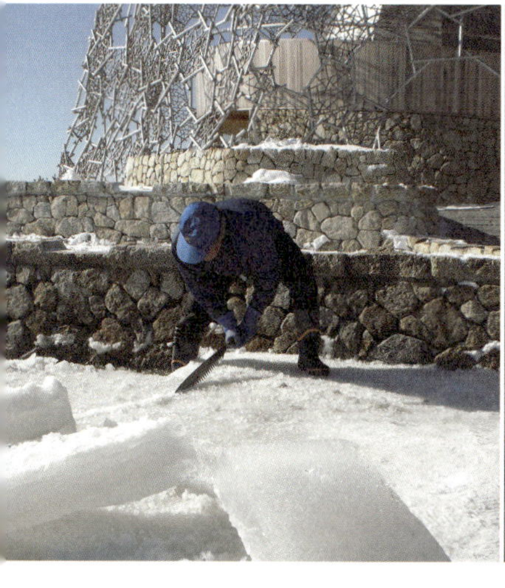

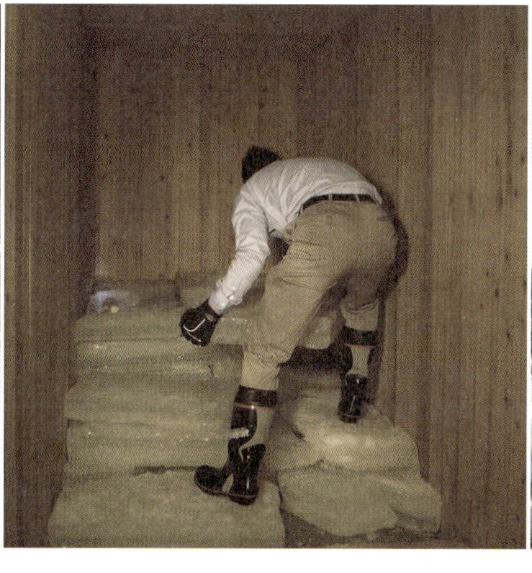

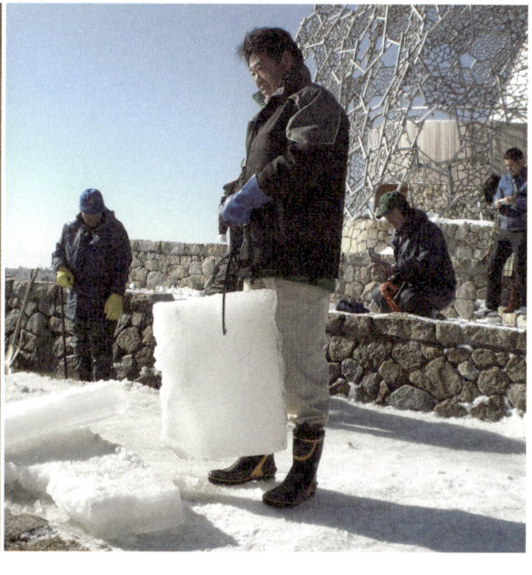

リサーチの結果、樹氷は、湿度ほぼ100％、温度マイナス5℃以下の水蒸気が風速5m/s程度で、枝などの物質に衝突し、衝撃振動を受けることによって、結晶化していくことが立証された。どれかひとつでも欠けると着氷は見られない。

展望台の枝葉のディテールはこの樹氷を着氷させることから導き出されている。枝葉の太さや構成は周囲の樹木に倣い、風が抜け、振動が起こることで樹氷が着氷しやすいディテールとした。

展望台周囲の地形には雨水を貯えられる氷棚を設け、地下に氷室がある。冬に氷を採取し、夏まで氷を保つためである。古くから六甲には、氷室の文化があった。この氷の文化を継承している。氷棚の広さと氷室の容積、ディテールは氷の液化の速さと量から導き出されている。冬の氷は夏まで貯え、氷が冷気をもたらしてくれる。夏が終わる頃すべて解けて水となる。内部中央の形状は、それら空気を吸い上げる幹のような形状をしている。

空気、氷、水、樹氷、すべて六甲の動く素材による建築である。

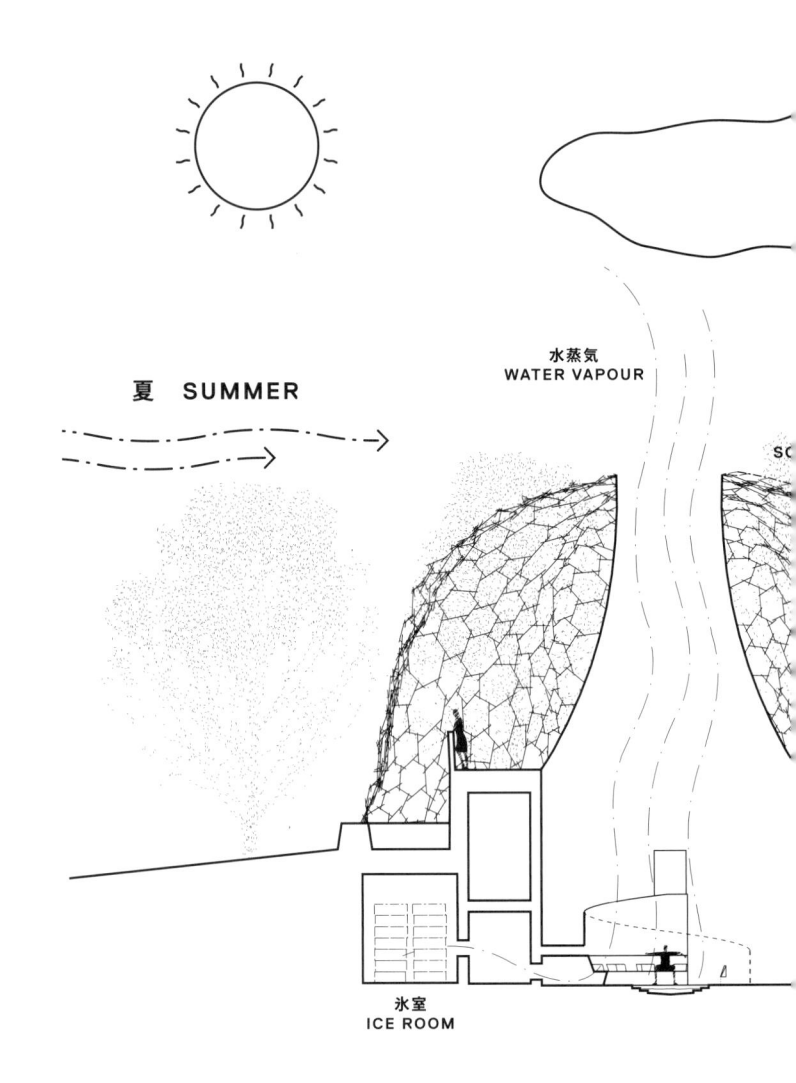

夏　SUMMER

水蒸気
WATER VAPOUR

氷室
ICE ROOM

冬 WINTER

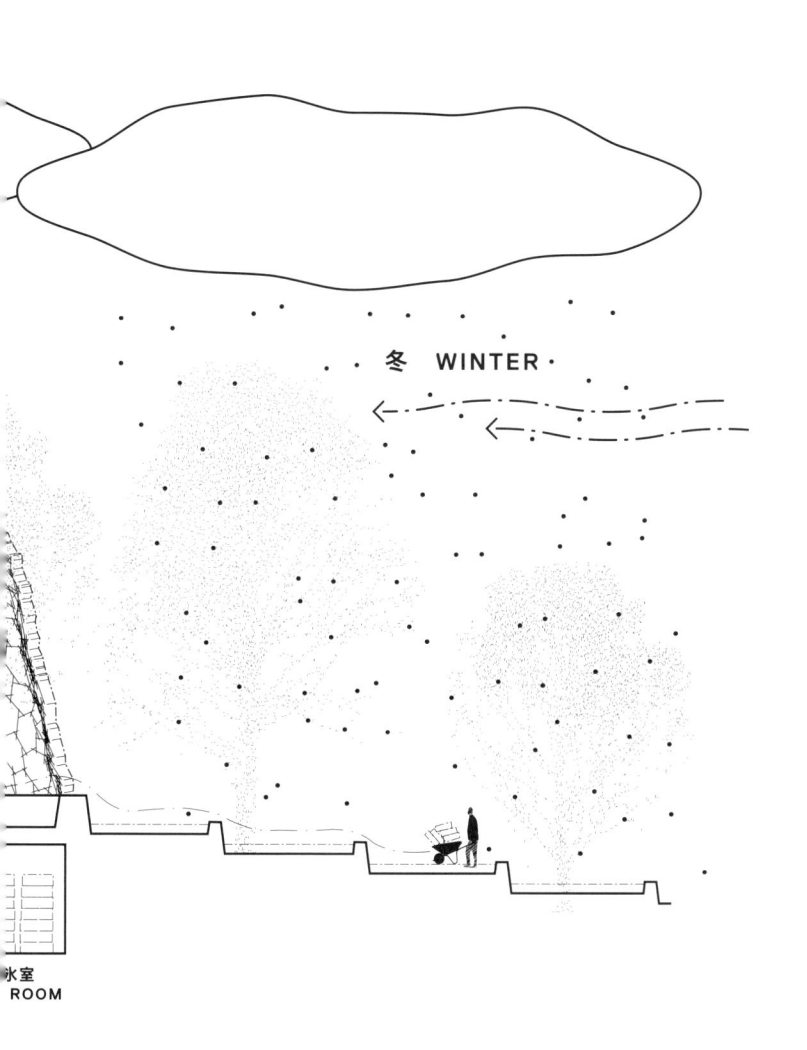

氷室
ROOM

It was demonstrated through research that the formation of rime on trees requires approximately 100% humidity, vapour with a temperature of -5°C or less, and wind speed around 5 m/s, and crystallization occurs due to impact vibrations in solid material such as tree branches. When even one of these factors is missing, the ice coating will not occur.

The foliage-like details of the observatory were derived from the way that ice forms as rime on trees. The thickness and composition of this foliage imitates the neighbouring trees, allowing wind to pass through and cause vibrations, details that make it easy for rime to accrete.

An ice shelf to collect rainwater has been established in the terrain around the observatory, and there is an ice room underground. This for the collection of ice in winter to be stored until summer. The culture of ice rooms has existed in the Rokko region since ancient times. This is an inheritance of that ice culture. Details such as the width of the ice shelf and the capacity of the ice room were derived from the quantity and speed of ice liquefaction. The winter ice is saved until summer, and it provides cooling. It melts into water just as summer ends. The core has a form like an air extraction shaft.

Air, ice, water, rime. All the moving materials of Rokko are expressed in the architecture.

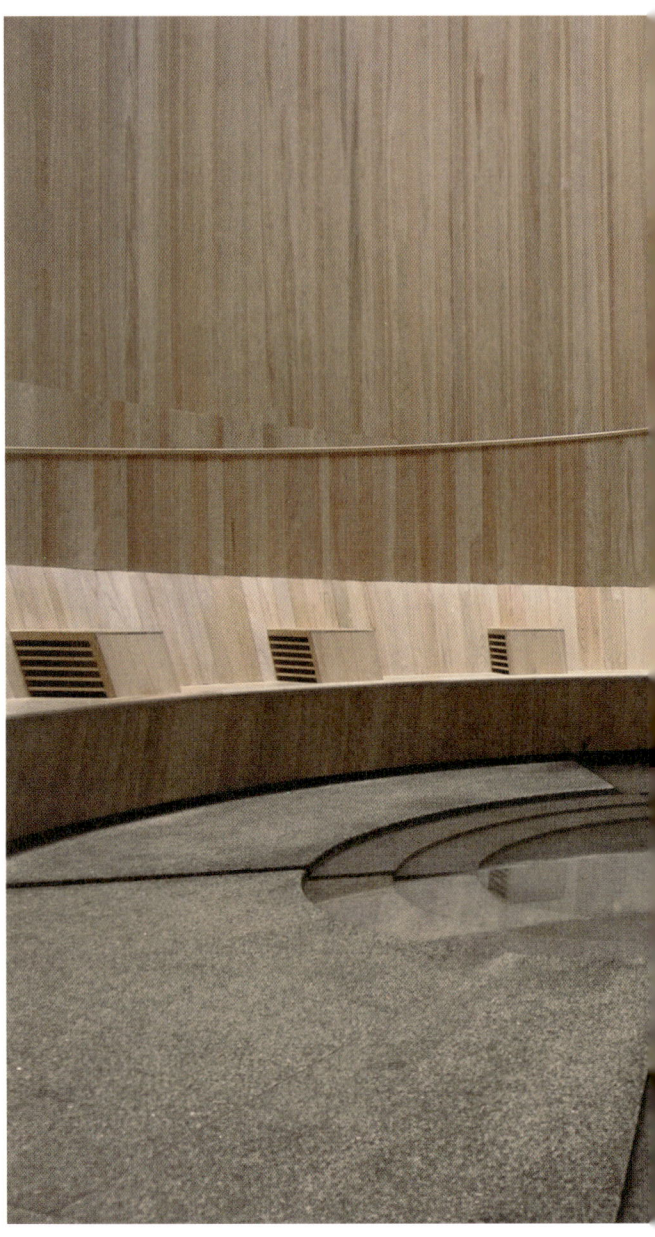

冬から夏へ。水は、再び固体から液体へ変わる。水は、地球上のすべての生命にとって、最も重要な素材である。ここでは、解けた氷が空間の熱を奪ってくれる。涼しい風が肘掛けから流れてくる。その後また気体へと変わり、トップライトから空へ戻って行く。水は常に地球を循環している。

From winter to summer, water changes from solid to liquid. Here, the melting ice removes the heat of the space. Cool breezes emanate from the armrests. Thus changing to gas it returns through the top light to the skies. On Earth, water is in endless circulation.

ある一定の条件がそろうと、六甲山の木々には樹氷が着氷する。同じように展望台にも樹氷は木々に着氷する。この時、建築は地球の一部と言える。

When all conditions are aligned, the trees of Mount Rokko are covered in soft rime, and so is the observatory. In that moment the architecture can be said to be a natural part of our Earth.

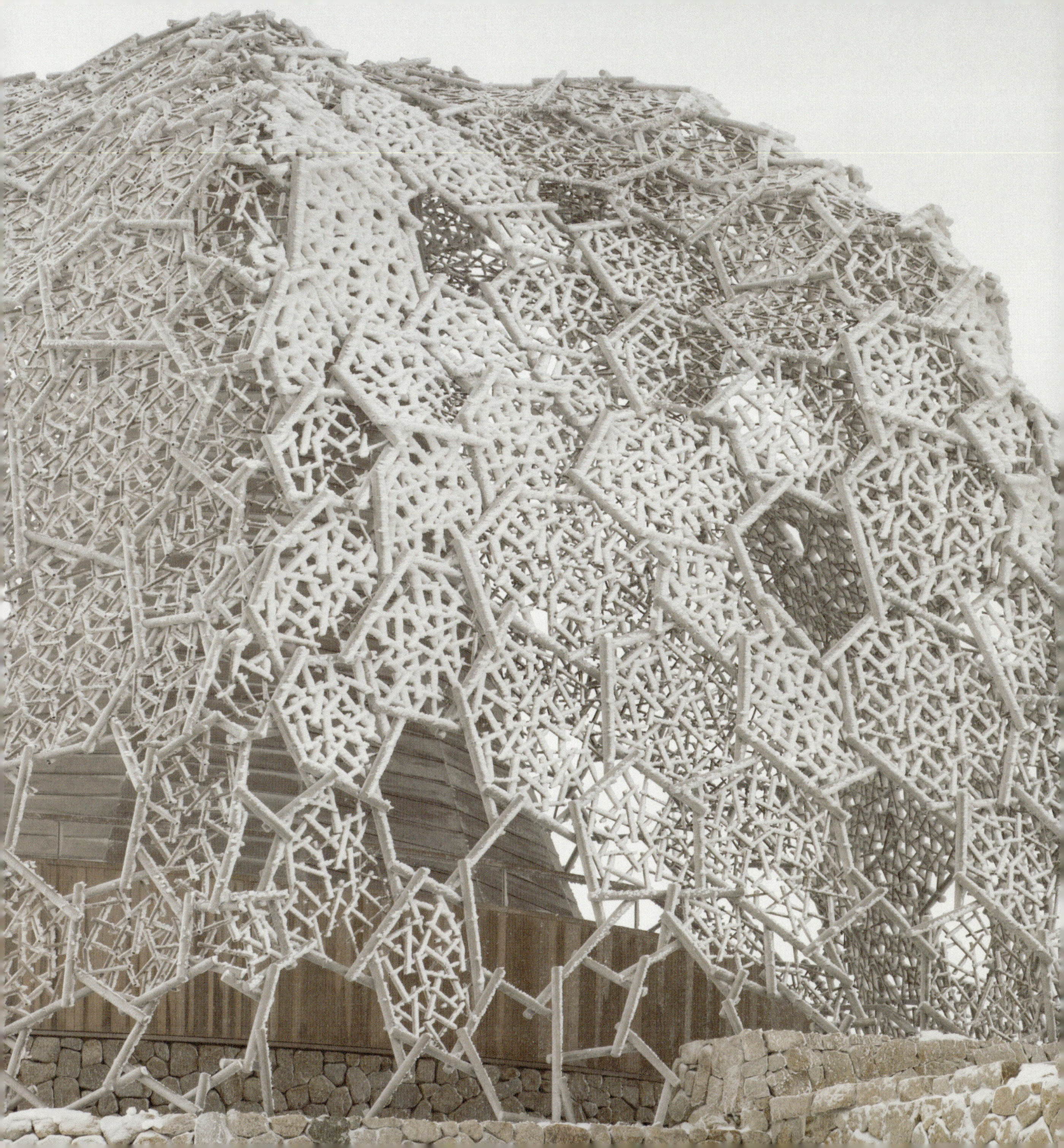

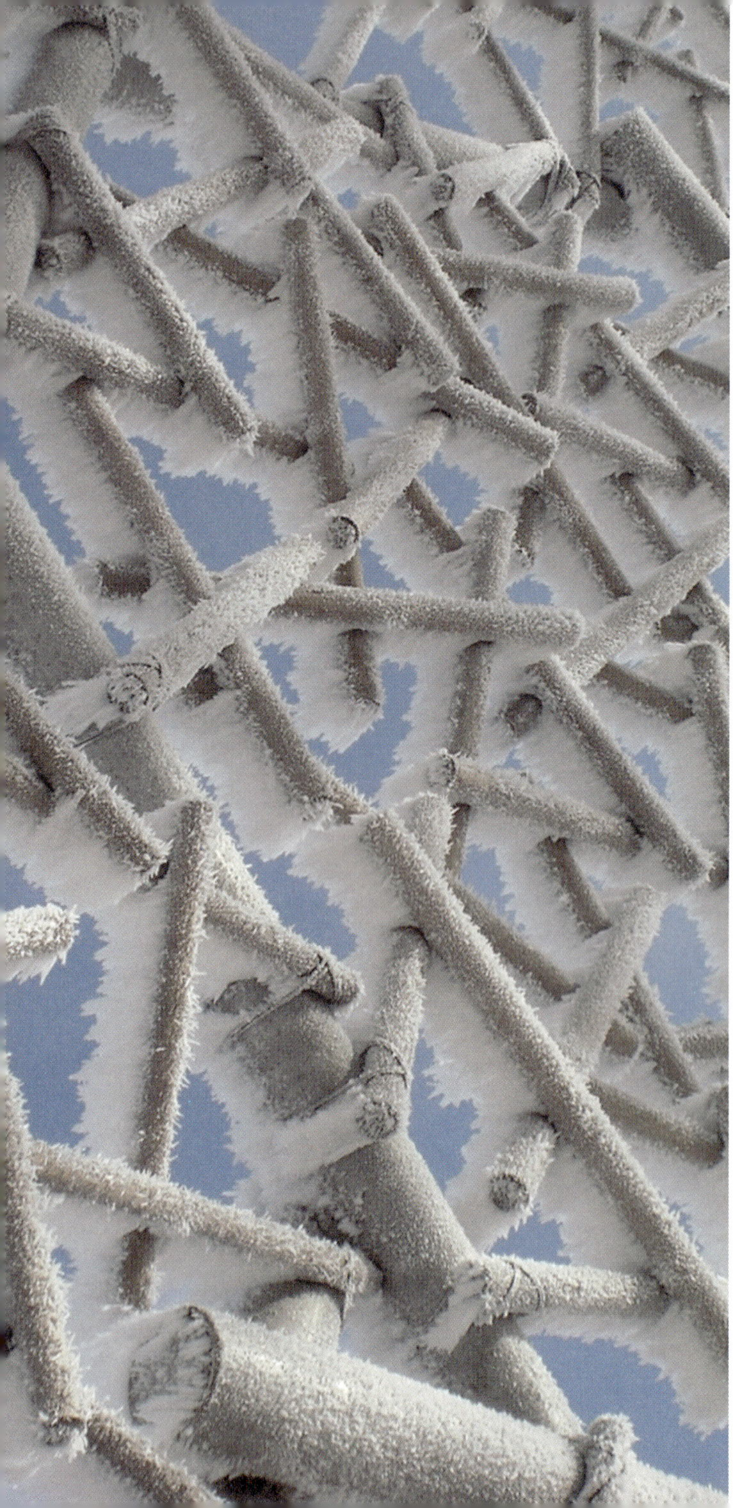

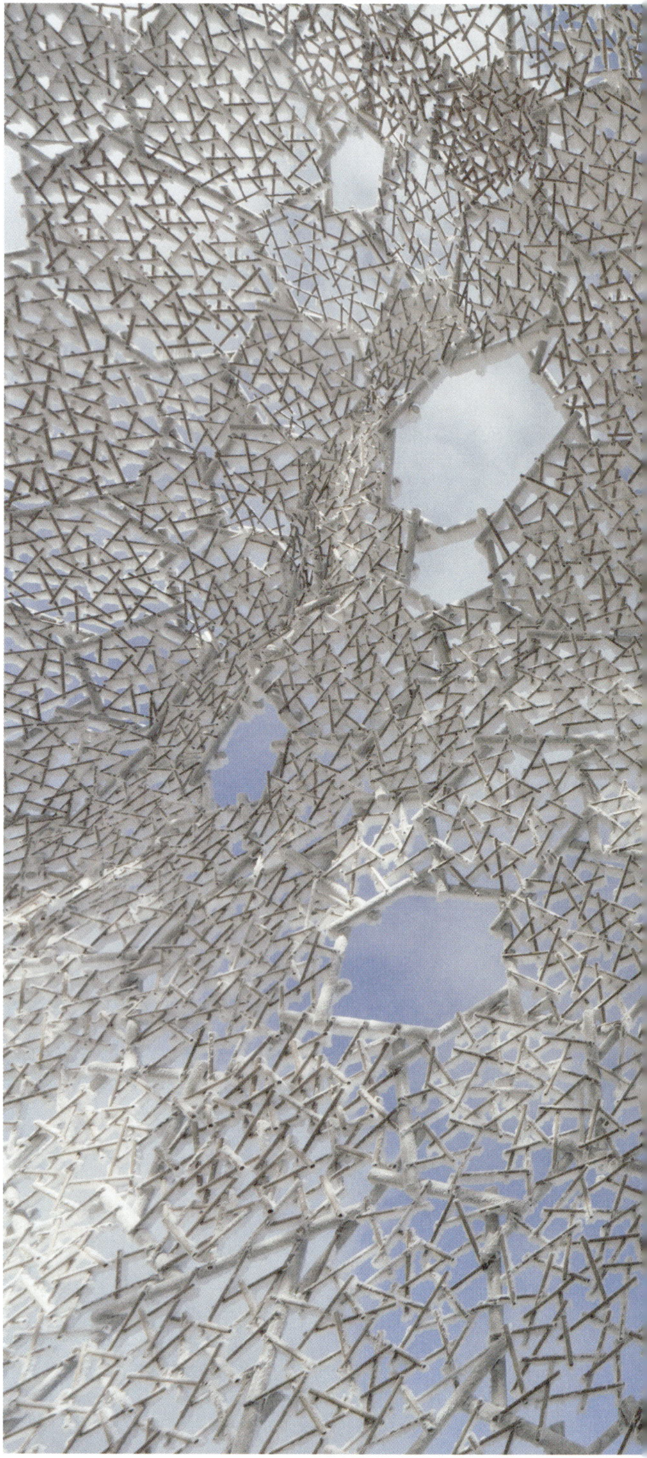

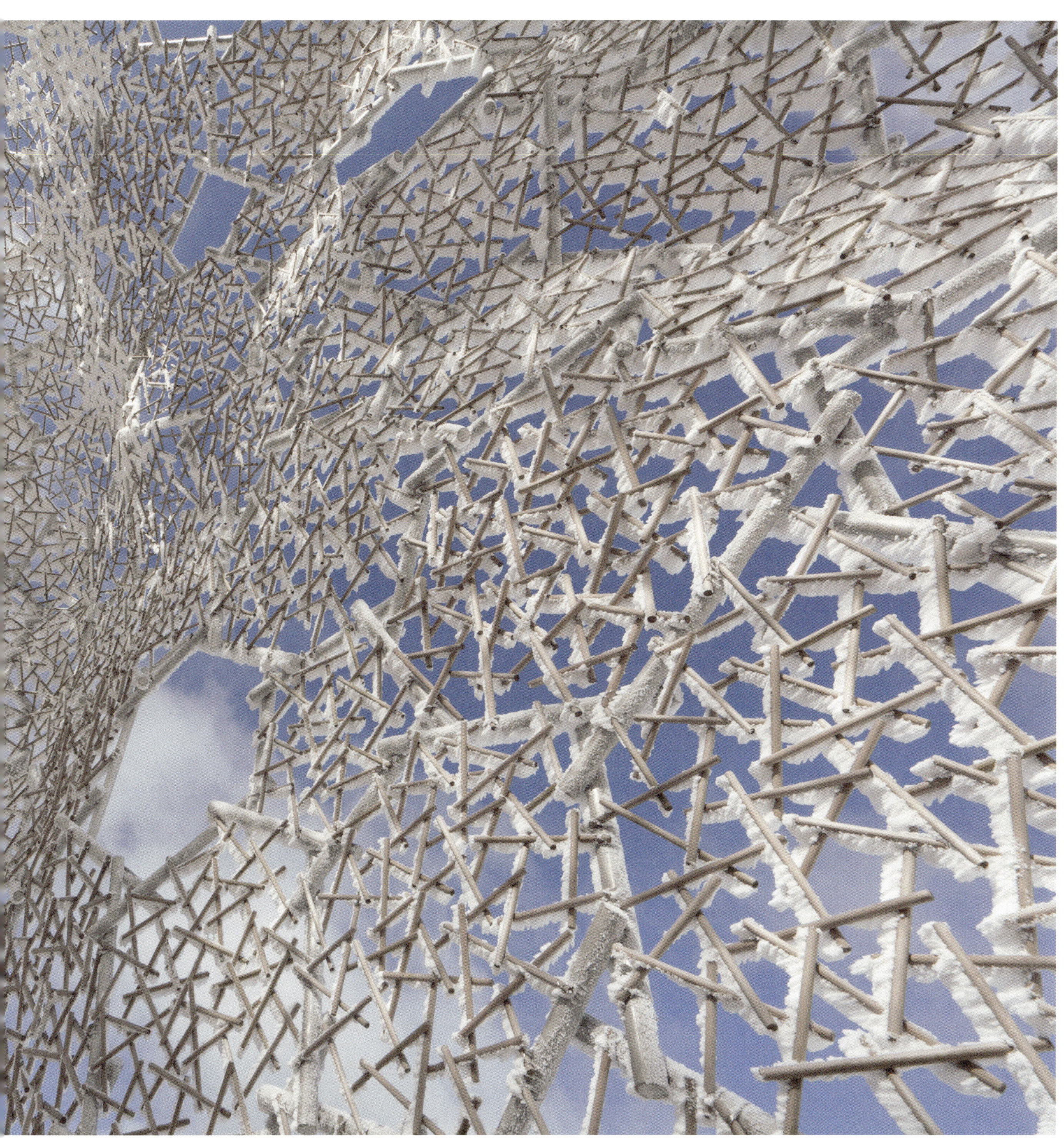

ウッツォンの後継者
モーエンス・プリップ=ブース／建築家

三分一博志に初めて会ったのは2010年、コペンハーゲンでのことである。場所は大手の建築事務所のひとつで、午後遅くに彼は自作を紹介する講演をそこで行った。互いに交わした言葉はほんのわずかだったが、それすら必要なかった。なぜなら、すべてはあまりに明確で、正しく、建物には真実が表現され、そこにあるすべての要素同士は関連し合い、結び付き合っていたからだ。立地条件理解のまさにお手本だった。

私は、ヴィルヘルム・ヴォラートやヨーン・ウッツォンのもとで長い間仕事をしてきたが、結局ウッツォンの仕事や思想はほとんど理解されてこなかったというのが実感である。ところがここにとうとう、彼の辿った道をさらに先へ進もうとする建築家を見出したと思った。そのアプローチは、素材や自然を深いところまで理解し、基礎的な自然の諸力と、それらが人や人の活動にとってもつ重要な意味を認識し活用しようとするものである。私にしてみれば、これはウッツォンの思想と仕事を積極的に継承することに等しい。残念ながら、ウッツォン自身には、そうした仕事を全うすることが許されなかったし、またその機会にも恵まれなかった。要するに、その晩私は幸せな気分だった。これで再び何もかもが可能になる、先へ続く道がはっきりと示されたと、そんな風に思えたからである。

翌日、三分一にヨーン・ウッツォンの建物をいくつか見せて回った。キンゴーの集合住宅、フレーデンスボアの集合住宅、そしてヘレベッグのウッツォン自邸である。たいてい彼はひとりで歩き回り、観察していた。時折われわれをじっと見つめると、うなずきながら微笑みを浮かべることがあったが、何も言わなかった。

われわれがウッツォンの仕事場と呼んでいた場所も見せた。ヘレベックの森と浜辺である。浜辺は、水際まで木々が生い茂り、ウッツォンのお気に入りの場所のひとつであると共に、大いなるインスピレーション源でもあった。とはいえ、子供っぽいロマンチックな感傷を誘うだけの場所と言う人もあるくらいなので、三分一がどんな反応を示すか、私には興味津々だった。その彼は、長いこと身じろぎもせずに立ち尽くしていたが、やがて満面に笑みを浮かべて私のほうに歩いてきて――目には涙を浮かべていた、と思う――そのまま車に戻っていった。

三分一と最初の出会いをこんなふうに書くと、少しばかり個人的な感想に偏りすぎるように見えるかもしれない。残念ながら、私は三分一の建物を自ら体験する、つまり住んでみる機会にはまだ恵まれていない。でも、作品の背後にいるのがどんな人物かは分かったし、その人と自分の間には強いつながりがあると感じたので、図面や写真からでも実物の建物が生き生きと浮かび上がってくるように思えた。そこから、私は、自分がいつも講演を締めくくる際の、「建築とは立地条件の真実にほかならない」という言葉の正しさを確信した。

そもそも、建築とは何のためにあるのだろうか。この問題は、ことに建築学校では、文字を使って、それも純粋にアカデミックな用語を使ってしばしば論じられるのだが、人びとの幸福な生活の追求に根差した建物なり建築プロジェクトを

通して、そうした問い掛けに答えようとすることは稀である。暮らしを幸福にするための環境とは、つくる人間が素材に通暁(つうぎょう)し、その生活が行われる、まさにその場所に適した建物へとその素材を構成することで創り出されるのである。

ウッツォンはこのことを、「最も奥深い存在としての建築」というエッセーの中で次のように述べている。

…

　　最も奥深い真実の存在としての建築とは、自然界における種子に比べることができる。自然界の成長原理における不可避的な在り様は、建築の根本概念とならねばならない。種子が草や木に成長する時のことを考えるなら、もし個体間の成長能力にさほど違いがなく、しかもどの個体にも等しく妥協なしに成長してゆける力が備わっているとすれば、同属内のすべての個体はみな同じように成長してゆくだろう。それぞれに置かれた条件が異なるからこそ、類似する種子は相互に甚だしく異なる生体へと成長してゆくのである。

…

　　また、別の箇所ではこう書く。

…

　　自然はいかなる妥協も知らず、すべての困難を受け入れる。困難を困難としてではなく、単なる新たな要因として受け入れ、やがてそれは何ら衝突や対立の兆候も見せることなくひとつの全体へとすんなり進化してゆく。

…

以上の引用を含む1948年のこのウッツォンのエッセイは、ぜひ、一読を勧めたい。それは、三分一とウッツォンの制作方法の驚くべき類似性を明かす証言である。もっとも、三分一のアプローチの方がもっと科学的ではあるかもしれないが。

ほかにも多くの人が人間の創作活動に対する自然のもつ重要性について語ってきた。およそ900年前に、クレルヴォーのベルナルドゥス(聖ベルナール、1090-1153)はこう言った。「これは間違いないことだが、人は書物などより木からはるかに多くのことが学べるものだ。木や石は、偉い師匠からは学べぬことを教えてくれる。」

時代が下り、近代になるとヨハン・アウグスト・ストリンドベリは、こんな警句じみた言葉を残している。「自然を模倣せよ、然り、ぜひとも、しかし決して奴隷にはならずに。何よりも、自然自身の創造のやり方を真似るのだ。」

この論理に従えば、われわれに必要なのは理論でないことは明らかだ。なぜなら理論はわれわれを狭い殻に閉じ込め、未だ見ぬさまざまな可能性を発見する妨げとなるから。パリで教えていた時のことだが、大きな円筒形をした広告塔を初めて見た時のことは忘れない。私は学生たちに、男がひとりそんな広告塔の周りを、両手を広げながら、大声で「助けてくれ、俺はここから逃げられない!」と叫んでぐるぐる歩いているドローイングを見せた。建築家の仕事は、立地条件というものを、そのあらゆる可能性を想定して理解することにある。建物を取り巻く条件とは何か。建物の構成要素とは何か。そして、建物は人間活動にどんな可能性をもたらすのか。繰り返そう、鍵は、「条件、要素、活動」だ。

この短文で私が言えることはただひとつ、三分一が建築に

もたらしたものは重要であるという確信だ。そして本書を読むことで、彼の思想や、彼の完成した、もしくは制作予定の作品に関する知識をもっと増やせるだろうと期待している。存在するもの、またわれわれがつくるものはすべて、どんなにいいものであろうと、常に改良の余地があり、また乗り越えられる可能性がある。だからこそわれわれの格闘には決して終わりがなく、あくまで戦い続けなければならないのだ。それこそが創造というものなのである。

たぶんこうした動かし難い信念をもって仕事をしてきたからかもしれないが、ある建築学校から突然の申し出があった時には、最初は驚いたものだ。「ウッツォン・ワークショップ」と銘打たれた講座を担当してくれないかと言われたのである。確かに私は、長年ウッツォンと共に働いて、彼との友情や付き合いは彼が他界するまで続いた。彼は、私の人生に決定的な重要性をおよぼし、今でも私は、彼の建築知識を世に知らしめようと活動している。にもかかわらず、私はその申し出にこう答えたのである。ウッツォンはもはやこの世の人ではないし、彼のもっとも重要な作品ははるか以前に完成されてしまっている。しかし、彼の建築観は今日、三分一の作品の中に生きているのだから、彼を呼んで学生を教えてもらうというのが、たぶんいいのではないか、と。

今でも私の判断は間違っていないと信じている。

SUCCEEDING UTZON
Mogens Prip-Buus, architect

I met Hiroshi Sambuichi in the late summer of 2010 in Copenhagen. Our first meeting took place at one of the larger architects offices, where he late in the afternoon gave a presentation about his works. There were only a few words, and these were in fact unnecessary, for everything was so clear, so obviously right, truths expressed in buildings in which everything connected. Understandings of situations.

After having worked many years for Vilhelm Wohlert and Jørn Utzon and later witnessed how little Utzon's of works and thoughts had been understood, here I found an architecture that finally showed a path ahead, an approach that went deep into the understanding of materials, of nature and its fundamental forces and their significance to people and their activities. For me, this was a positive continuation of Utzon thoughts and works, things which he sadly was not allowed to or had the opportunity to complete. In short, I was happy, everything seemed possible again, the road ahead was clear.

The following day, we showed Sambuichi some of Jørn Utzon's buildings: the Kingo Houses and the Fredensborg Houses and Utzon's home in Hellebæk. Mostly he walked around alone, observing, once in a while he would look at us, nodding with a smile but without saying a word.

We also showed him what we called Utzon's workshop; the forest and beach in Hellebæk. This beach, where the beech trees meet the water was one of Utzon's favourite places and his great inspiration. Others have described this as an almost infantile romanticism, so I was curious to see Sambuichi's reaction. He stood for a long time on his own, without moving, and then he came towards me with a radiant smile and I think with a tear in his eye, walking back to the car.

This description of my meeting with Sambuichi is perhaps a bit too personal. Sadly I have not had the opportunity to experience - to live in - his architecture, but my understanding of the person behind, and the close connection I felt between us, makes the illustrations and pictures of his works come to life and confirm for me the ending words of my lectures: Architecture is the Truth of a Situation.

For what is architecture really? This question is often debated, especially at the architecture schools, in writing and in purely academic terms and only rarely during projects and buildings based on the wellbeing of people in surroundings created through knowledge of materials and their compositions into constructions suitable for the life that will take place - at exactly this place.

Utzon described this in his essay *"The Innermost Being of Architecture"* in which he states:

...

The true innermost being of architecture can be compared with that of natures seed, and something of the inevitability of nature´s principle of growth ought to be a fundamental concept in architecture. If we think of the seeds that turn unto plants or trees, everything within the same genus would develop in the same way if the growth potentials were not so different and if each growth possessed within itself the ability to develop without compromise. On account of differing conditions, similar seeds turn into widely different organisms.

...

or

...

Nature knows of no compromise, it accepts all difficulties, not as difficulties but merely as new factor´s which with no sign of conflict evolve into a whole.

...

In addition to these couple of quotes I highly recommend this Utzon's testimony from 1948 that shows striking similarities between the working methods of Sambuichi and Utzon, notwithstanding that Sambuichi in his approach may be more scientific.

Many others have spoken about the great importance of nature to human creativity. About 900 years ago, St. Bernard of Clairvaux said: *"Believe me, you will find more lessons in the woods than in books. Trees and stones will teach you what you cannot learn from masters."*

More recently, Johan August Strindberg said, almost cautionary: *"Copy nature, yes, by all means, though never slavishly. Above all, imitate nature's own way of creating."*

Following this logic, it should be obvious that we do not need theories, for we risk that they shut us in, preventing us from discovering the yet unseen possibilities. I remember, from my time teaching in Paris, discovering the large cylindrical billboards. I showed the students a drawing of a man walking around one with outstretched arms shouting: "Help, I'm trapped!" The work of an architect rather lies in the understanding of a situation with all of its possibilities. What are the conditions? Of what elements is it composed? And what possibilities does it give for human activities? I repeat: Conditions – Elements – Activities.

With these few lines I can only express my conviction of the importance of Sambuichi's contributions to architecture, and I look forward to reading this book to expand my knowledge of this thoughts and works, those completed and those to come. Whatever there is and whatever we do, no matter how good, it can always be improved. Our struggle will never end and we must strive on. This is creation.

It was perhaps in the light of this final view, that I surprised myself with a proposition that shocked me at first. I was asked on the possibility of conducting an "Utzon workshop" at a school of architecture. I have worked with Utzon for innumerable years and our friendship and contact lasted until he passed away. His significance is crucial to my life and I still work to promulgate the knowledge of his architecture. Nevertheless, I replied that Utzon was no longer alive and that his most important works were completed a long time ago, but that his view on architecture lives on today in the works of Sambuichi, so perhaps it would be a good idea to ask him to come and teach the students.

I still believe so.

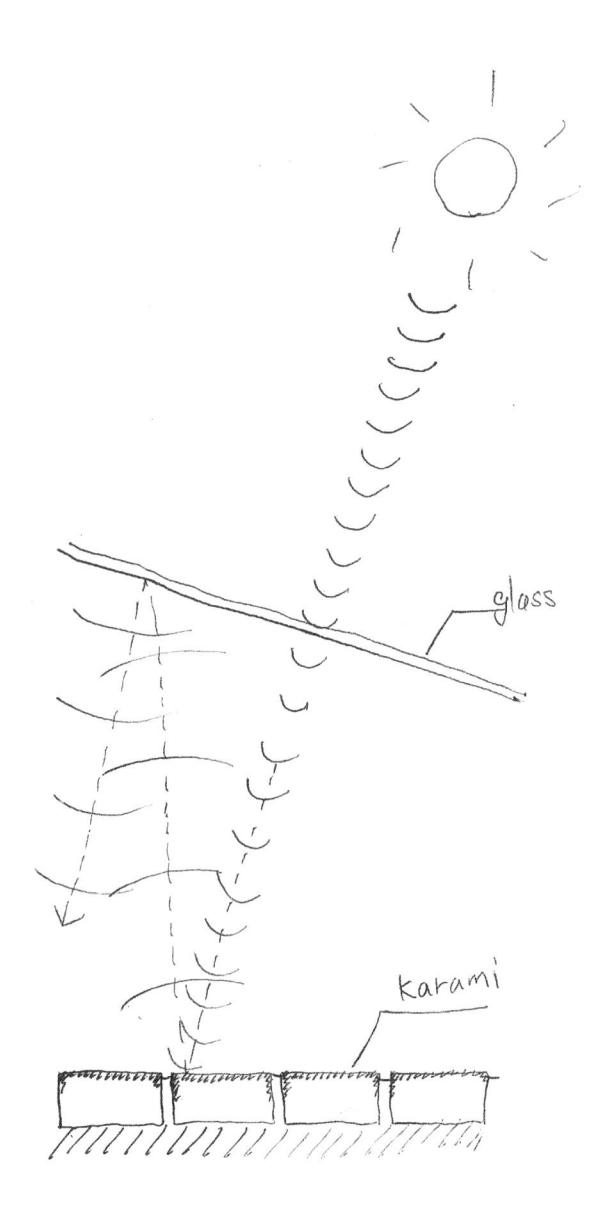

犬島

INUJIMA

太陽
SUN

0・54k㎡の小さな島は、かつての産業により傷付けられていた。

A small island of 0.54 square kilometres once marred by profitable ravages of industry.

島の東に銅の製錬所跡。島全域には、石切り場の跡が池として点在している。深さ40mの池も存在すると言われている。犬島すべてが岩盤の島で池の水密性は高く、完全な真水である。小さな谷にはいくつかの集落がある。人口は最盛期には3,000人とも5,000人とも言われているが近年島から若者は去り平均年齢は75歳となっている。島の一部は自然にのみ込まれ廃墟愛好家やアーティストが時々訪れる程度で長い間社会から見放されていた。

In the east of the island are traces of a copper refinery, and around the entire islands traces of a quarry are dotted as ponds. These are said to be up to 40 metres deep and as all of Inujima is of bedrock the water permeability is low, thus the ponds are filled with fresh water. Several settlements are situated in the small island valley. It is said that at its heyday the island accommodated a population of three to five thousand, but as young people have since moved from the island the average age is now 75. The island was for long time neglected, occasionally visited by artists and ruin enthusiasts finding beauty in the structures succumbing to nature.

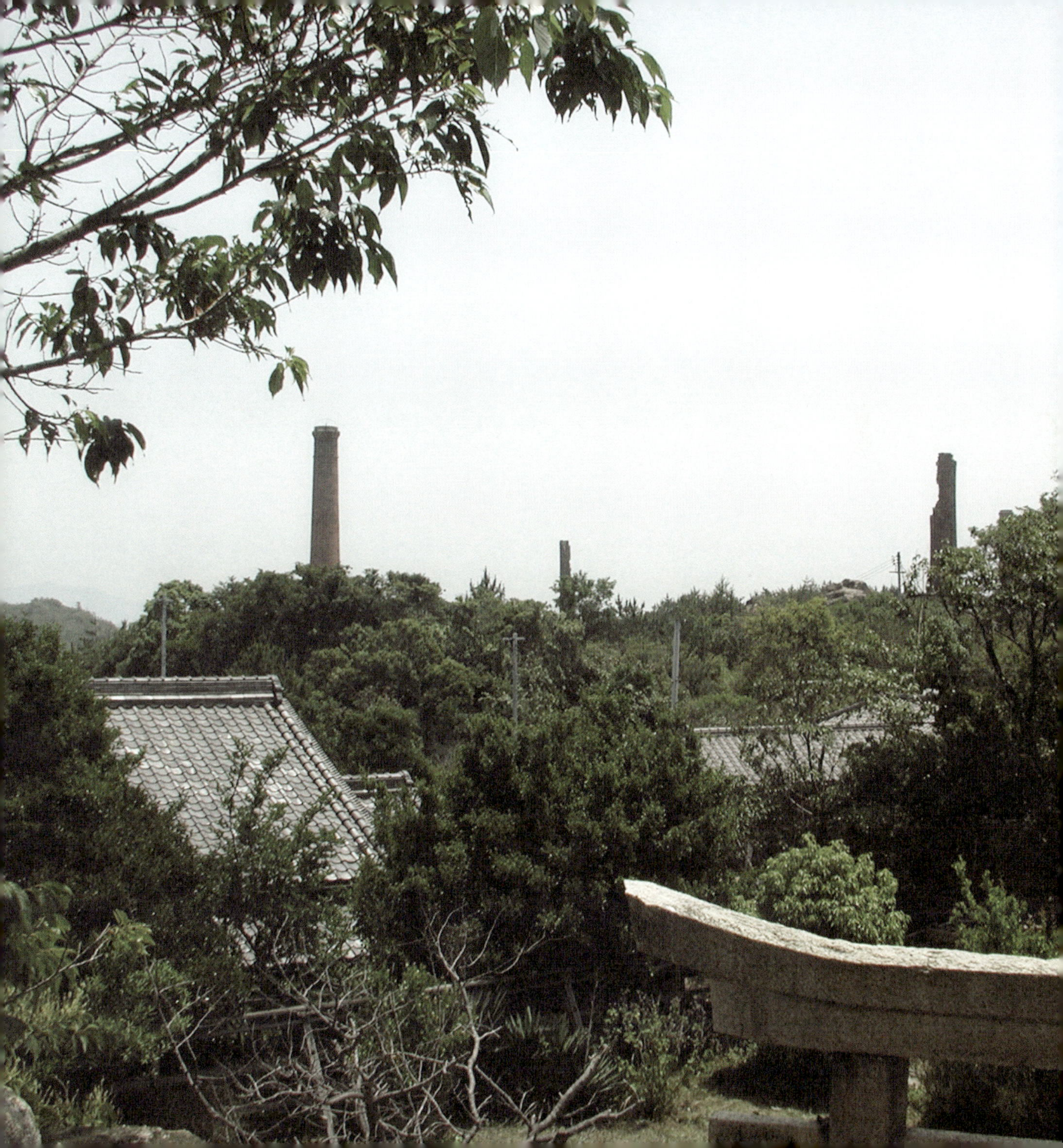

遠くからでも、最高40mの6本の煙突により島の輪郭が容易に理解できる。

Even from a distance the island is easily profiled by its six chimneys reaching up to 40 metres, remnants of abandoned industry.

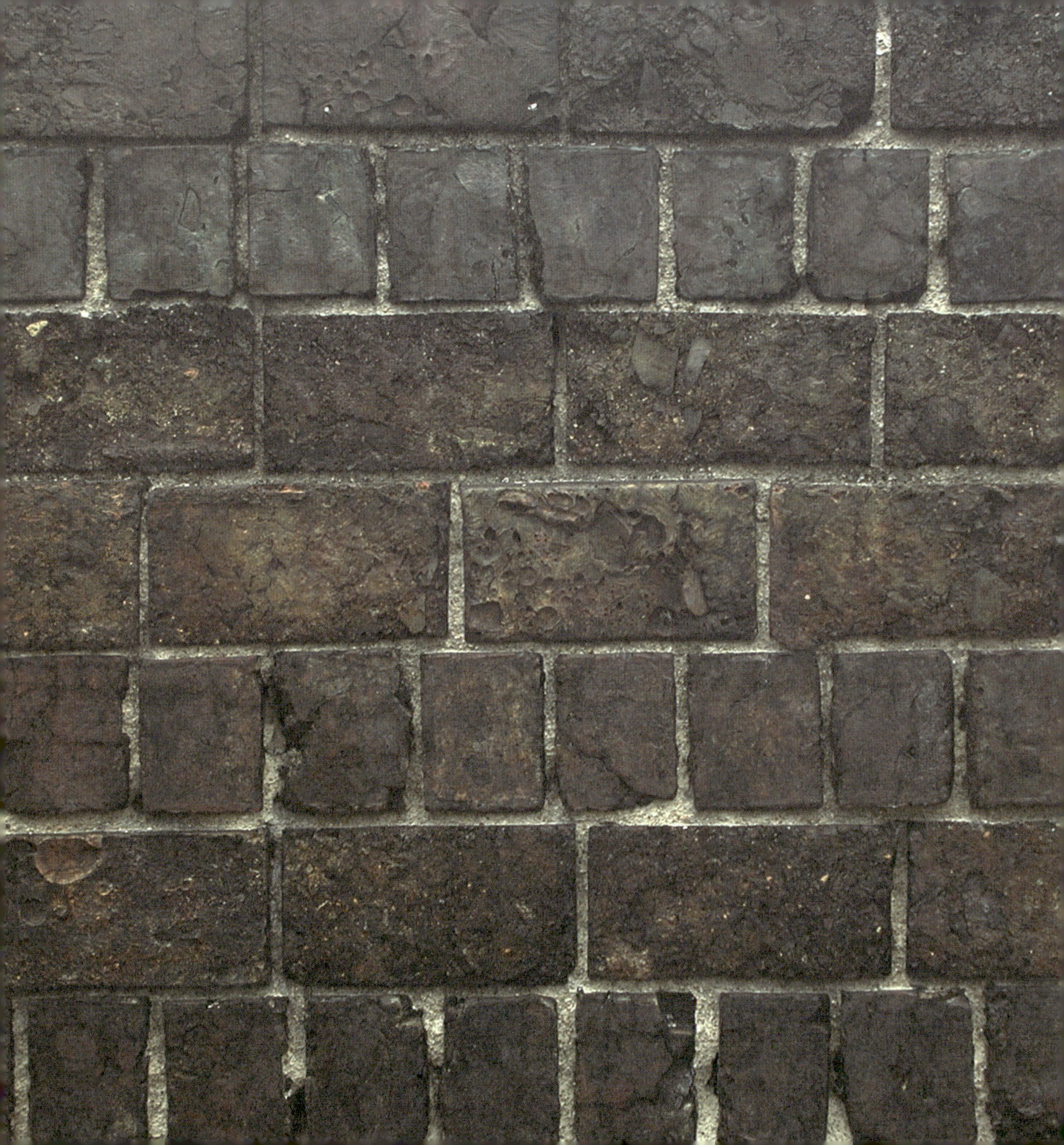

島を調査して目についたのは東の岸に沿って、黒い煉瓦とスラグ（鉱石を製錬する際の副産物）が散乱した今まで見たことのない光景であった。

Surveying the island, unusual blocks appeared scattered along the eastern shore and in mysterious ruins rising up through heaps of slag.

深さ約40mの垂直の穴は水で満たされている。島にはこのような穴が点在している。

The landscape is dotted with great water filled holes, some with depths up to 40 metres.

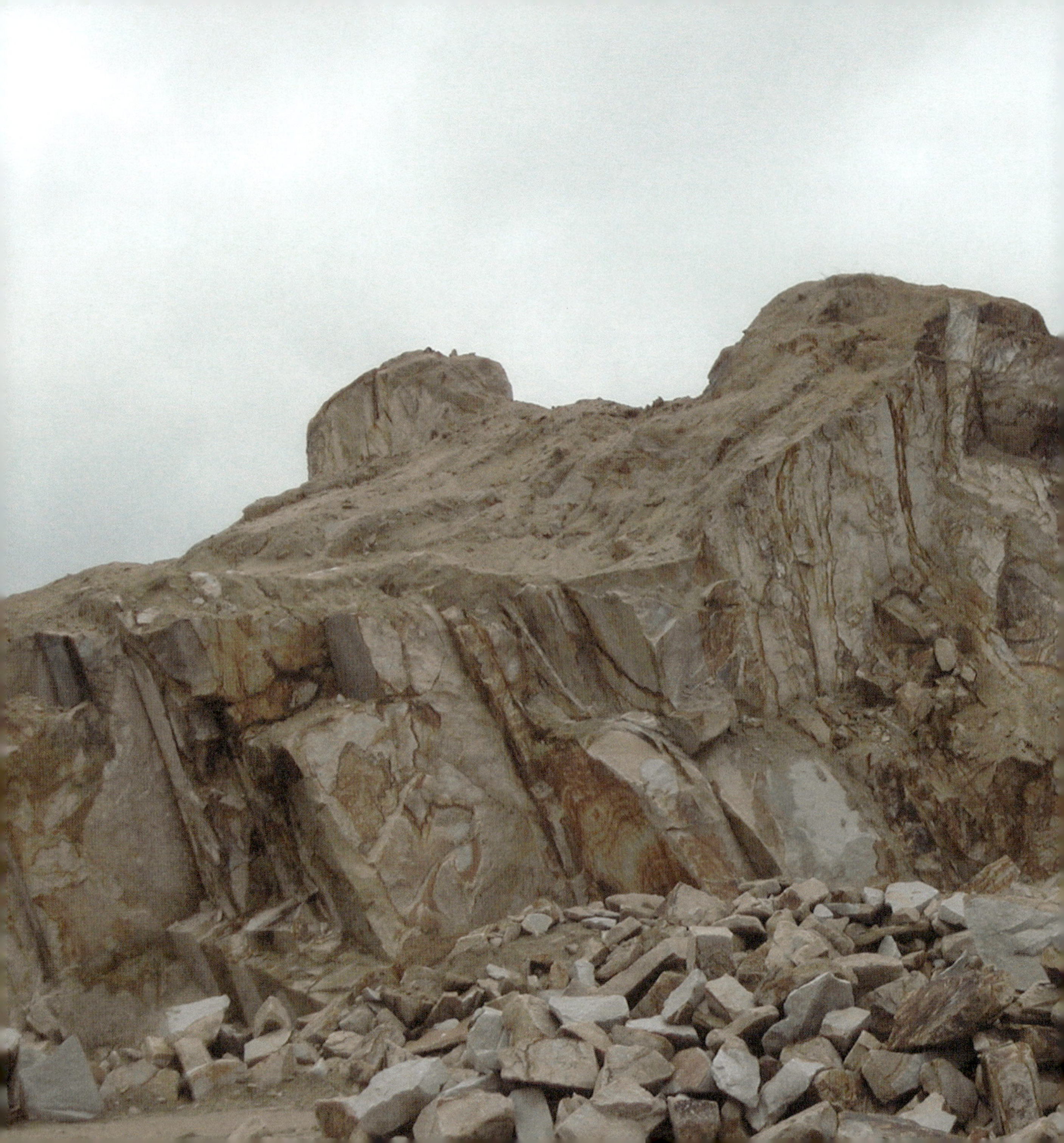

これらの穴は犬島の花崗岩が日本各地で使われた証しである。大阪城の巨大な石垣にも使用された。

The water filled holes are marks of Inujima's past granite industry. Rocks from Inujima has been used in some of Japanese greatest stone structures like the massive stone walls surrounding Osaka castle.

カラミ煉瓦は100年前に行なわれていた銅の製錬の際に出た副産物である。それらは大量の鉄やガラスを含み、非常に特殊な熱特性をもっていることが分かった。

Century old byproducts of copper smelting, the recovered *karami* slag bricks contained large amounts of iron and glass. As such they were found to have very special thermal properties.

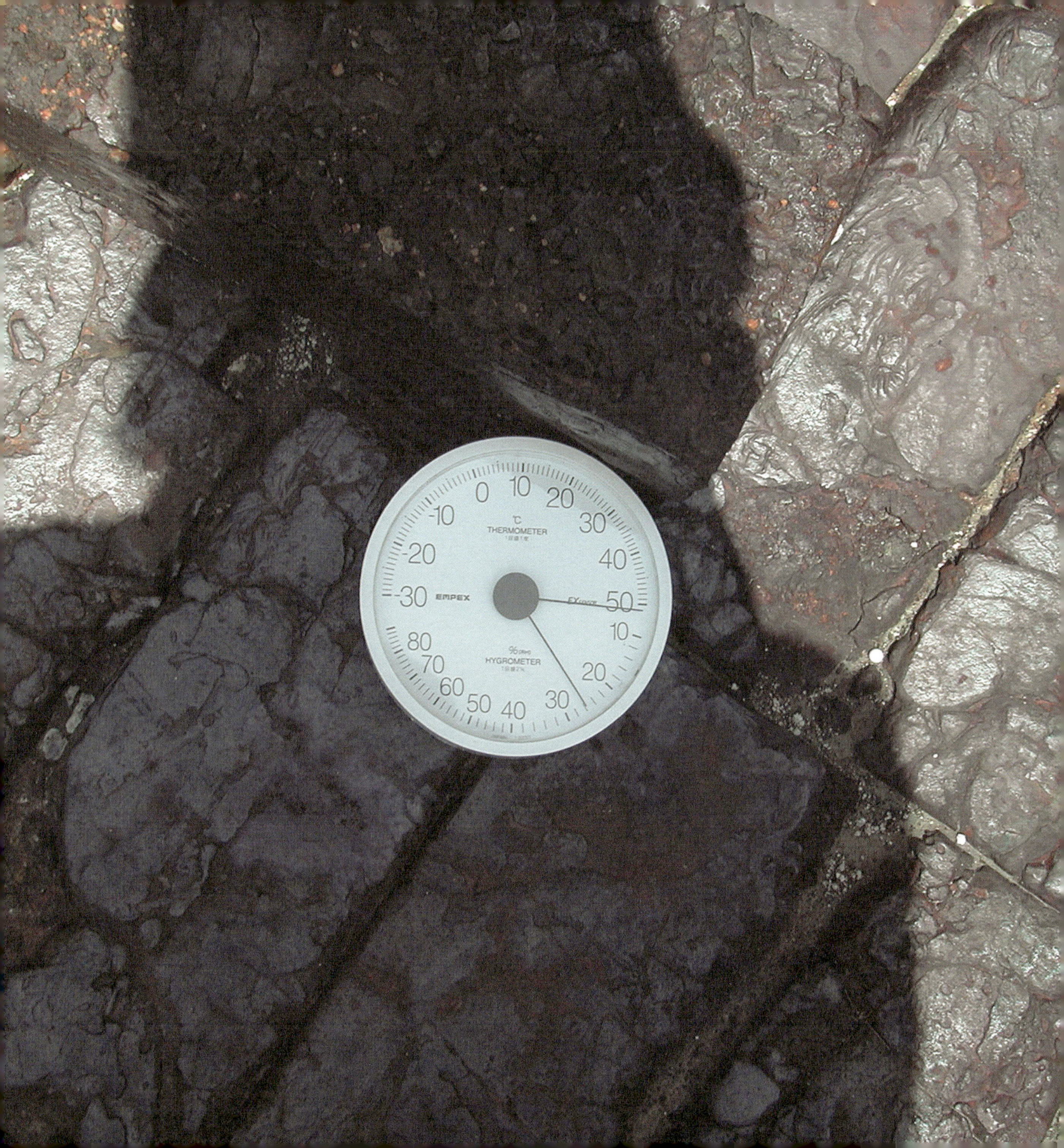
℃
THERMOMETER
EMPEX
HYGROMETER

煙突も産業の遺産である。ほとんどの煙突の風洞が東側を向いている。

The chimneys too were structures of this industry and with them were found numerous east oriented ducts.

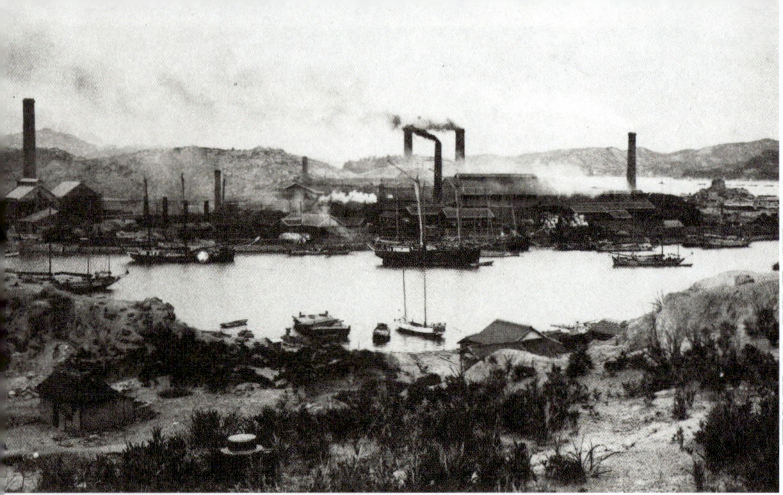
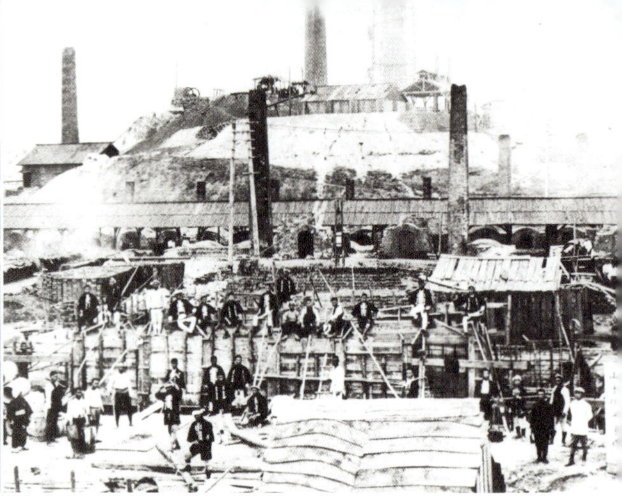
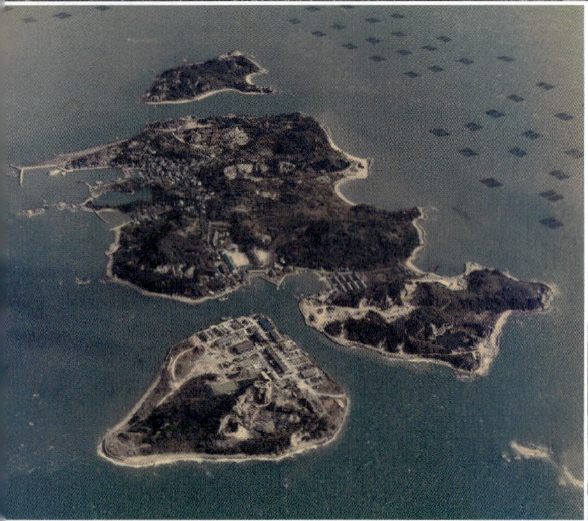
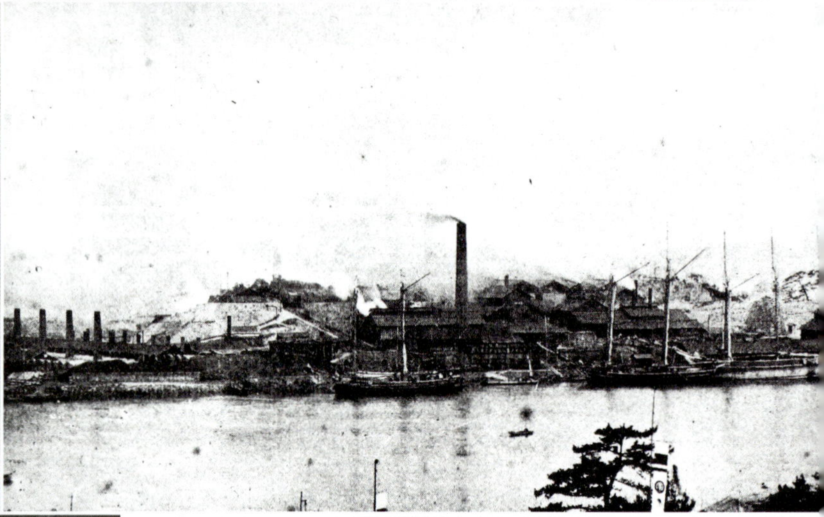
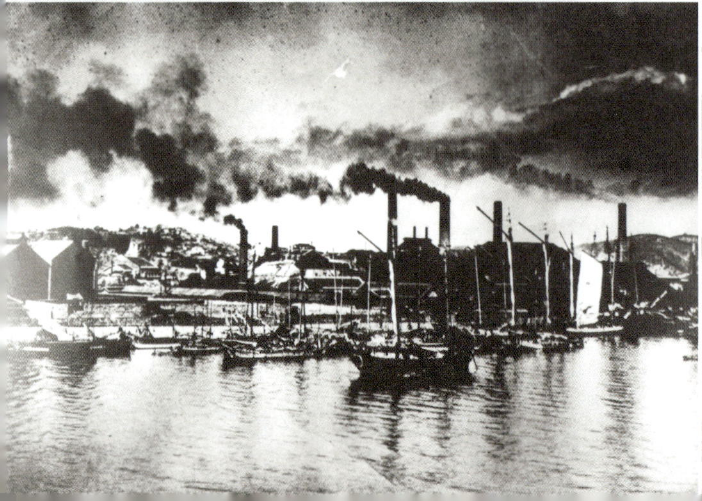
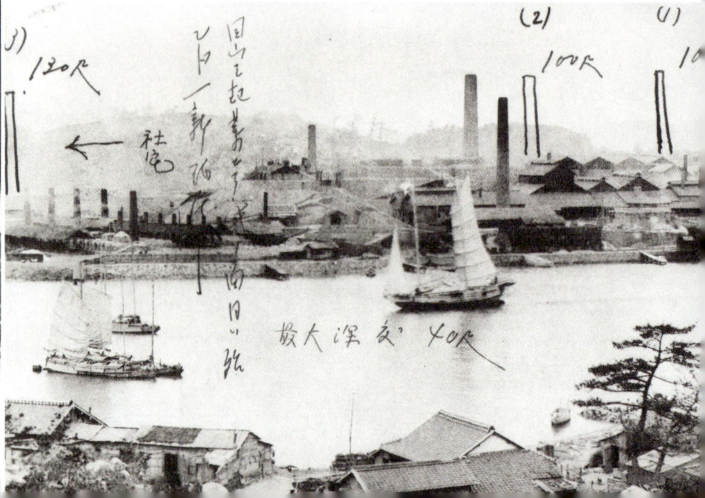
(2)
(1)
120尺
100尺
社宅
最大深度 40尺

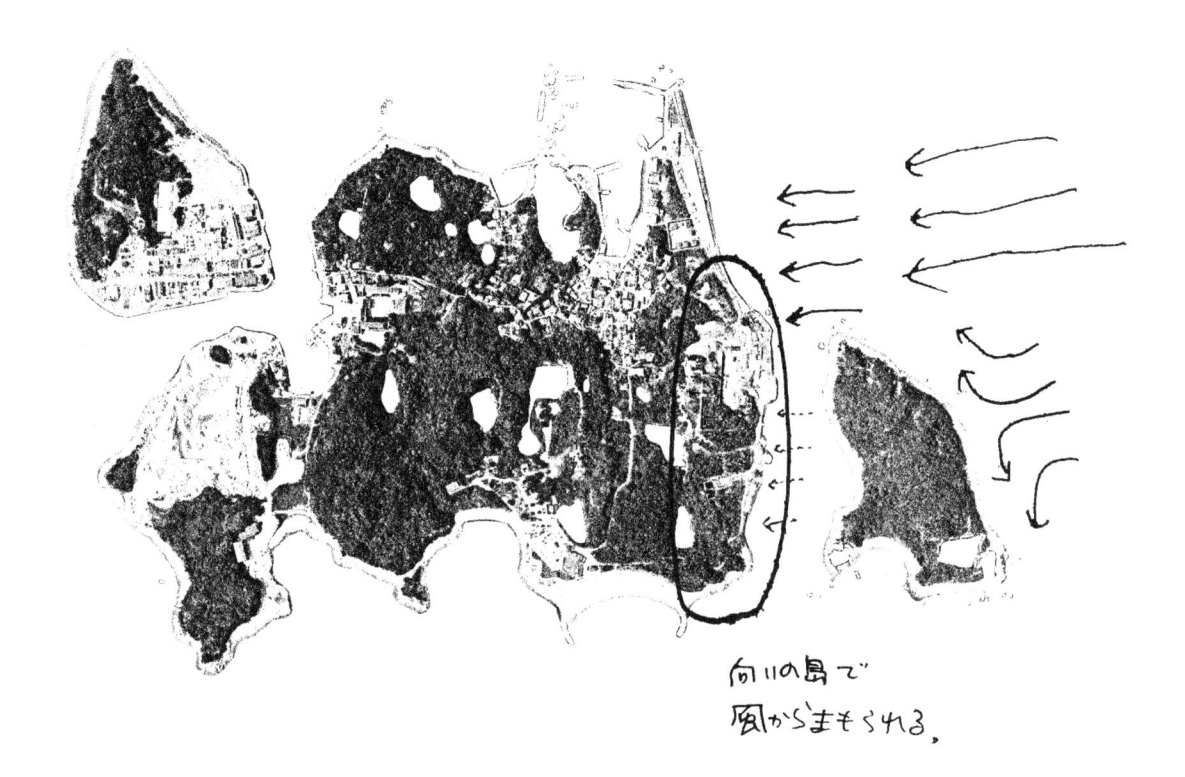

私は古い写真からも動く素材を読み取る。古写真を見ると煙突からの煙はほとんど西へなびいていた。このことから敷地の卓越風が東からの風であることが読み取れた。煙突の東側に向いた風洞はさらなる証拠であった。製錬所の位置を確認すると犬島に隣接する小さな島の風下に配置されていた。それは強風から製錬所を保護するためである。製錬所の設計は風によって決められていた。

Looking at old photos of the refinery an interesting pattern emerged - the smoke from the chimneys always floated to the west. Inspections on site confirmed that the dominating wind direction was from the east. The east oriented ducts of the chimneys were further proof. The placement of the refinery also confirmed this, placed alee of the small island adjoining Inujima, it lay protected from the stronger winds. Certainly the planning of the copper refinery was made with the winds as a determining factor.

west

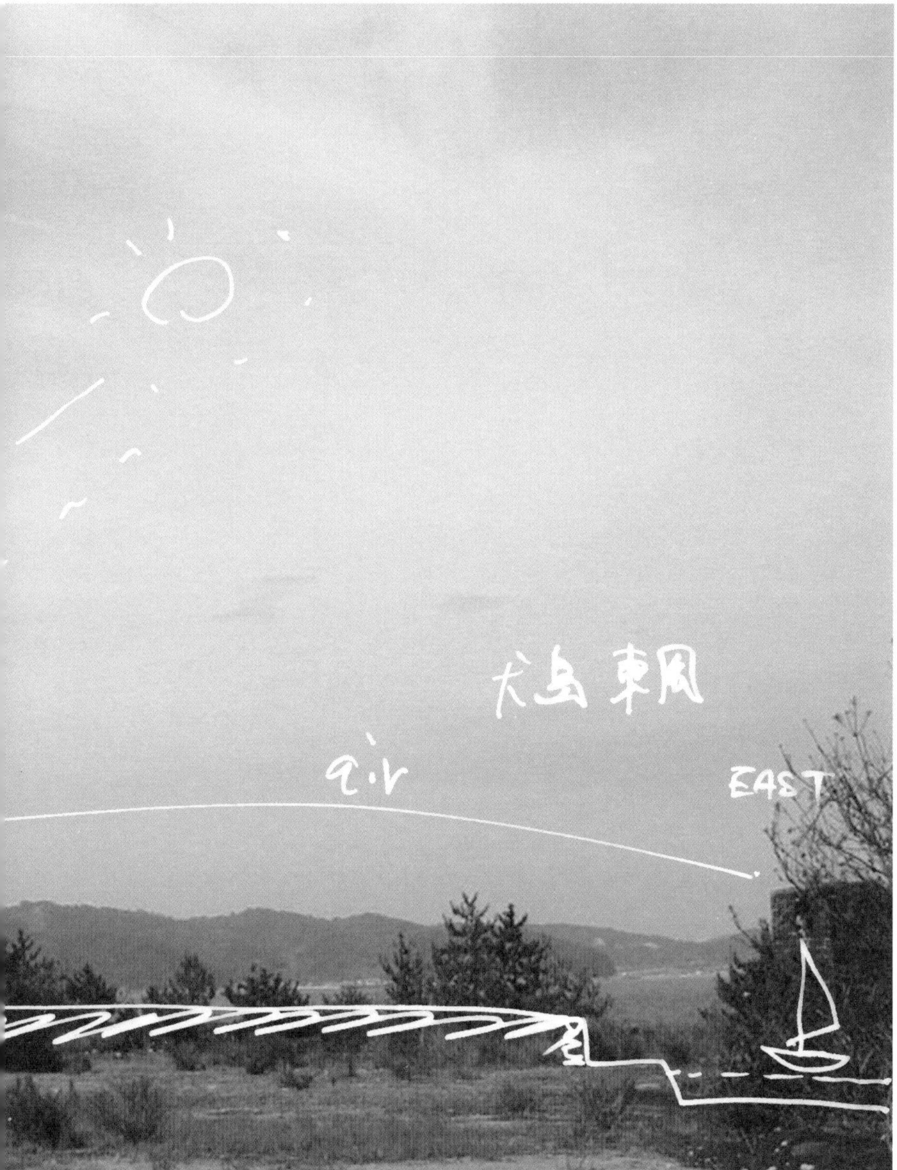
犬島東風
air
EAST

hall A

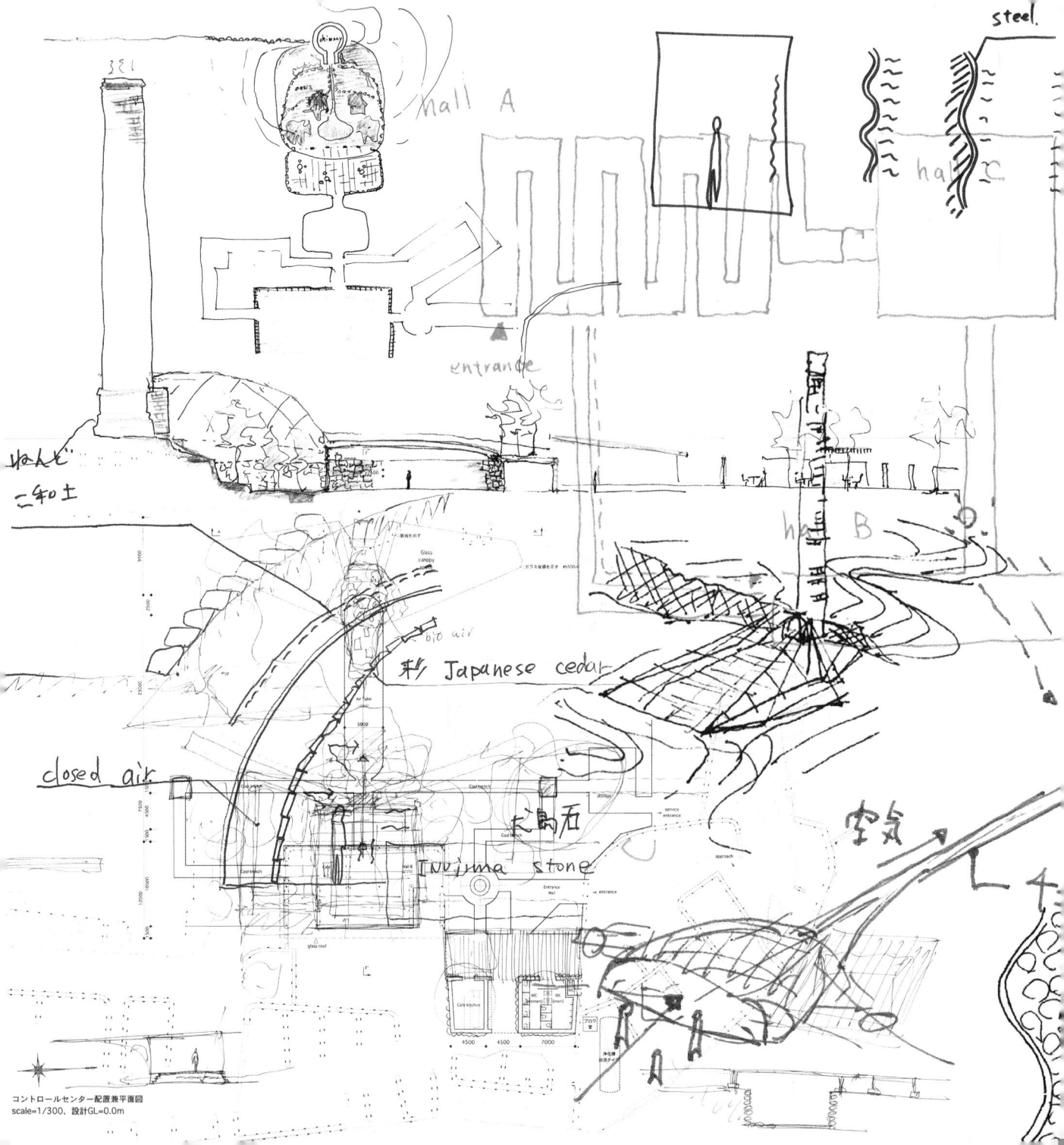

steel.

hall C

entrance

ねんど
三和土

closed air

Glass canopy

bio air

杉 / Japanese cedar

犬島石 Inujima stone

hall B

空気

service entrance

approach

Cafe kitchen | WC women's | WC men's

コントロールセンター配置兼平面図
scale=1/300, 設計GL=0.0m

B-B'断面図　scale=1/300
設計GL=0.0m

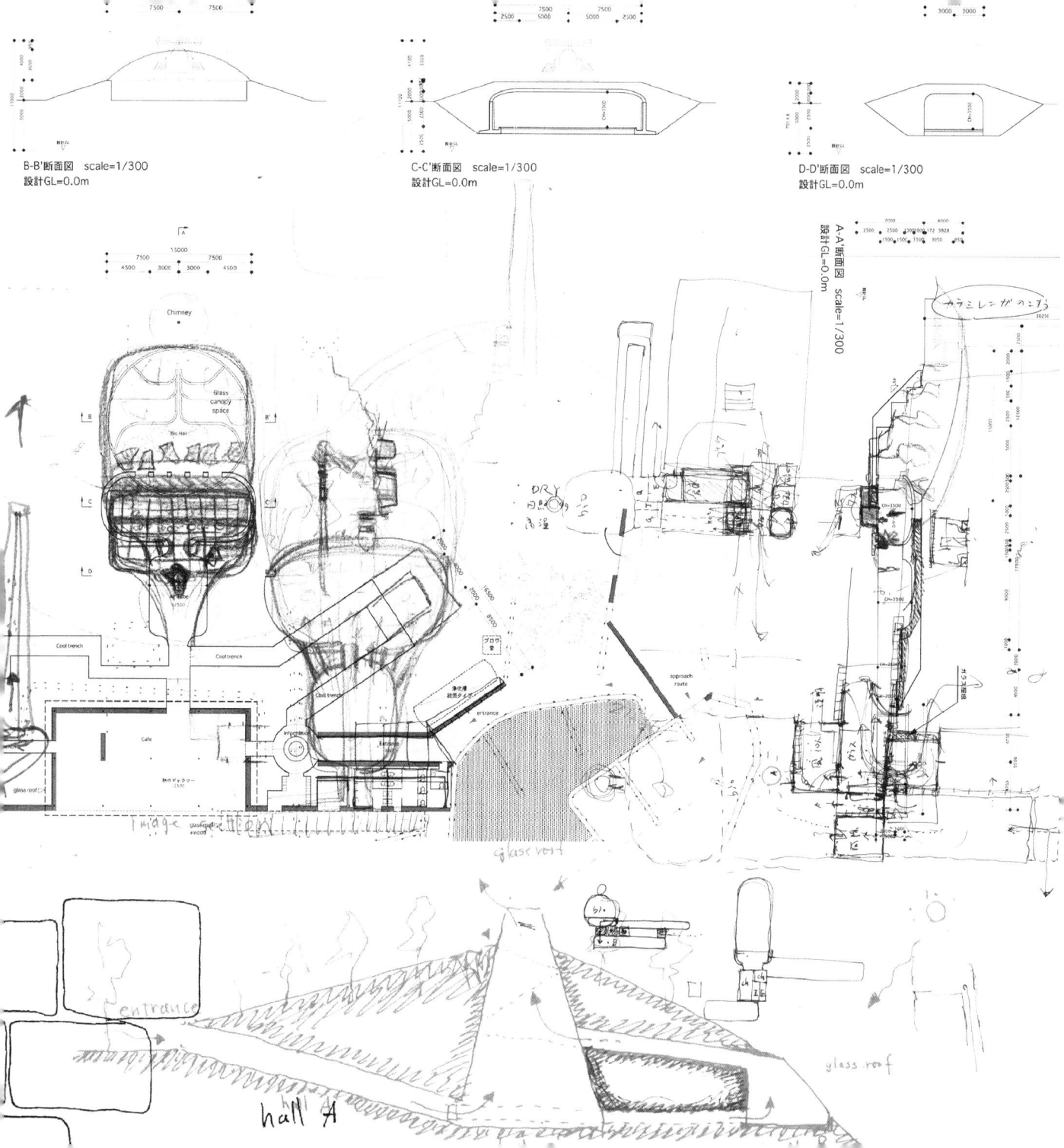

C-C'断面図　scale=1/300
設計GL=0.0m

D-D'断面図　scale=1/300
設計GL=0.0m

A-A'断面図　scale=1/300
設計GL=0.0m

hall A

上昇気流

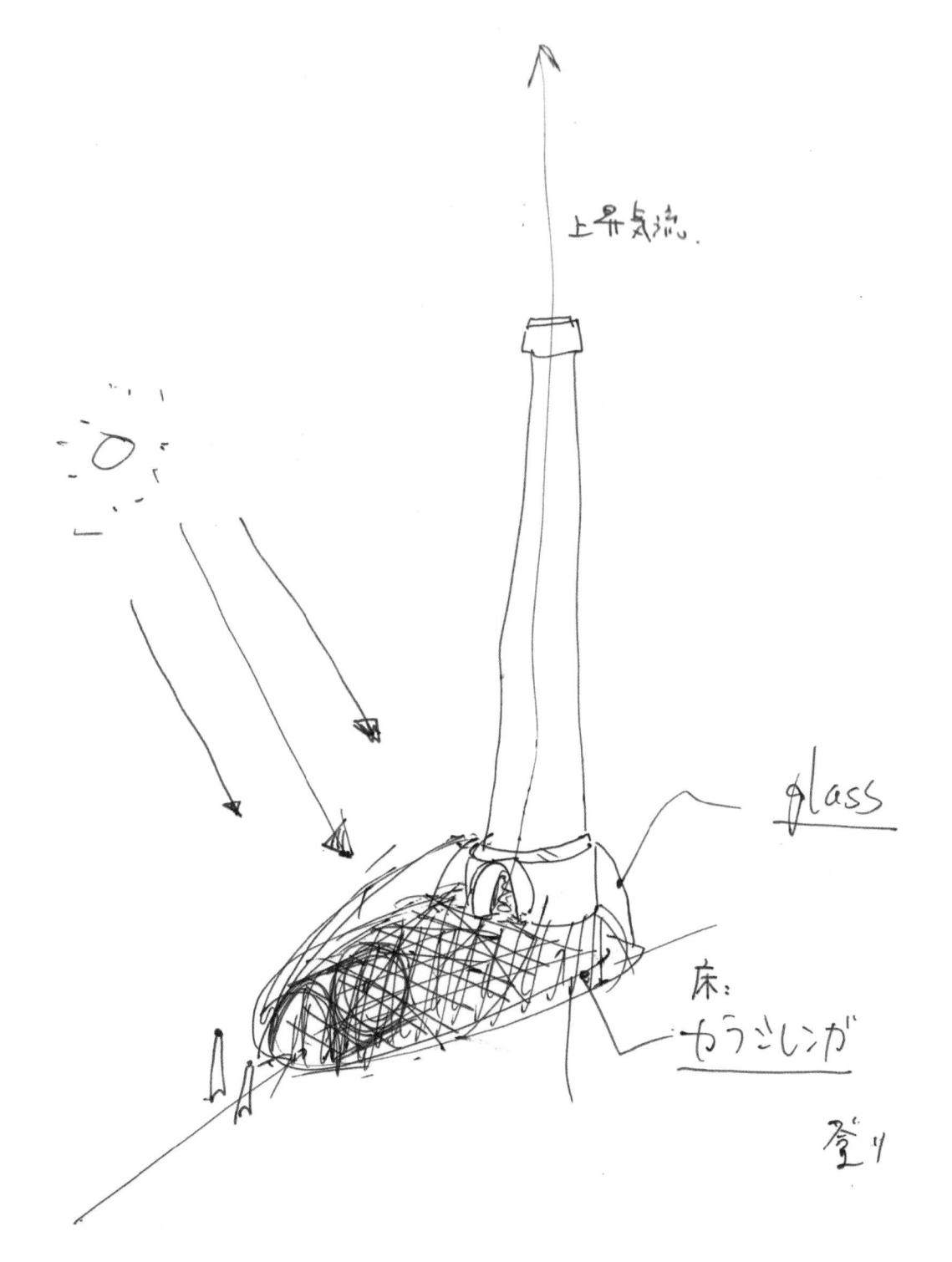

glass

床：
もうこしんが

登り

犬島精錬所美術館

ここで伝えたかったことは、地球の動く素材の動力源を司るのは太陽であること。そして最後に頼るべきものは、大切にすべきものは、この永遠に変わらない価値であるということだ。そう思えるようになったのは犬島との出合いで、さまざまな経済的価値観に翻弄され、搾取、破壊された島の歴史を目の当たりにしたことがきっかけだった。変わらない価値、すなわち太陽による島の再生。それが犬島での試みだった。

江戸期の犬島は石の産業で栄え、大阪城をはじめ各地へ運び出された。島が繁栄する一方で、一説には島の3分の2が切り取られてしまったとも言われている。石切りの最盛期を終えると、1909年には銅の製錬所が設けられ急激に日本の近代化の波に呑まれていく。莫大な資金と人が投入され、犬島最大の繁栄期を迎える。しかしわずか10年で銅の暴落やさまざまな経済的価値の変化によって製錬所は閉鎖されてしまう。その後100年近く廃墟として放置され、犬島は衰退の一途を辿った。

私がこの犬島において再生の可能性を見いだすきっかけとなったのが島民との出会いだった。私の知る瀬戸の風景とは全く異なる製錬所跡も彼らにとっては生まれた時から遊び場であり、当たり前にそこに「在る」ものだった。「在る」ものの可能性を求めて、どこにも「無いもの」をつくる新しい挑戦が始まった。

私は製錬所煙突群と太陽の組み合わせは、犬島の空気を動かすための有効な動力源になると直感した。さらに島を調査していると、海岸一帯に廃棄された多くの黒い塊があった。これは銅の製錬の副産物であり、カラミ煉瓦と呼ばれていた。太陽の熱を素早く吸収し、多く蓄えられる性質をもつことがその後の分析で分かってきた。太陽の熱で空気を暖める新しい素材との出合いであった。

製錬所操業当時の古い写真を確認していると、どの写真も煙突の煙が東から西へなびいていた。私は写真から「動く素材」を読み取った。実際に各煙突、煙突跡を調査するとすべて東側に入り口が設けられていた。私は美術館の入り口と風の入り口を、東側と決定した。

空気は太陽と煙突によって美術館の中へ引き込まれる。夏は地中の通路によって冷やされ、冬はカラミ煉瓦のサンルームで太陽によって暖められる。ふたつの空気が出合うホールには犬島の石切りの歴史を伝える巨石が置かれている。熱を蓄える石の特性を生かし、空間の夏の温度を安定させる。動く素材と一緒に巡る美術館である。

私がこの時代において取り組んでおきたいことは、いつまでも変わらない価値とは何か、建築を通して世の中に示すことである。

この美術館は太陽がなくならない限り地球の営みの一部として永遠に空気が動き続けるだろう。

INUJIMA SEIRENSHO ART MUSEUM

What I wanted to convey here is that the sun controls the power sources of the moving materials of the Earth. What we should ultimately rely upon, what we should treat with great care, is this eternally unchanging value. It was my encounter with Inujima that caused me to think in this way, having seen with my own eyes the island's history of being buffeted, exploited, and destroyed by multiple economic forces. The island may be revived by an eternal value, that is to say, by the sun. That is what I am trying to do in Inujima.

During the Edo period, Inujima prospered due to the quarries, and its stone was distributed to many places, including Osaka Castle. On one hand, the island was prosperous, but from another viewpoint, it is said that two-thirds of the island was excavated. A copper refinery was established in 1909, after the golden age of quarrying, and was suddenly engulfed by the wave of modernization of Japan. Vast amounts of money and people were invested, and Inujima's population experienced their greatest ever prosperity. However, after a mere ten years, the refinery was closed due to a sudden fall in the price of copper and various changes in the economy. It was abandoned as a ruin for almost the next 100 years, and Inujima followed a path of decline.

My encounter with the islanders was the impetus to find a possible means of reviving Inujima. The traces of the refinery were totally different from the scenery of Seto that I knew, but for them it had been a playground since they were born, and obviously there it was an "existing" thing. Pursuing the potential of "what exists," I began the new challenge of somewhere making "what is to be."

I felt intuitively that the combination of the sunlight and the refinery chimneys would be an effective power source for moving the air of Inujima. Furthermore, when I investigated the island I discovered many black lumps scattered across the entire shorefront. This was a byproduct of copper smelting, called karami brick. Through later analysis, I understood that it has the property of quickly absorbing and storing a great deal of solar heat. This was an encounter with a new material that can warm the air by means of solar heat.

With old photographs taken at the time when the refinery was operating, I ascertained that the smoke from the chimneys streamed from east to west. I deciphered the "moving materials" from photographs. Investigating each chimney and chimney ruin, I discovered that the entrances were all established on the east side. I decided to put the museum entrance and wind openings on the east side.

Air is drawn into the art museum by the sunlight and the chimneys. In summer, it is cooled by an underground passage, and in winter it is warmed by a sun gallery made of karami brick. A huge stone conveying the history of quarrying in Inujima has been placed in the hall where the two air flows converge. The summer temperature of the space is stabilized by making use of the heat-storage characteristic of the stone. It is a museum that circulates together with moving materials.

In this era, I want to grapple with eternal values, and somehow show them to the world through architecture.

Unless the sun disappears, air will continue flowing through this museum forever, as a part of the movements of the Earth.

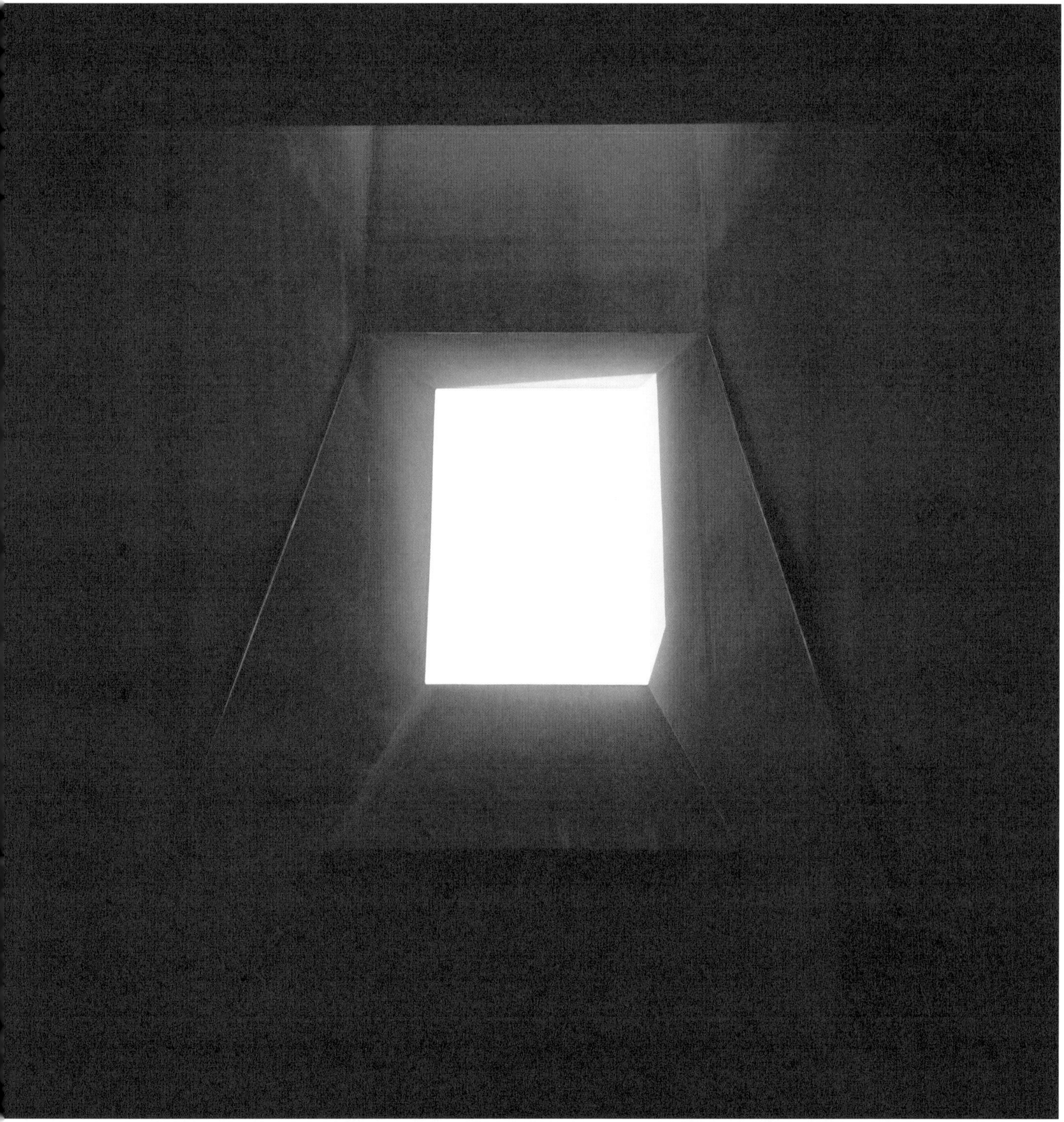

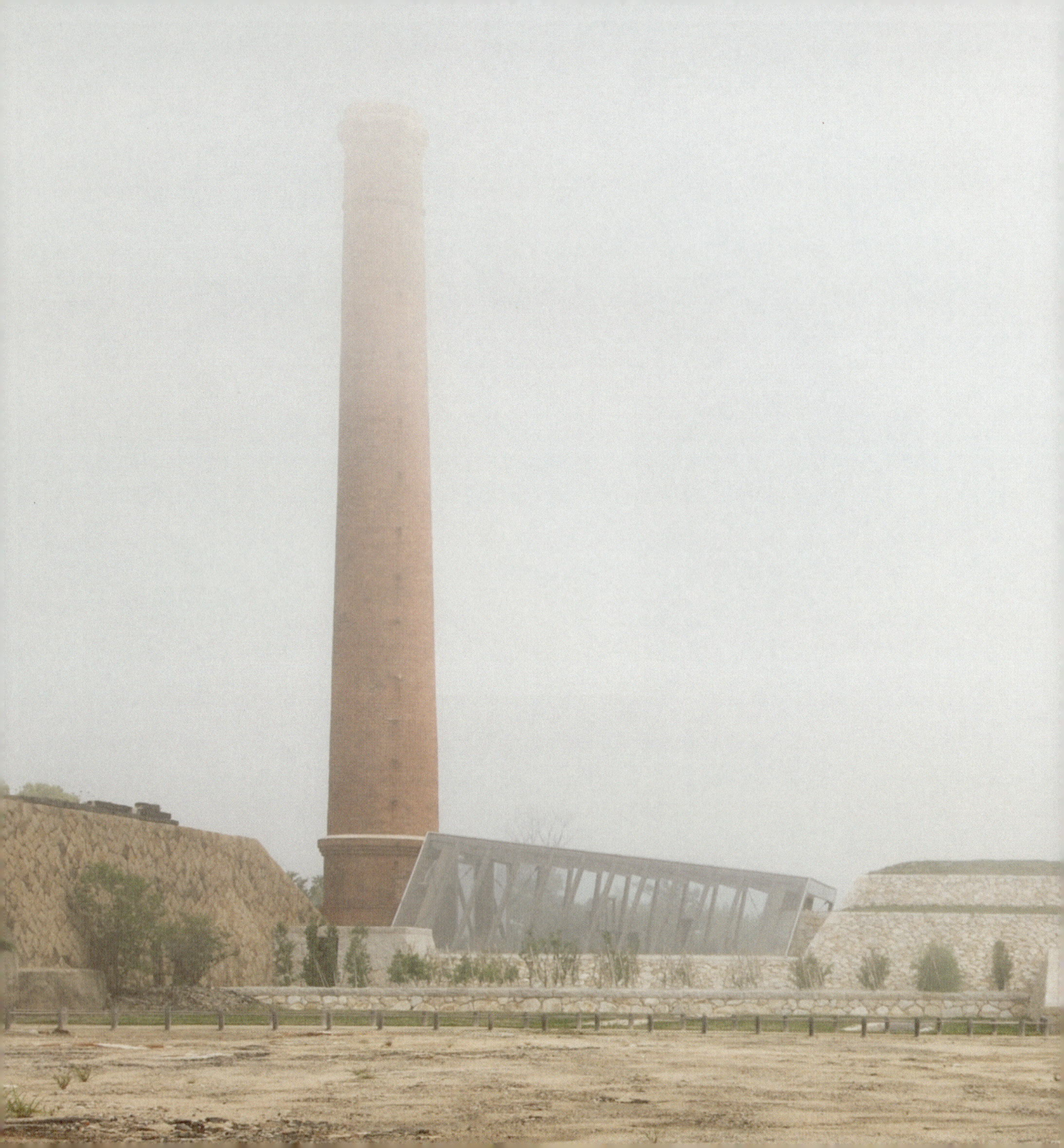

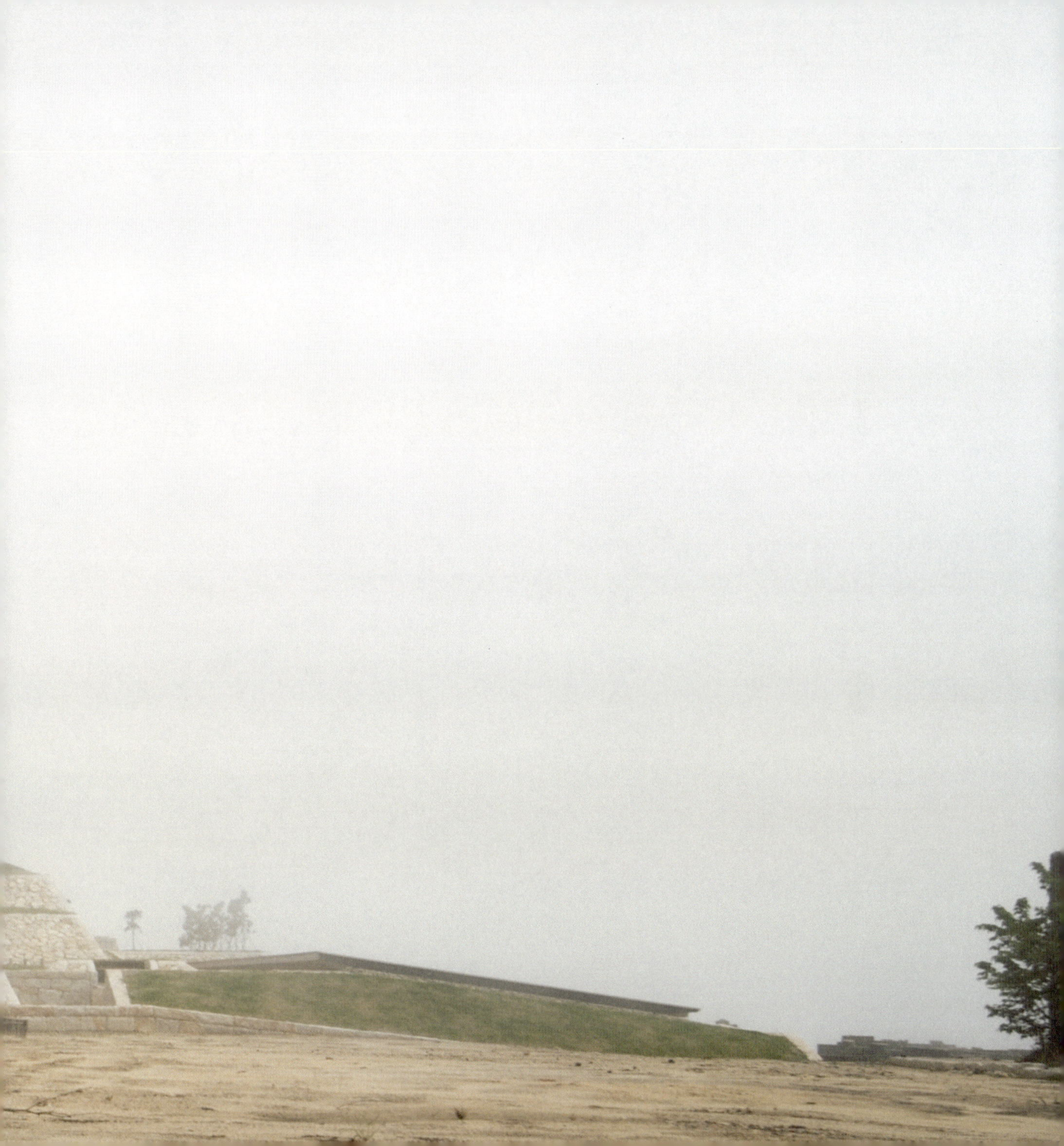

太陽がなくならない限り動き続ける空気。空気が人を導く美術館をつくりたかった。

Air moves for as long as the Sun is glowing. On Inujima air guides visitors at the museum.

カラミ煉瓦の壁は製錬所当時のオリジナルのままである。それらを抜けて、人と空気の入り口に辿りつく。

Passing through the untouched ruins, one arrives at the museum entrances for the air and people.

ウェーブしている鉄のディテールは構造と熱の両方から導かれている。

In the underground gallery, mirrors direct light from the sky and walls of corrugated iron hold earth pressure and maximise surface for heat transfer.

海岸などに廃棄されていたおよそ1万7000個のカラミ煉瓦を拾い上げ、壁や床に太陽の熱を集めるため再生した。

Around 17,000 bricks that were found on the island, were used in walls and floors to collect the heat of the Sun.

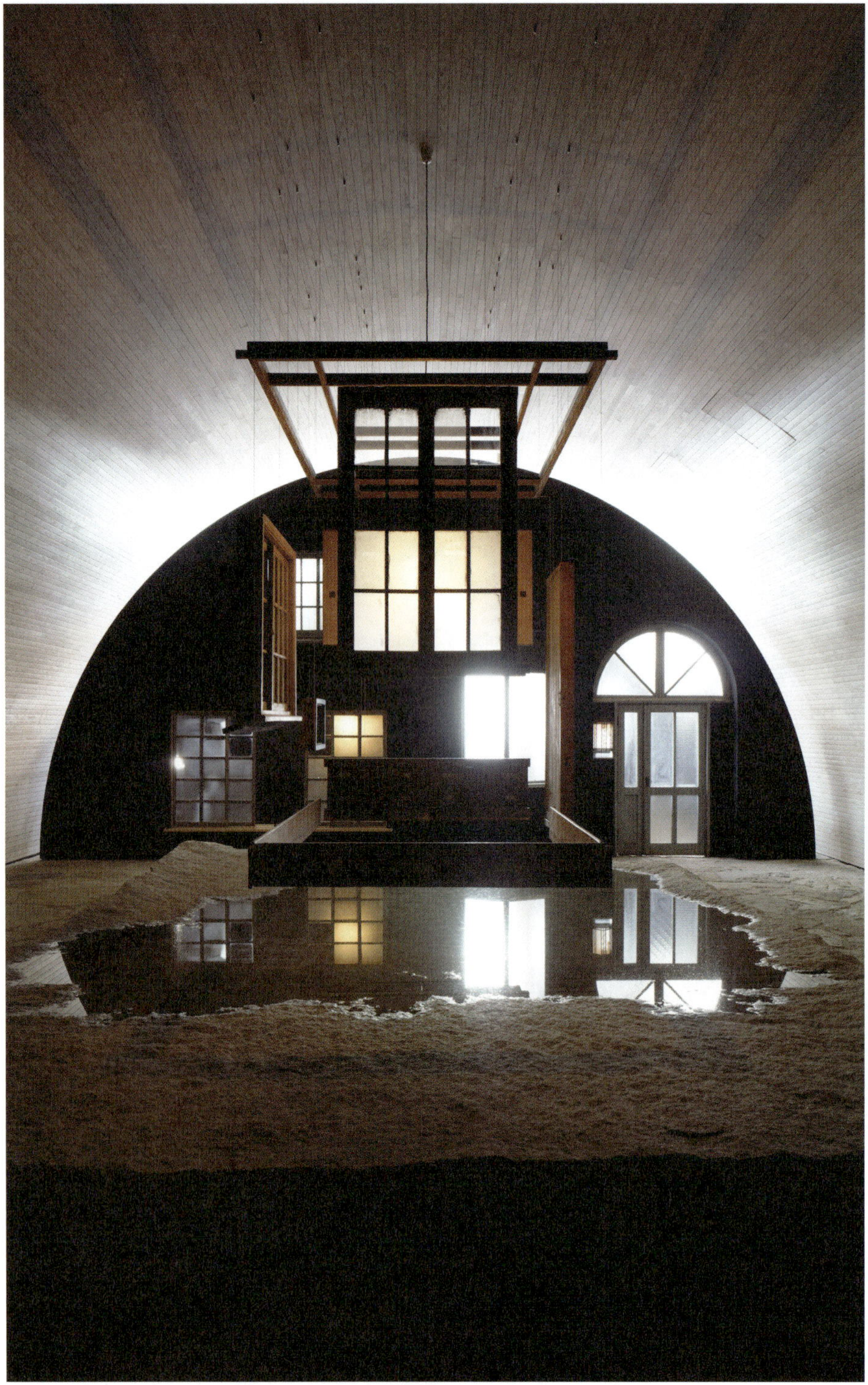
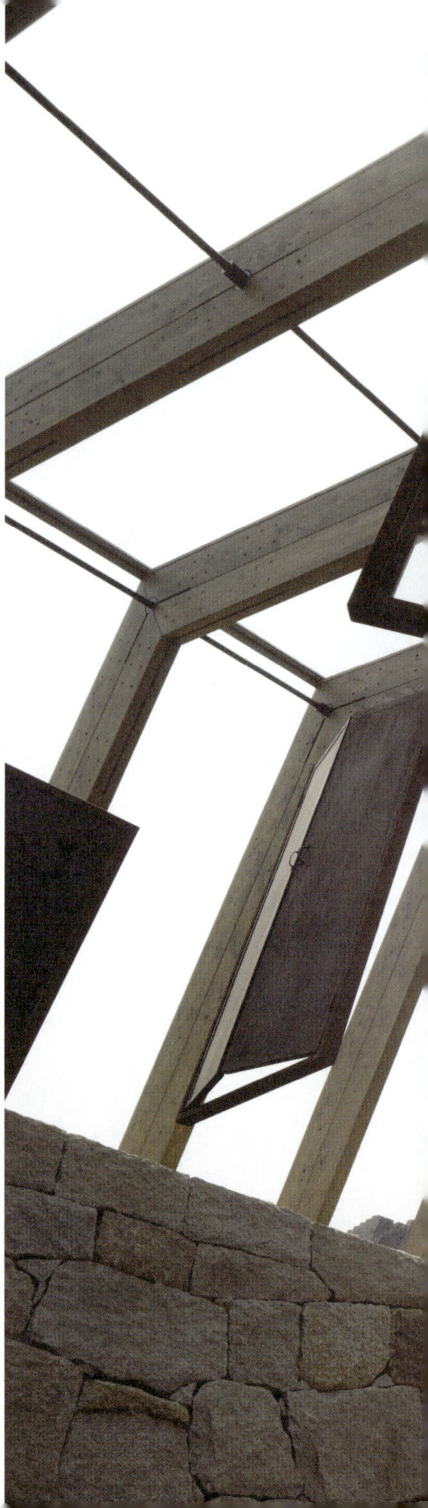

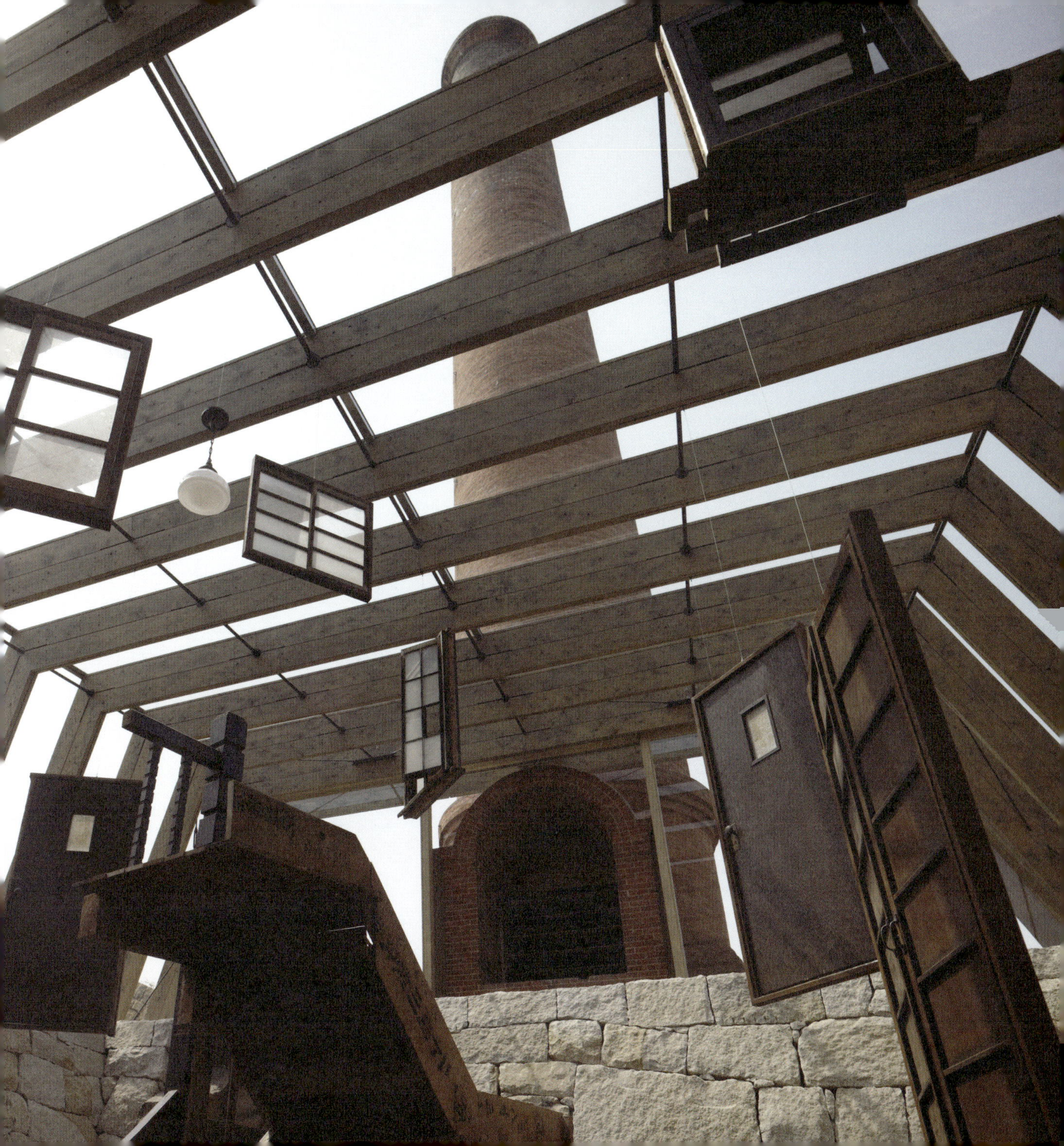

私は犬島に新しい空気を吹き込んだ。その動力は太陽であり、促すのは煙突やスラグなど犬島の素材であった。

犬島に残っていた6つの煙突のうち、最も美しく健全なものを選んだ。その煙突の足下にはガラスで覆われた空間を設け、スラグを敷き詰めた。スラグは銅の製錬の副産物であり、太陽の光を採り入れ、逃がしにくい性質をもつ。太陽と煙突、スラグ、ガラスの空間の力で空気を軽くし、その流れを高める。そこにある素材、捨てられた素材に新たな価値を見いだした。

エントランスはふたつある。ひとつは人のための入り口で、もう一方は空気のための入り口である。入り口から入った空気は地下2mにある約80mの長い廊下によって冷やされる。廊下の壁は鉄を選択している。地球とエネルギーを交換するためである。通路が折れ曲ったり、壁がウェーブしているのは「空気」から熱を奪うための必要なディテールである。

地中の通路のコーナーに鏡を置き、トップライトから光が反射しながら射し込む。ここを訪れる人は空気と一緒に光に向かって進む。

ここでは、来館者は単にアートや建築、自然を体感するだけでない。自然にも貢献する。人もまた地球の動く素材のひとつであると理解して欲しい。ここでは来訪者の排泄物は敷地内の植物の栄養分へ変換され、浄化され、建物を覆う木々の成長を助ける。成長した木々は、木陰によって土中の建物の環境をより安定したものへと導く。収穫される果実は、施設を訪れた人びとに水分や養分を与えてくれる。多くの人が訪れれば訪れるほど、犬島へ水と栄養がもち込まれ、緑が成長し続ける。美術館は手段であって、重要なのは、そこに建築が存在することで人類が植物や太陽・地形・水・空気などと共に地球本来の循環の一部となっていることである。すべてのディテールは地球に通じている。

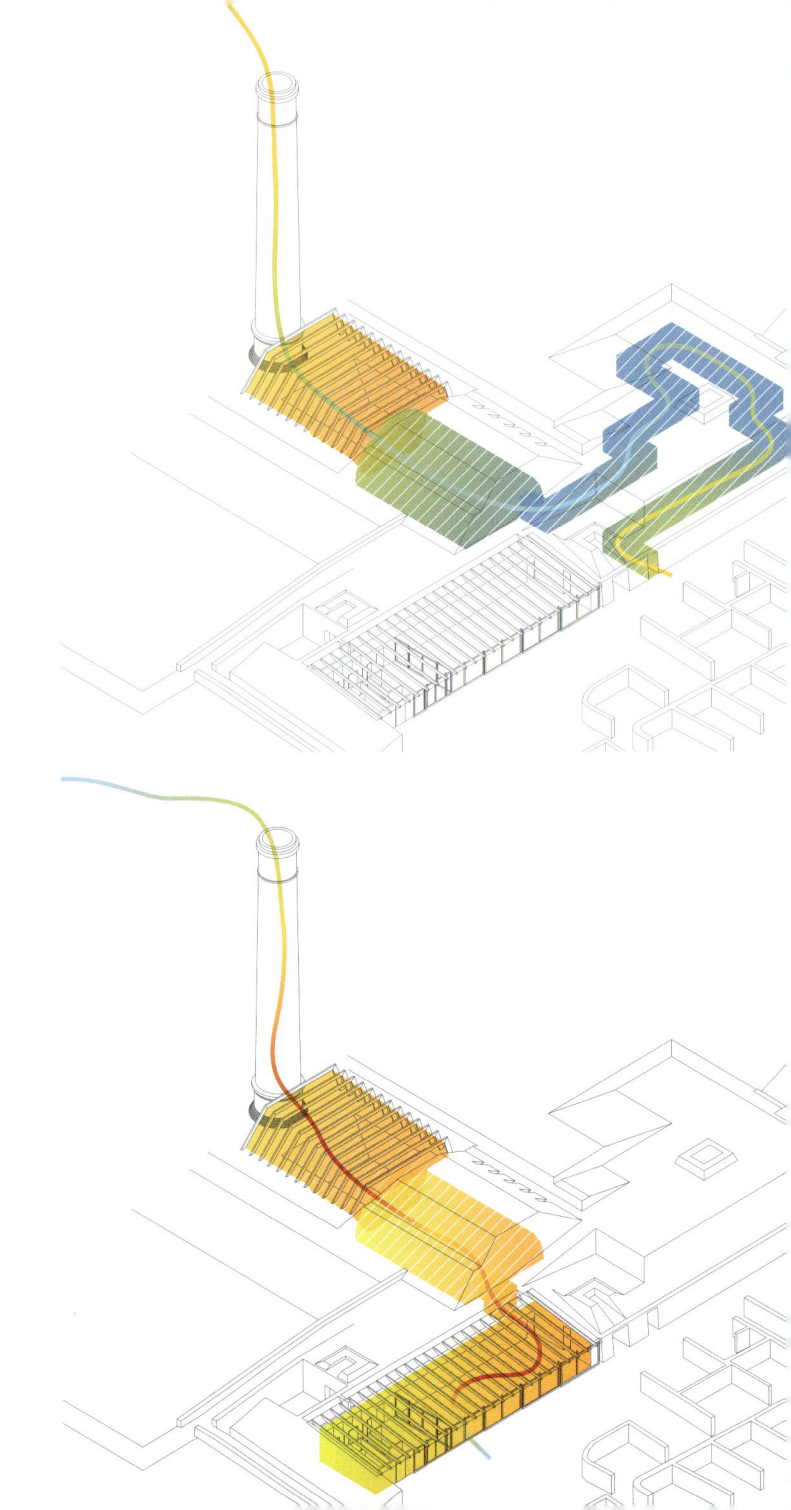

I am breathing new life new air into Inujima. The driving force is the sun, supported by the materials of Inujima such as the chimney and bricks of slag.

From the six chimneys remaining in Inujima, I chose the most beautiful, robust one. I established a glass-covered space at the base of the chimney, made of discarded bricks of slag. The slag is a by-product of copper smelting, and has the property of absorbing and retaining solar energy. The air is lifted by the combined power of the sun, the chimney, the slag, and the glazed space, all working together to enhance the airflow. New values have been discovered for existing materials and discarded materials.

There are two entrances. One is an entrance for people, and the other is an entrance for air. The air that enters at the entrance is cooled by a corridor approximately 80 metres in length, set 2 metres below ground level. Steel was chosen for the walls of the corridor. This is to transfer energy to the Earth. The passage bends back and forth, and the walls undulate, a necessary detail for extracting heat from the air.

Mirrors are placed in the corners of the underground passage, facing each other, while reflecting the light that enters through skylights. A person visiting here will advance with the air toward the light.

But visitors here do not just experience the art, architecture, and nature. They also contribute to nature. I want them to understand that people are part of the moving materials of the Earth. Here, the excrement of the visitors is converted and purified into fertilizer for plants within the site, helping the growth of the trees that conceal the building. The shade of the growing trees causes the underground environment of the building to be more stable. The harvested fruit gives moisture and nutrients to the people who visit the facility. Water and nourishment are brought into Inujima according to how many people visit, and the greenery continues to thrive. The important thing is that, due to the presence of the architecture, the art museum is the means by which human beings become part of the Earth's essential cycles, together with plants, sunlight, terrain, water, and air. All the details extend throughout the Earth.

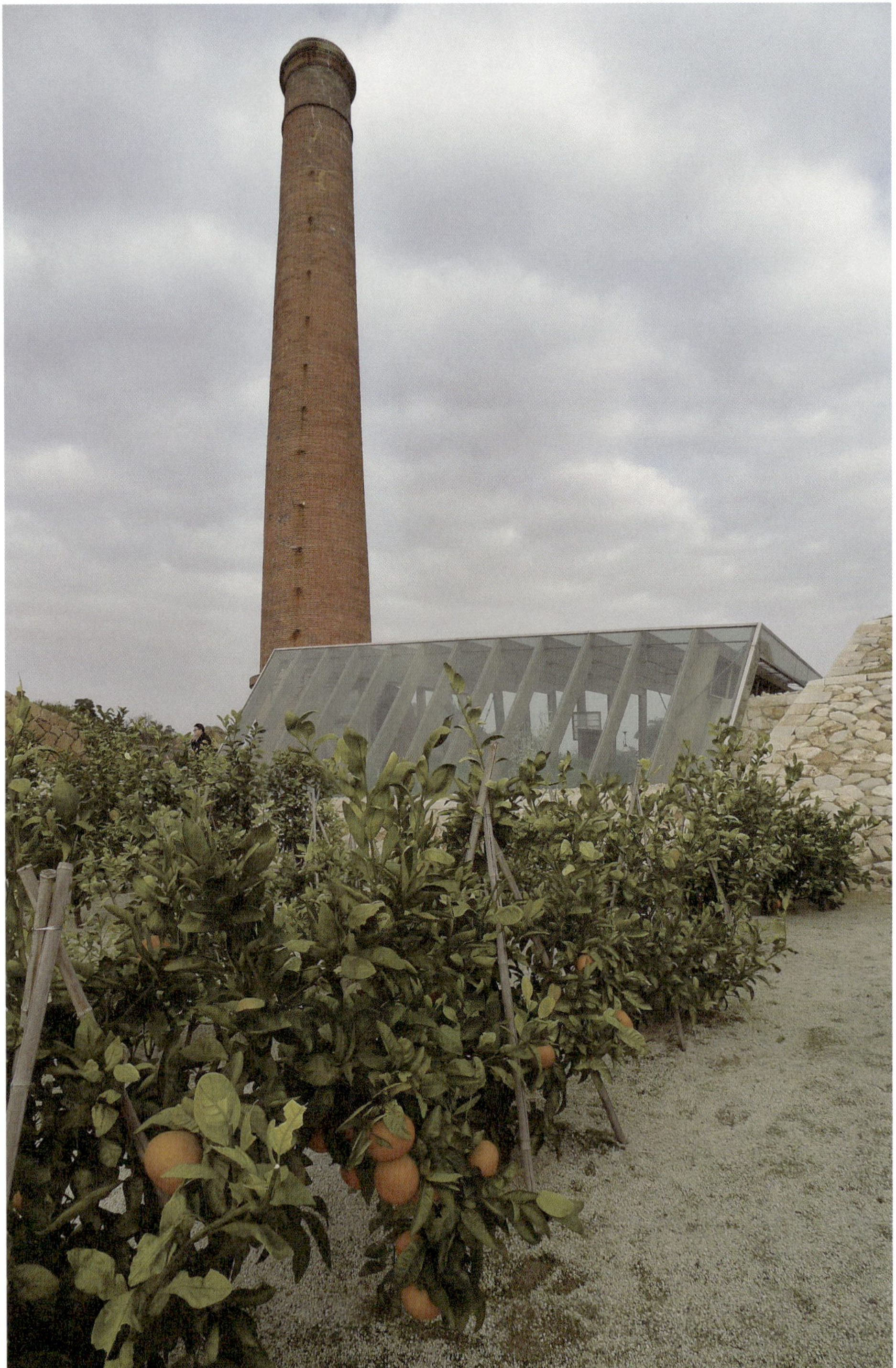

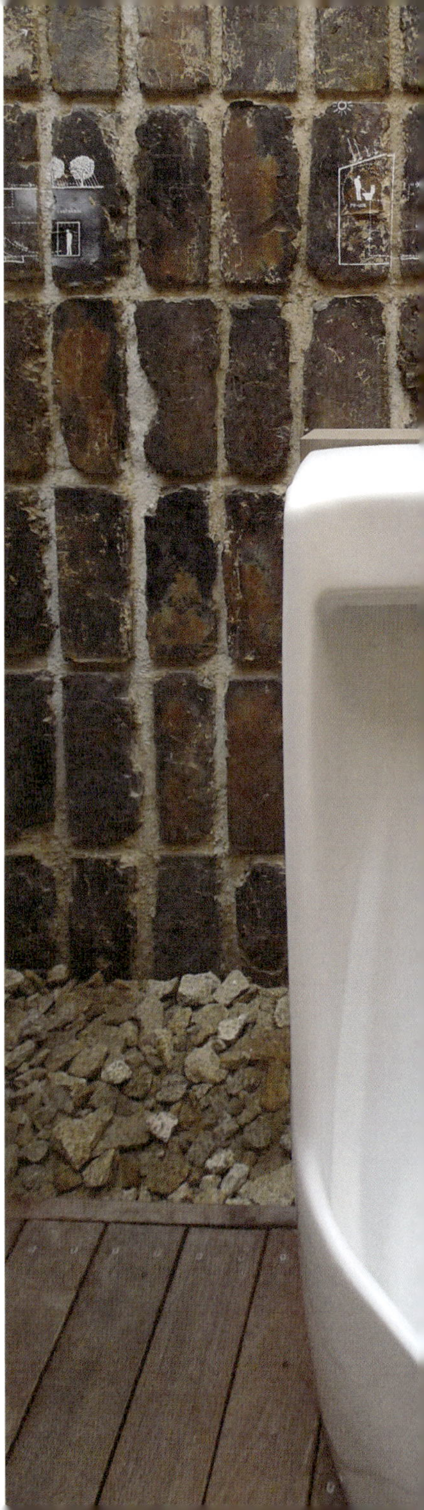

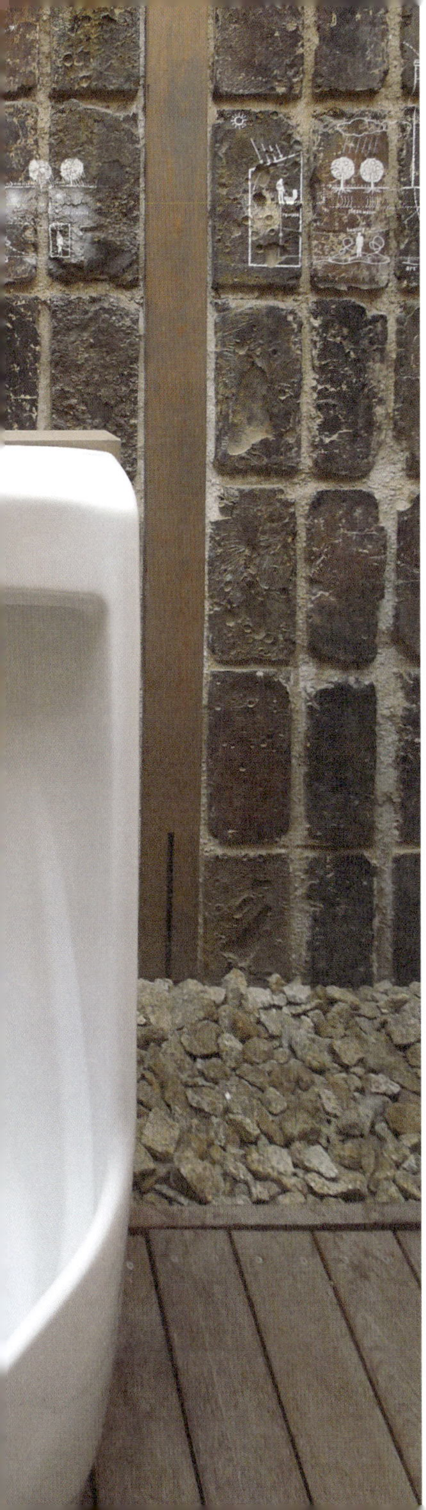

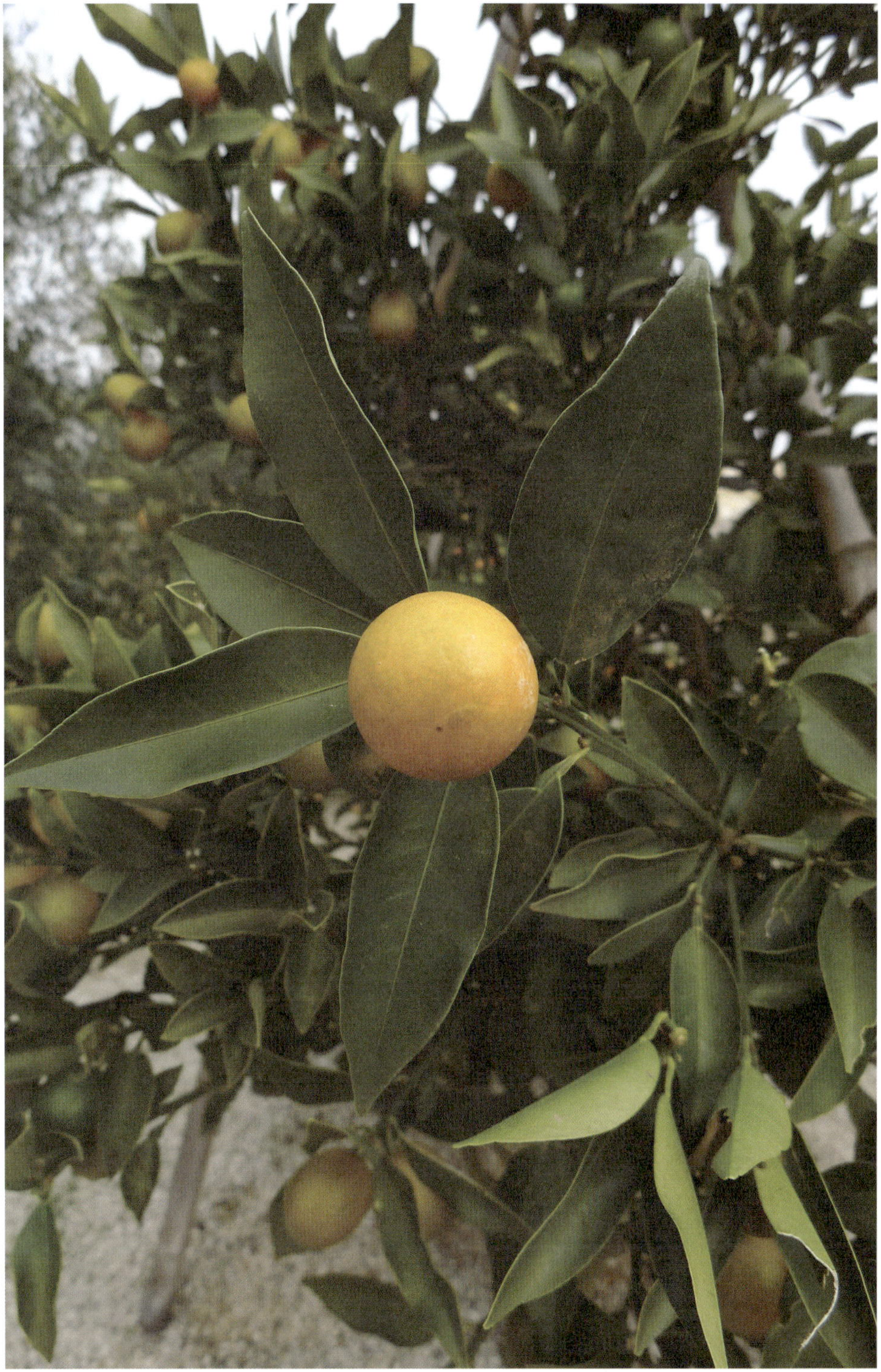

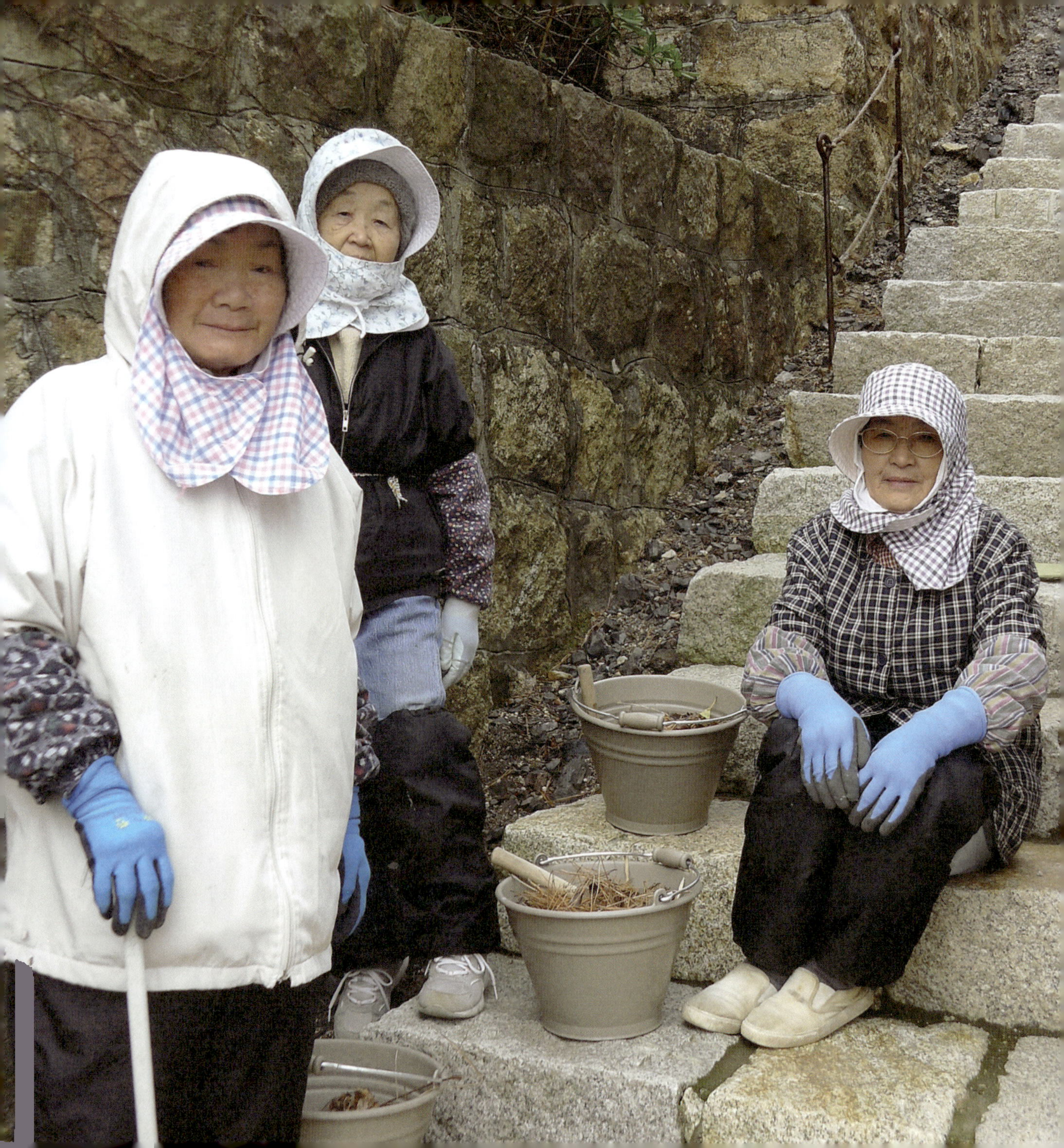

在るものを活かし、無いものを創る
福武總一郎／公益財団法人福武財団理事長

私は、若い頃は主に東京で生活をしていましたが、40歳の時に父が急逝したため、瀬戸内へ帰ることになりました。

父が進めていた直島でのプロジェクトを引き継ぎ、島の人びととの交流を深めながら瀬戸内の島々を回るうちに、瀬戸内海の美しさ素晴らしさと同時に、歴史や文化、島々に暮らす人びととのあり方など、その魅力を再認識するようになりました。

瀬戸内の多くの島々は、近代化の波に洗われていない、かつて日本人が本来もっていた心のあり方や暮らし方、地域の原風景が残っていました。

一方で、日本で最初の国立公園に認定されながらも日本の近代化や戦後の高度成長を支えるため開発が進み、その歪みや負の遺産を背負わされた場所でもありました。

瀬戸内の魅力を世界の多くの方々に知っていただこうと、直島を中心にアートや建築のプロジェクトを進めていきました。ただ私にとってそれらはコレクションのためではなく、またそれ自体が目的でもありません。

地域やそこに暮らす人びとの本来もっている魅力を引き出すための手段であり、純粋に瀬戸内が本来もっている姿を掘り起こし、世界に類をみない美しい風景やコミュニティの姿にしていきたいと考えています。

瀬戸内海の魅力を再認識する中で、東京での社会のあり方と比較すると、近代化のベースとなっている考え方である「破壊と創造」の文明、つまり「在るものを壊し、新しいものをつくり続け、肥大化していく文明」のあり方に深い疑念を憶えたのです。そうした、「破壊と創造を繰り返す文明」から、「持続し成長していく文明」に転換していかなければいけない。そうでなければ、文化の継承と発展はできないし、われわれのつくったものも、いずれ後世に抹殺されてしまうだろうと考えました。

「在るものを活かし、無いものを創る」。それこそが地方の、そして日本の再生の理念であると確信するようになりました。

その転機となったのが犬島と三分一博志さんとの出会いでした。

銅製錬所跡を抱えた犬島は、穏やかな風景の広がる瀬戸内海にありながら、採石で土地を削られ、銅製錬所からの煙害によって緑を失うなど、近代化の中で苦しめられてきた歴史をもちます。私はこの場所でこそ、日本が辿った近代化の道に疑問を投げ掛けるメッセージを発信できると考えました。

既にアート活動を行っていた直島とは同じ瀬戸内海にありながら、異なる環境や文化をもつため、ゼロからの始まりとなりました。

銅製錬所跡や周辺には、操業当時を彷彿とさせる痕跡が見られます。私たちは当時の様子を語り伝える地域の人びとに話を聞きながら島の歴史風土をひもといていきました。同時に建築家を探していました。この場所の魅力を引き出

すには東京の建築家ではなく、むしろ瀬戸内の地域・気候をよく理解し、地域の自然環境と一体となったメッセージを発信できる人と考えていました。結果、三分一さんに辿り着いたのですが、きっかけは瀬戸内の北側斜面に建つ住宅でした。それは、通常マイナス要因でしかない北斜面の地形を利用し、空気を循環させるという手法で建てられた住宅でした。固定概念を覆し、さらにそれを利用し発展させていく発想に魅力を感じました。

三分一さんはその場所の地形や気候を丁寧に読み解き水や空気など自然の動きを利用した設計を手掛ける新しい時代の建築家だと思います。「在るものを活かし、無いものを創る」を実践し続けていました。彼は、まさに私の考え、そしてメッセージを犬島の美術館の建築を通して具現化してくれました。

近代以降、人の生活とエネルギー問題は切り離すことができません。犬島の環境に負荷を与えないよう設計し、見事に調和した「犬島精錬所美術館」は、自然破壊を省みない経済至上主義に疑問を投げ掛けるだけでなく、環境との関わり方を提案し、新しい社会のあり方について考えさせる場所に生まれ変わったと思っています。

地域再生における次の取り組み
「直島プラン」

地域再生にとって重要なことは自立性です。アートや建築を通してその地域の価値を世界にみせていくと、その先に見えてくるものは、個性・魅力によって文化・経済的に自立し、持続する地域づくりです。

私は特に「食とエネルギーの自立」に取り組もうと考えています。「瀬戸内海の島々の自立」という大きな目標を考えていく上で自然の力を上手く利用した、無理のない街づくりという課題を次の取り組みとして定め、現在、直島の本村地区における新しいプロジェクトを三分一さんにお願いしています。

私は彼の取り組みを、もう10年以上もの長い間見てきました。その手法は2年も3年も掛けてその場所を細やかに調査し、地域を理解し、地形・気候・歴史など、さまざまな要素によりその土地がもつ潜在的な力を掘り起こそうとするものです。

例えば、本村は400年前に城下町としてつくられました。それらは、風や水、太陽などの自然エネルギーから導かれた碁盤目状の集落だと分かってきました。これまで「家プロジェクト」[1]ではその残っていた家とアートを結び付けてきましたが、三分一さんはその家々がどのような背景をもってそこに「在る」のかを浮き彫りにしようとしています。おそらく、「直島の家またべえ」[2]や「直島ホール」に実際にお越しいただくと、島の人びとや島を訪れた方々も建築を通し自然から導かれた直島像を具体的に理解してくれるでしょう。その結果、直島が本来もっている魅力が島の人びとに理解され、直島の誇りとなる生活スタイルがこれからも続いていくことを願っています。それはかつて日本人が本来もっていた自然の力をうまく利用し、生活、文化、芸術の発展につなげてきた営みの姿／風景でもあります。

近代化や都市化を否定するつもりはありません。日本にも、東京のマネではなく、もっとそれぞれの地域の歴史と文化を生かした都市が生まれることによって、都会と田舎、そしてお年寄りと若者、男と女、そこに「住む人びと」と「訪れる人びと」とが互いに交流し、お互いの良さを発見し、認め

合うことができます。そのことが都市に住む人びとにとっても良い影響を与え、過疎と言われる地域もよみがえり、それぞれの地域のもつ多様で豊かな文化を生かしていく「バランスの取れた価値観の社会」ができることを期待しています。

そして「在るものを活かし、無いものを創っていく」という21世紀の新しい文明観を、ここ瀬戸内海から、世界に発信していきたいと思います。

(1) 直島・本村地区において1998年より展開するアートプロジェクト。点在していた空き家などを改修し、人が住んでいた頃の時間と記憶を織り込みながら、空間そのものをアーティストが作品化。現在7軒を公開。

(2) 個人宅のため通常は非公開。

USE WHAT EXISTS TO CREATE WHAT IS TO BE
Soichiro Fukutake, chairman of the board, Fukutake Foundation

In my youth I lived mainly in Tokyo, but returned to the Seto region when I turned 40 following my father's sudden demise.

I took over the Naoshima project that he had initiated, and while travelling around the islands of the region and deepening my ties with their residents, I developed a renewed appreciation for the history, culture, and way of life of the people living on the islands, at the same time taking in the exquisite beauty of the Seto Inland Sea.

Many of the islands in the Seto region have not been touched by the waves of modernization, so Japan's traditional spirit, way of life, and primeval landscapes still remain.

On the other hand, though declared the first national park in Japan, through developments supporting Japan's modernization effort and the post-war period of high economic growth, it is also a place that was forced to bear the distortions and negative legacy thereof.

I am developing art and architecture projects in and around Naoshima so that many people across the world would be made aware of the charms of the Seto region. In doing so, I do not act for the sake of my collection, nor are the projects the actual purpose.

I think of them as a means to draw out the charms of the region and the people that live there, to reclaim the original appearance of the authentic Seto region, and its uniquely beautiful scenery and community.

While rediscovering the charms of the Seto Inland Sea, and comparing the region with society in Tokyo, I became deeply dubious about the way of thinking that forms the basis for modernization; a civilization of "scrap and build" or, in other words, an ever-expanding civilization that destroys what exists in order to constantly create new things. We must shift from this "civilization of scrap and build" to a "civilization of sustainable growth." If not, the inheritance and development of culture will be impossible, and the things that we create will inevitably be obliterated by future generations.

I became convinced that, for the revitalization of this region and of Japan, our ideal should be to "use what exists to create what is to be."

The turning point was an encounter with Inujima and Hiroshi Sambuichi. Though Inujima sits in the expansive and calm scenery of the Seto Inland Sea, it contains the ruins of a copper refinery and has a history tormented by modernization, its land carved up by quarrying, and its greenery destroyed by emissions from the refining activities. Precisely from this place I thought I could convey a message that questions the path of modernization followed by Japan.

Even though Inujima is located in the Seto Inland Sea just like Naoshima, where art activities were already underway, it has a distinct environment and culture, so we began from zero.

In the ruins of the copper refinery and its surroundings, there are visible traces that are vivid reminders of the days when it was operational. While listening to local people passing down stories about circumstances back then, we unravelled the history and climate of the island.

At the same time, I was looking for an architect. To draw out the charms of this place, rather than using an architect from Tokyo, I was thinking about an architect with a good understanding of the Seto region and climate, and who would be able to convey a message of unity with the local natural environment. This eventually led me to Sambuichi, the impetus being a house built on a north-facing slope in the region. North-sloping terrain is usually considered a negative factor, but this house makes use of this characteristic to circulate air. A preconceived idea was thus not only overturned, but further built upon, which I found very interesting.

I think that Sambuichi is an architect of a new era, one who designs by carefully reading and comprehending the terrain and the climate of a place, and utilising the natural movements of water and air. He constantly puts into practice the notion of "using what exists to create what is to be." He gave physical shape to my thoughts and to my message through his architecture for the art museum on Inujima.

Since the beginning of the modern era, human life cannot be separated from energy issues. Designed so as to avoid placing any burden on the environment of Inujima, I think that the wonderful harmony of the Inujima Seirensho Art Museum not only questions the principle of economic supremacy unconcerned by natural destruction, but also reinvigorates a place so as to propose a relationship with its environment and thus induces thoughts about new forms of society.

The next step
in regional revitalizaion:
"The Naoshima Plan"

What matters for regional revitalization is self-reliance. Revealing the value of this region to the world through the medium of art and architecture, it became clear that what lies ahead is the sustainable and independent development of the region's culture and economy through its own attributes.

In particular, I want to tackle the challenge of food and energy independence. Aiming ultimately for the self-reliance of the Seto Inland Sea islands, I decided to focus on a community development model that would skilfully use the powers of nature, and asked Sambuichi to develop a new project in the Honmura village of Naoshima.

I have been observing his activities for more than ten years now. His technique is to gently investigate a place over a period of up to two or three years, comprehend the region, then unearth the latent power of the land embodied by various elements, including its terrain, climate, and history.

Honmura, for example, was built 400 years ago as a castle town. We came to understand that the village's grid plan derived from natural energies such as wind, water, and sunlight. In the "Art House Project"[1] undertaken previously, existing houses were linked with art, but Sambuichi intends to shed light on the background of the "existence" of these very houses.

Probably, if island residents and visitors from outside see the Matabe house[2] and Naoshima Hall, they will gain a concrete understanding – through the architecture – of the extent to which Naoshima was shaped by nature. As a result, Naoshima's inhabitants will come to realize the value of their island, and it is my hope that the lifestyle that is the pride of Naoshima will carry on. This is also a manifestation of the skilful use of the powers of nature, which the Japanese once mastered to develop their livelihoods, culture, and art.

It is not my intention to reject modernization and urbanization. In Japan also, through the rise of cities based on their specific regional histories and cultures, rather than simply imitating Tokyo, it is possible to encourage mutual exchange and recognition between city and countryside, young and old, men and women, as well as "inhabitants" and "visitors." This can have a very positive impact on people living in the cities, contribute to the revival of so-called depopulating rural areas, and make good use of the rich cultures that have arisen as a consequence of regional diversity, thus my hope for a "society with a balanced sense of values."

"Use what exists to create what is to be." This is the new civilizational paradigm for the 21st century that I want to convey, from the Seto Inland Sea to the world.

1) An art project that has been underway in the Honmura village of Naoshima since 1998. It entails the renovation of scattered, unoccupied houses, in which the spaces themselves are turned into works of artists while incorporating memories of the times when people lived in them. Currently, seven houses are open to the public.

2) Private home. Not open to the public.

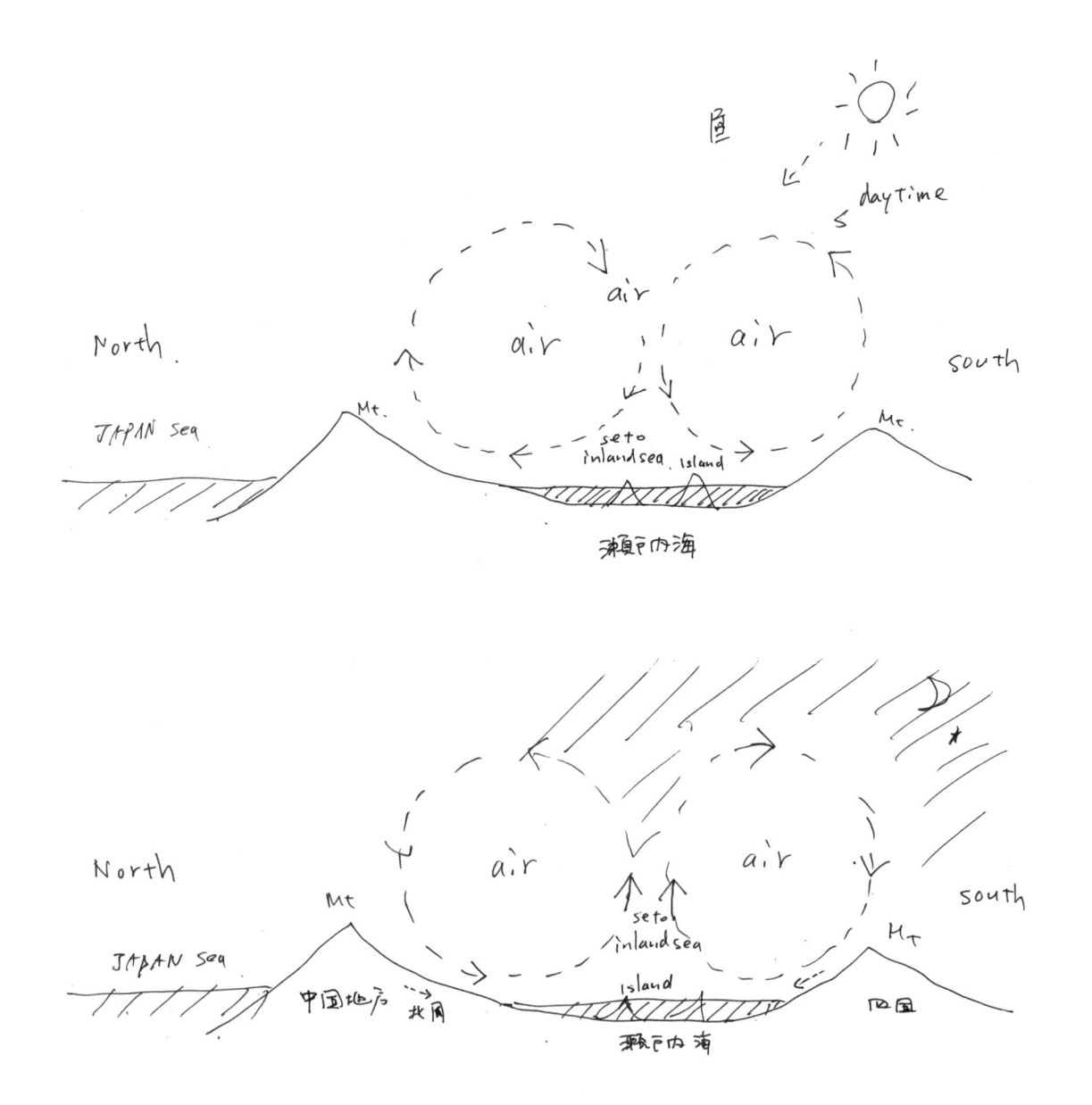

直島

NAOSHIMA

風
WIND

現代アートによって新たな価値を創造してきた直島。

Naoshima - a model for local revitalization through contemporary art and architecture.

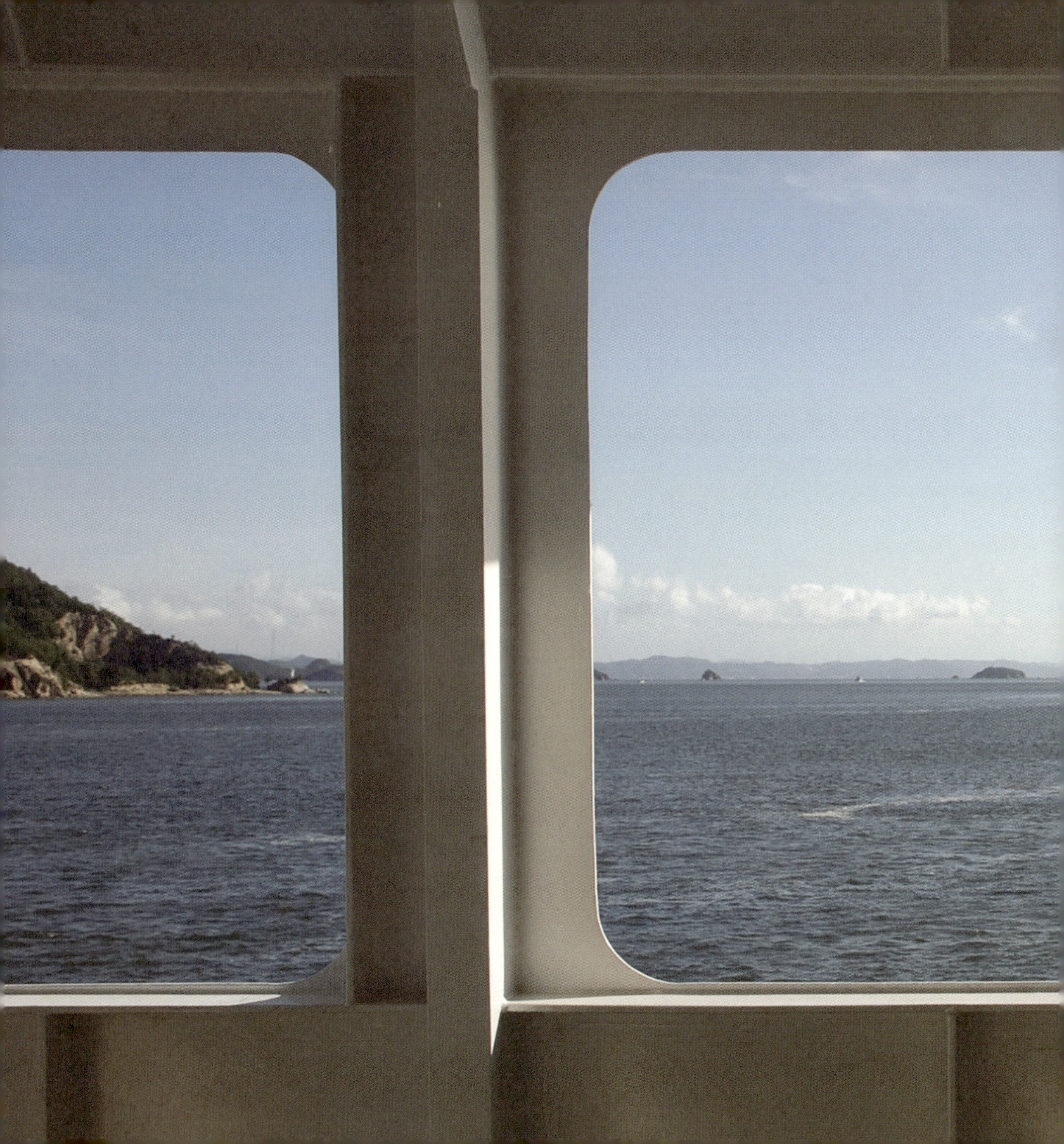

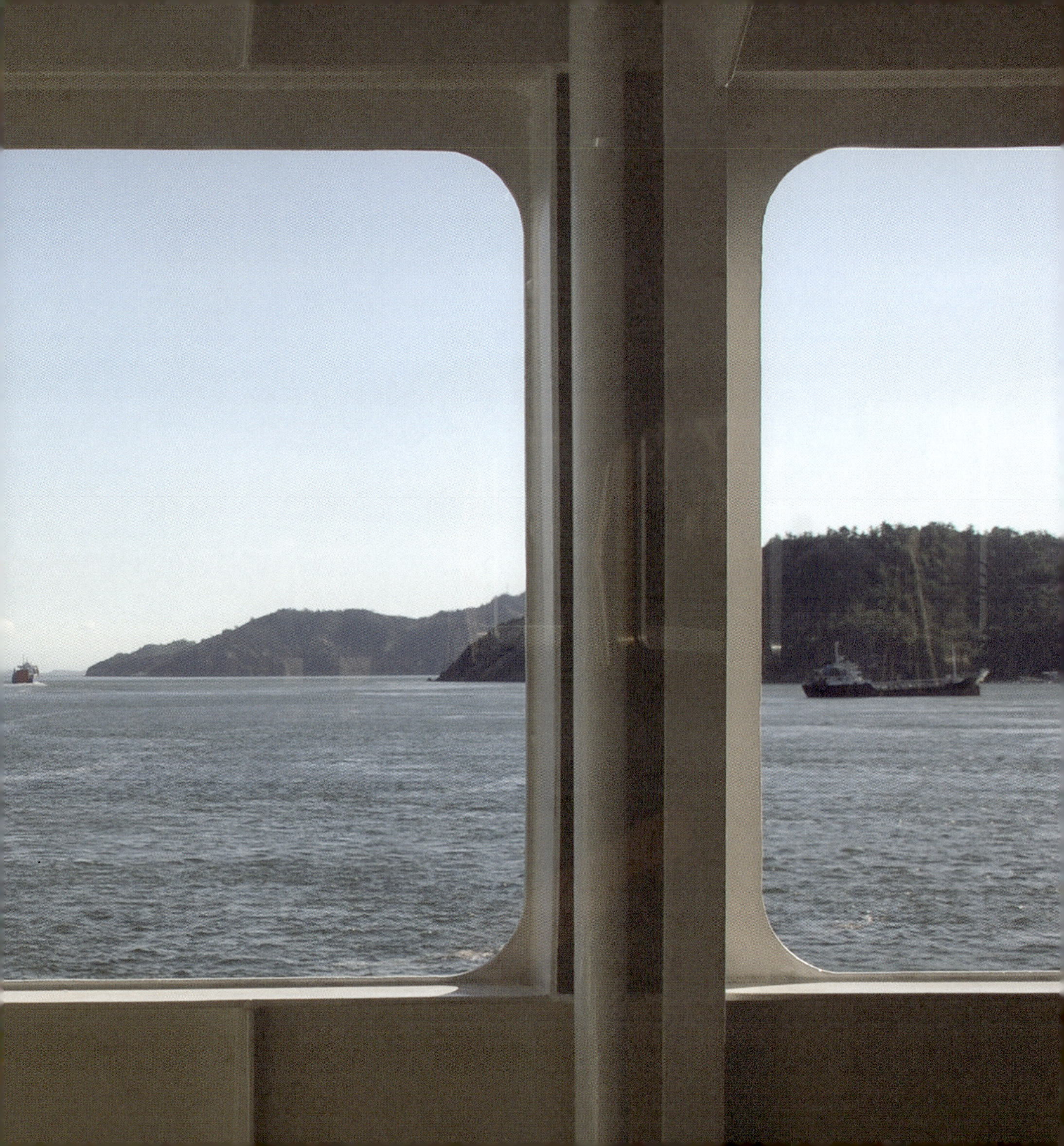

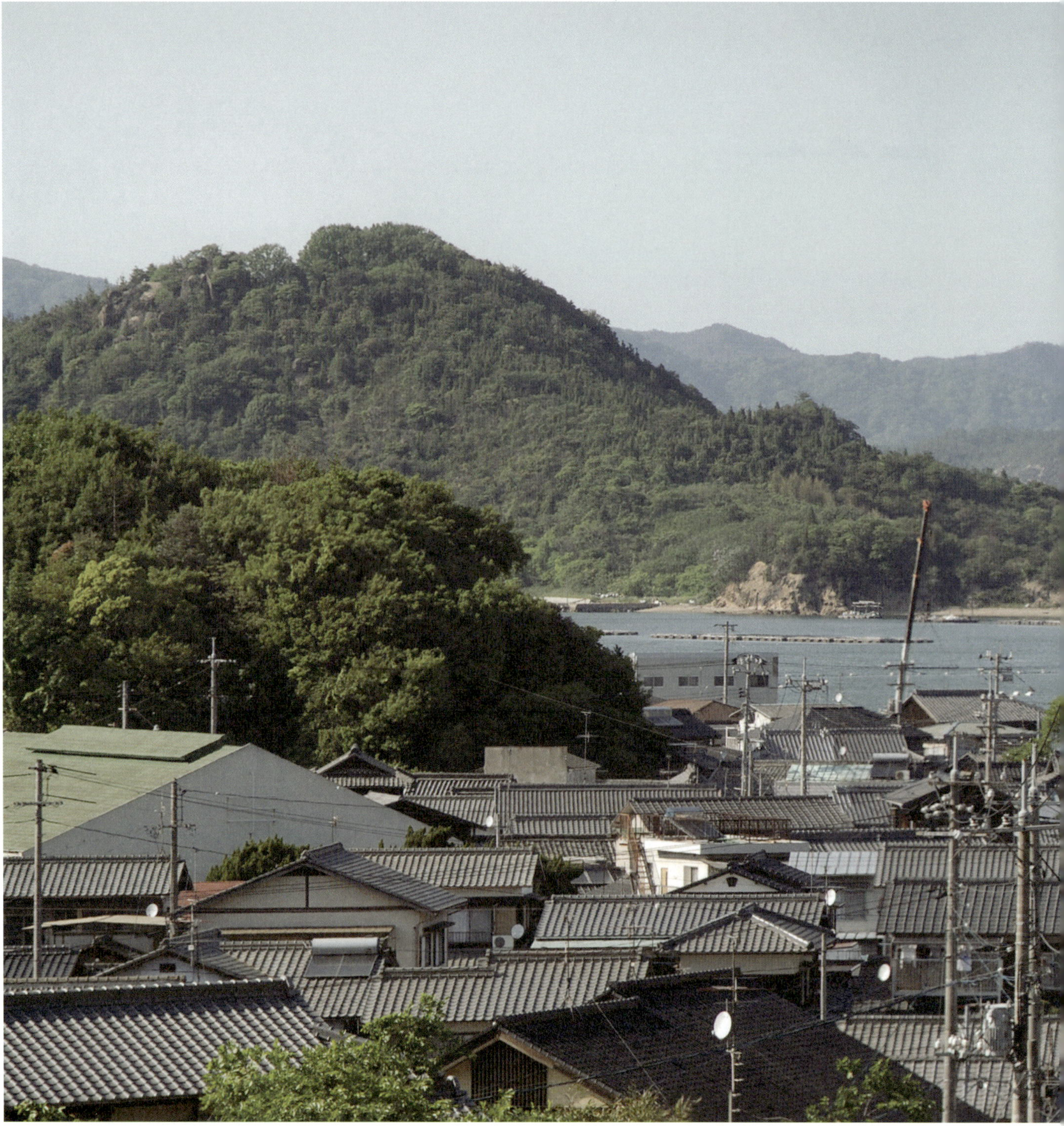

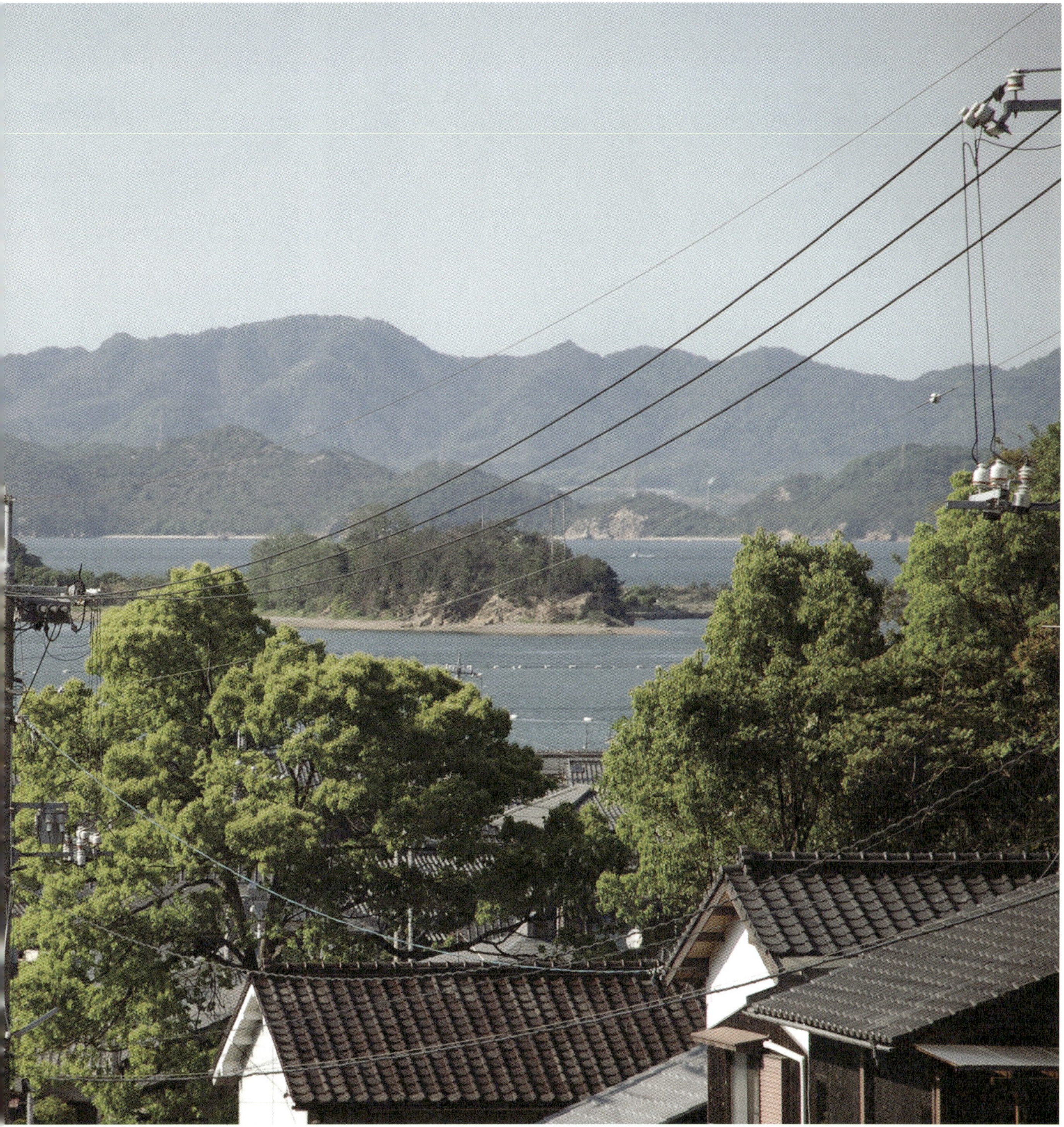

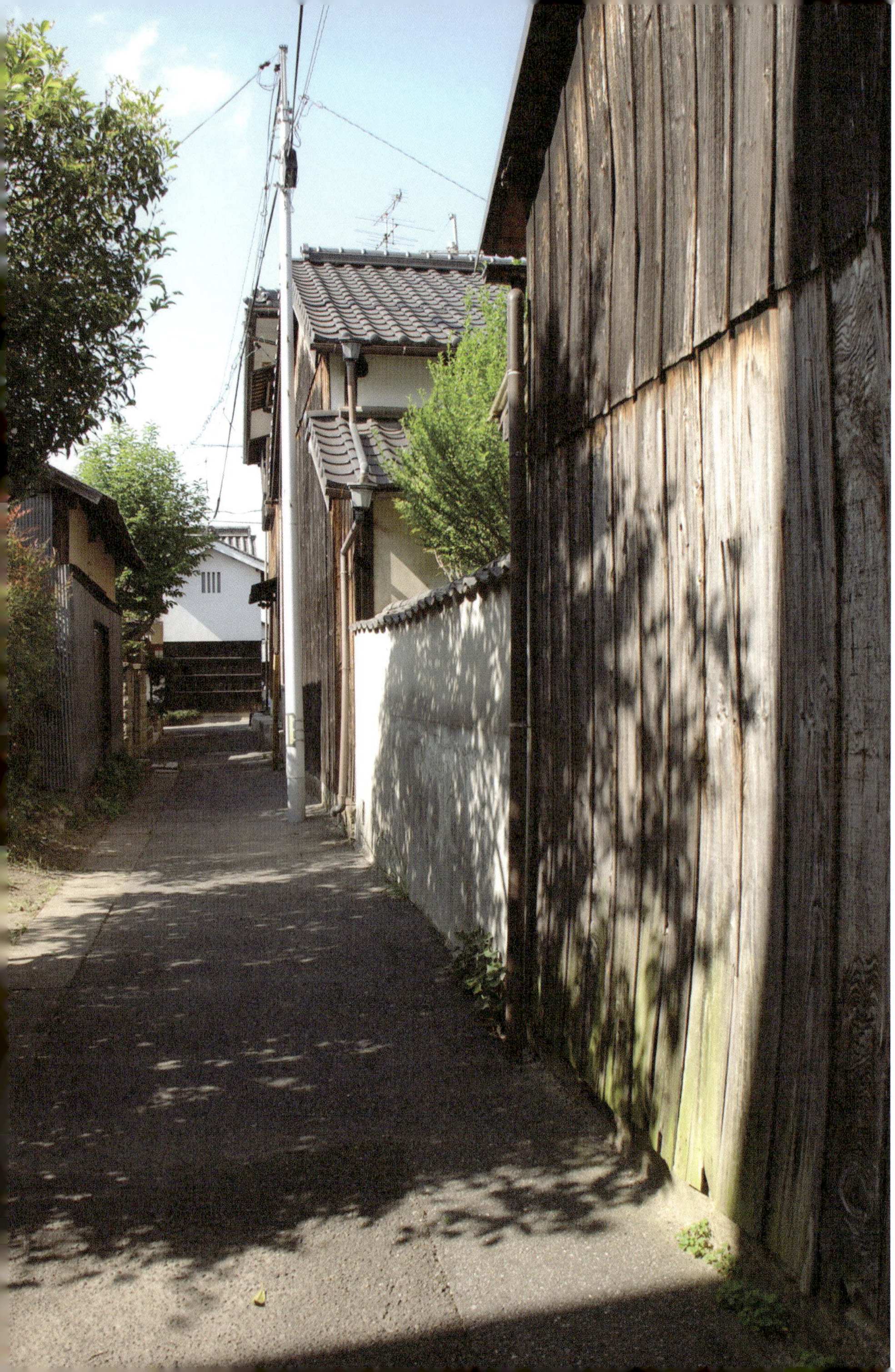
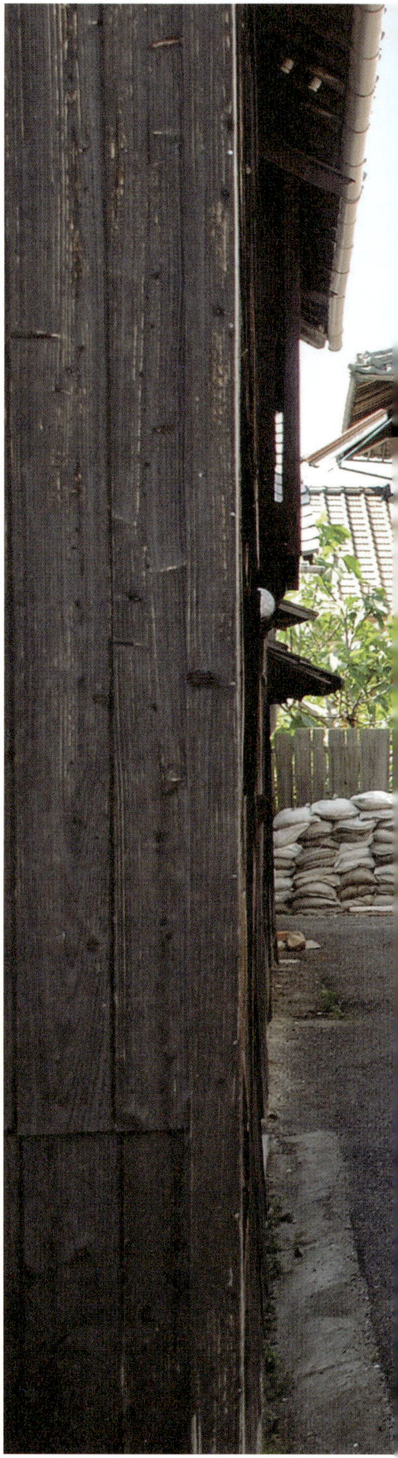

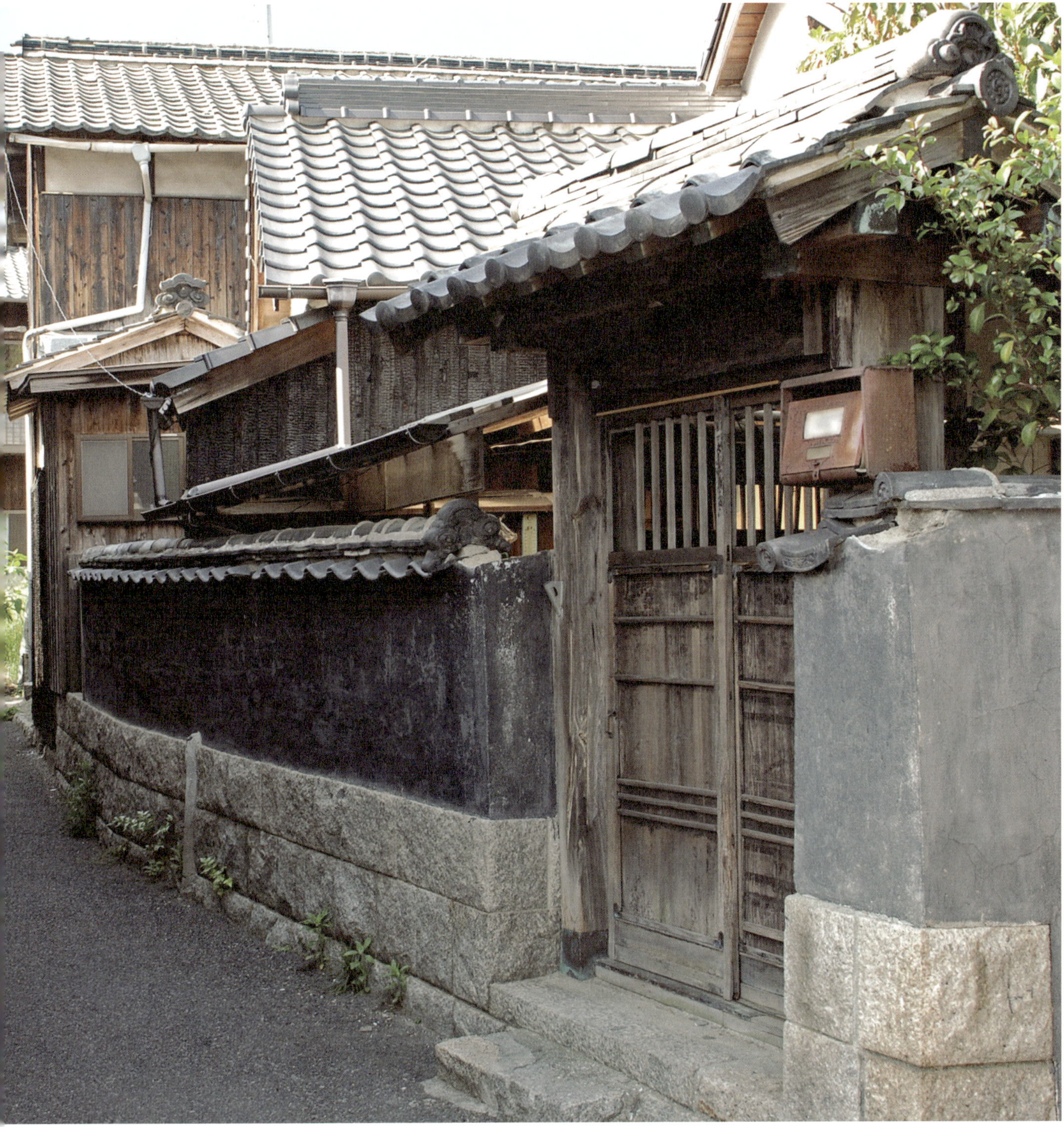

2年半におよぶ直島本村集落の調査の中で私に見えてきたものは、中世から脈々と受け継がれてきた風・水・太陽などの動く素材や地形によって導かれた集落の姿だった。

With more than two and a half years of research, it became apparent that Honmura village on Naoshima had been planned under the direction of the moving materials of wind, water and the Sun.

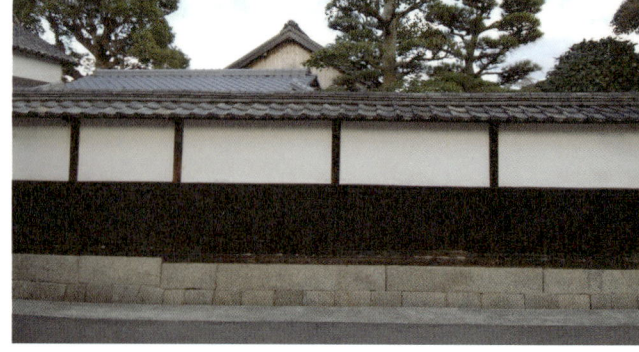

それぞれが塀で囲まれた屋敷造りとなっている。込み入った集落の中で、塀がそれぞれの民家の独立性を確保していた。

Every house was built with a surrounding wall. In this intricate town settlement, the wall ensured the privacy of each home.

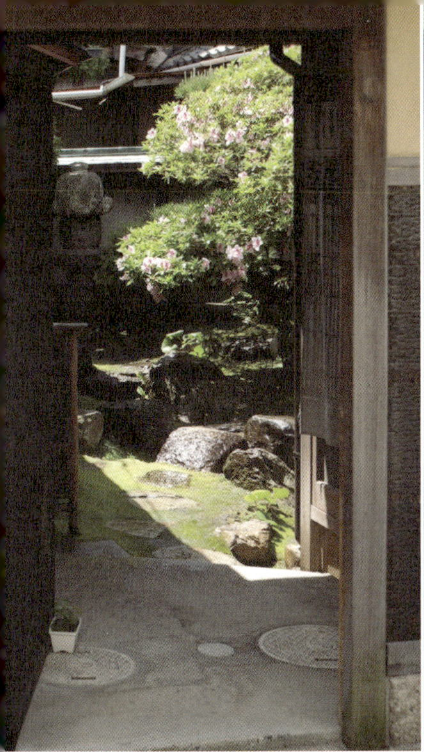
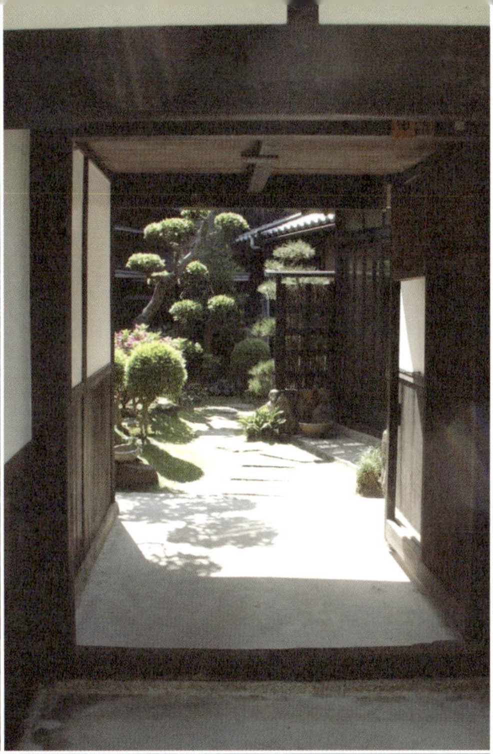
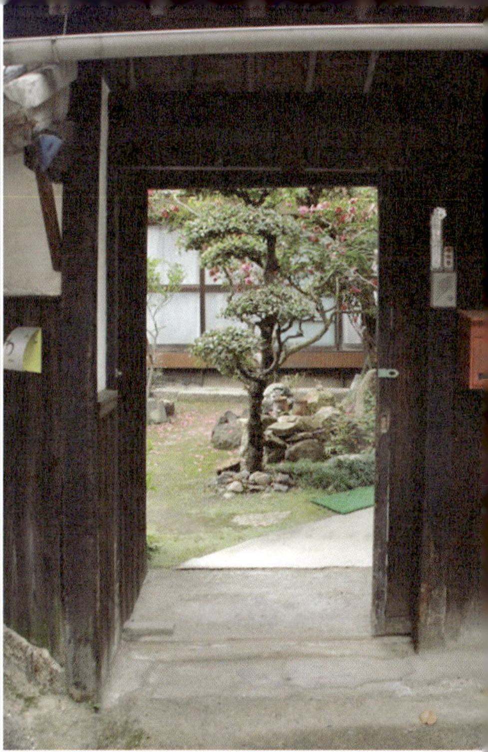
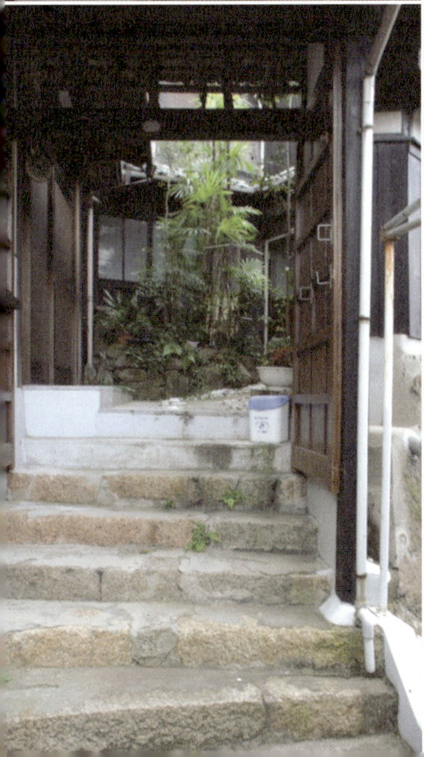
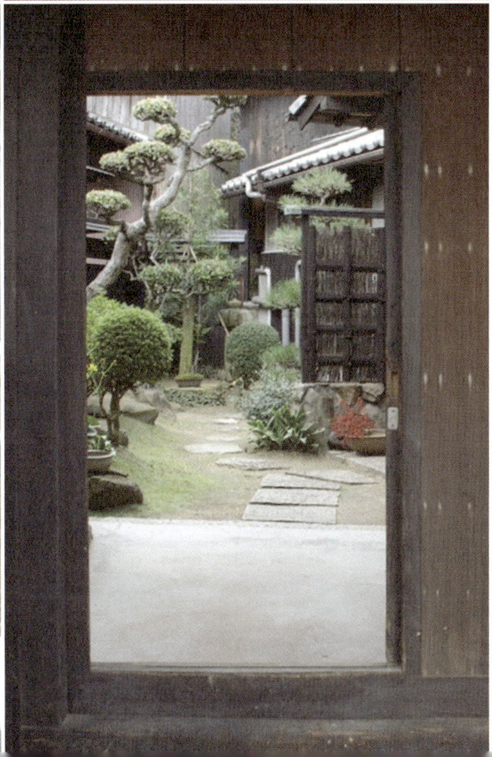
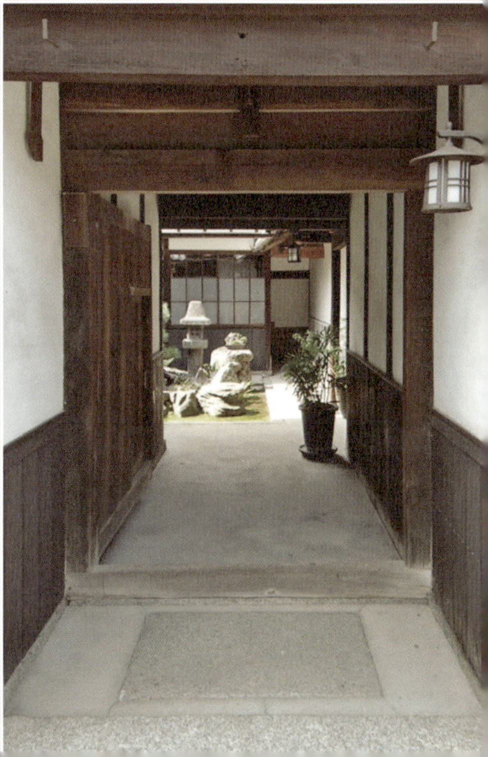

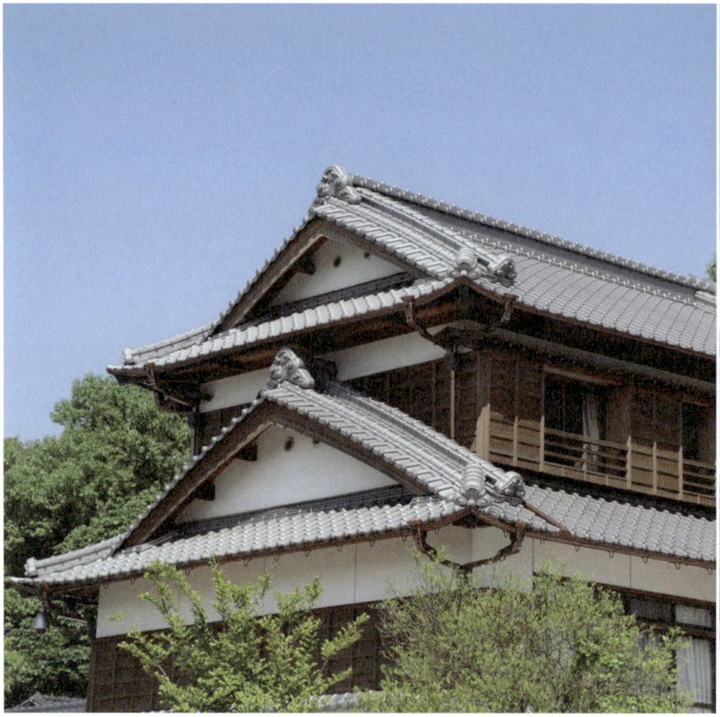
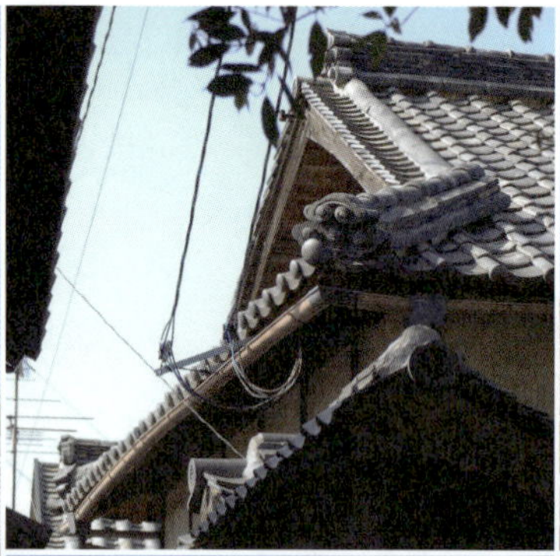
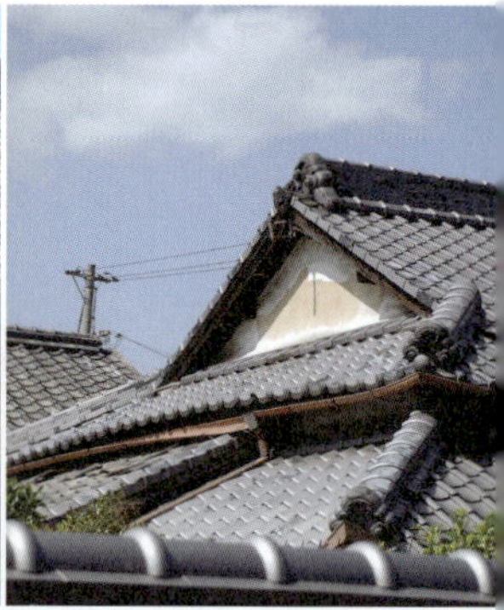
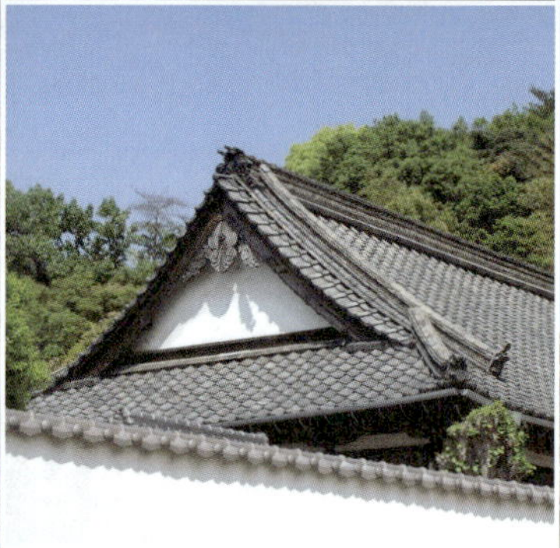
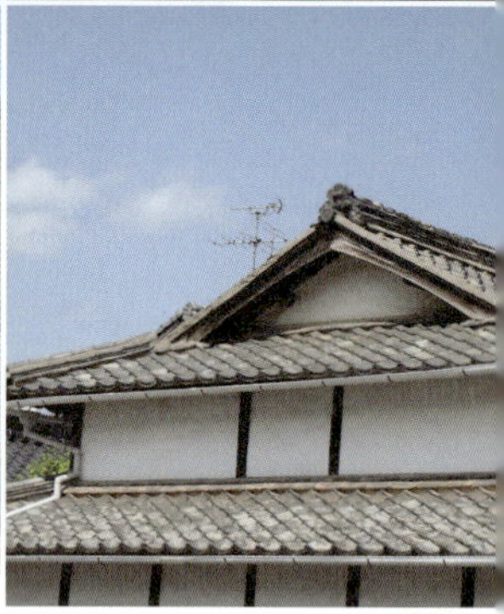
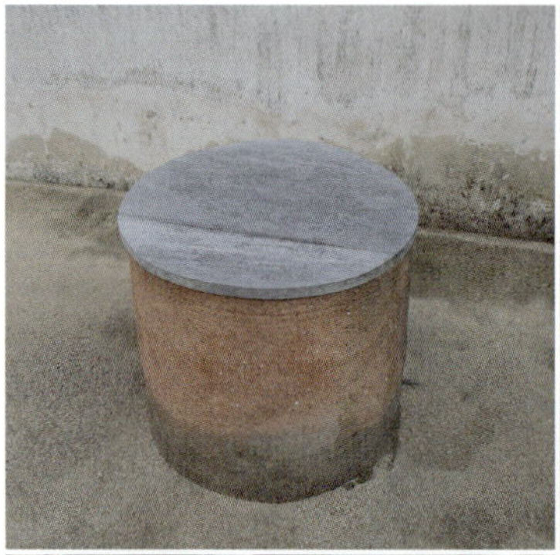
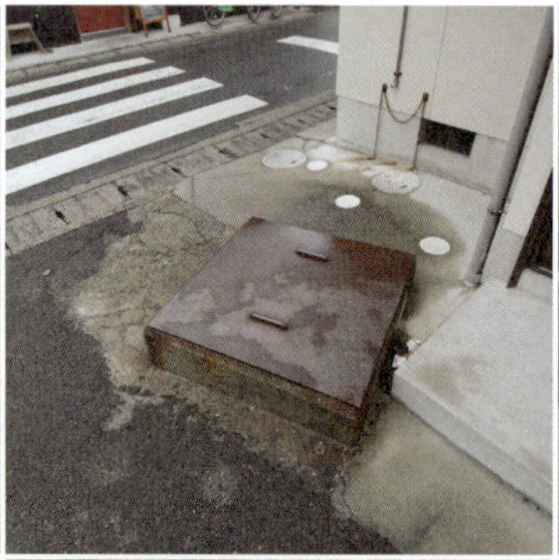
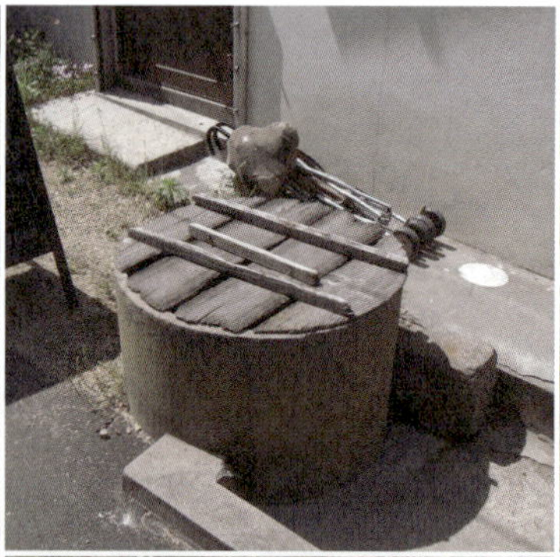
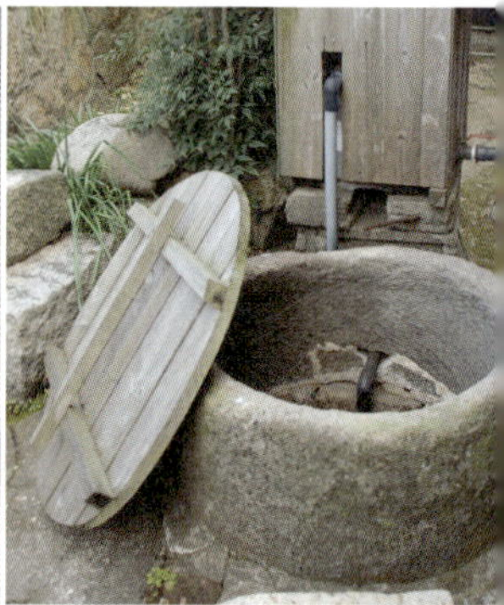
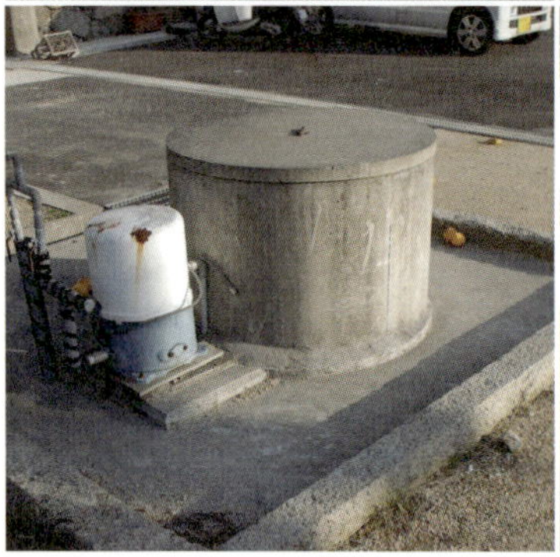
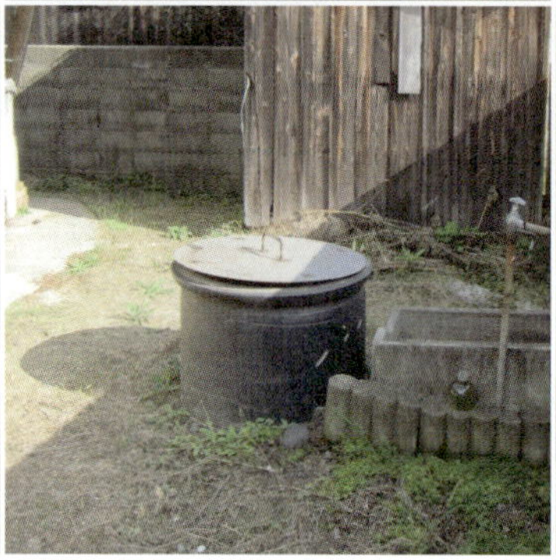
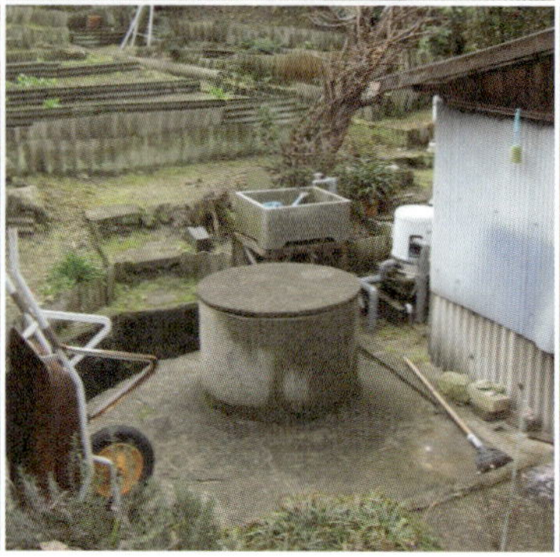
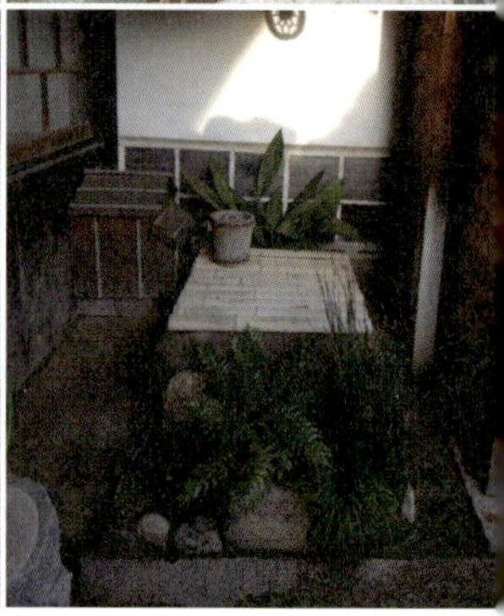

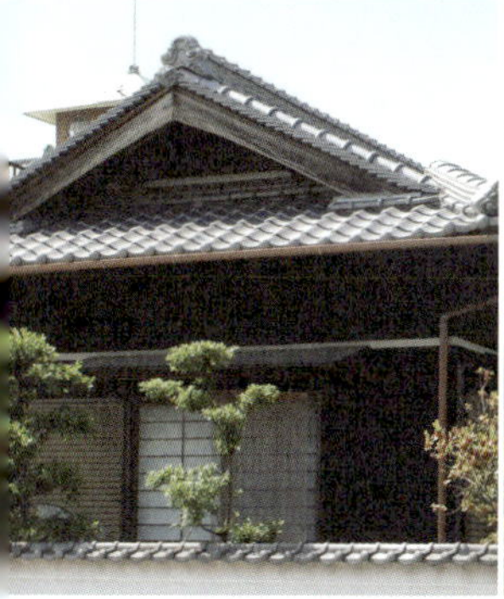
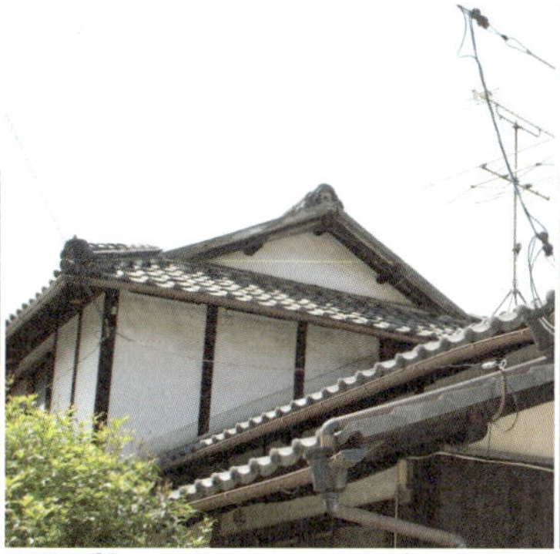
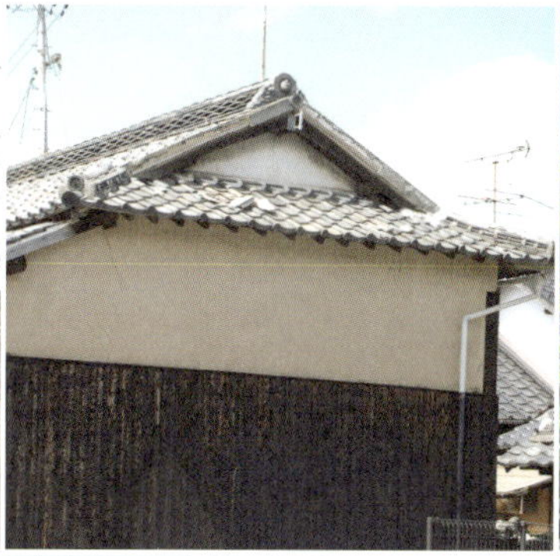
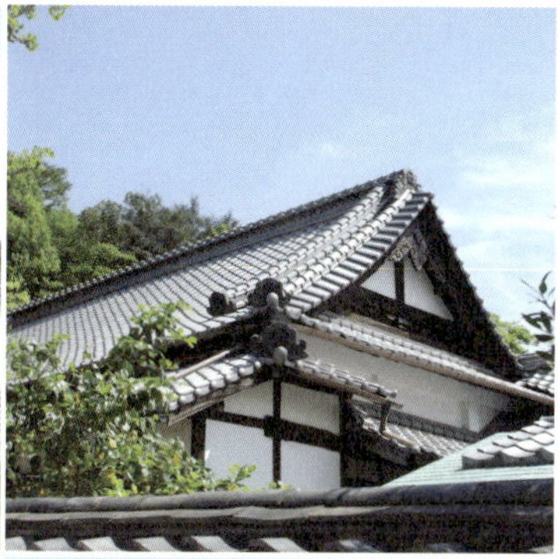
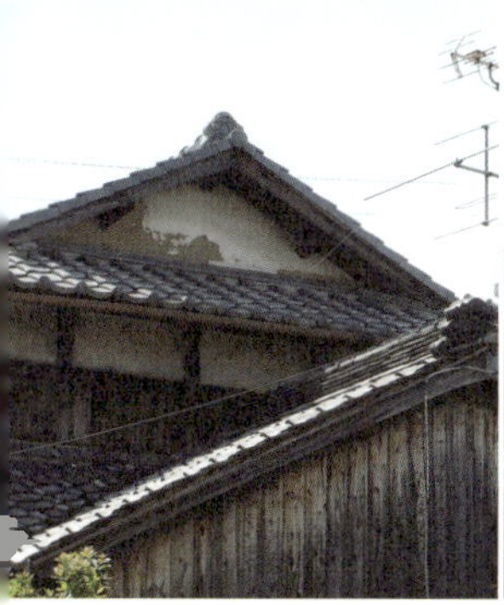
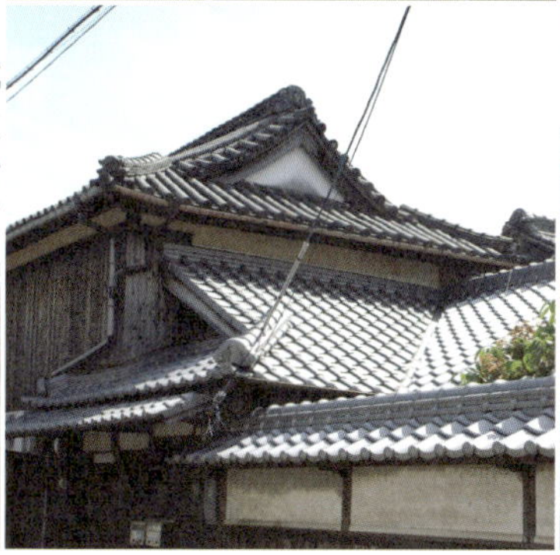
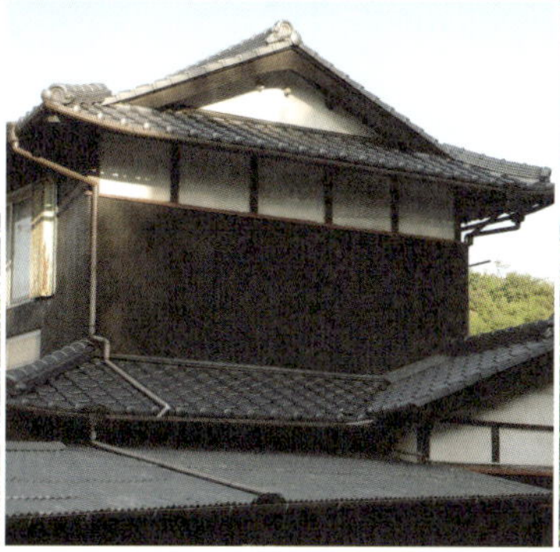
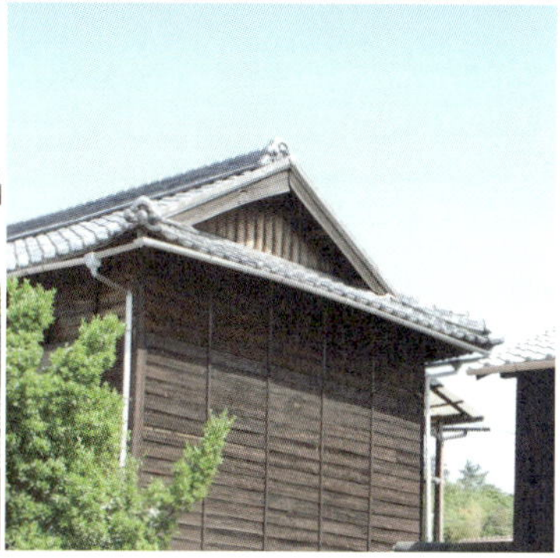
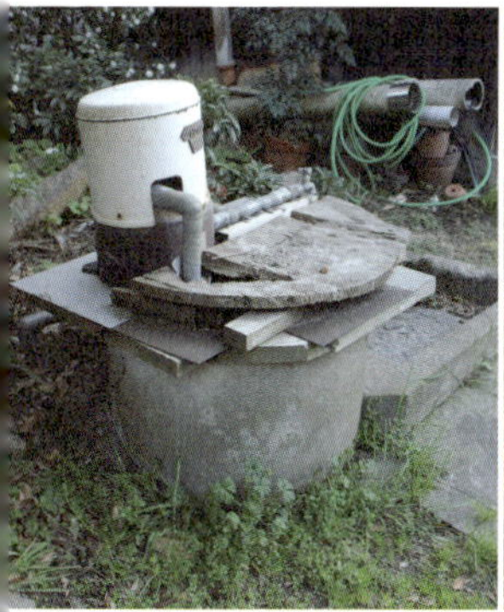
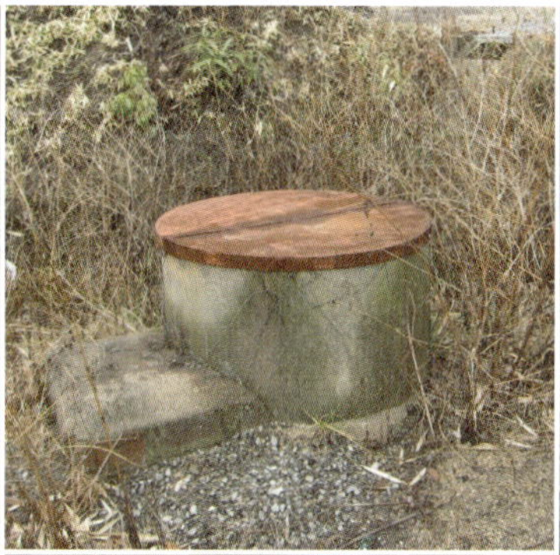
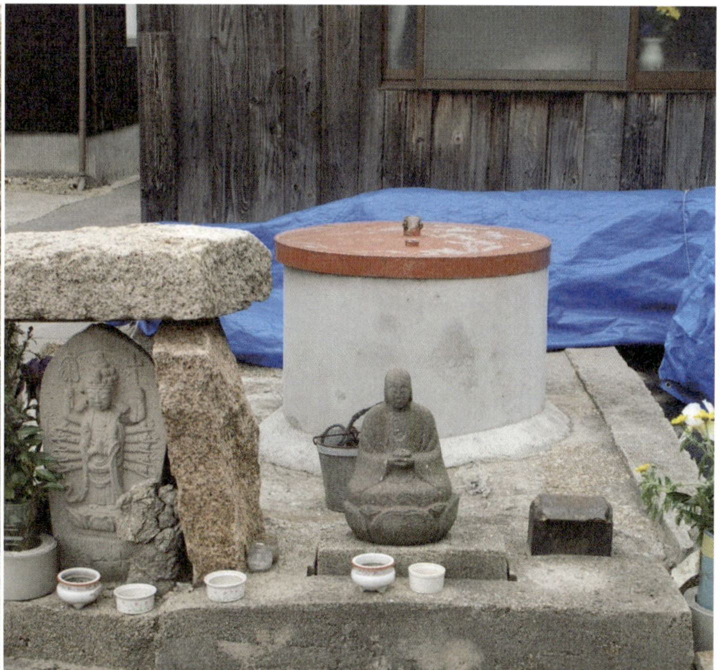
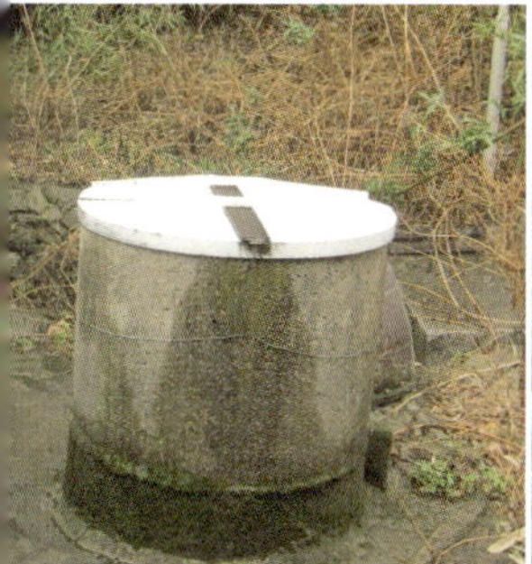
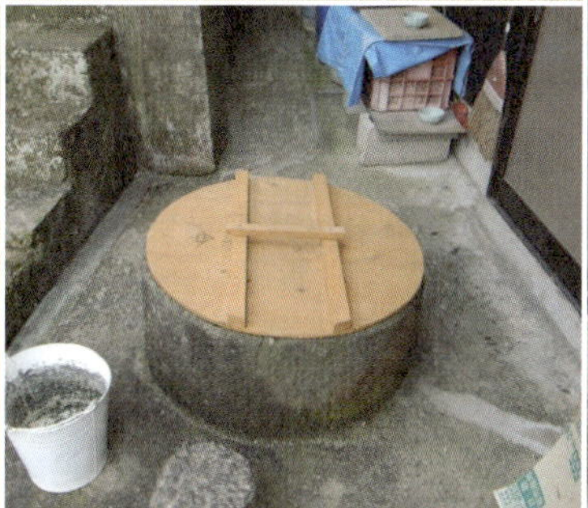

集落の水は上流の水源である溜池より、集落内の水路を通って、海へとつながっている。集落を通る水は地下にもある。水道が対岸から供給されるまで集落各所にみられる井戸は重要な生活用水だった。

Water flows through the village leading to the sea but it also flows underground. Wells throughout the village were important sources of water for domestic use.

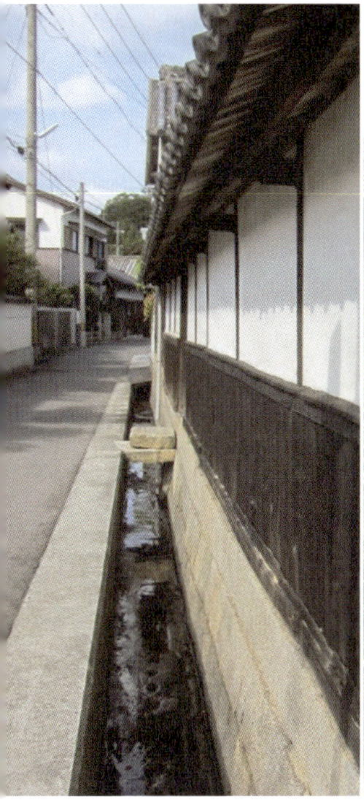
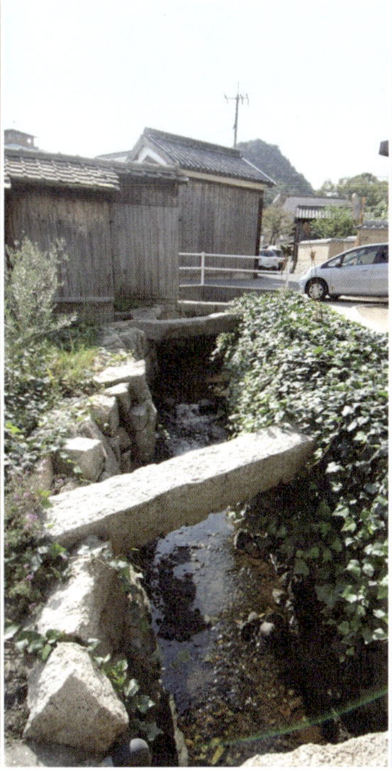
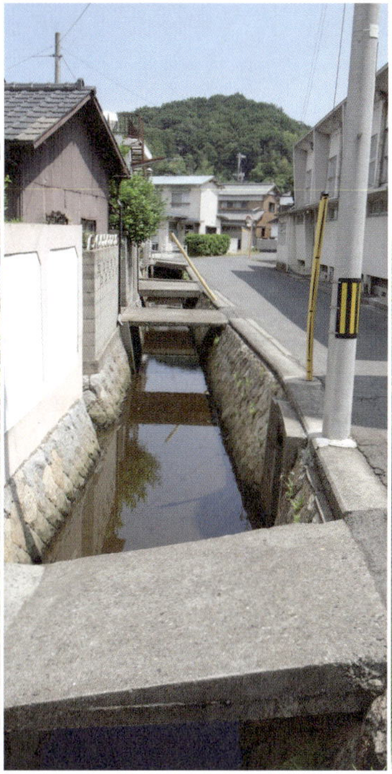
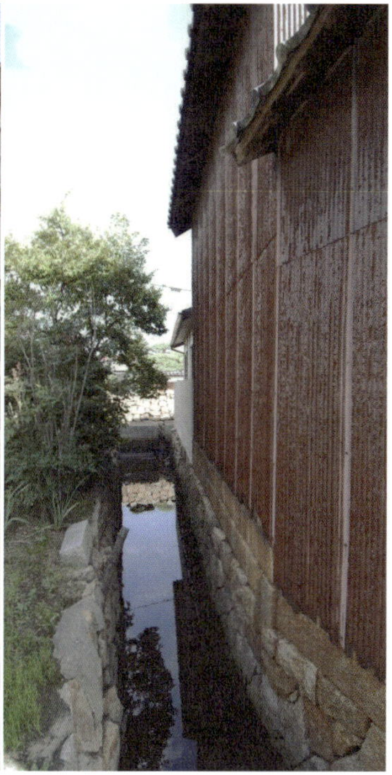
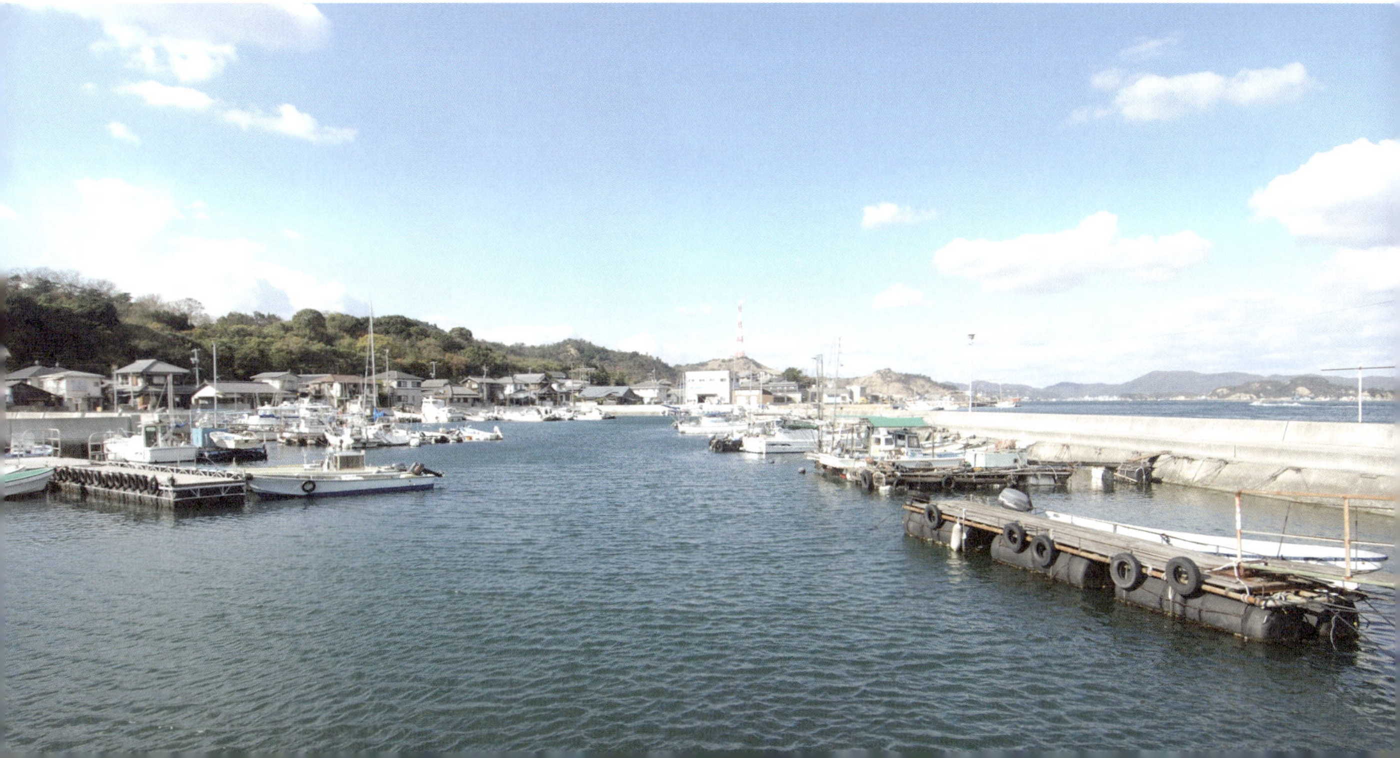

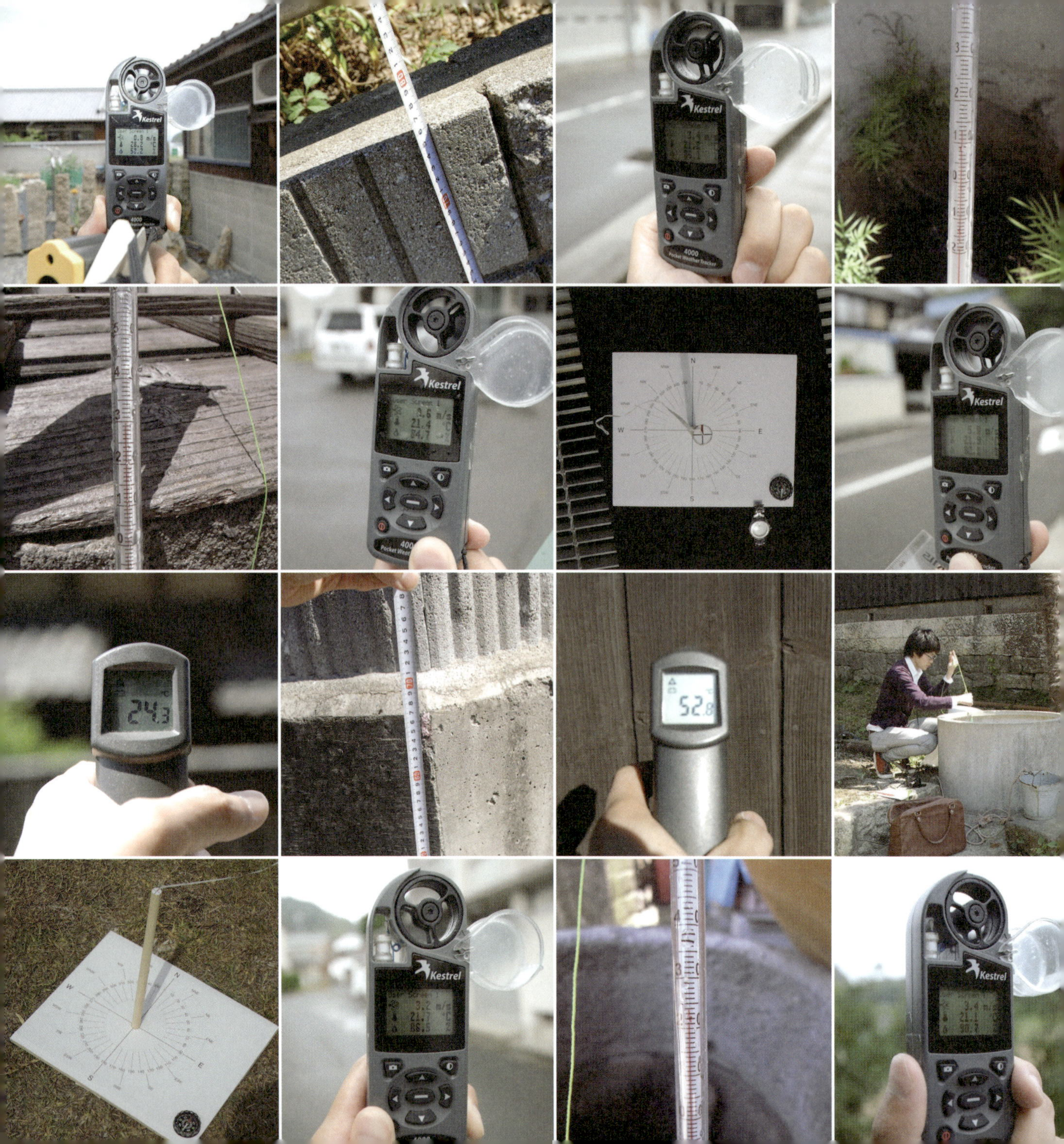
Kestrel
4000
Pocket Weather Tracker
24.3
52.8

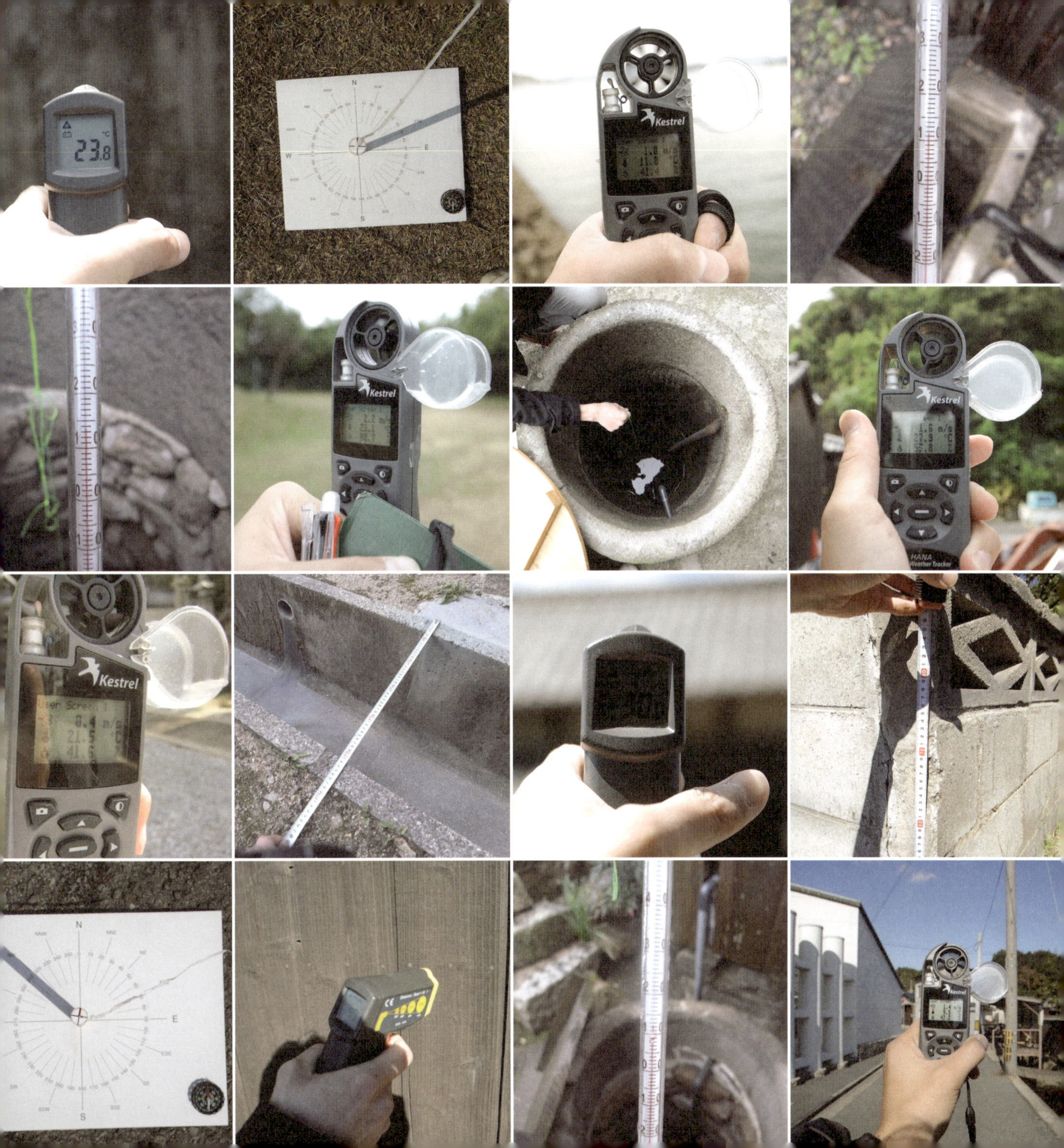
Kestrel

直島プラン

私は動く素材を整えていく感覚が日本人の根底にあるのではないかと思っている。例えば、狩猟や遊牧の文化とは異なり、谷を流れる水の速度を変えて水田にしていった文化がある。人びとは暮らしのために、動く素材の速度を調整する必要があった。

「直島プラン」は、個々の建築や街区、水路などを通して、島全体の水や空気など「動く素材」を浮き上がらせ、その美しさや大切さを再認識してもらう試みである。さらに将来、棚田や水路の修景のレベルを超えた、動く素材を整えることで地形までも含めた集落固有の姿形に迫る。それは、直島においても私個人においても、これまで以上に広がりをもった、新たな挑戦である。

今や直島は世界中の人びとから現代アート・現代建築の島として認知されている。しかし私が直島に通い、周辺の風・水・太陽の動きや植生、集落の調査を2年半行ない見えてきたものは、はるか中世から脈々と受け継がれている自然に寄り添った直島の暮らしの知恵と街区、建物のつくりの美しさであった。

他の瀬戸内の集落と異なり本村は城下町であったため、集落が碁盤目状に整理され、一つひとつの建物が塀に囲まれた屋敷型となっているのが特徴である。その中で、風・水・太陽から建物配置、平面計画が成されている。

ある民家の客間でお茶をいただいた時、とても心地良い風が流れていた。そこは南北に並んだ続き間を介して南北ふたつの庭がつながる間取りとなっていた。他の民家も気になり、調査していくと、多くの民家で同じように庭と続き間がセットとなり、谷に平行な南北軸に沿った風を導くつくりとなっていた。

次に集落の水系を見ていった。本村が中世に「高田の浦」と呼ばれる意味がよく理解できた。本村の谷の上には溜池があり、その水は棚田、集落の水路、海へと順々に利用されていたこと、さらには谷に沿った地下水脈は、集落の重要な生活水源として井戸を潤していたことが分かった。井戸には今でも水が満たされていた。

これらの調査を通して、直島はまさに風と水と太陽の島であることが見えてきた。建物や集落のつくりそのものが数百年の時を超えて直島の固有の動く素材を後世の私たちに伝えてくれているように感じた。

そのメッセージを後世へ向けて丁寧に受け渡すことが今の時代に生きる私の役目であると考えられるようになった。

THE NAOSHIMA PLAN

I think that sensitivity to the arrangement of moving materials might be ingrained in the Japanese people. For example, unlike nomadic or hunting cultures, this is a culture of rice paddies and the varying speeds of water flowing through valleys. For people to survive, they had to regulate the speeds of moving materials.

The Naoshima Plan is an attempt to show the moving materials (water, air, etc) of the entire island manifested in individual buildings, and to make people once again recognize their beauty and importance. Furthermore, beyond the level of this landscape of terraced fields and waterways, in the near future I will engage the inherent form of the village, which includes the terrain, by adjusting the moving materials. For Naoshima, and for me personally, this is a new challenge of greater breadth than before.

Naoshima is now recognised by people all over the world as an island of modern art and modern architecture. However, I visit Naoshima frequently, and what I have witnessed in the two-and-a-half years of investigations of the wind, water, sun movement, vegetation, and villages is the beautiful way that the lots and buildings have been made, and the wisdom of the local way of life, which comprises an intimacy with nature in an unbroken succession since distant medieval times.

Because Honmura was a castle town, unlike villages in other parts of the Seto region, it is organized in a grid and characterized by a residential form in which each building is surrounded by walls. The building locations and floor plans have been laid out in accordance with the wind, water, and sun.

When I received tea in a certain private house, a very comfortable breeze drifted though the guest room. The layout connects two gardens at the north and south through a series of linked, adjacent rooms (separated by operable shoji panels) aligned north–south. I was curious about other private houses, and when I investigated, most of them had the same arrangement of linked gardens and rooms, a format guided by the wind, which also follows the north–south axis parallel to the valley.

Next, I observed the water system of the village. In medieval times, the people of Honmura had a good understanding of the meaning of the area named *takada no ura* (terraced rice fields above a bay). There is a reservoir above the Honmura valley, and its water is used sequentially from the terraced rice paddies to the village waterways, and then to the sea, and furthermore the underground water channels that follow the valley supply the wells, which are an important water source for life in the village. Even now, the wells are filled with water.

Through these investigations, I saw that Naoshima is undoubtedly an island of wind and water and sunlight. I feel that it is the making of buildings and villages over several hundred years that conveys the island's native moving materials for posterity.

I believe it is my duty, as someone born in the present age, to carefully deliver this message for posterity.

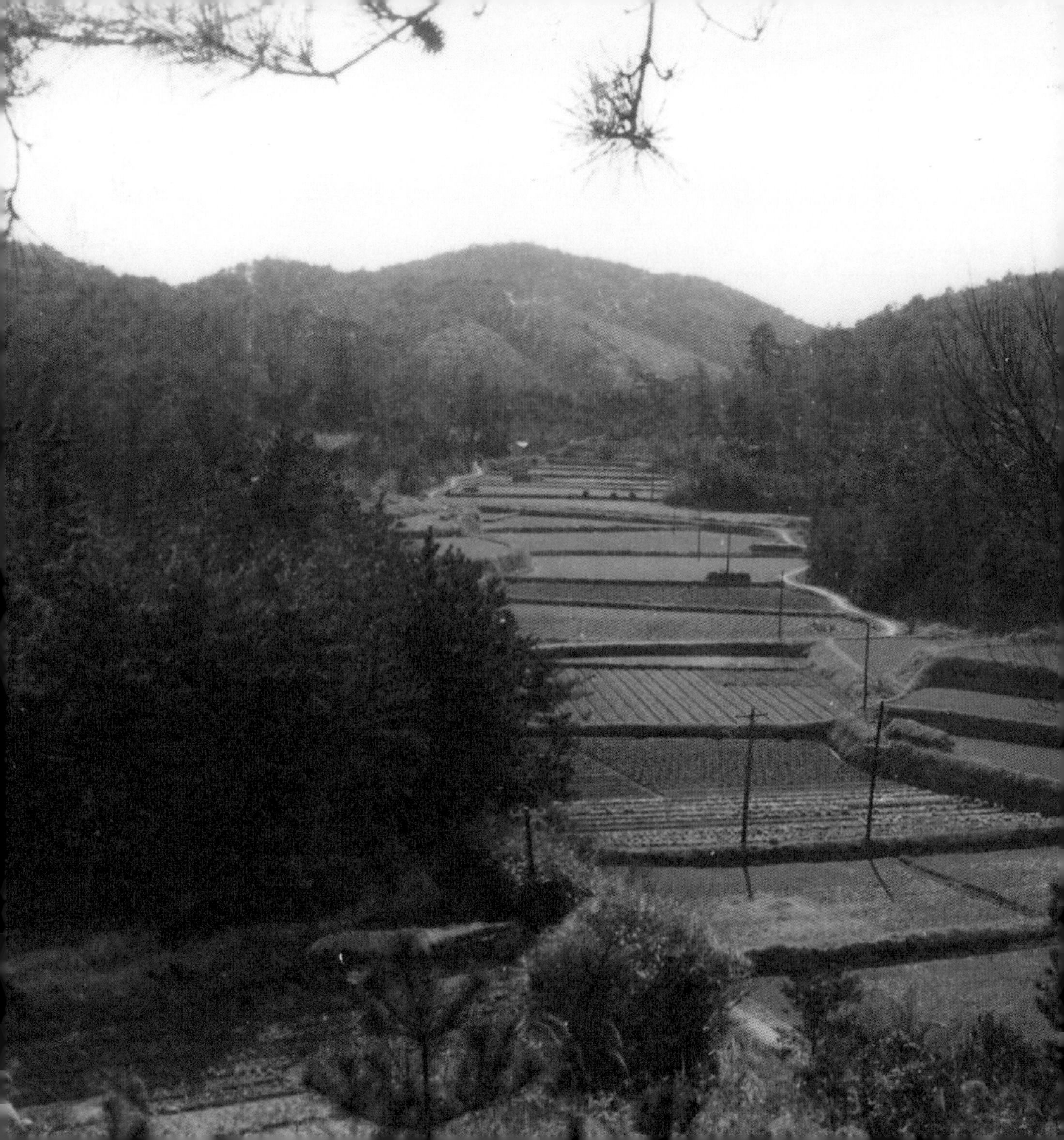

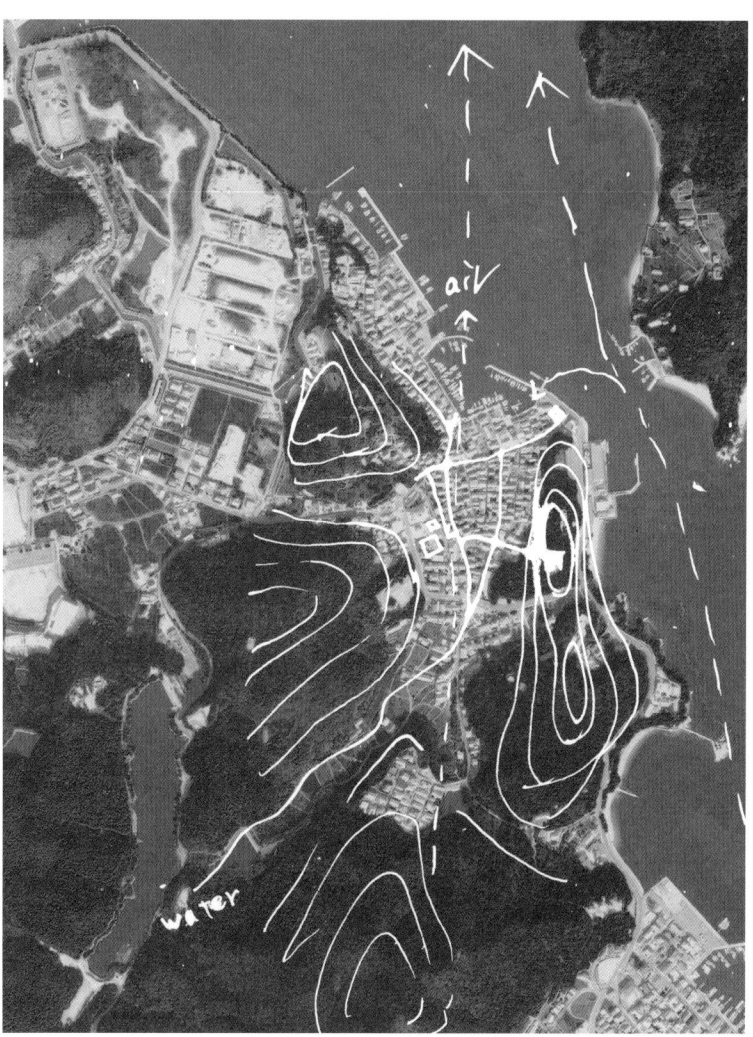

本村集落の上流部には棚田があり、溜池からの水は棚田を潤し、集落へと注がれていた。棚田は単に稲の収穫という恵みをもたらすのみならず、南からの風を冷やし、集落へ心地良い風を運んでいたと思われる。

Upstream from Honmura are terraced rice fields. Water from a pond further up nourishes the rice fields and flows on into the village. These rice fields not only gives the blessing of rice harvest, by the evaporation of water it also provides a cooling southern breeze to the village.

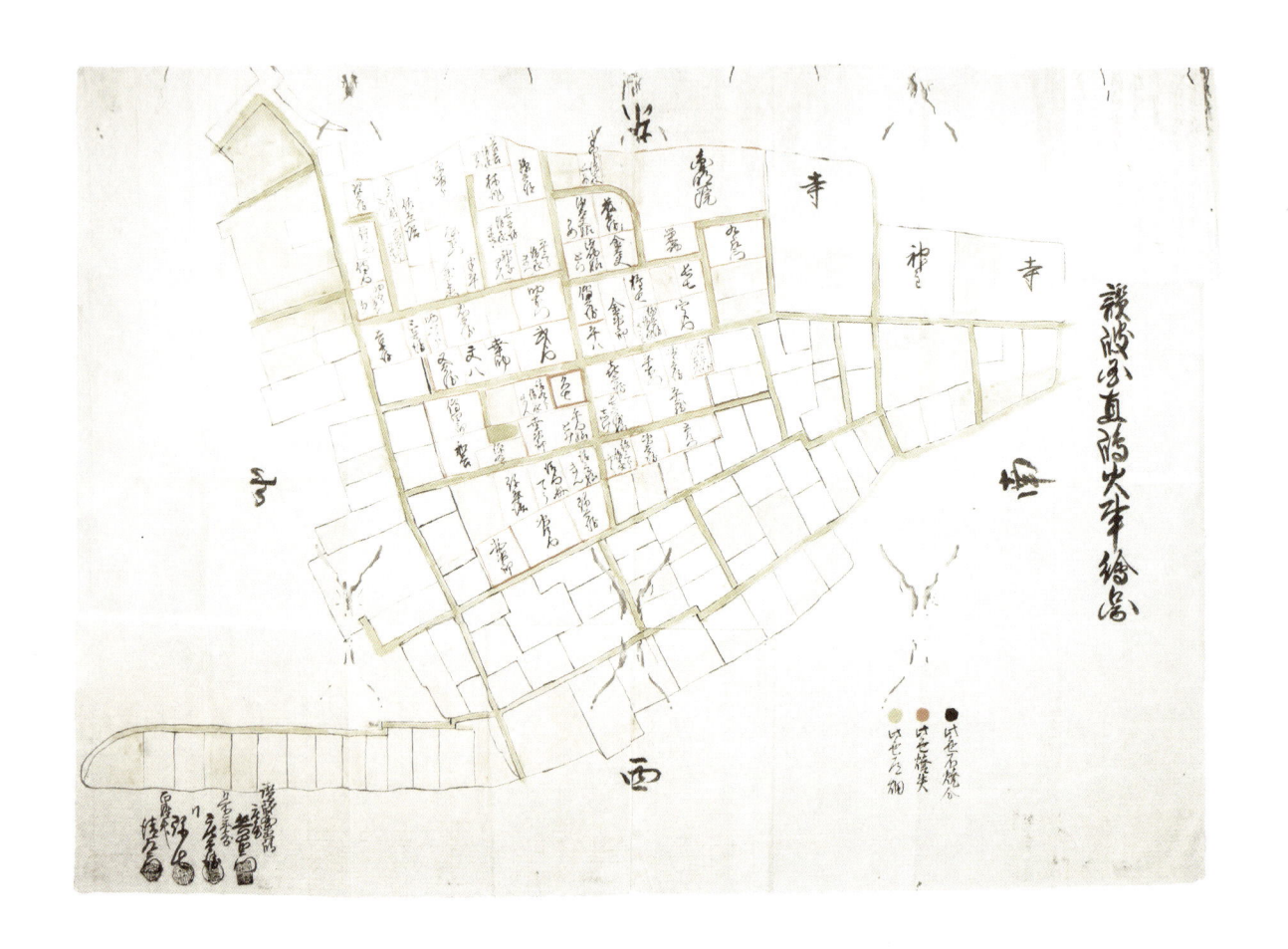

江戸時代の古地図を見ると、当時より変わらぬ碁盤目状の街区が今も受け継がれていることが分かる。上空より見ると、塀で囲まれた街区には南北に庭が設けられ、庭、南向きの建物、庭と、ひとつのパターンを織り成していることが分かる。

Looking at a map of Honmura from the Edo period (1603-1868), it is evident that the the town grid has been preserved unchanged until today. Seen from above, a distinct pattern becomes clear. Within the walls surrounding the houses, two gardens, one north and one south, is the common standard.

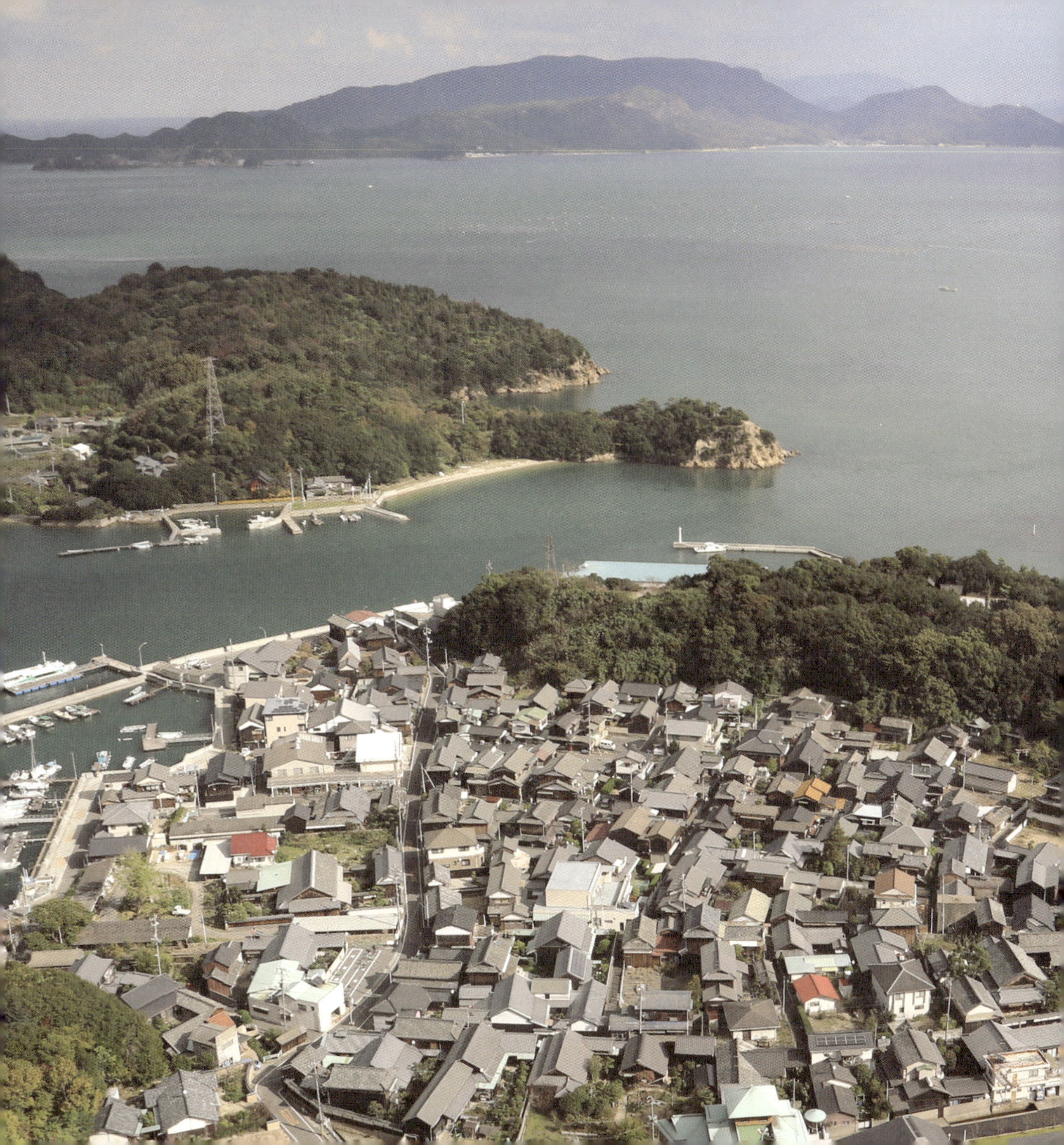

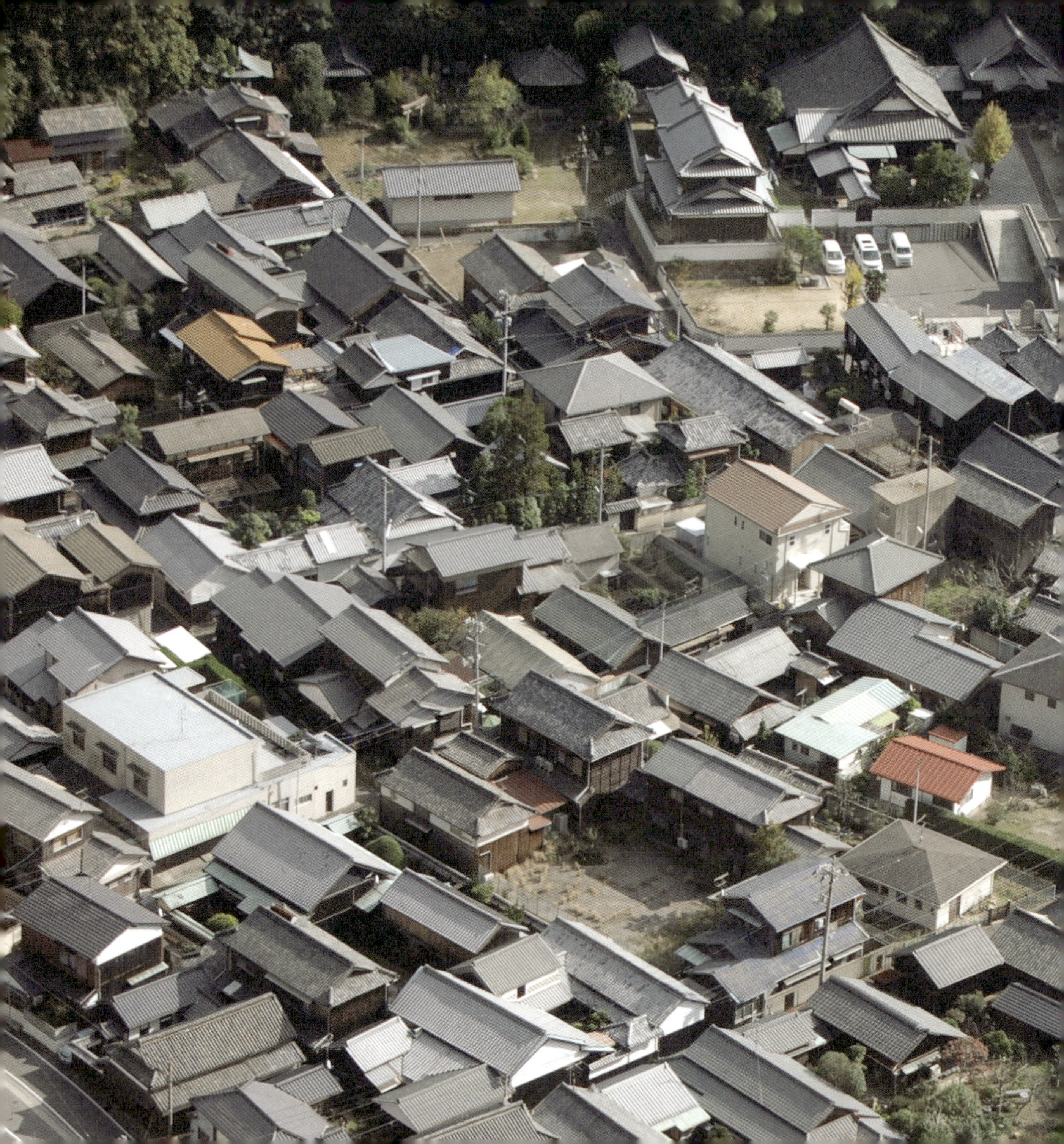

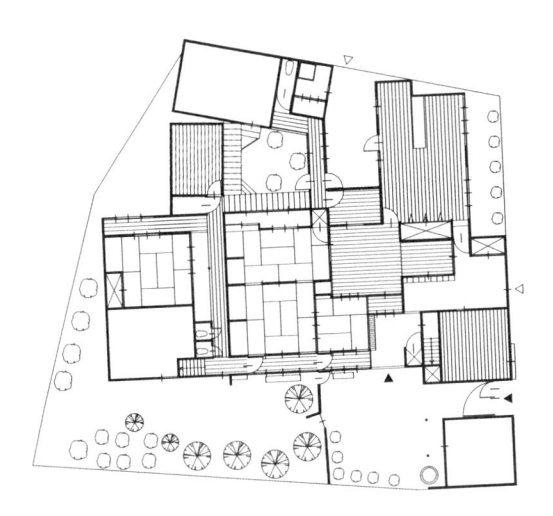

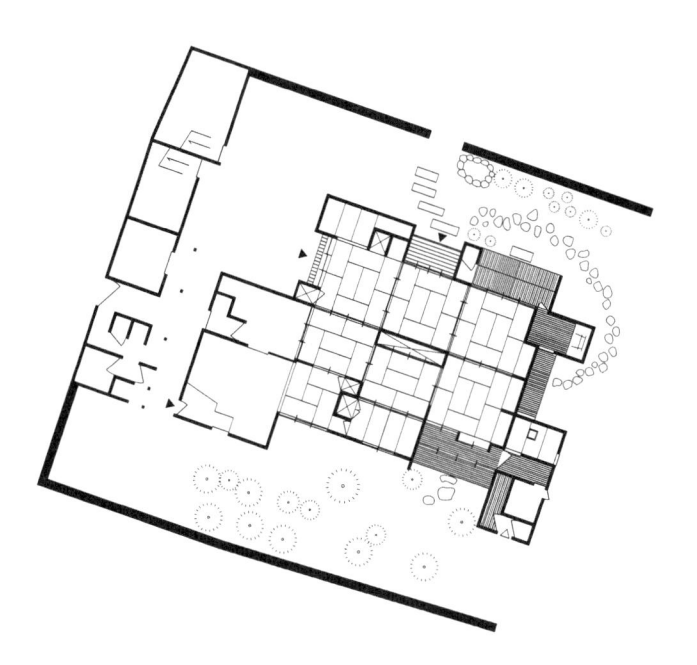

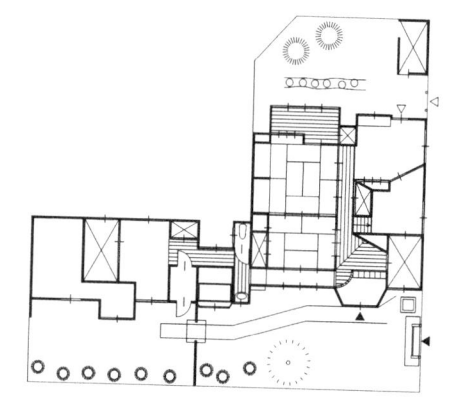

直島の民家の調査をしていく中で、南庭、南北続き間、北庭の構成によって、本村の南北軸の谷を流れる風が集落内で受け渡されていくことが見えてきた。

Investigating the planning of the homes, it became clear that the placement of the north and south facing gardens allows for the predominant gentle south-north wind to continue its flow through the houses to cool them.

0 5 10M

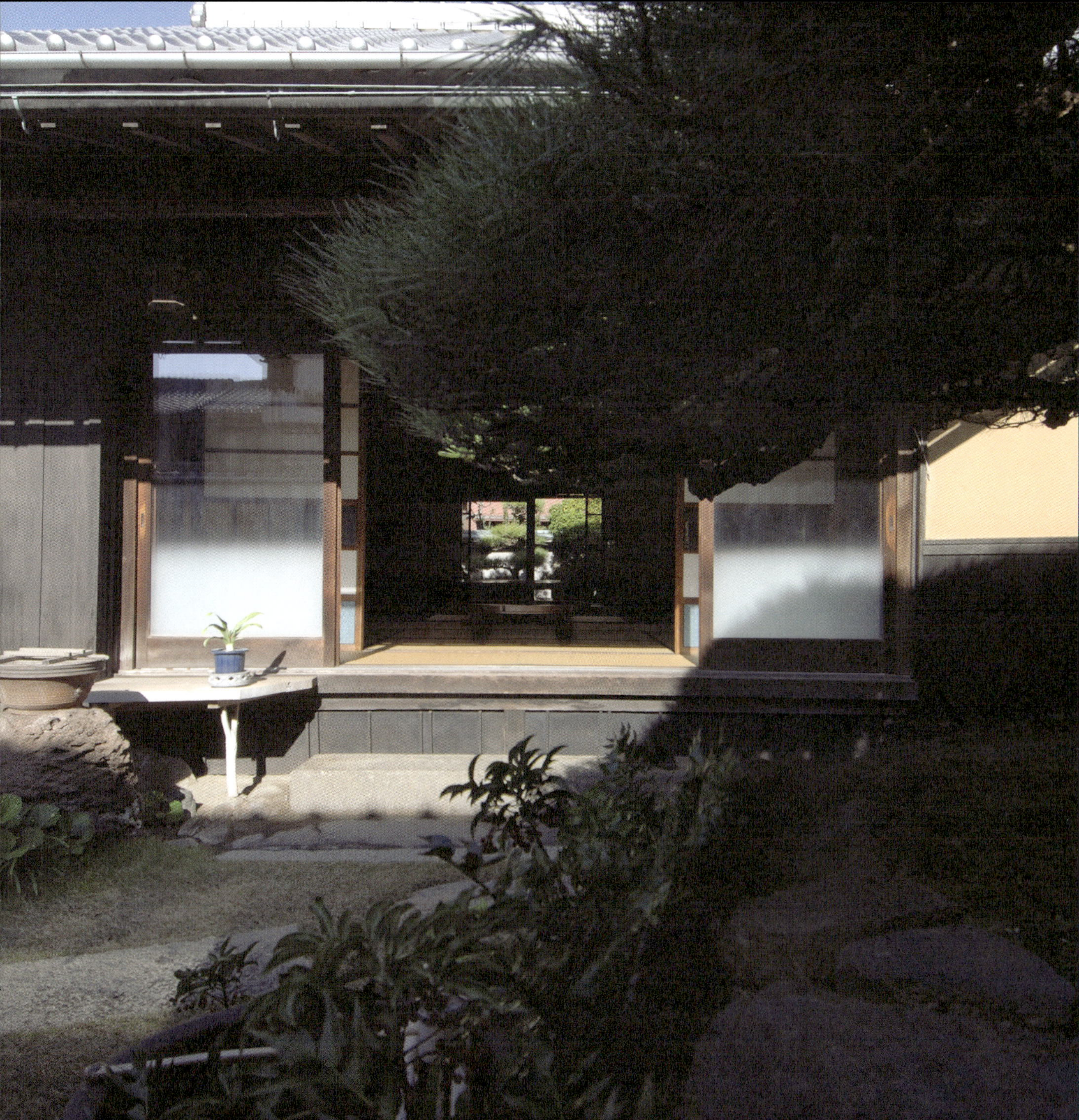

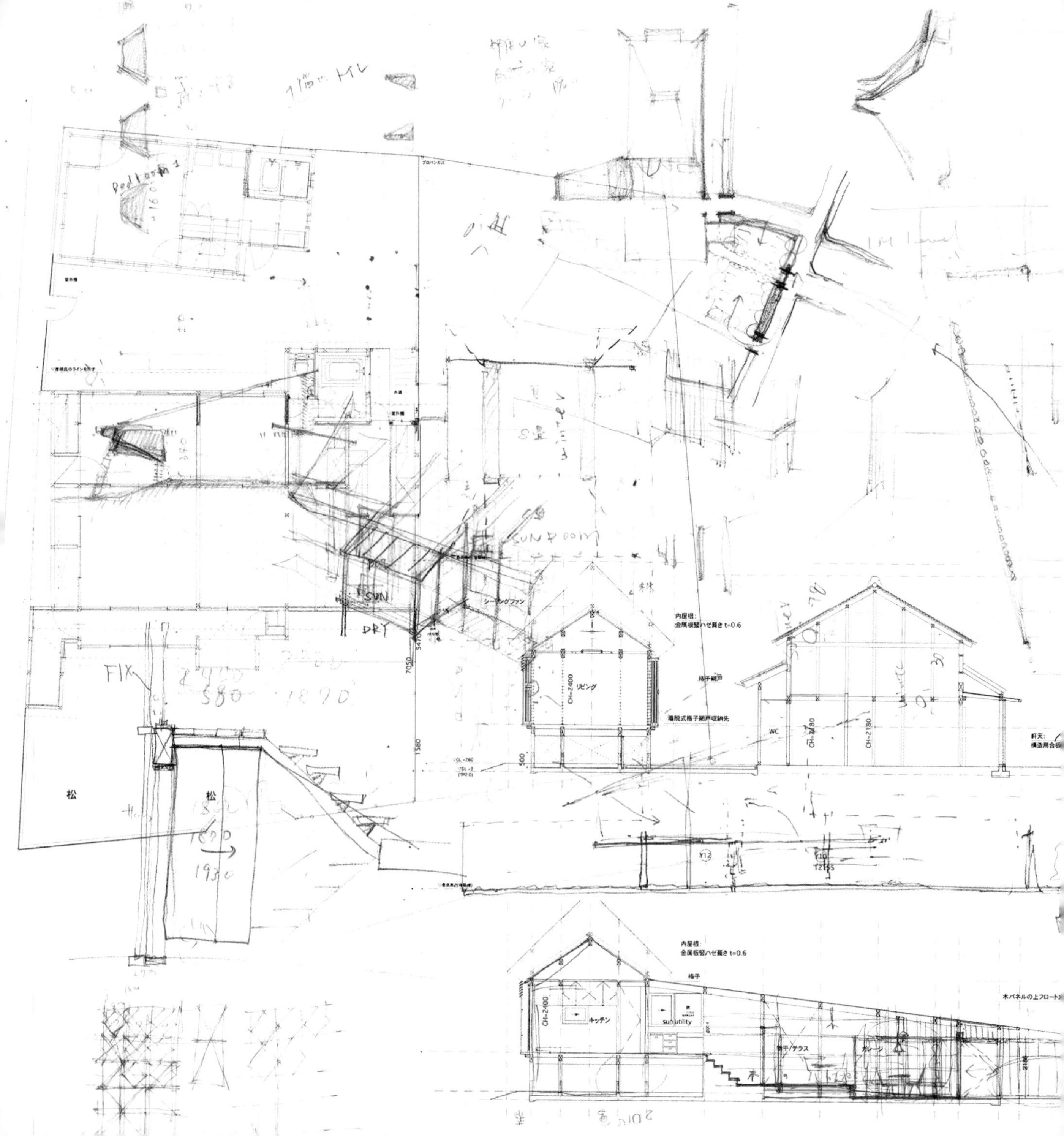

プロパンガス
室外機
Bedroom 1
FIX
SUNROOM
SUN
DRY
シーリングファン
内屋根:
金属板竪ハゼ葺き t=0.6
格子網戸
リビング
CH=2400
WC
CH=2180
軒天:
構造用合板
松
松
7050
5470
1380
500
Y12
Y10
格子
キッチン
sun utility
物干/テラス
ガレージ

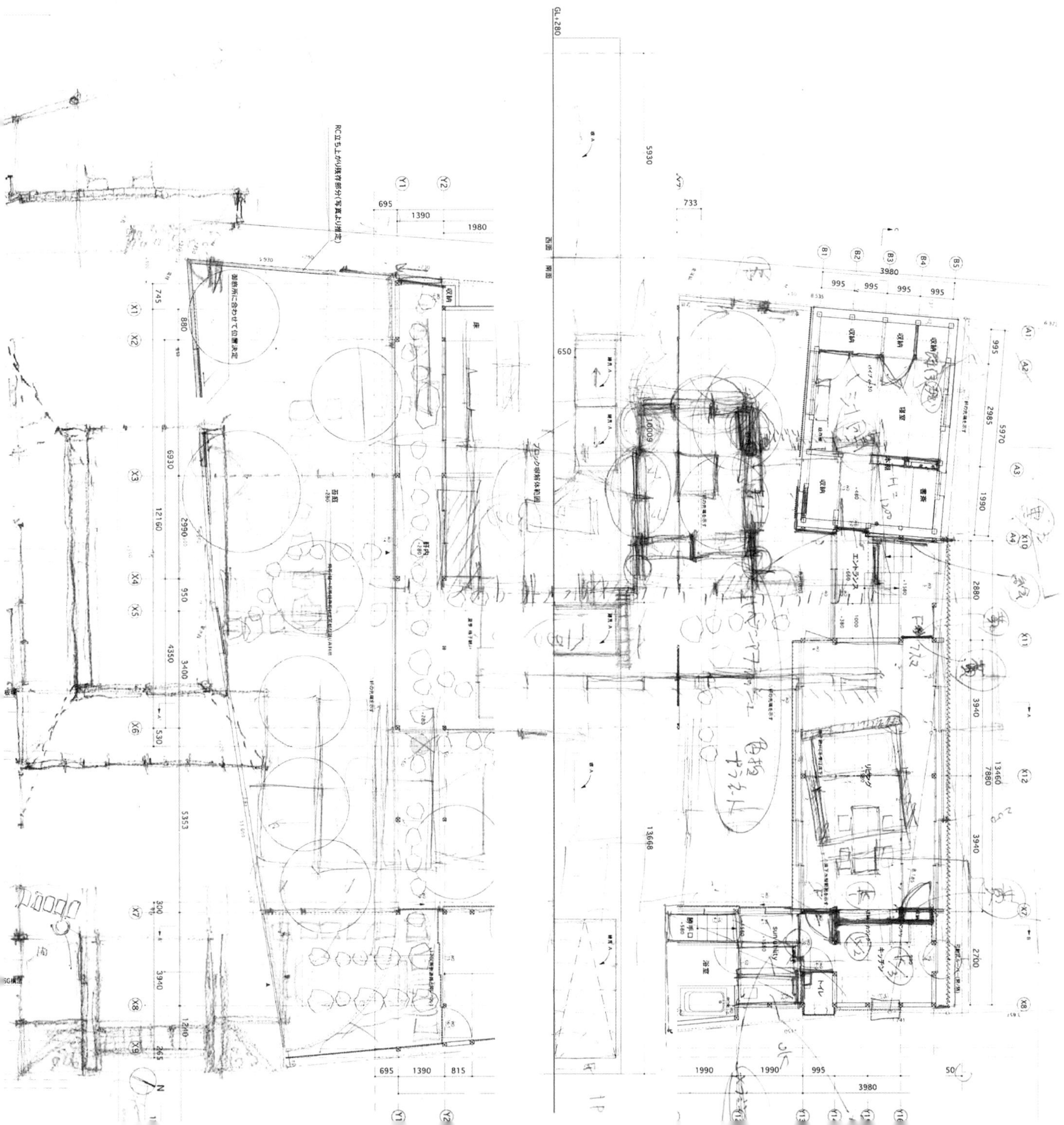

GL+280
RC立ち上がり既存部分(写真より推定)
既存所に合わせて位置決定
ブロック塀解体範囲
収納
寝室
書斎
エントランス
リビング
キッチン
トイレ
浴室
勝手口
695
1390
1980
815
733
995
3980
5930
13668
12160
5353
2880
3940
7880
13460
2700
5970
2985
1990

air

water

直島の家またべえ

「直島の家またべえ」は母屋の再生と「離れ」の新築の2棟で構成される。「直島プラン」の民家における実践として直島の風や水をいかに集落全体へ、さらには時代を超えて後世へリレーするかがテーマとなった。

中世から続く直島本村の集落の風との付き合い方は南北続き間と庭の関係に現れている。それぞれの民家の塀の内側に風の通り道が存在し、それらが連なることで集落全体へ風がリレーされていることに気付いた。

「またべえ」の既存の「母屋」も、本村集落の特徴である「南北に抜ける続き間、縁、南北の庭」といった従来のスタイルへ戻し接客の間とした。南北には苔庭を設け、本村の他の屋敷と同様に空気と水を調整する庭へと再生した。「離れ」は、高床とすることで太陽の光を十分に受け、かつ床下を抜ける風が母屋や隣の家へと風をリレーしている。また高潮対策としても効果を発揮する。

本村の集落の水との付き合い方は、上流の溜池から続く水路とその下を流れる水脈を利用した井戸との関係に現れている。井戸の水は上流から下流までひとつの水脈をリレーしていることを意識し、上水が引かれる現代まで、清潔にかつ大切に公共の財産として利用されてきた。

近年飲み水としての利用価値の薄れた井戸の価値の再認識と後世にリレーする手法として、井戸水の新たな活用を試みている。

「離れ」の特徴は8層で構成された屋根に現れている。特に低い水温の井戸水による冷却層が特徴で、真夏の熱気を建物から奪っていく。中世から培われてきた感性に倣い、動く素材に丁寧に対応することで導かれた姿形は直島らしさを有するものになり、その考えが直島の固有の植物のように再び本村に根付き、未来へリレーされていくことを望んでいる。

HOUSE IN NAOSHIMA - MATABE

House in Naoshima - Matabe comprises two buildings: a renovation of the main building and a newly constructed building. As a private house implemented within the Naoshima Plan, the theme became how to relay the wind and water of Naoshima to the whole village, and furthermore how to transcend the era for posterity.

Since medieval times, the adaptation to the wind in Naoshima's Honmura village is manifested in the north-south relationship of adjacent rooms and gardens. Wind passages exist on the inner faces of the walls in each private house, and we noticed that, due to their extension, wind was relayed to the whole village.

Matabe's existing main building also has a reception room that follows the conventional planning style, characteristic of the Honmura village, with gardens and engawa verandas on both the north and south sides of the building. Similar to the way that moss gardens are established in the north and south of residential sites in Honmura, gardens that will regulate the air and water have been revived. By raising its floor, the annex receives plenty of sunlight, and the wind passing below the floor relays wind to the main building and the neighbouring houses. In addition, it also helps to protect against sudden raised water levels due to storms.

The way water is dealt with in Honmura village is manifest in the relationship between the water channels that continue to the upstream reservoir, and the waterways flowing underground, which are used by the wells. The well water is carefully and hygienically used as a public asset, with an awareness that it is relayed from upstream to downstream along a single channel, and has been drawn on as a water supply right up until the present day.

In recent years, the value of using wells for drinking water has faded, so as a method for relaying to posterity a recognition of a new value for wells, I attempted to find new uses for well water.

The annex is characterized by a roof comprising eight layers. Notably, there is a cooling layer that uses the cool well-water pumped up to the roof to extract midsummer heat from the building. In accordance with a sensitivity that has been cultivated since medieval times through careful interactions with moving materials, the form thus derived has a Honmura-esque quality. I hope that this way of thinking will again take root in Honmura, like the native fauna of Naoshima, and be relayed to the future.

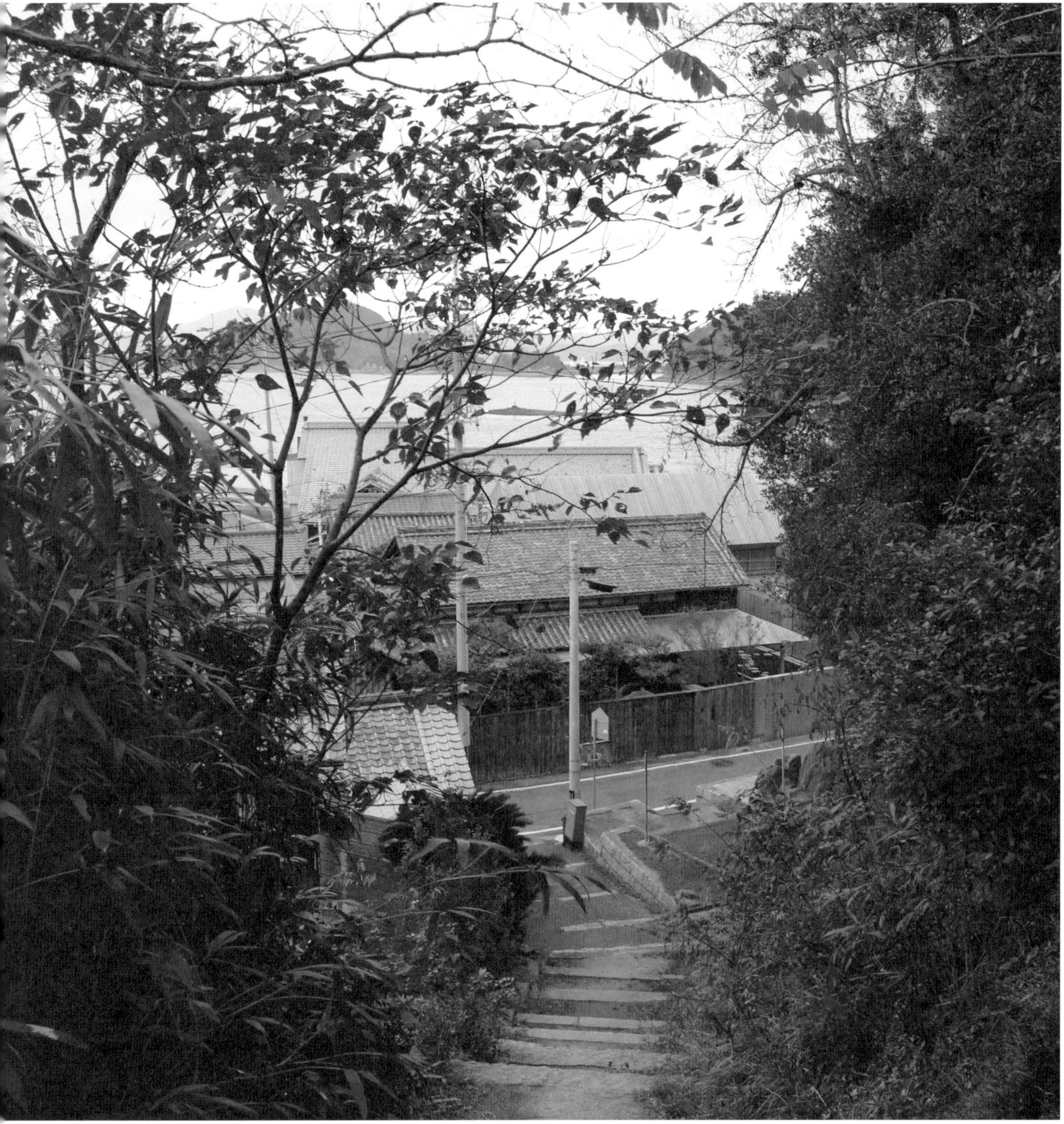

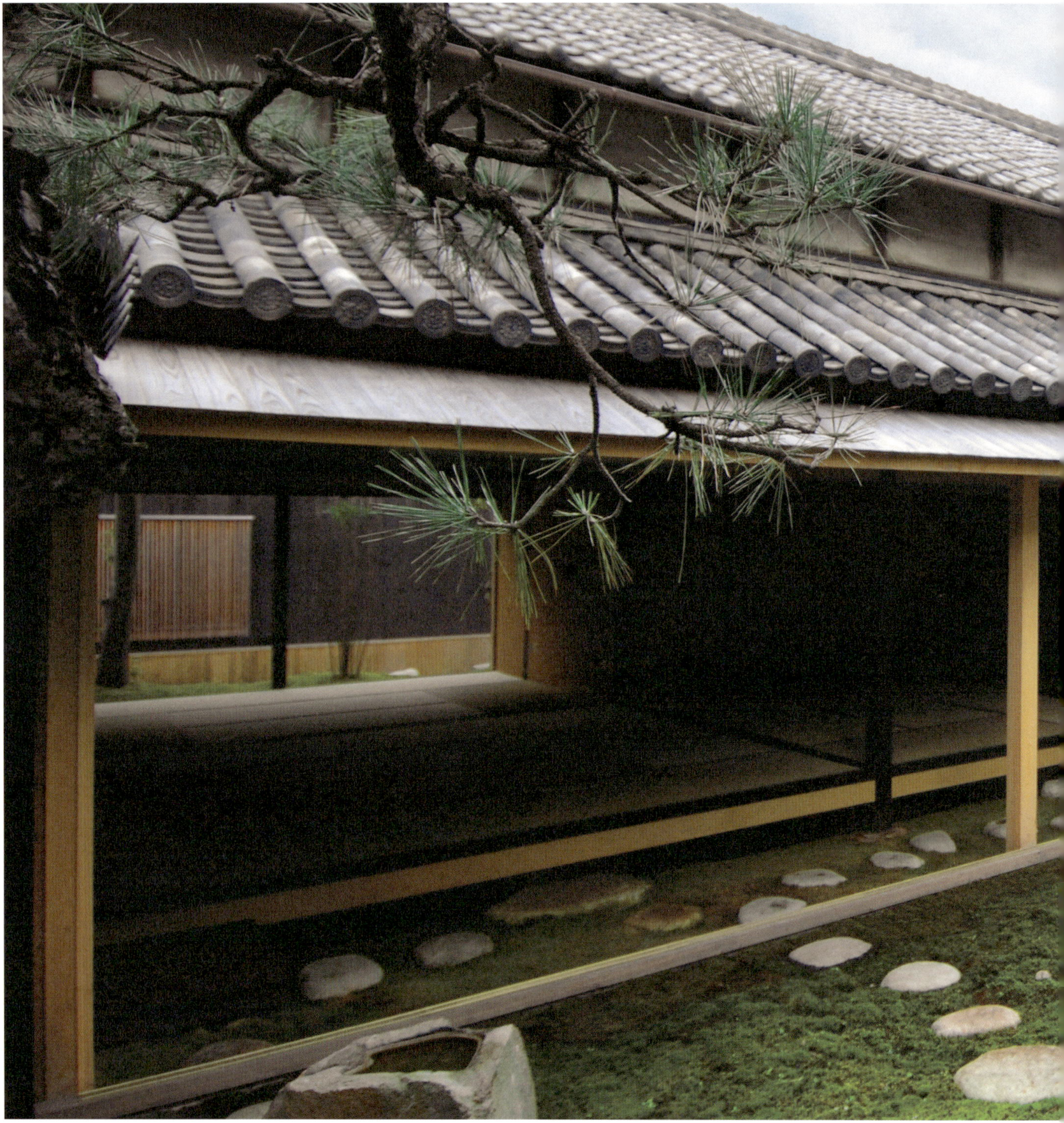

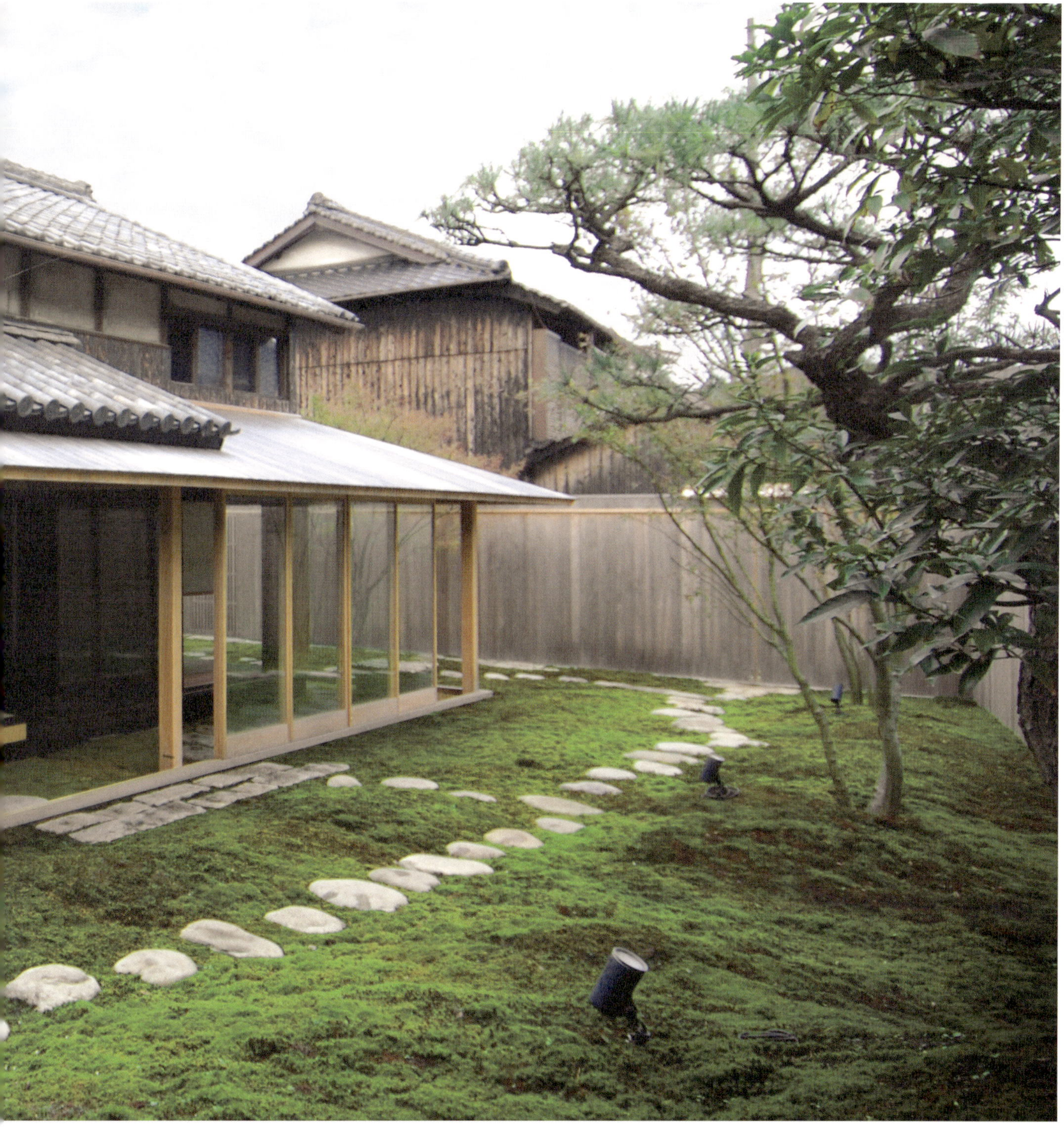

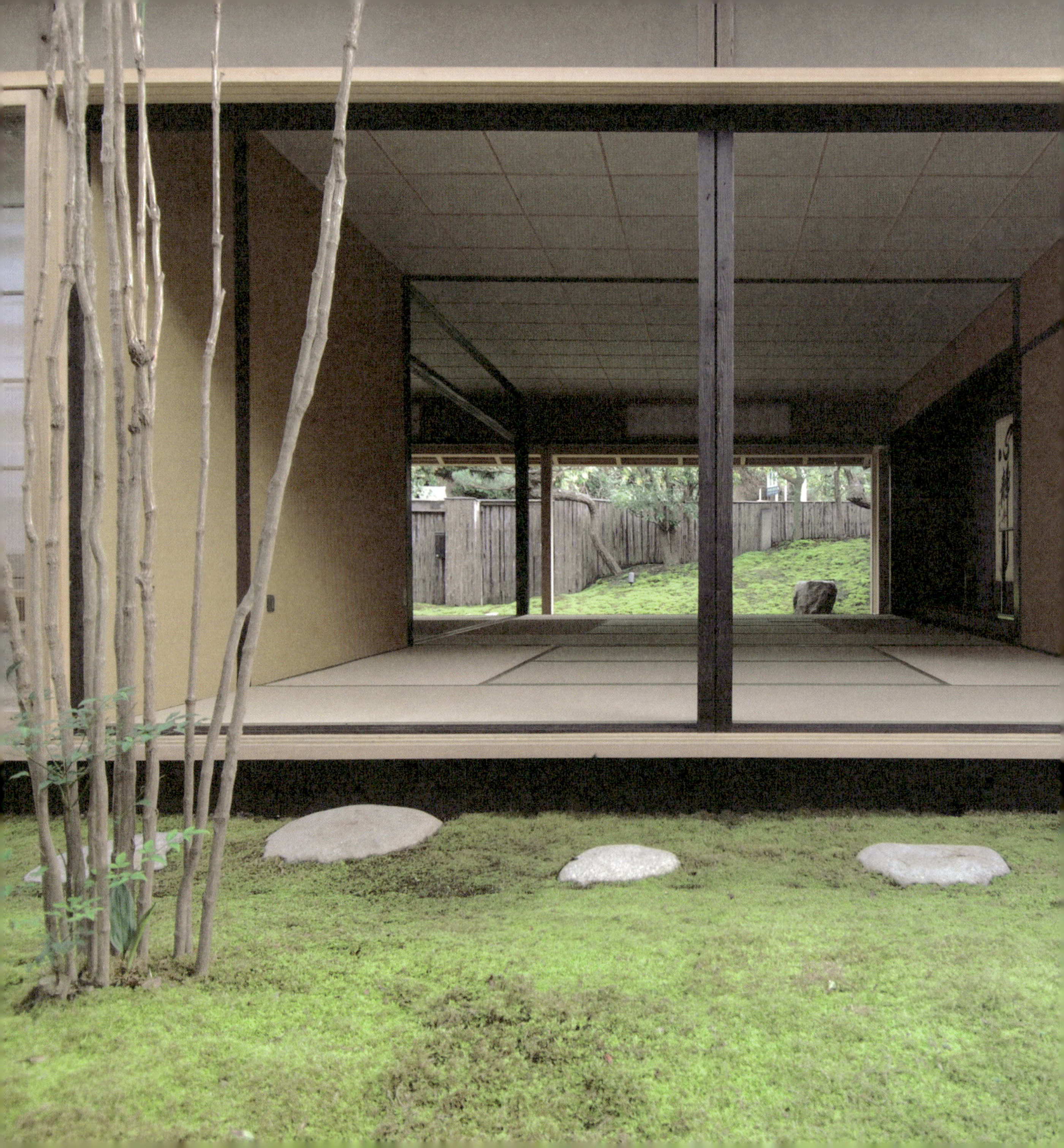

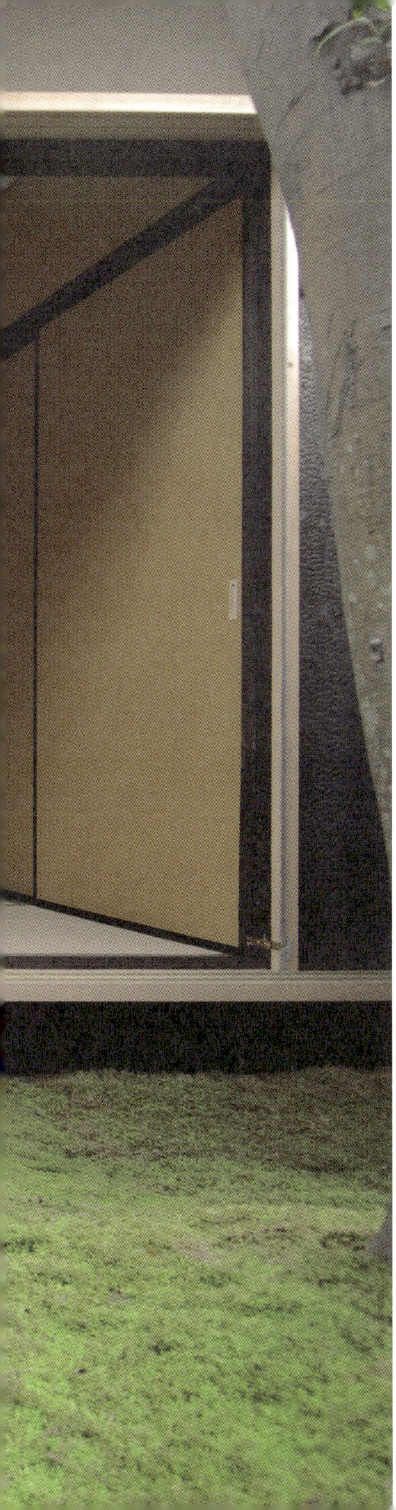

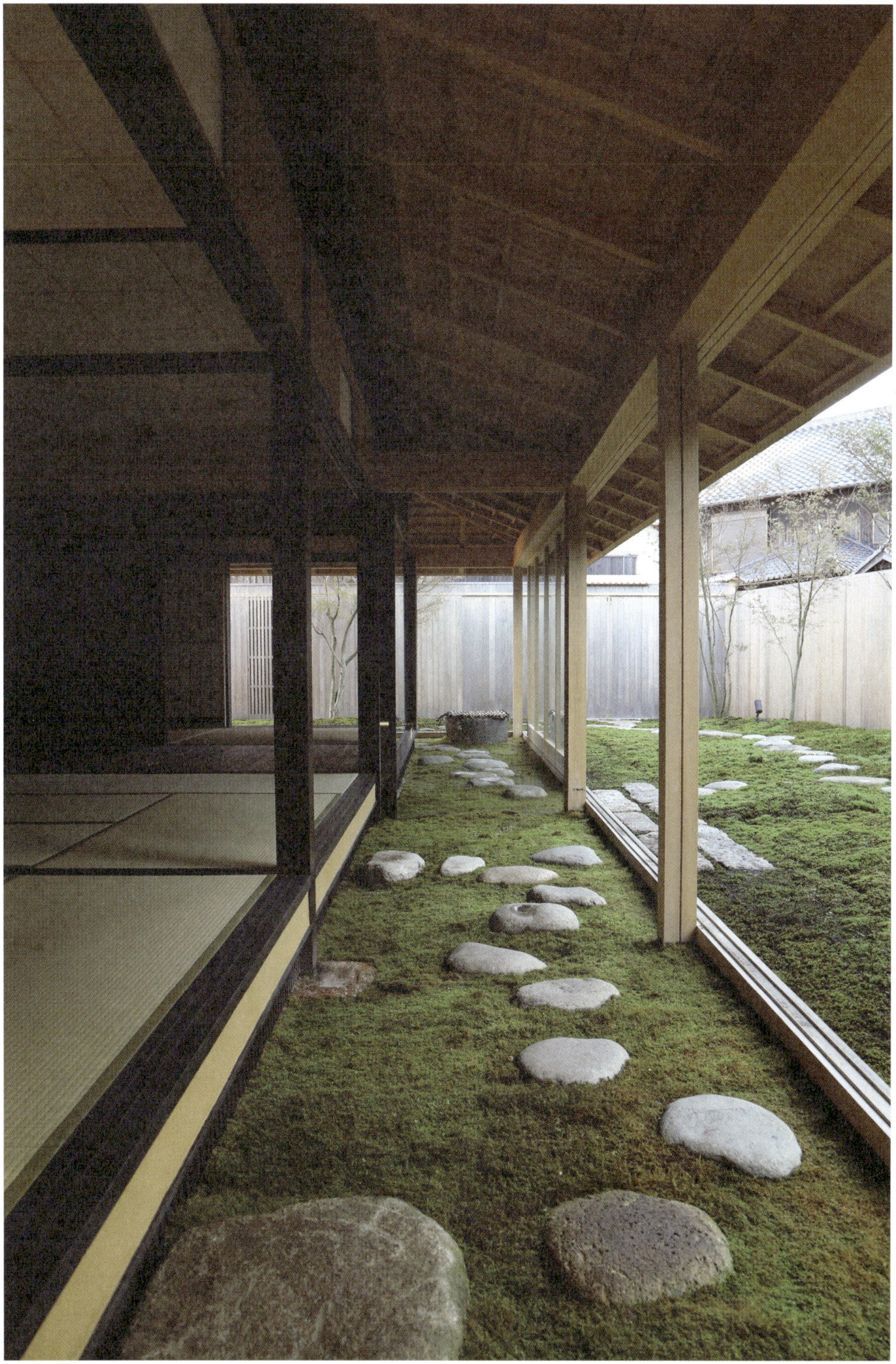

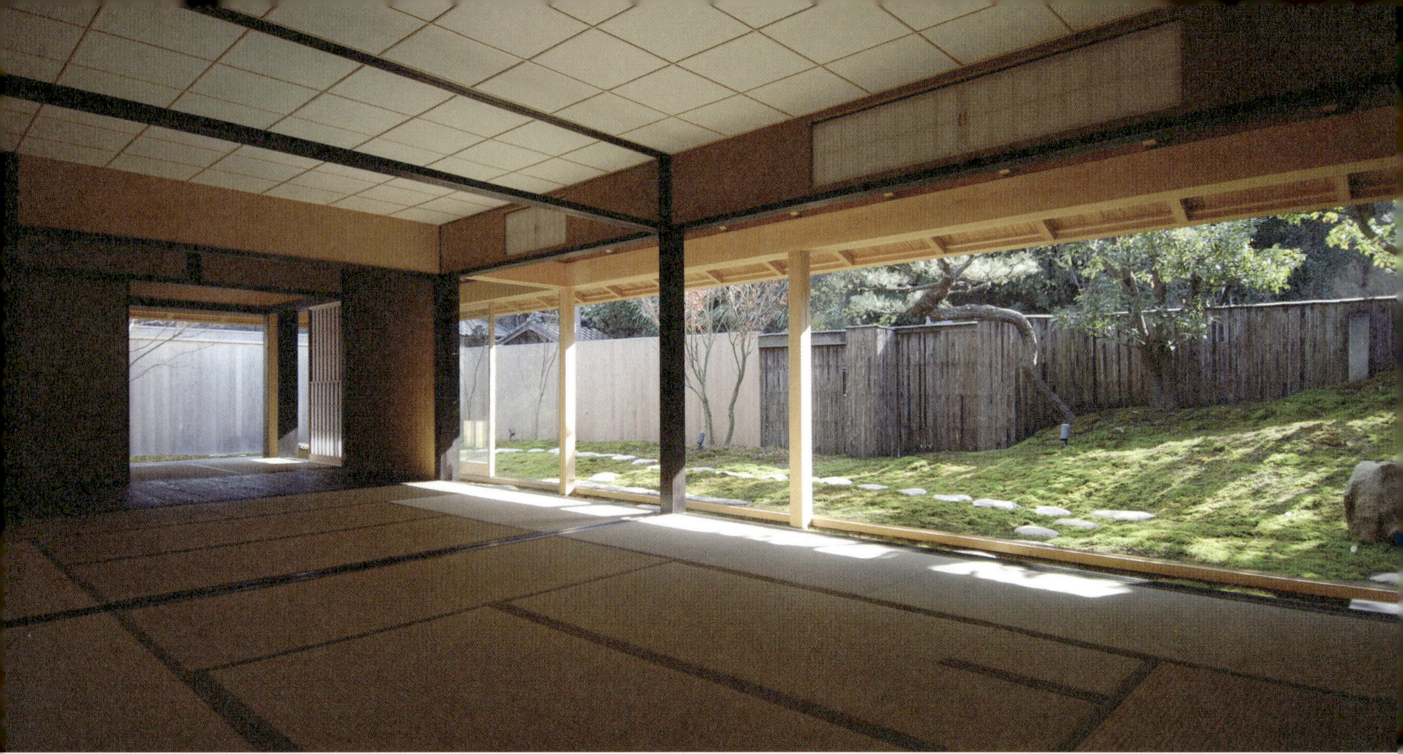

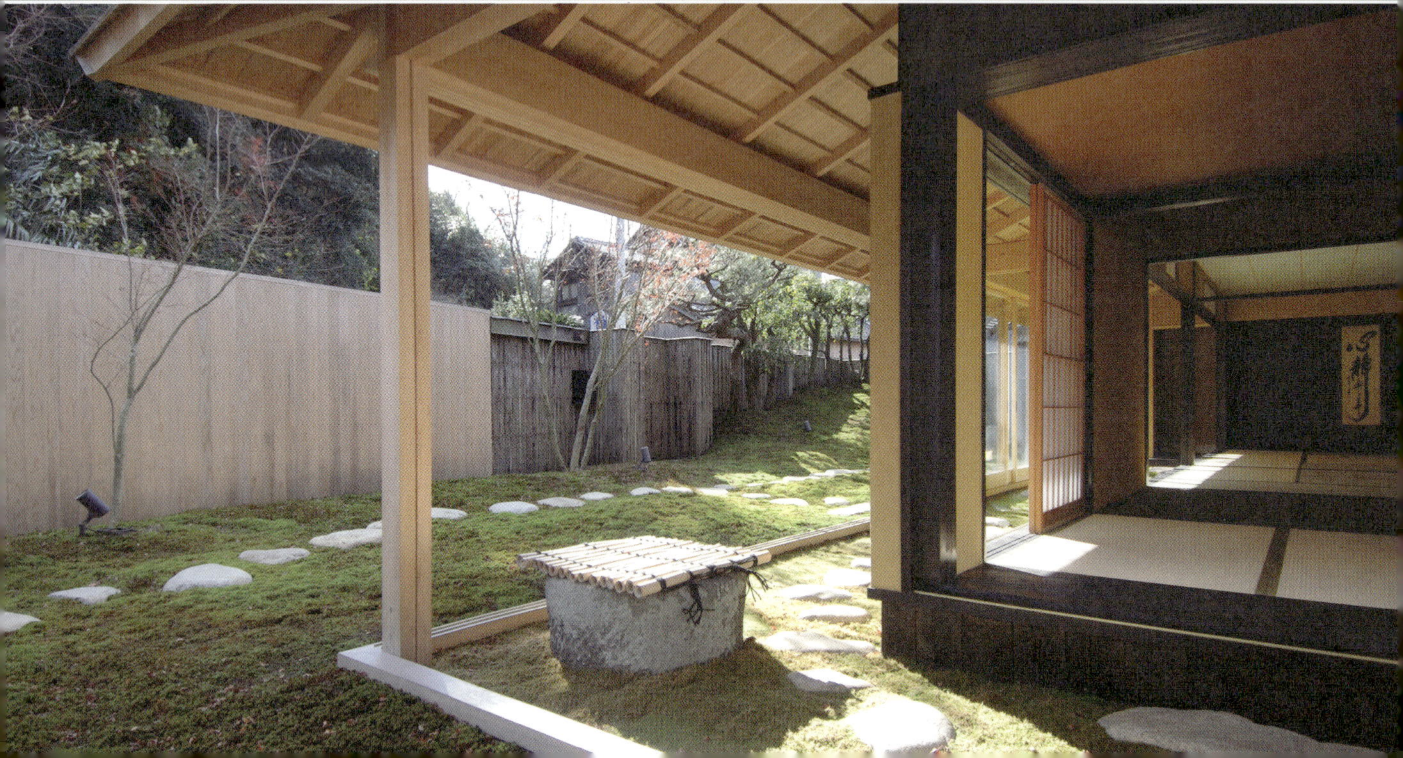

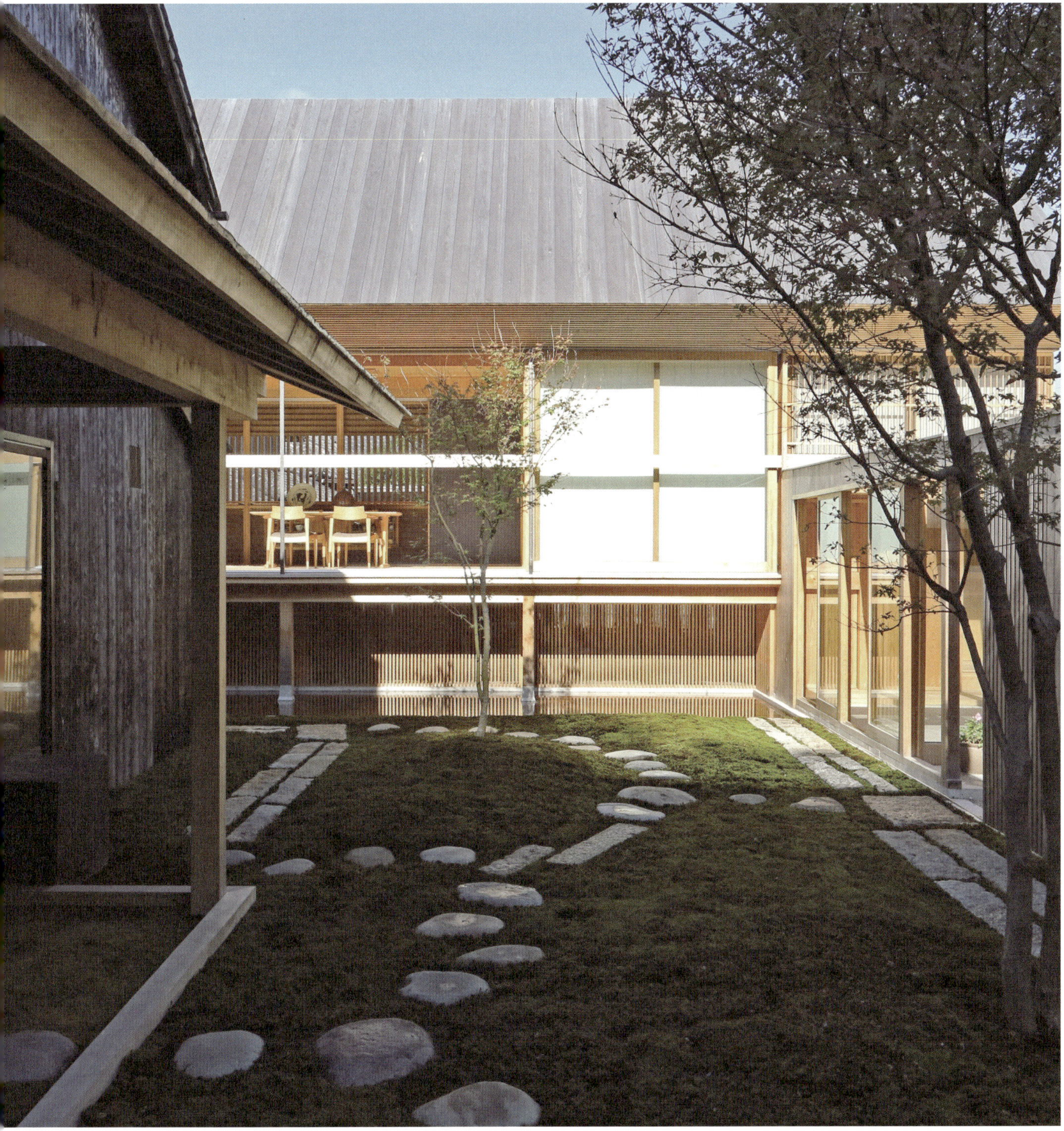

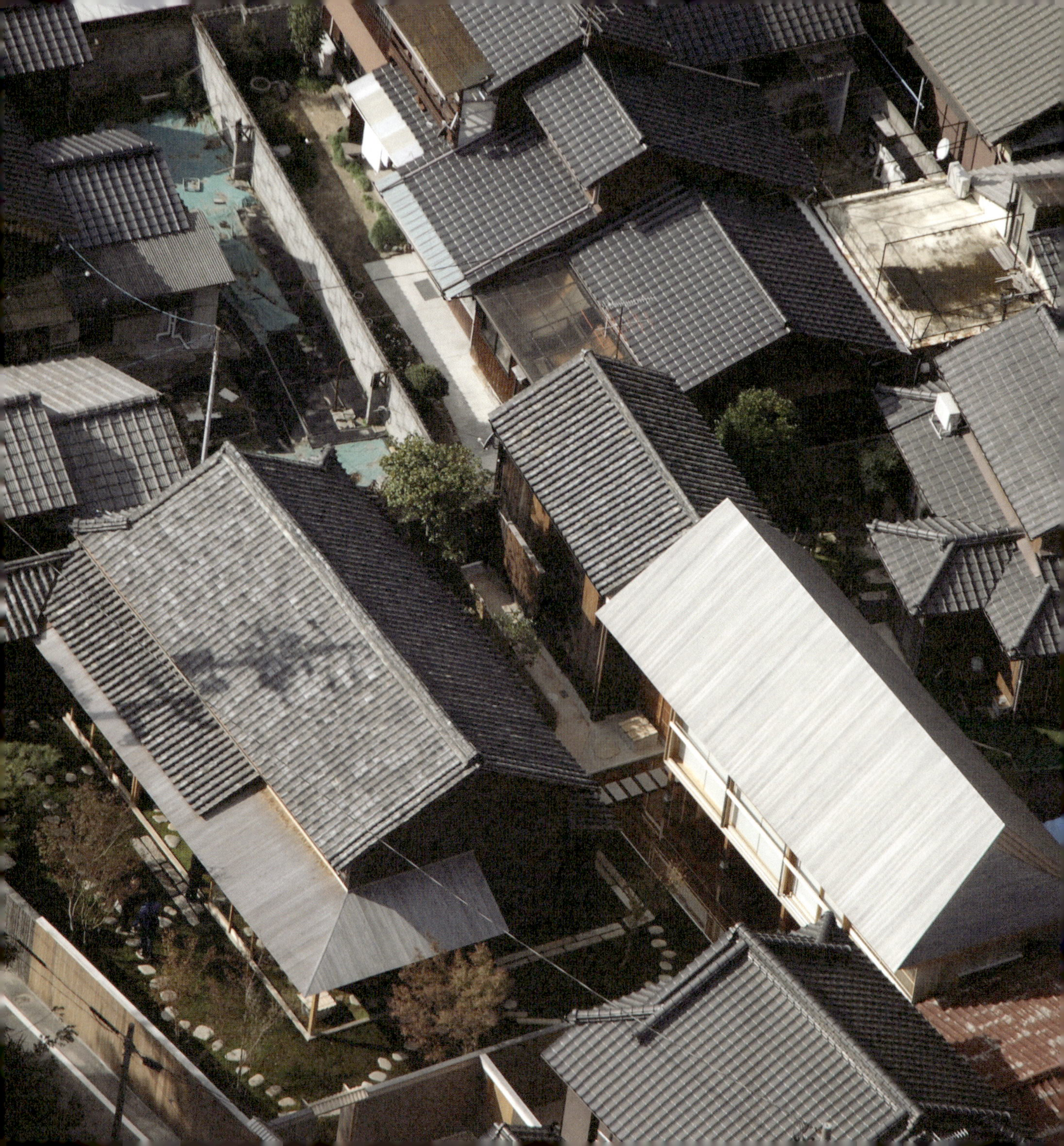

ANNEX

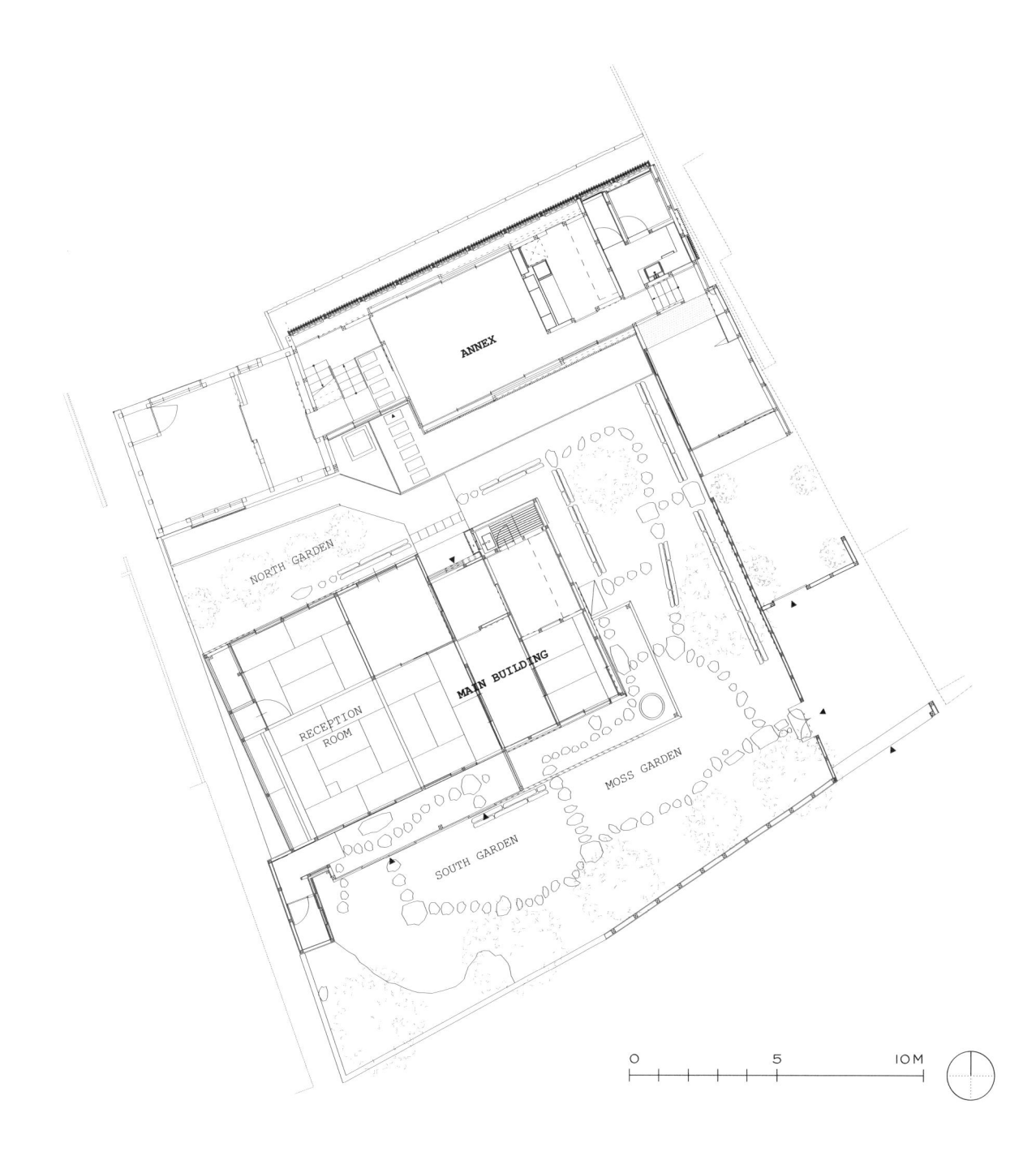

NORTH GARDEN

RECEPTION ROOM

MAIN BUILDING

MOSS GARDEN

SOUTH GARDEN

0　5　10M

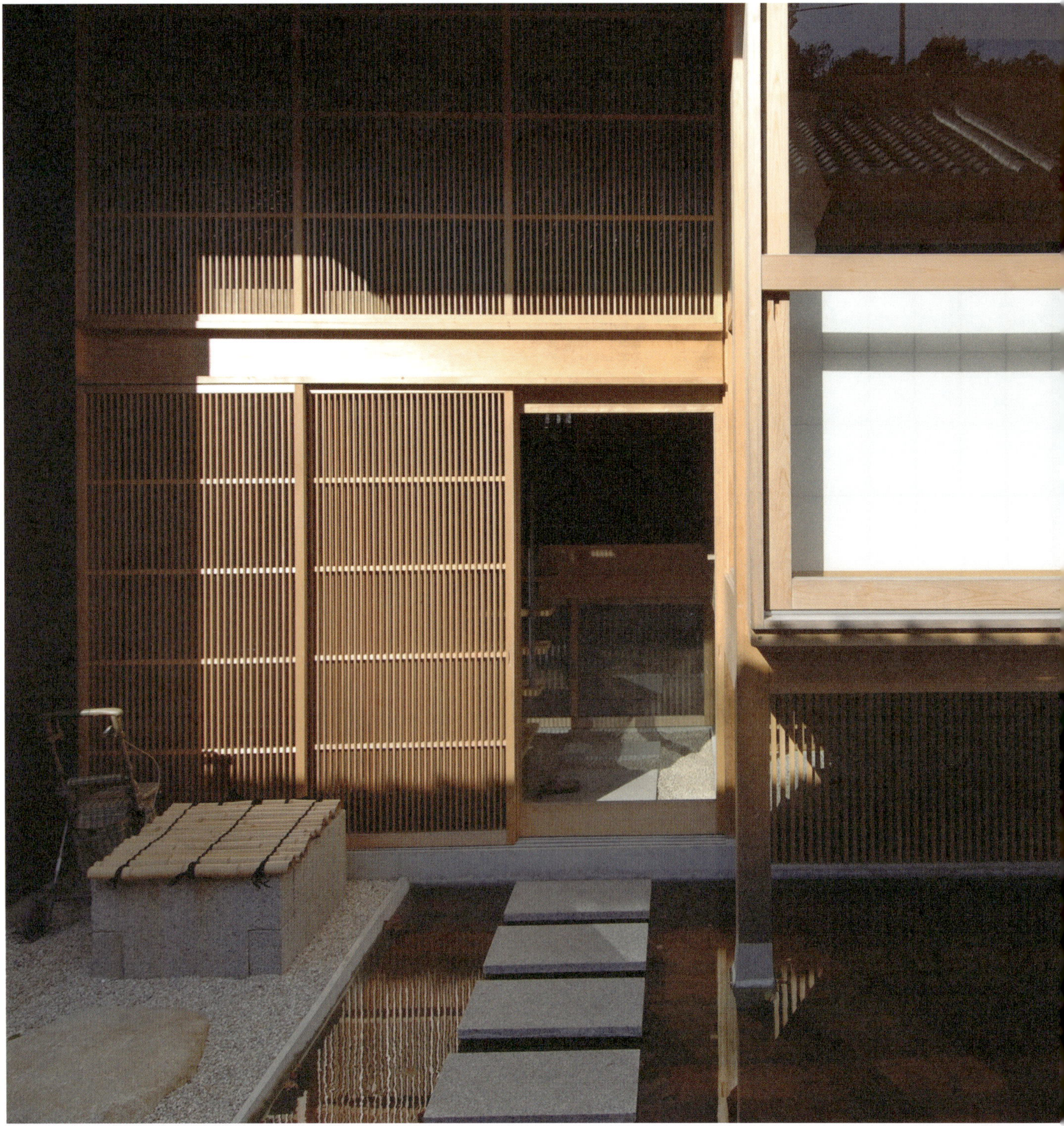

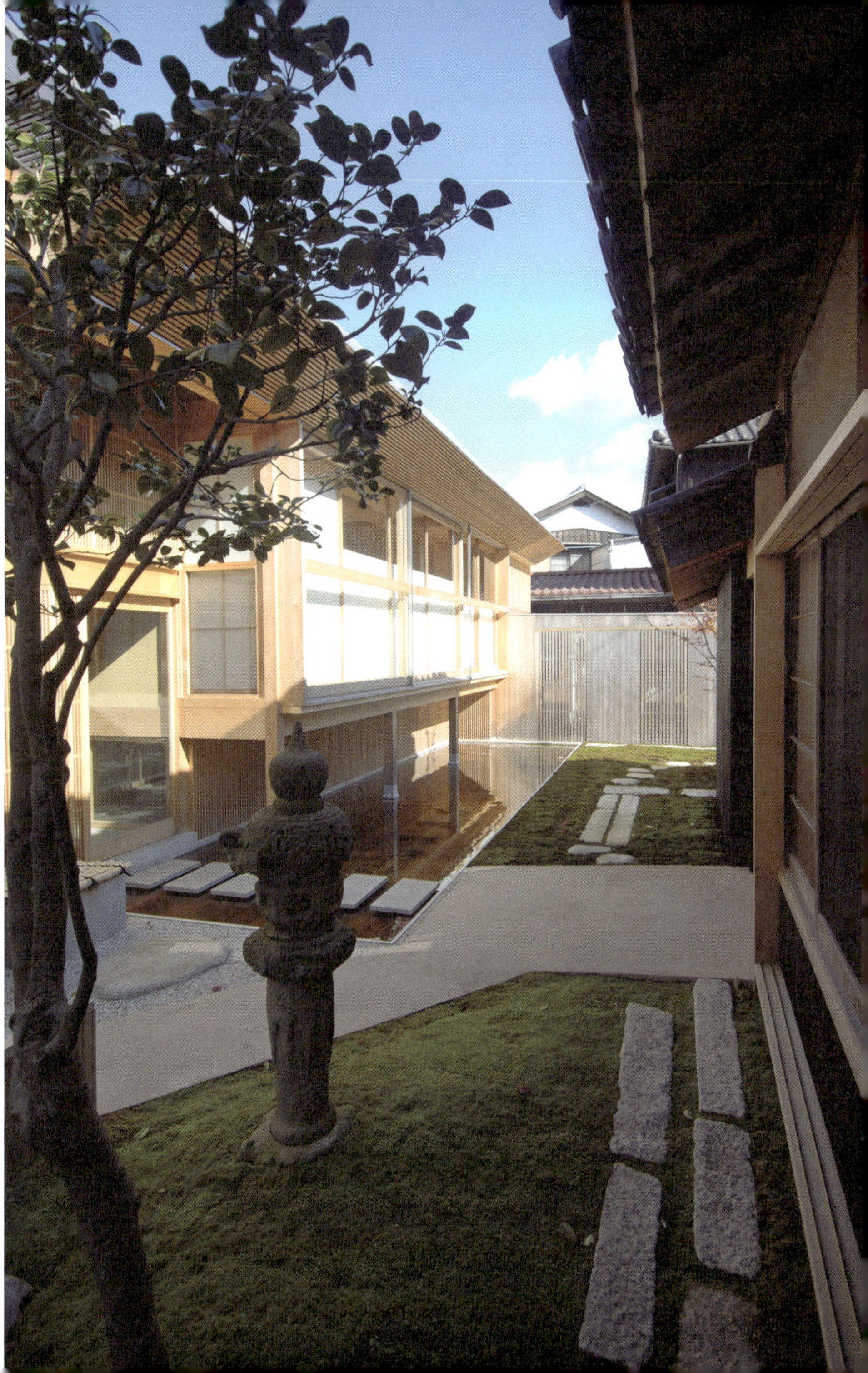

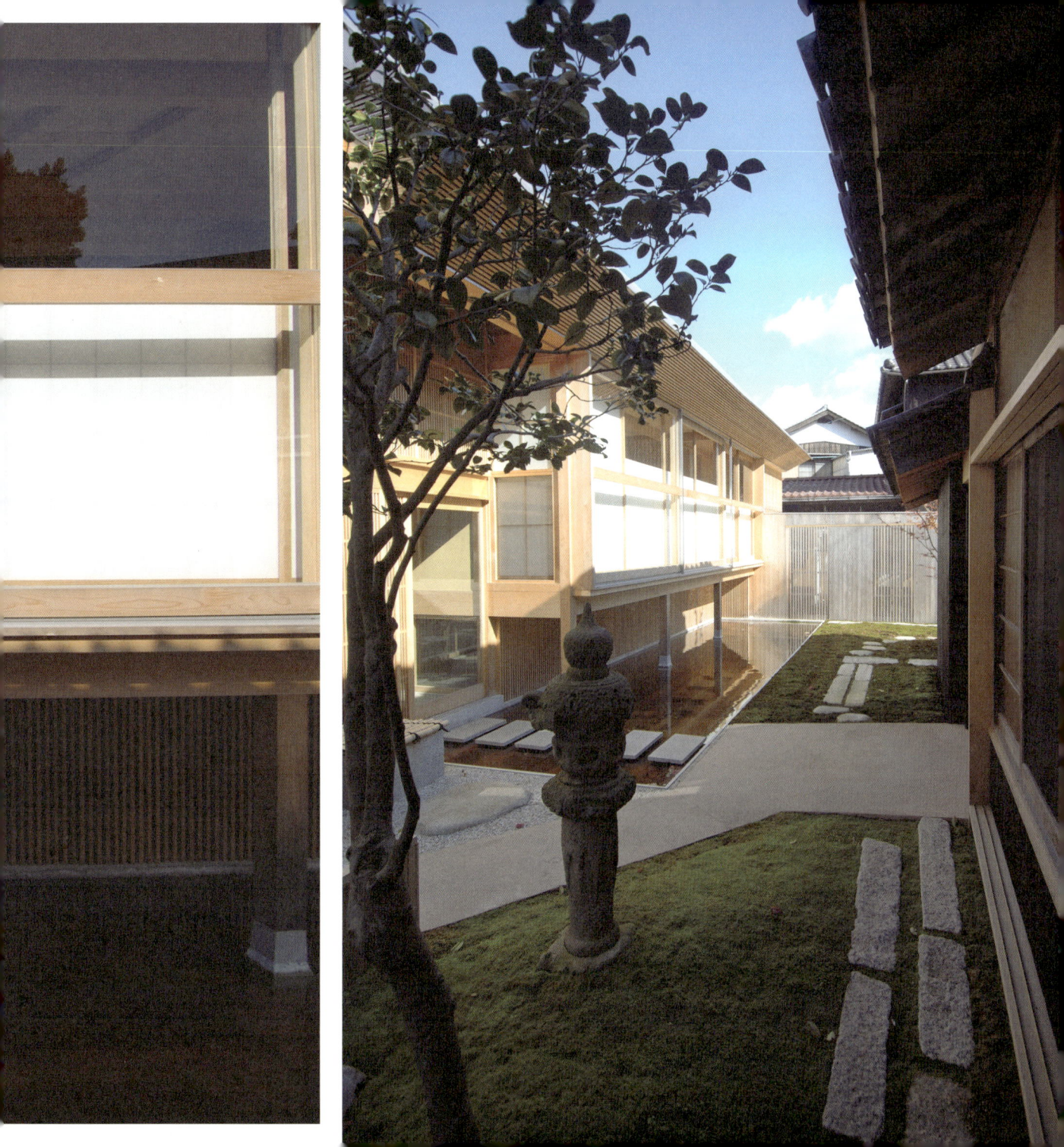

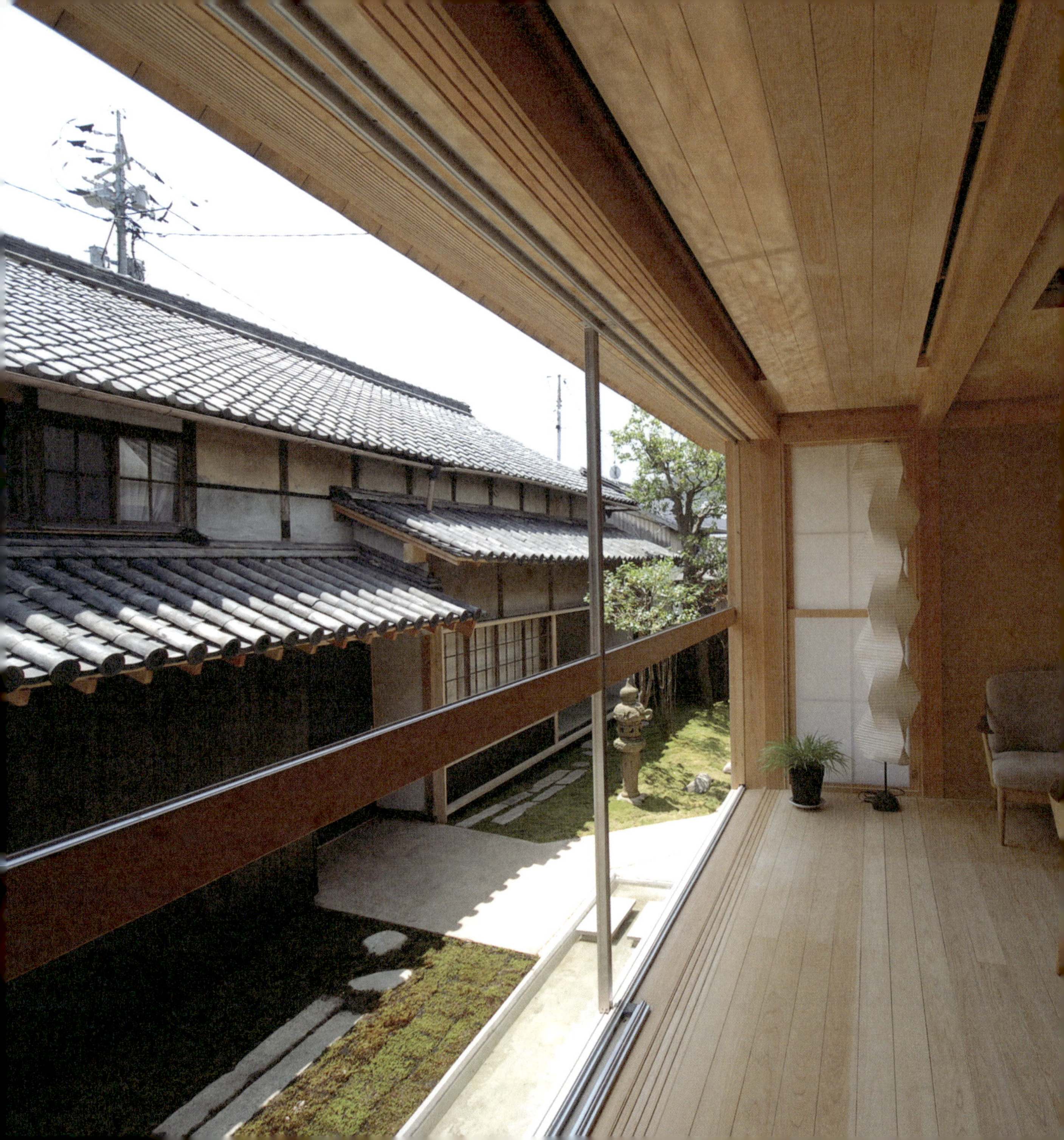

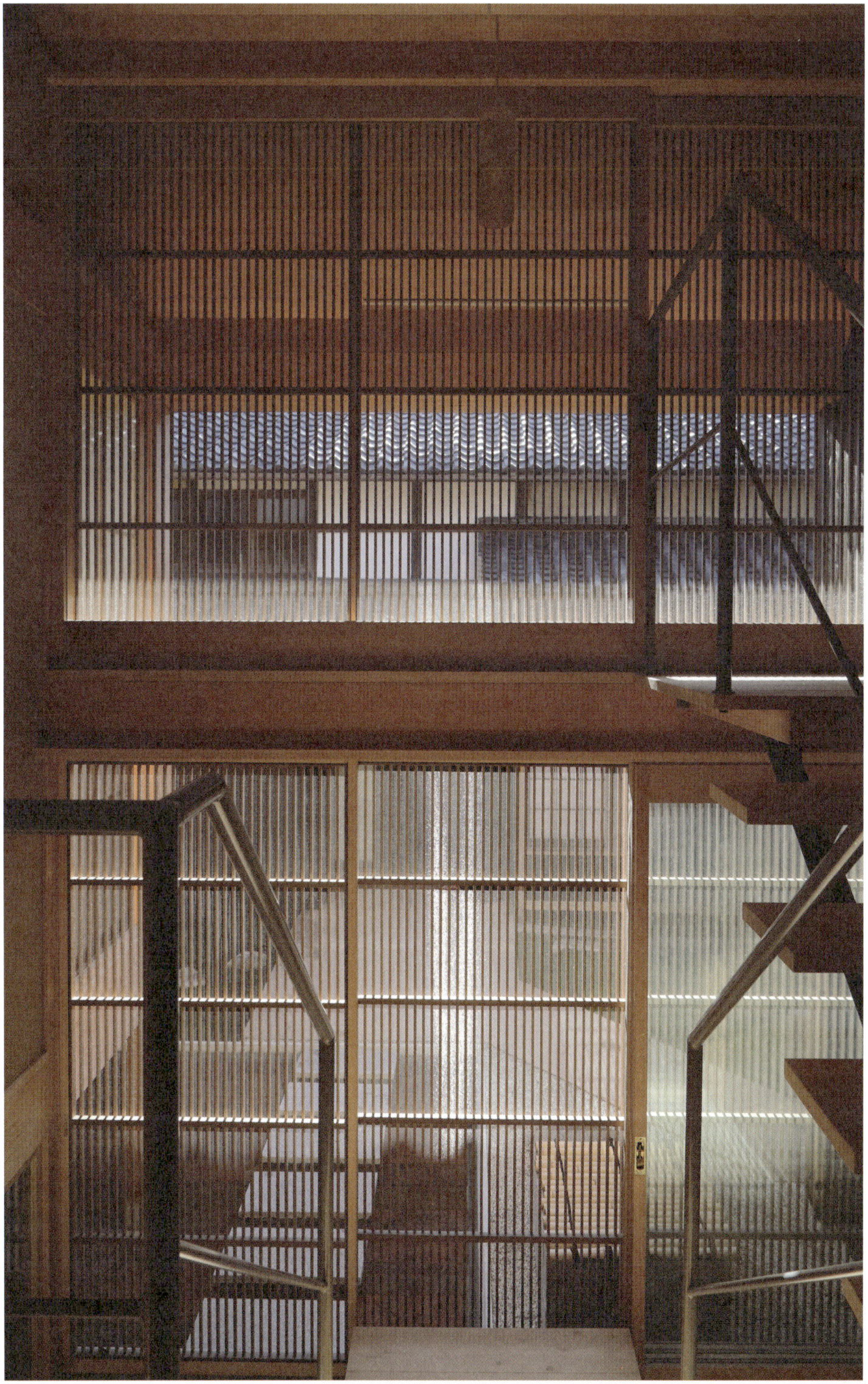

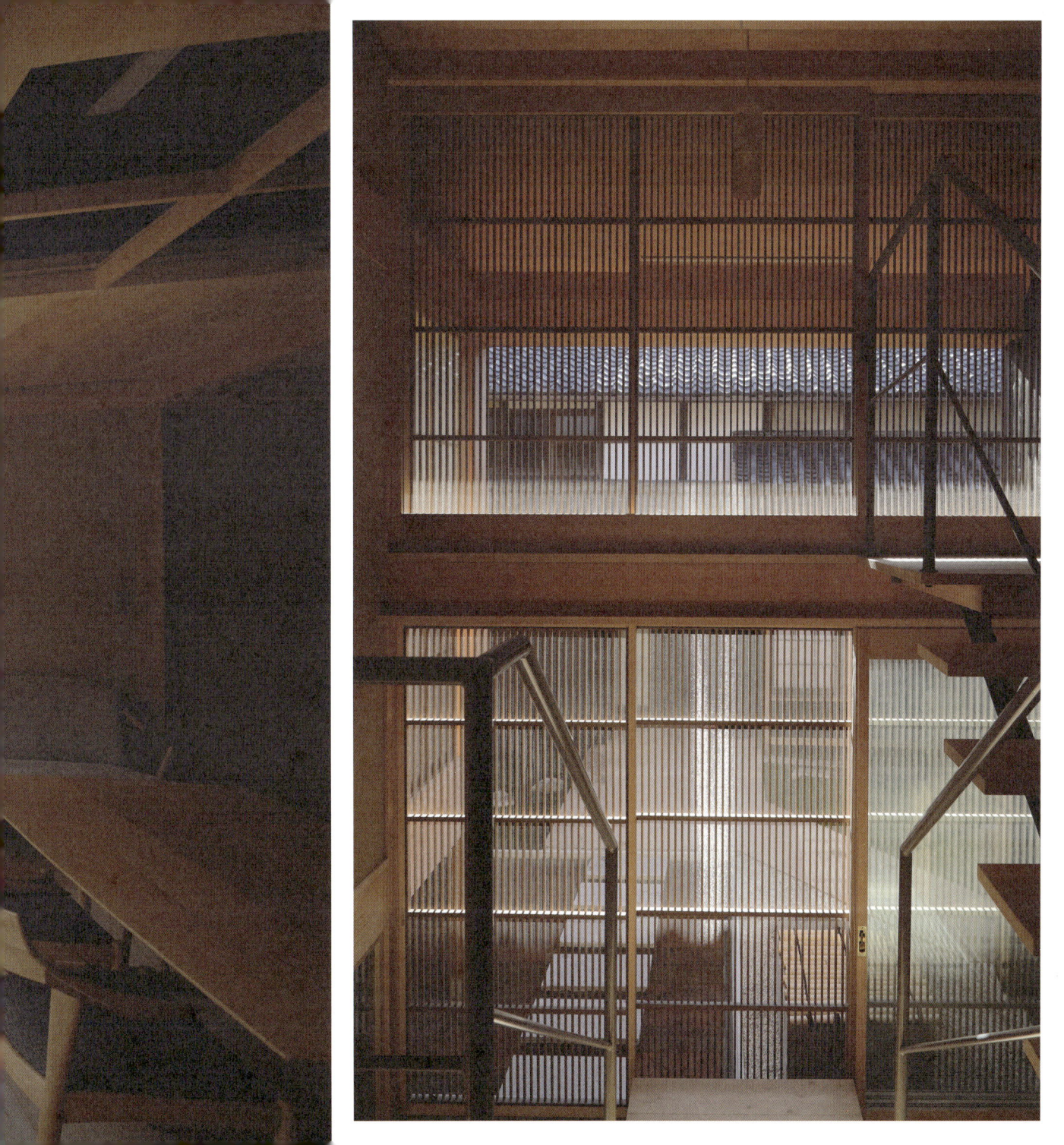

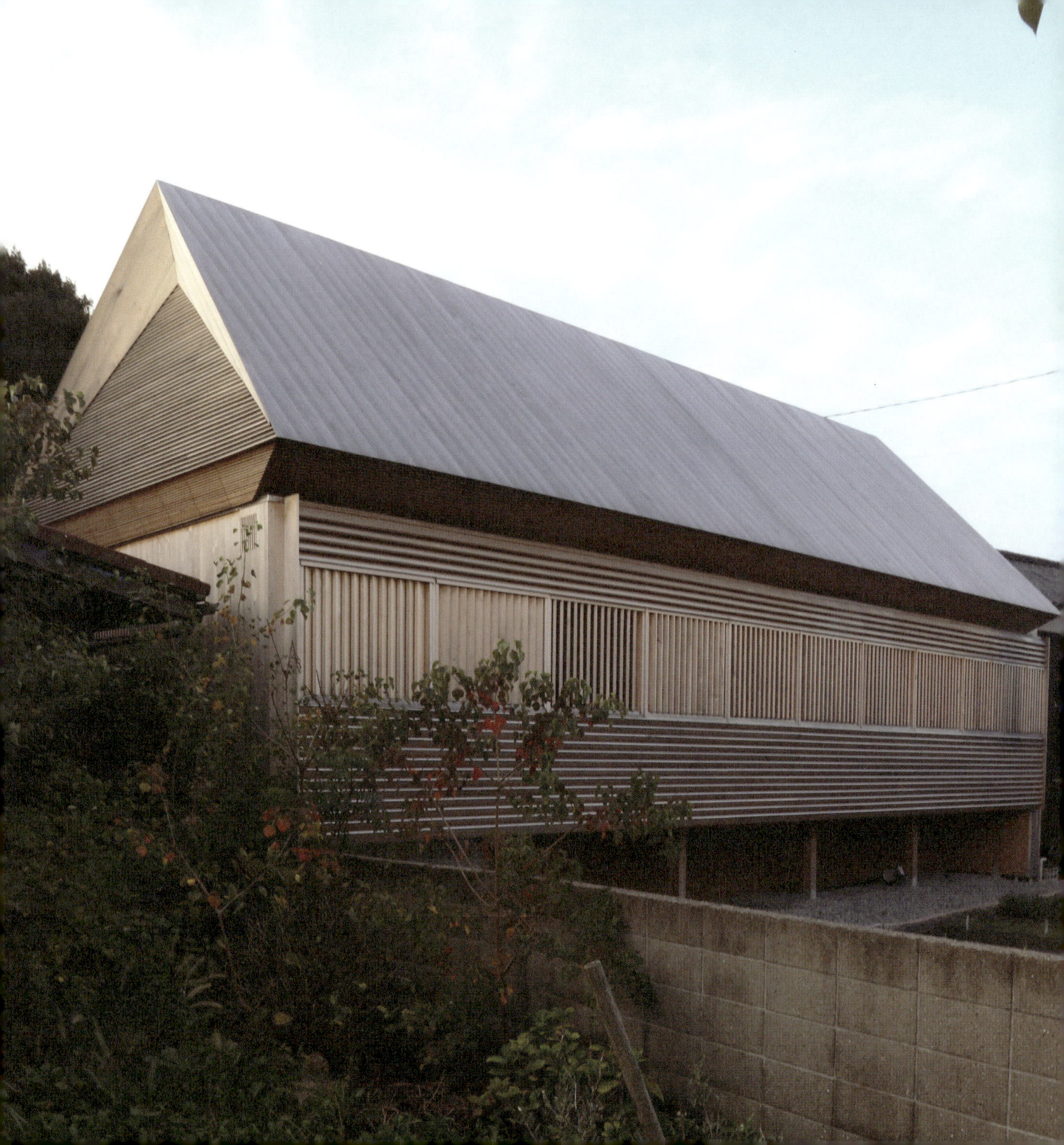

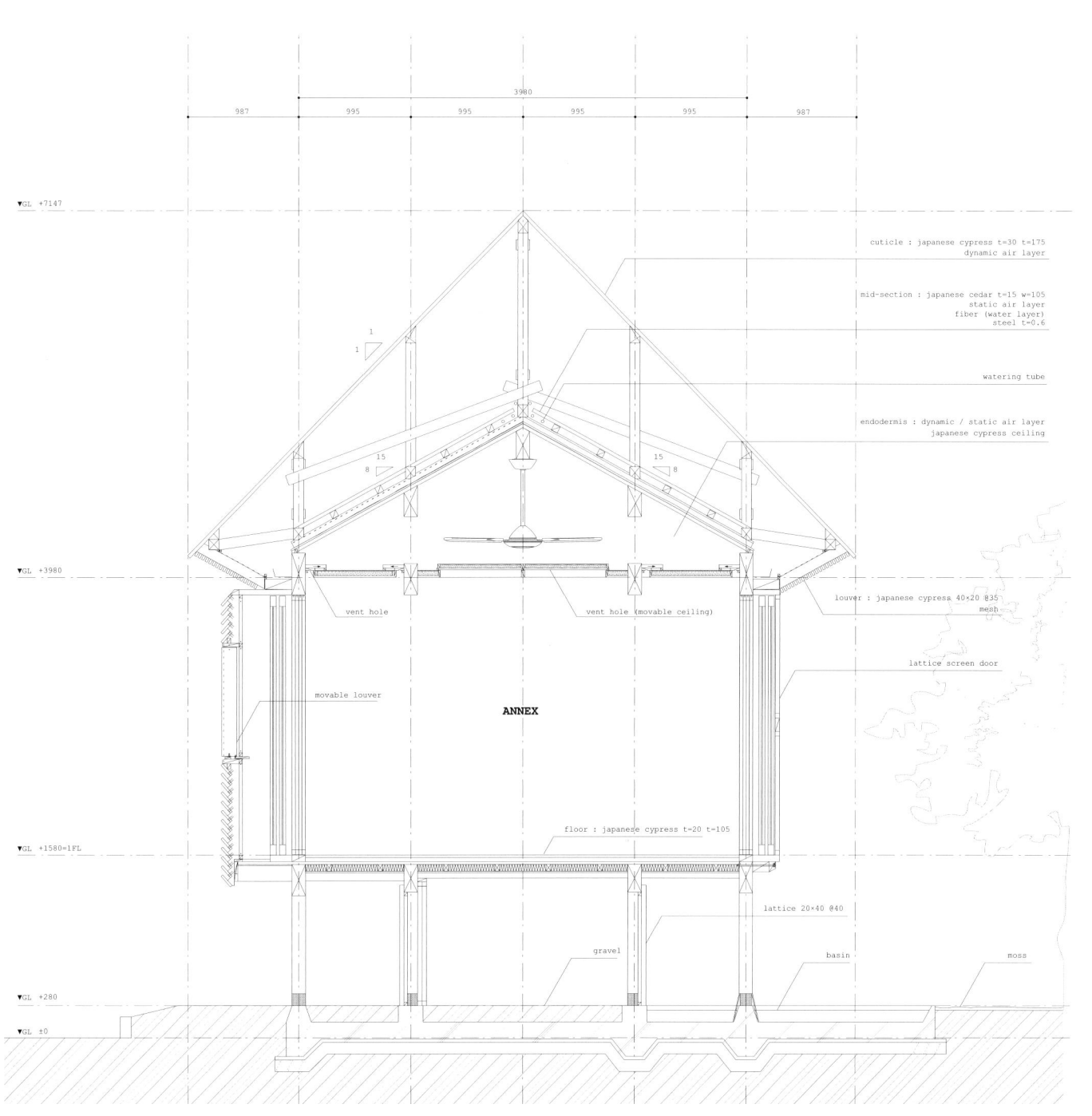

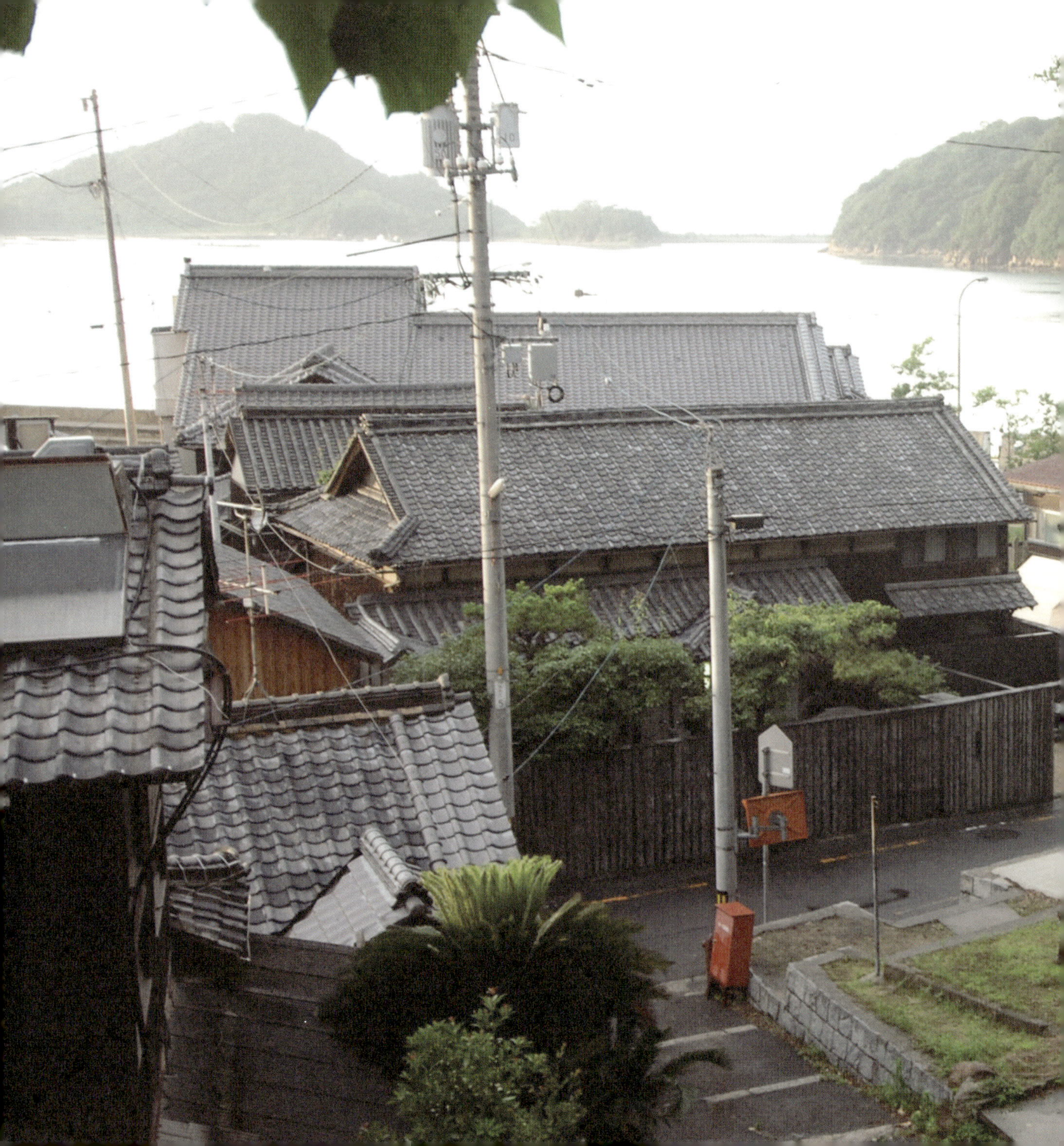

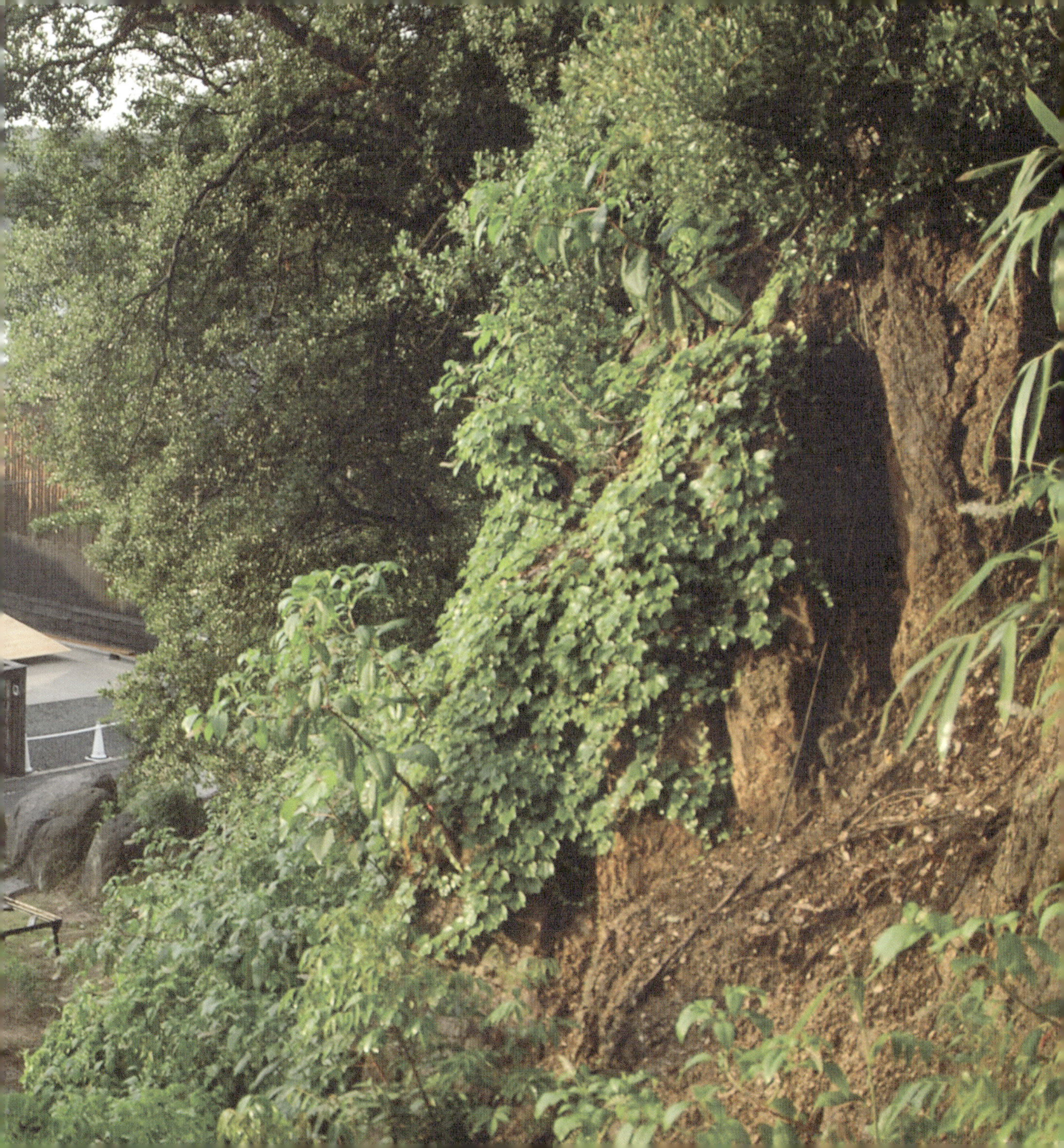

無り 板係 土間

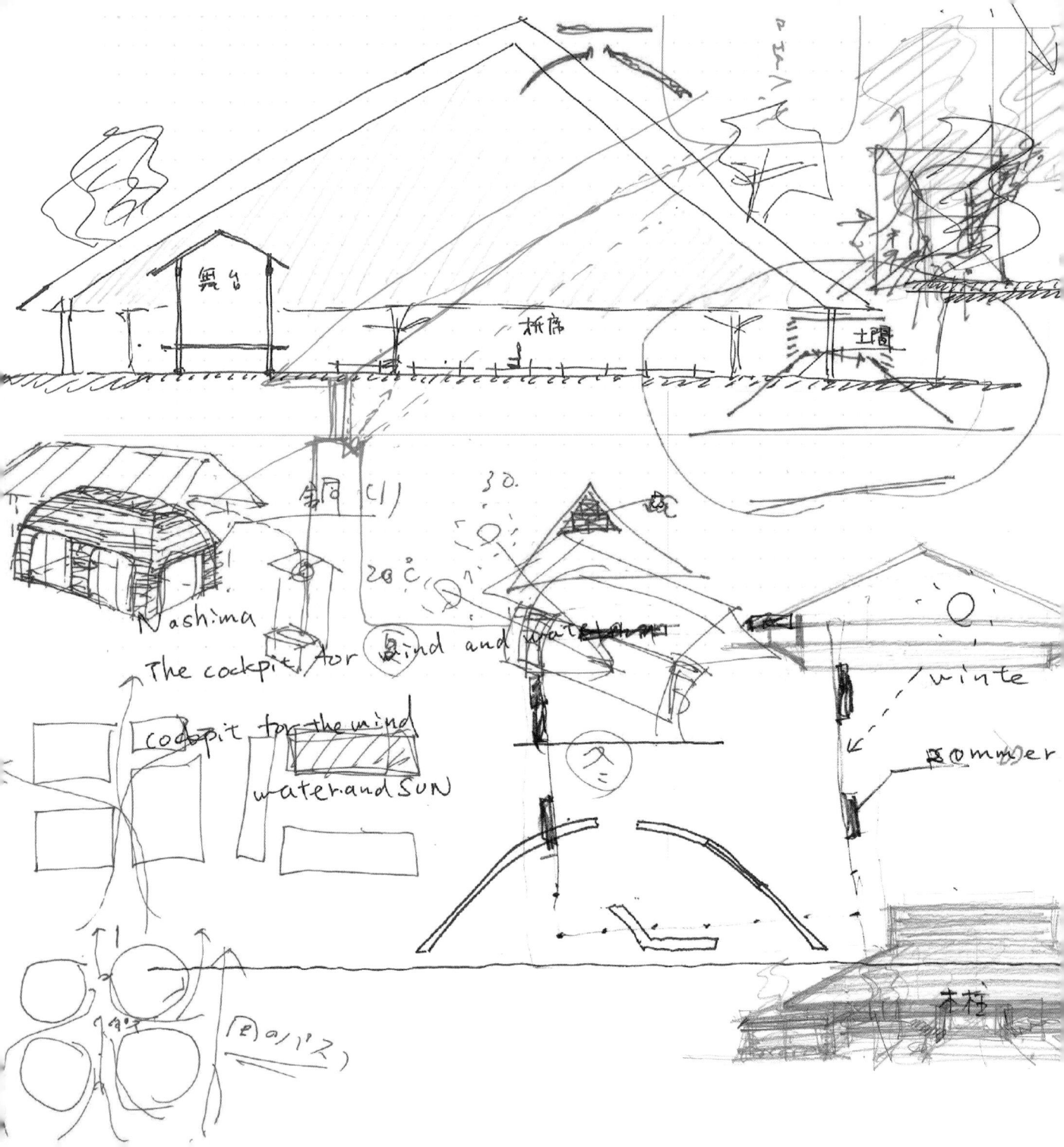

Nashima
The cockpit for wind and water

cockpit for the wind
water and SUN

冬

winter
summer

木桓

20℃ 30℃

風のパス

air

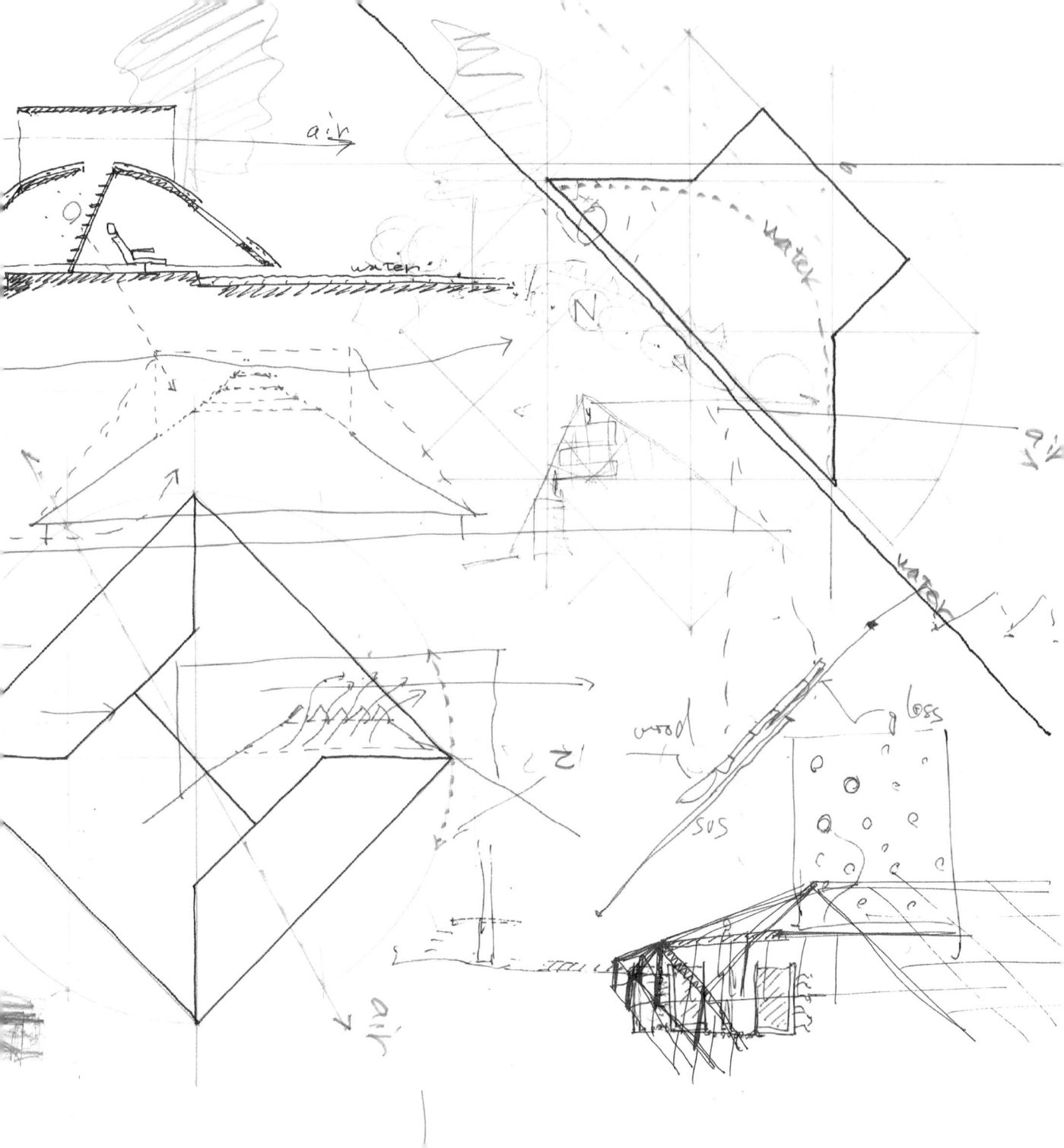

water

water

water

air

loss

air

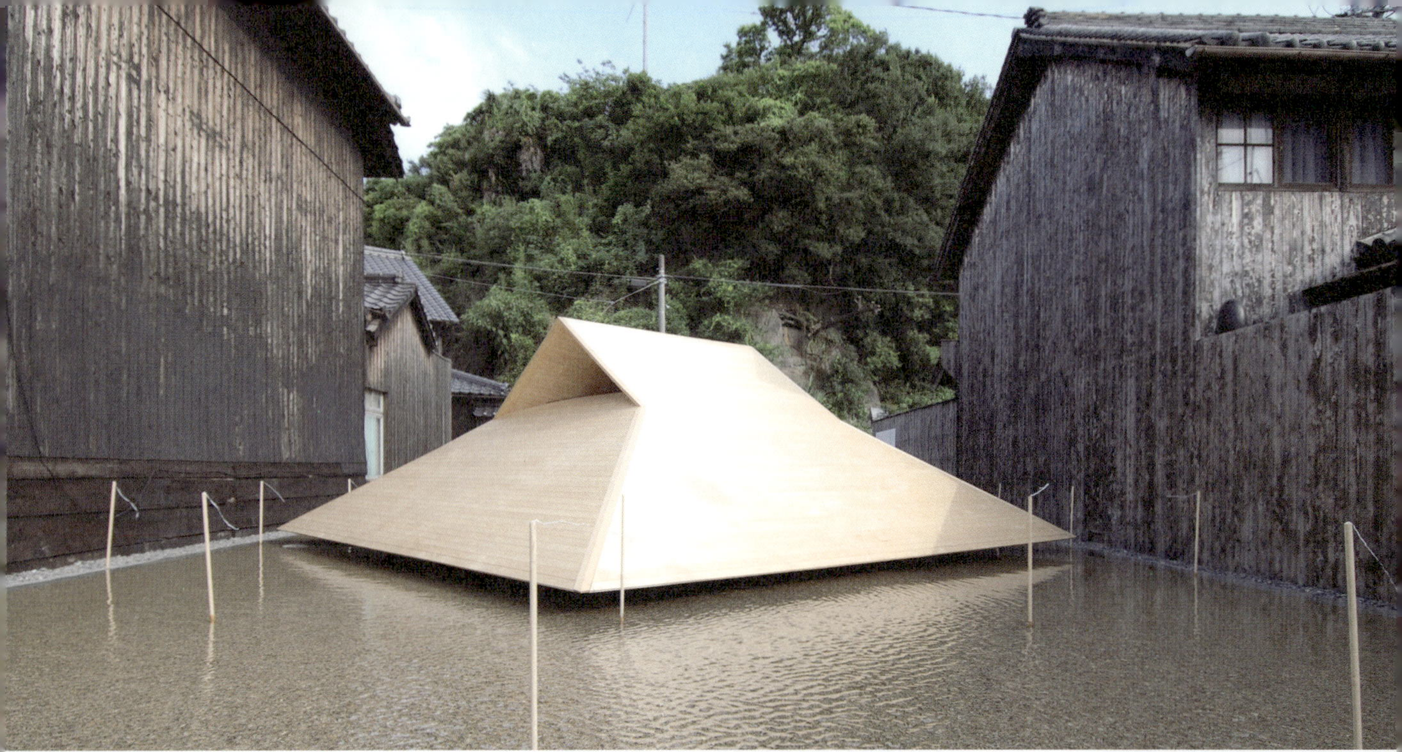

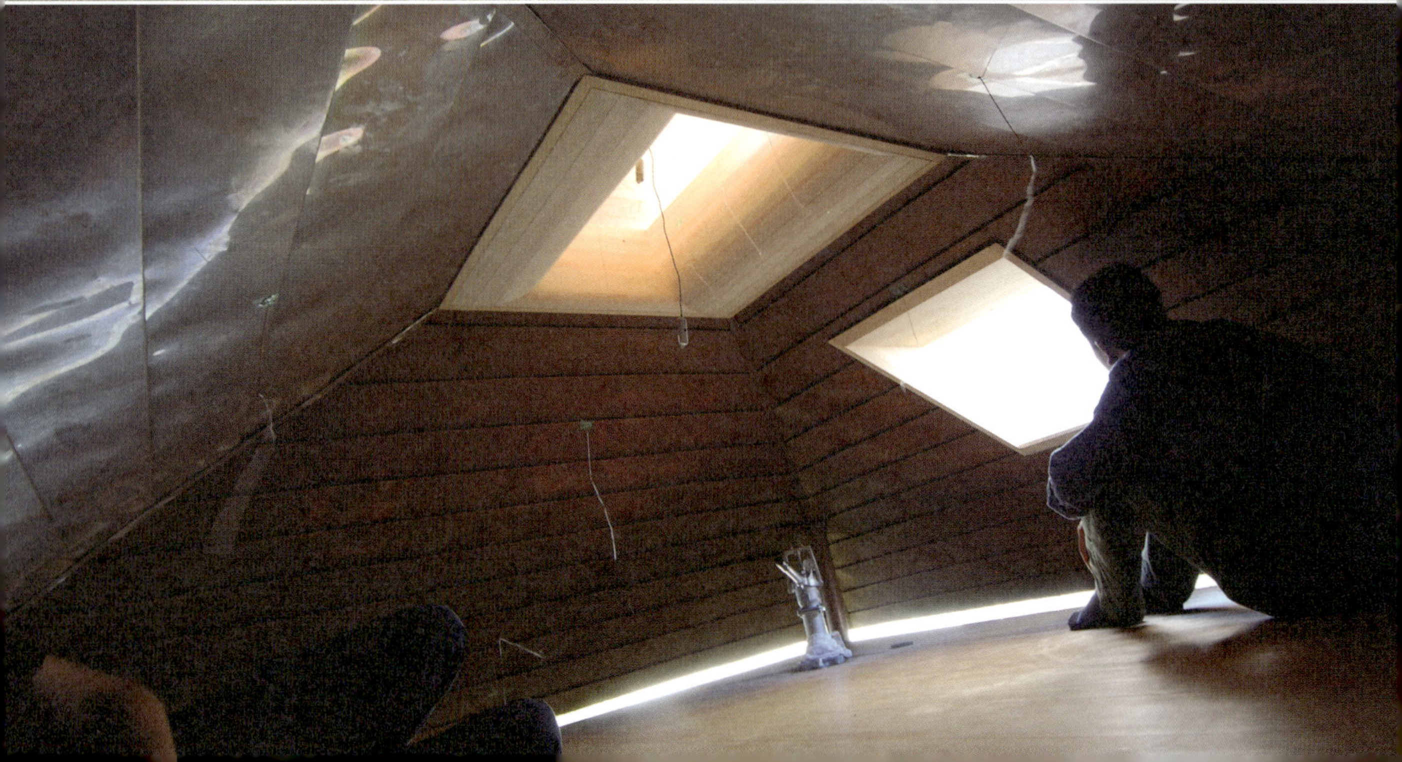

集落の風に適応した姿形を風洞模型、モックアップ、CFD解析とさまざまな角度から検証し、屋根の形状や風のディテールを決定していった。「瀬戸内国際芸術祭2013」では6分の1のモックアップ「風と水のコックピット」を直島に製作し、集落の風の中で検証を重ねた。

Wind tunnel experiments and mockups adapted to the winds in the village and additional simulations of computational fluid dynamics gradually determined the shape and wind details of the roof of the Naoshima Hall project. For the Setouchi Triennale 2013 a 1:6 scale model, a "cockpit for wind and water" was produced, providing vital validation of the local winds.

風洞実験模型により繰り返しテストされた空気の流れ。

The flow of air was tested in wind tunnel experiments through multiple design iterations.

空気の流れの解析。

Analysis of the air flow by computational fluid dynamics simulations.

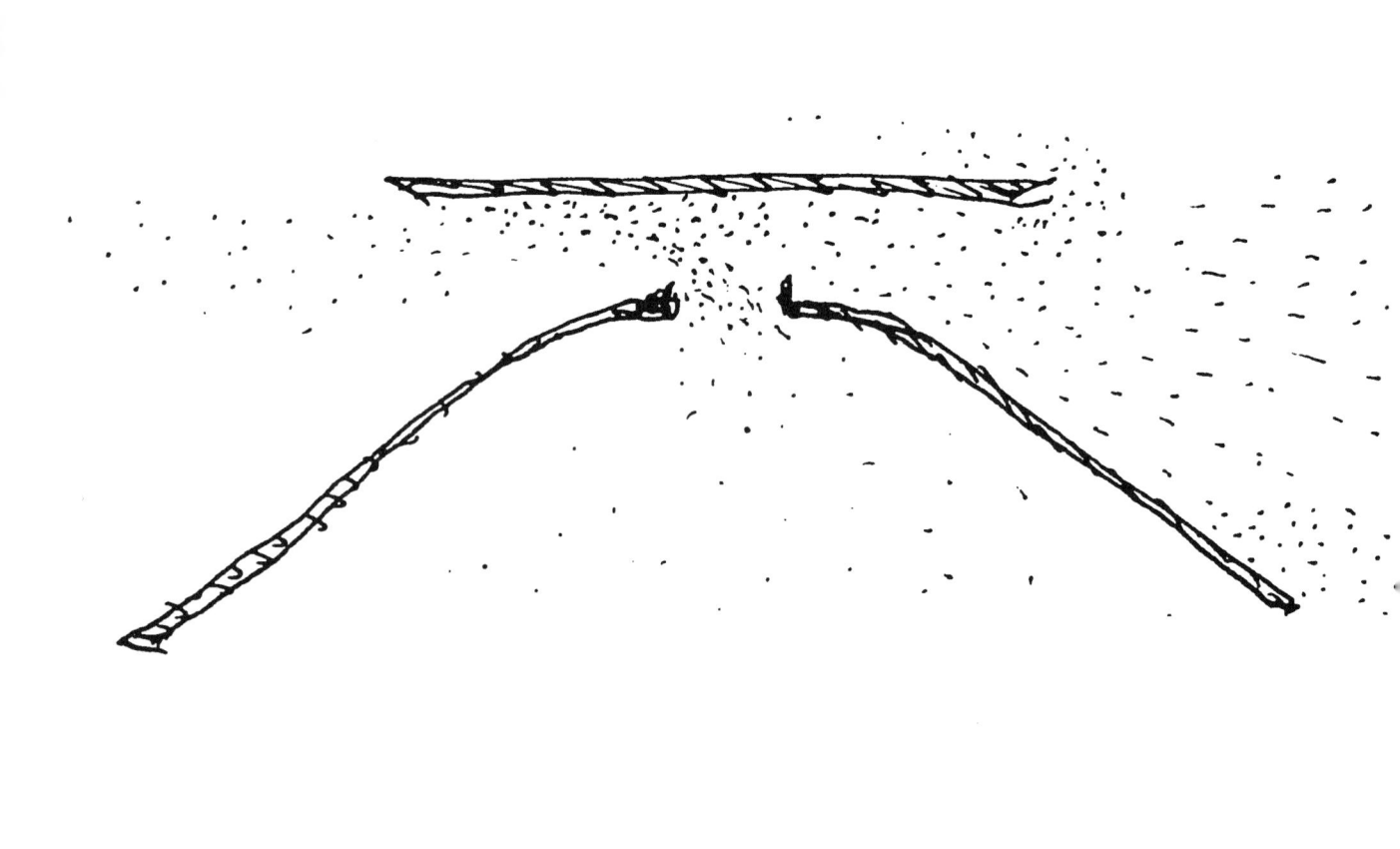

直島ホール

「直島ホール」はホール、集会所、庭園で構成され、2棟の異なる檜の大屋根が特徴である。「直島プラン」の公のプロジェクトにおいて直島本来の動く素材の「流れ」をいかに次の世代へ伝えるかが大きなテーマであった。

ホールの大屋根は総檜葺きで直島の集落に多く見られる伝統的な入母屋形状に直島の風向に即した風穴が開いている。この形状は、直島の動く素材の流れを可視化すると同時に空気の圧力差を生み、ホール内の空気を循環させる。夏に窓を閉じても空気が緩やかに動くことで熱気が抜け、さまざまな活動ができるよう工夫されている。流体形の天井は漆喰、壁は土壁、体育室の床は総檜、その回りは直島のにがりを使った三和土(たたき)など天然素材で構成される。舞台は四国や瀬戸内に多く見られる農村舞台、特に近世芸能の人形芝居の舞台小屋形式を継承し、香川県指定有形・無形民俗文化財の直島女文楽の練習場としても利用される。

集会所の大屋根は、総檜の寄せ棟形状で2重のルーバー屋根とトップライトで構成される。雨からは守られ、空気は緩やかに通すつくりである。日本の茅葺き屋根の原理を継承している。大屋根の下には4棟が配されている。各棟は内縁や土間を介してつながり、お祭りの際には大屋根で囲われた半外部空間が多目的に利用できる。畳の間は、直島の伝統的な形式に倣って南北に庭や縁を設け、風が抜けるつくりになっており、本村の民家に流れる風の特徴を継承している。特に天井内の地下水循環が特徴で、夏場に屋内を涼しく保つ手助けをしてくれる。近年利用価値の薄らいでいた井戸水の新たな価値への試みである。

庭園には苔庭と紅葉が広がり、花見ができる枝垂れ桜(直島枝垂れ)の巨木は集落のシンボルとなることだろう。水に浮かぶ桟敷はステージや、茶会、観劇の場としても多目的に利用できる。特に建物周囲の苔で覆われた盛り土が特徴である。苔の保水力の高さは盛り土と共に、建物を夏の暑さと冬の寒さから守っている。私の建築は地形も建築の一部であり、建築も地球の一部である。

今後「直島ホール」が島民や観光客にとって集いや憩い、さらには地球鑑賞の場として直島の中世より受け継がれてきた文化、芸術を世界に伝える場となると共に400年前から届けられた本村の谷の「風のメッセージ」をこの大屋根がさらに後世へ届けてくれることを願っている。

NAOSHIMA HALL

Naoshima Hall comprises a hall, a community centre, and a garden, and is characterized by two different roofs made of hinoki (Japanese cypress). As a public project in the Naoshima Plan, the major theme is how to convey to the next generation the original material "flows" of Naoshima.

Clad in hinoki, the large roof of the hall is a traditional hipped shape that is often seen in the villages of Naoshima, and has a vent opening aligned with the prevailing wind direction. This shape is a visualization of the flow of moving materials in Naoshima, and simultaneously produces a pressure differential that causes air to circulate in the hall. Even with the windows closed in summer, heat is removed by the gentle movements of the air – a device that allows various activities to take place. The fluidly shaped ceiling is stucco, the walls are adobe, the floor of the gymnasium is solid hinoki, and the surrounding areas are composed of natural materials, including hard-packed earth that uses *nigari* (bittern) left over from salt production in Naoshima. The stage is similar to the agricultural stages often seen in Shikoku and the Seto region, in particular the hut-shaped stages used for public puppet shows in early modern times, and also used for practicing Naoshima Onna Bunraku, which has been designated an Important Tangible and Intangible Folk Cultural Property of Kagawa prefecture.

The large roof of the community centre is a *munakata* (gabled ridge beam) shape made of solid hinoki comprising a double layer of louvres and a skylight. A structure that provides protection from rain while allowing breezes to gently pass through, it inherits the principles of the Japanese traditional thatched roof. Four buildings are arranged below the large roof. Each building is connected by its inner *engawa* (veranda) and *doma* (earthen floor), and the semi-exterior space sheltered by the large roof can be used for many purposes, for instance during festivals. Emulating the traditional layouts found in Naoshima, gardens and verandas are placed at the north and south, so that breezes will pass through the tatami rooms, inheriting the characteristic style of the *minka* (private houses) of Honmura. Like the Matabe house, water from underground is circulated within the ceiling to help keep the rooms cool in summertime. This is an attempt to find new ways of utilizing well water, which I have been working on in recent years.

Moss and maple trees are spread through the garden, and cherry blossom viewing parties can take place under the large *Naoshima-shidare* (weeping cherry tree), which might even become a symbol tree of the village. A multi-purpose stage floating in the water can be used as a tea ceremony venue, a theatre, and for other activities. Another unique feature is the moss-covered berm surrounding the building. The high moisture-retention capacity of the moss, together with the berm, protects the building from summer heat and winter cold. The terrain is also a part of my architecture, and my architecture is a part of the Earth.

From here on, Naoshima Hall will be a place for islanders and tourists to gather and relax, and furthermore a place for appreciation of the Earth, from which to transmit to the rest of the world the culture and art of Naoshima that has survived from medieval times. The 400-year-old "message of the wind" from the Honmura valley is expressed by this large roof, and I hope that it will be further conveyed to future generations.

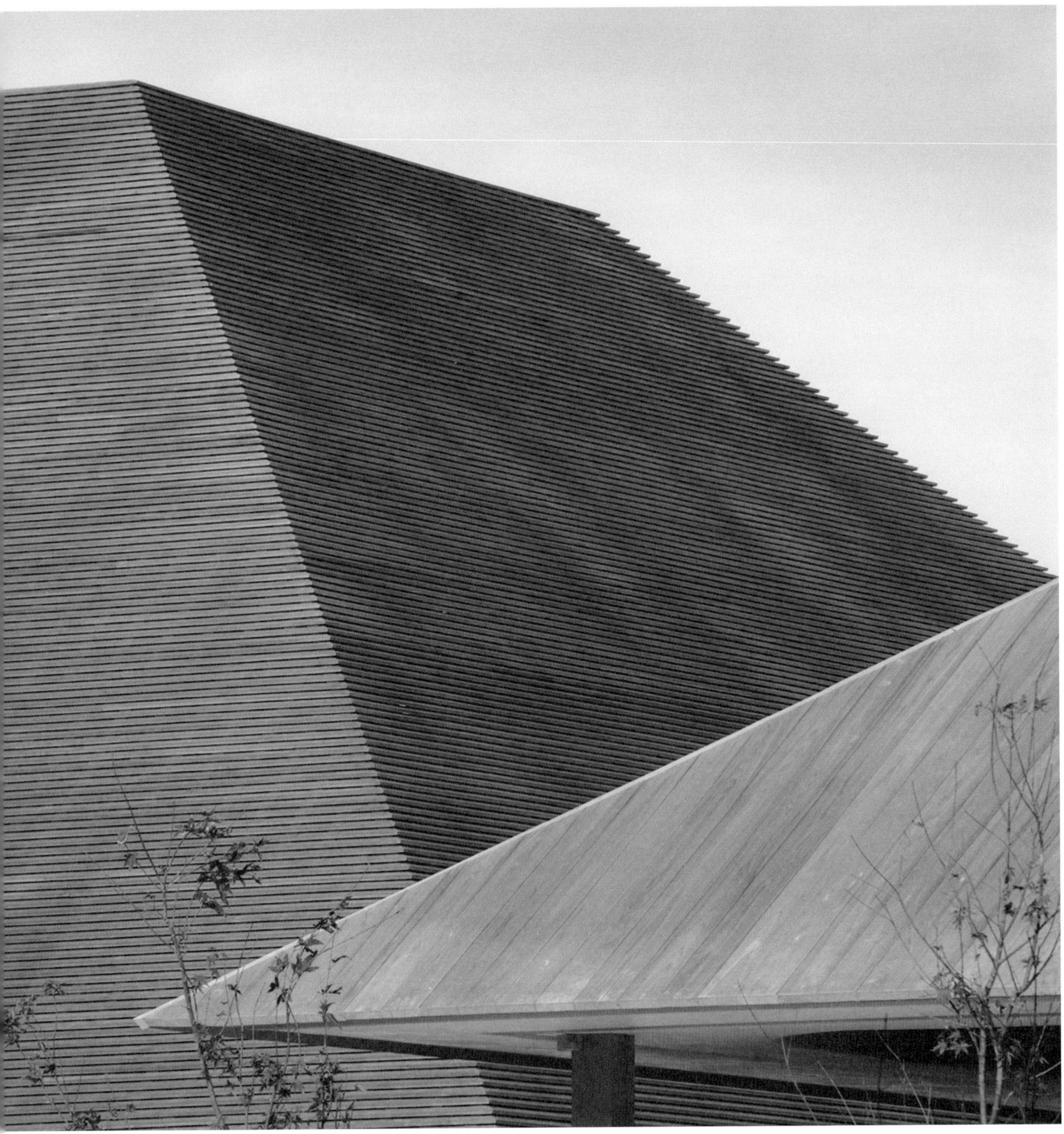

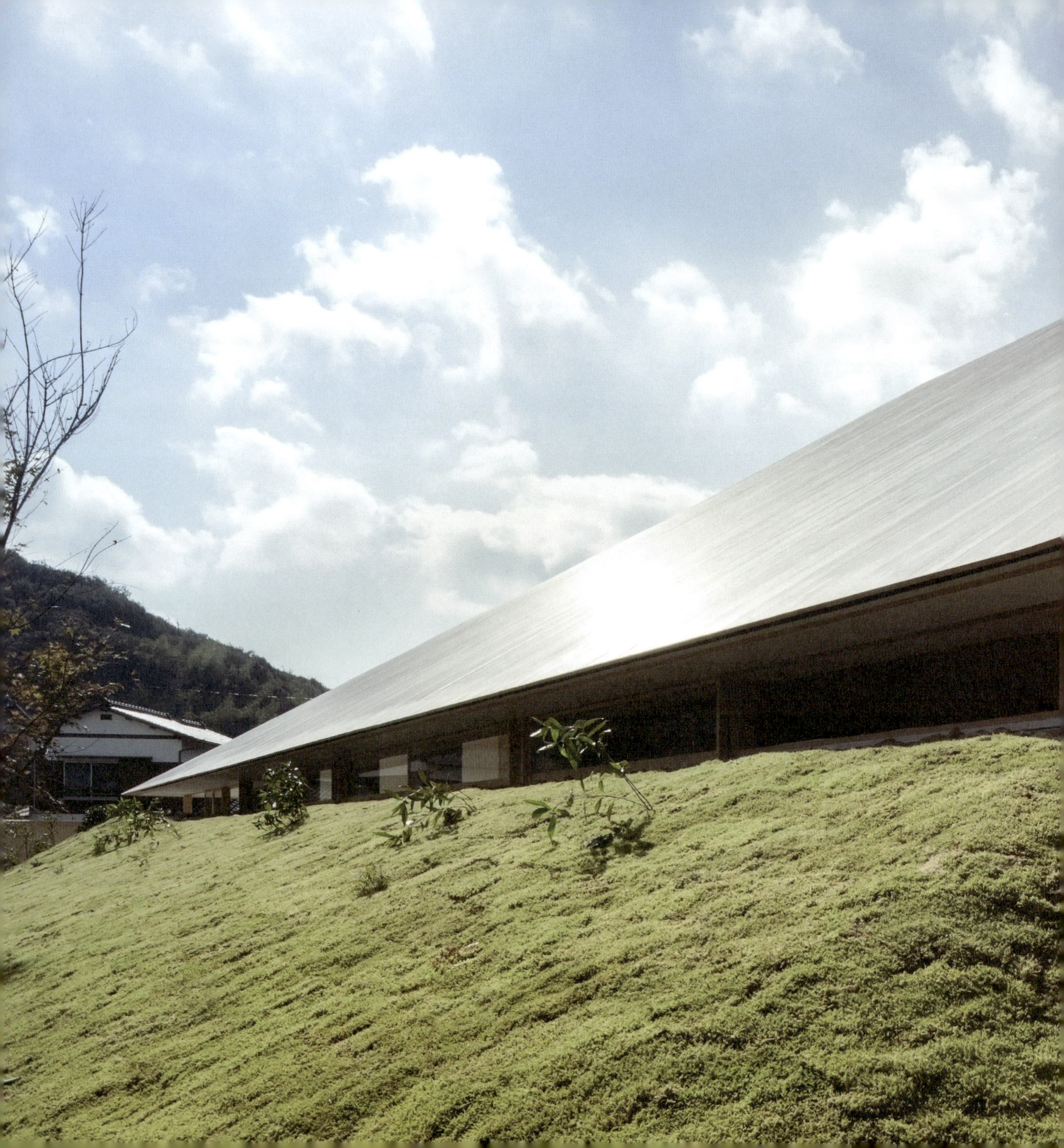

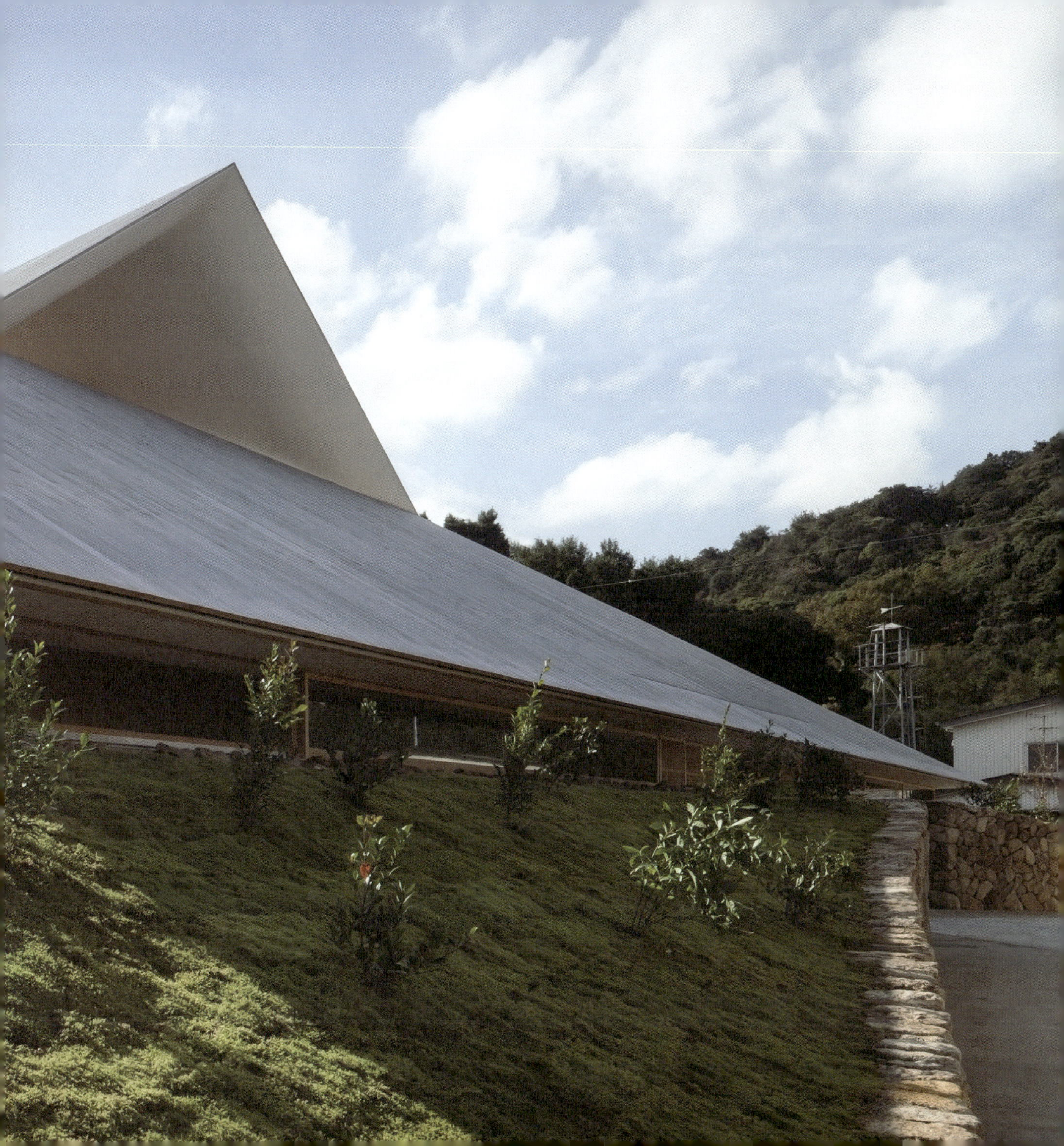

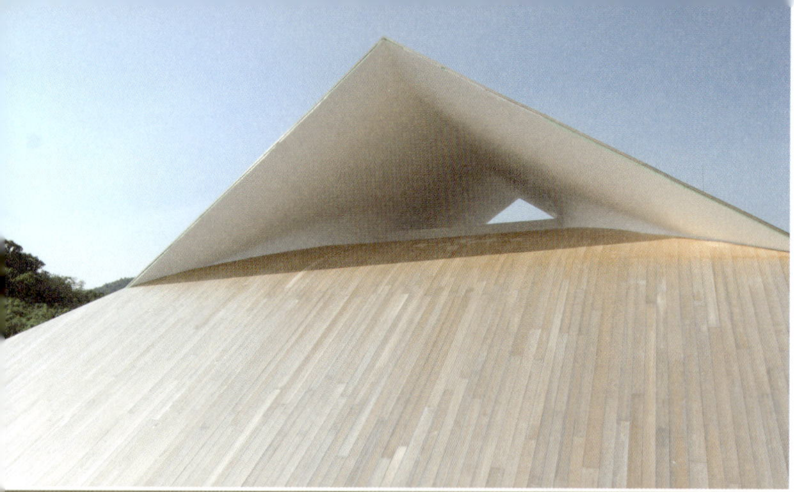

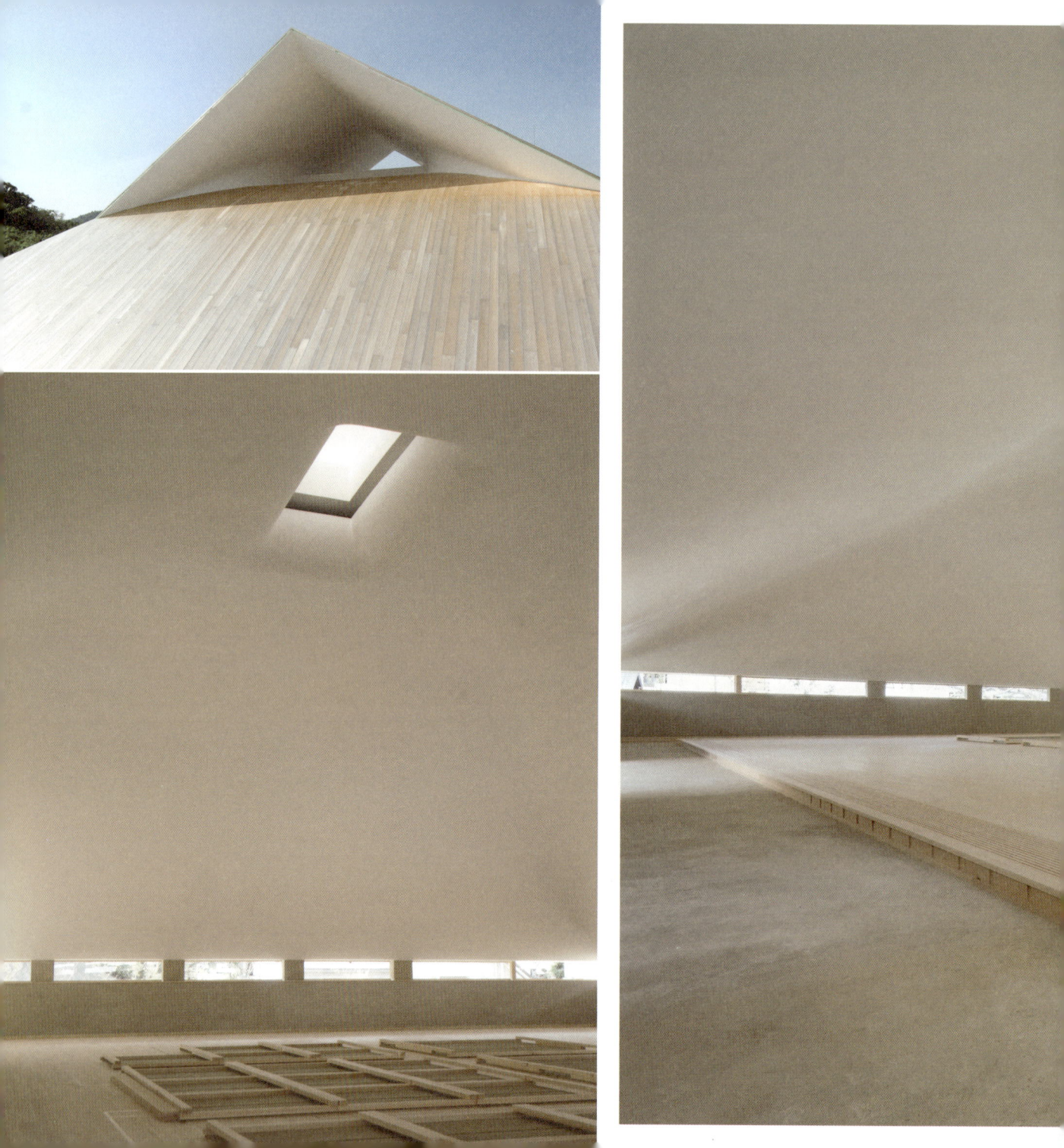

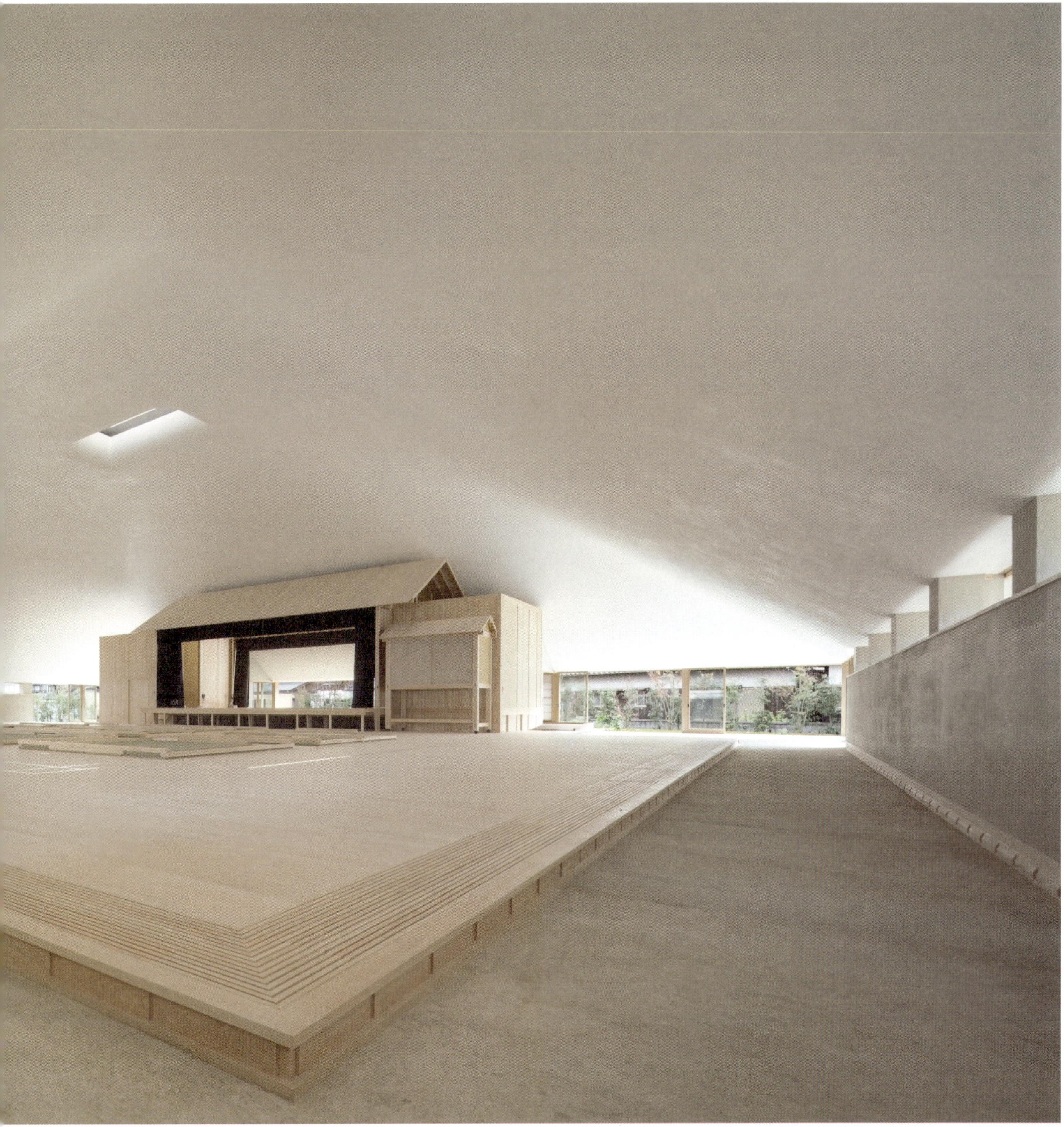

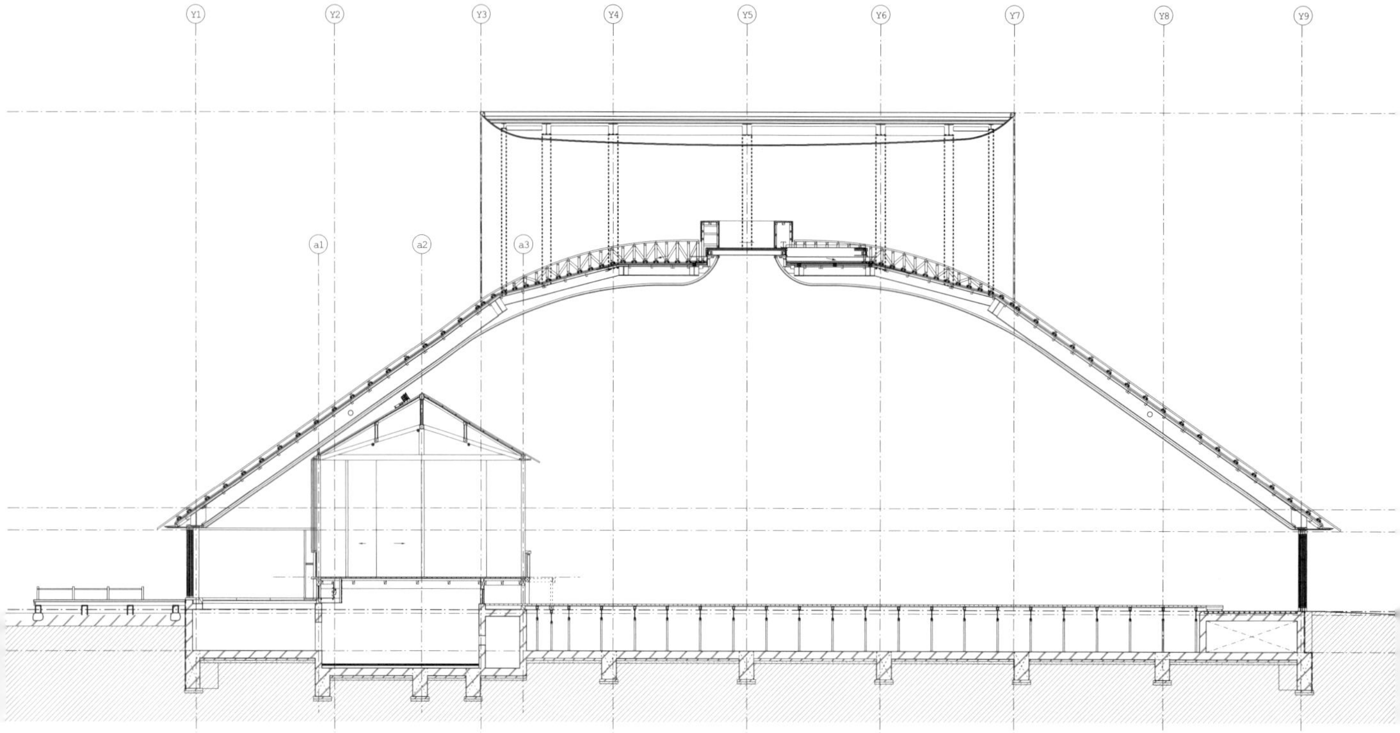

Y1
Y2
Y3
Y4
Y5
Y6
Y7
Y8
Y9
a1
a2
a3

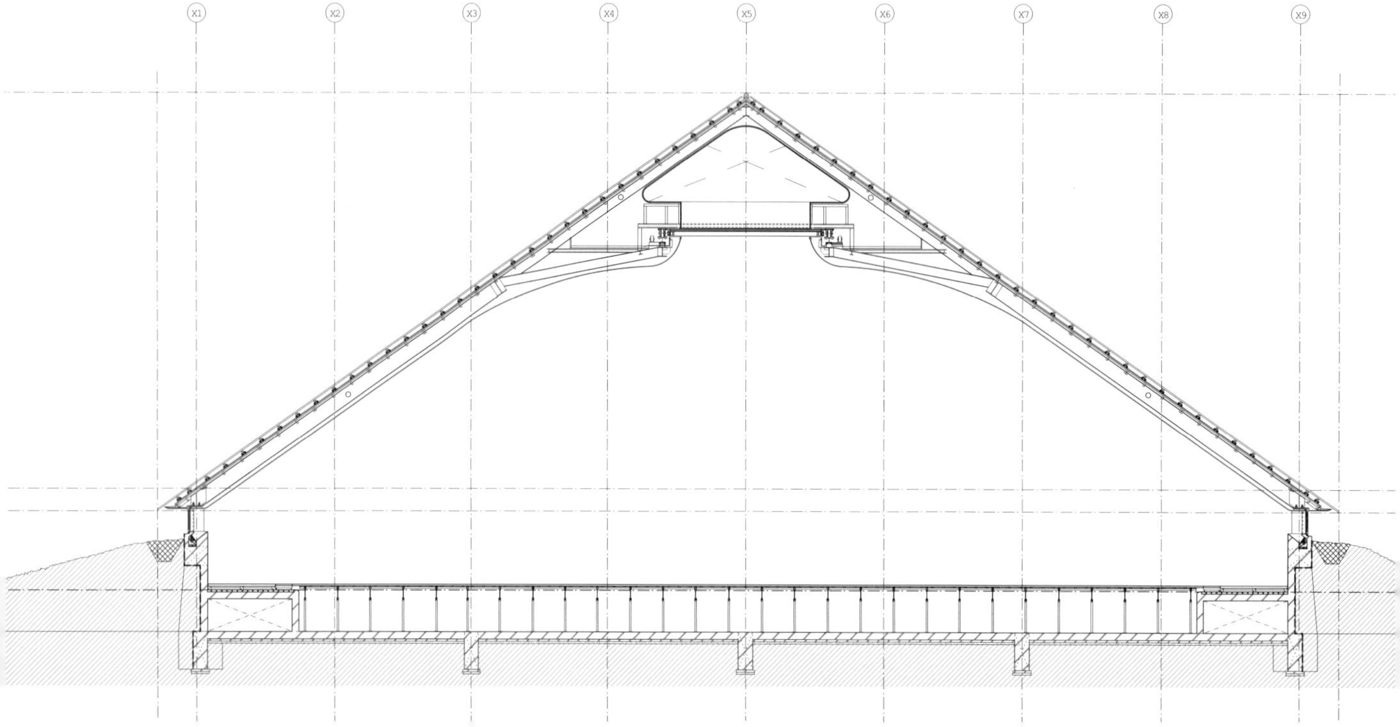

X1
X2
X3
X4
X5
X6
X7
X8
X9

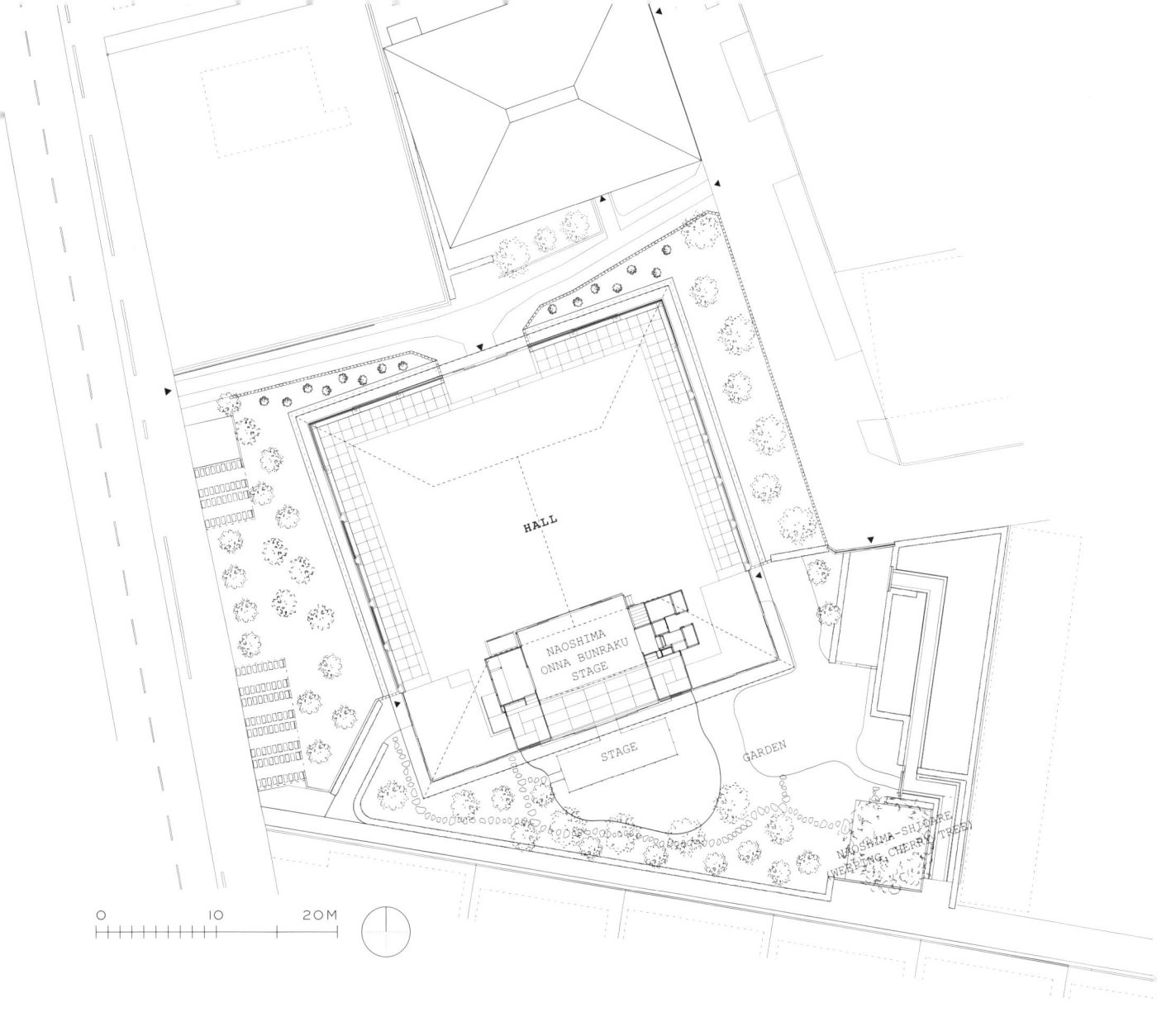

室内の空気をゆっくりと常に吐き出すことが求められた。その上で雨が入らないこと、空気の逆流が起こらないこと、この条件を満たす開口の立ち上がり、面積、曲率、形状などが、風洞の形状・ディテールを決定していく上で重要であった。

A steady and slow ventilation was required for the interior space. Furthermore it should shelter from rain and inhibit reverse air flow. To satisfy these conditions, the development of the ceiling opening, the size the curvature and the overall shape was heavily dependent on wind tunnel experiments.

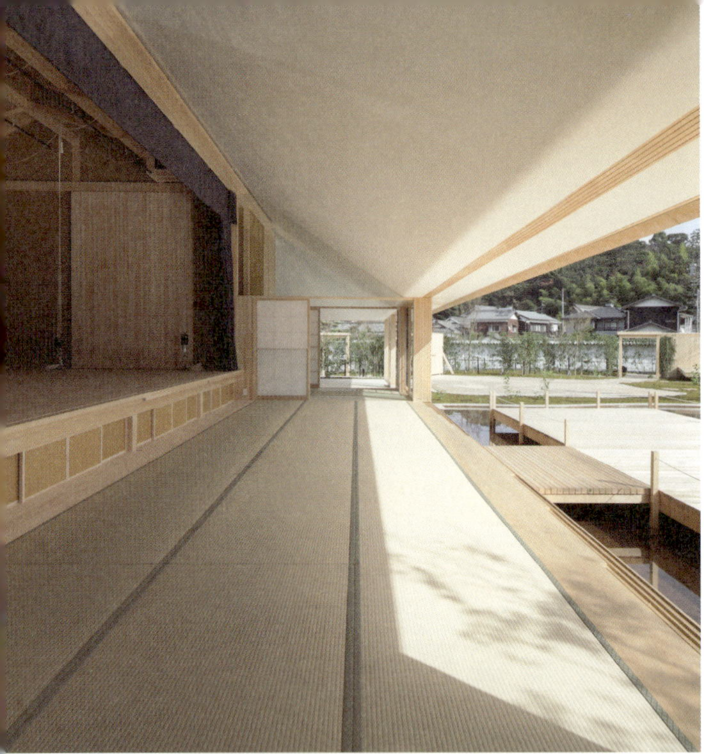
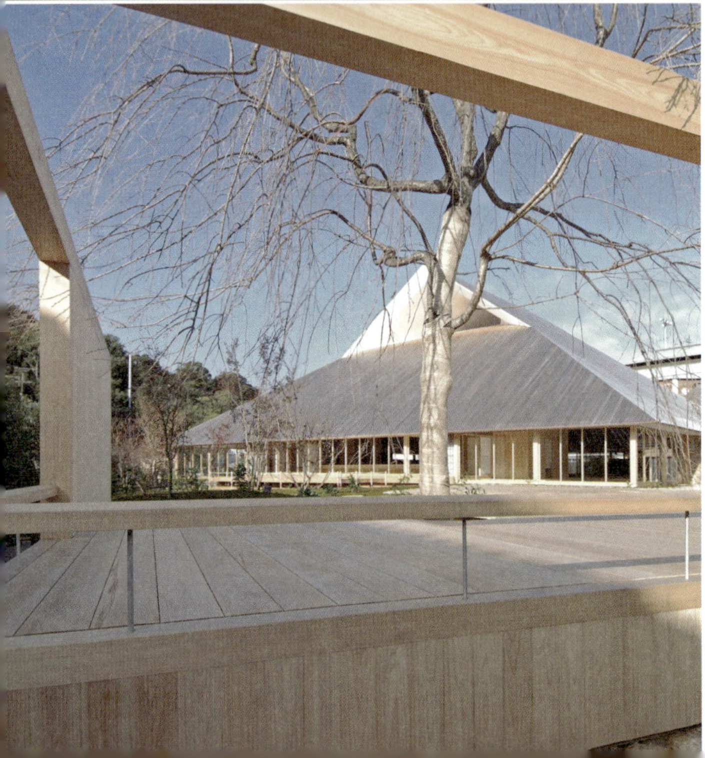
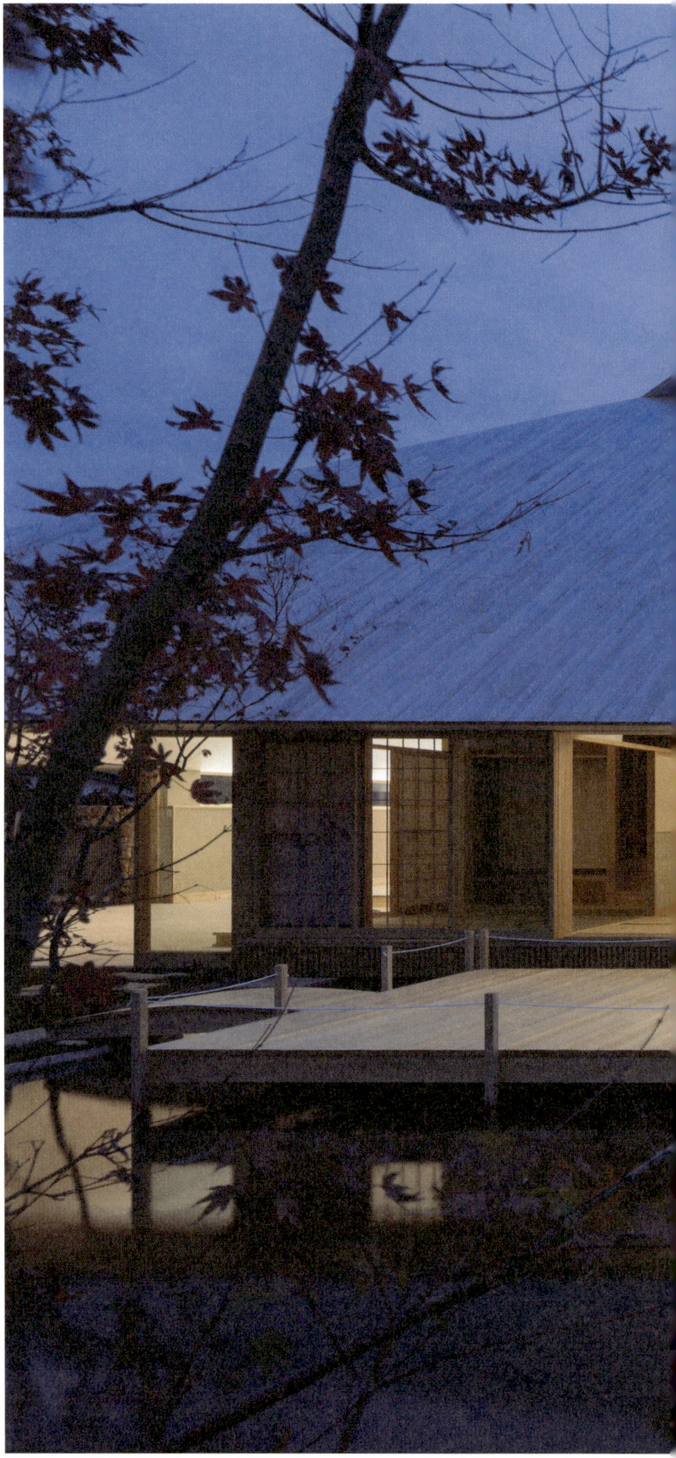

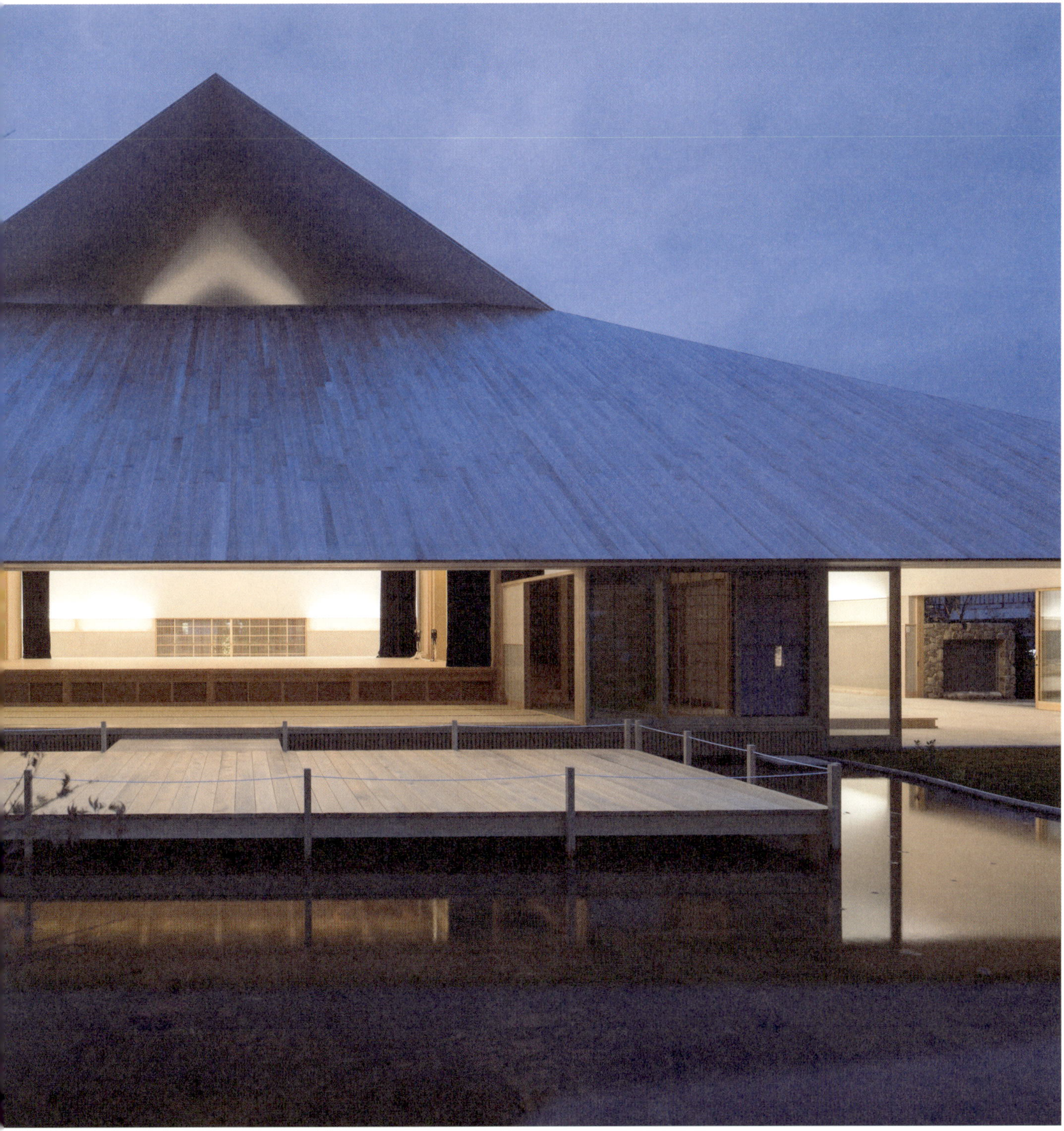

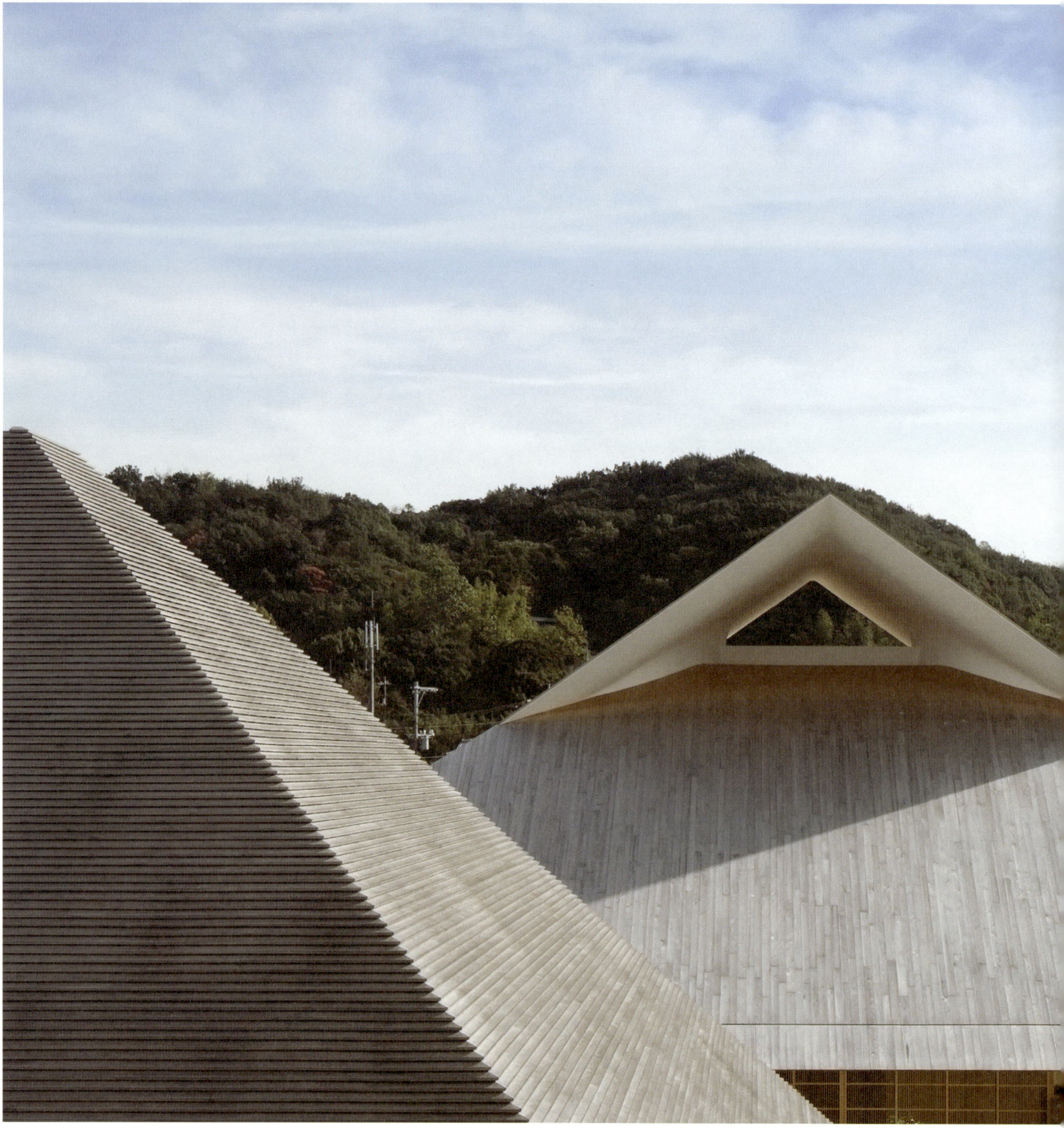

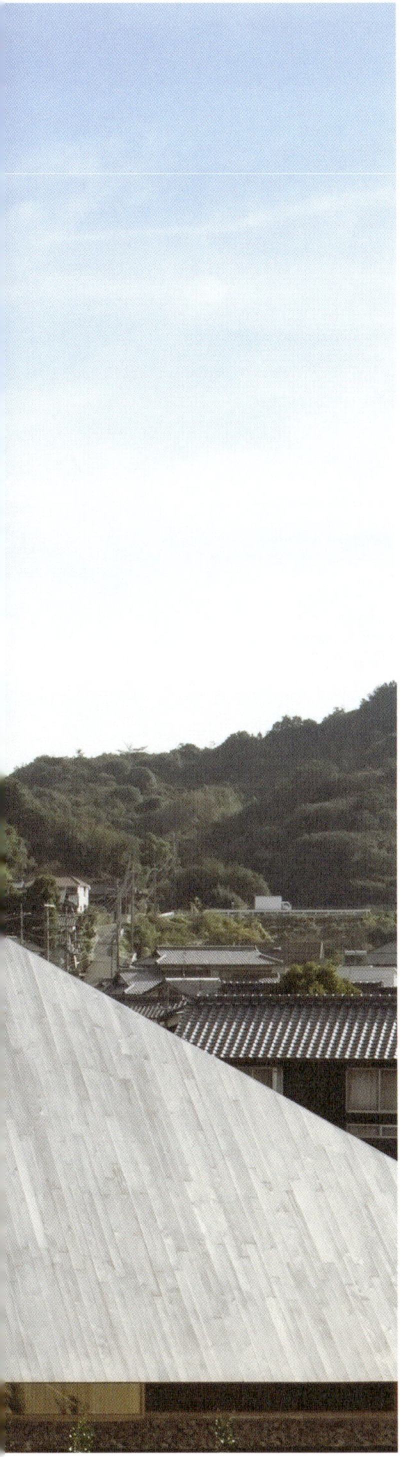

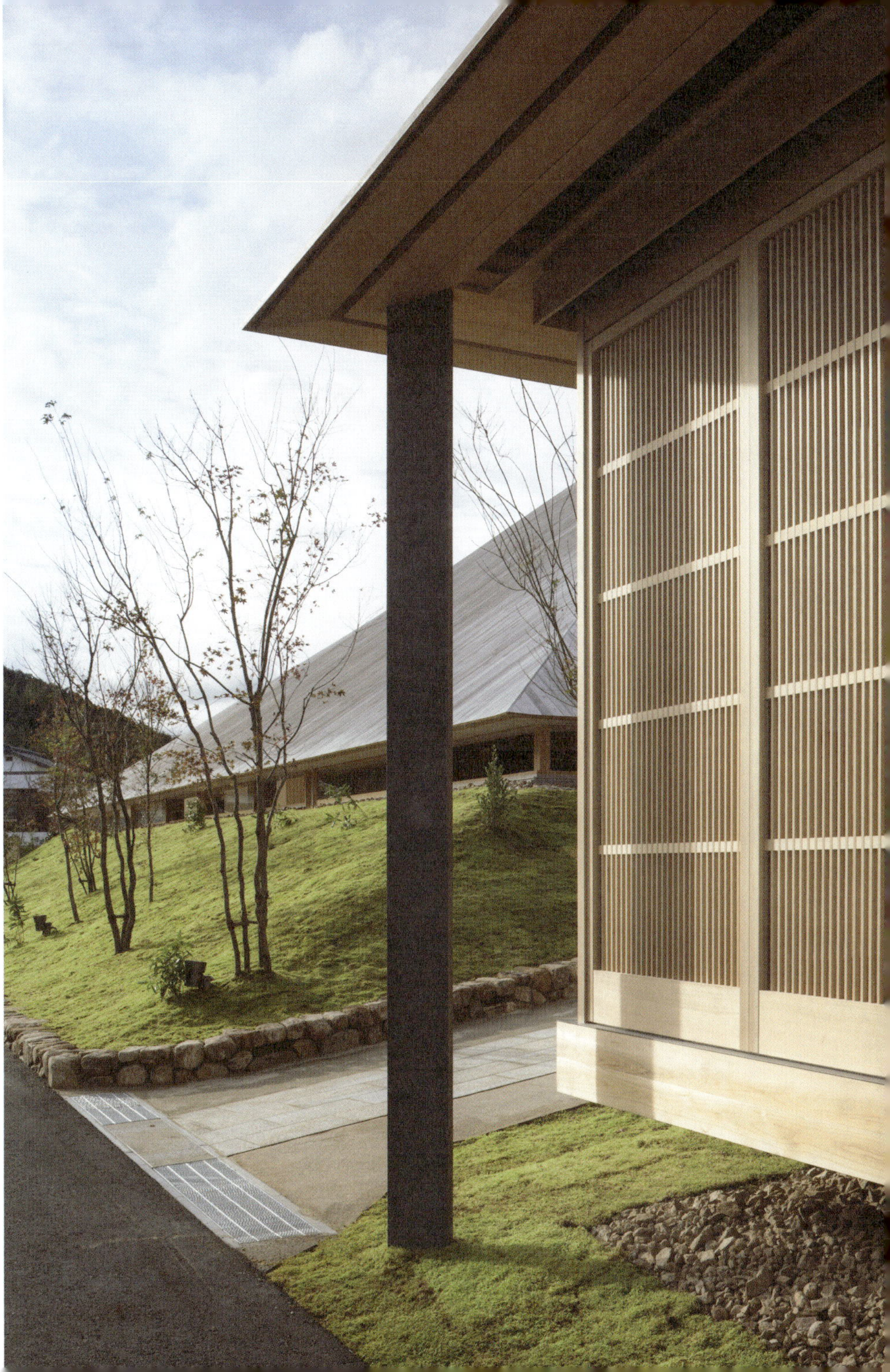

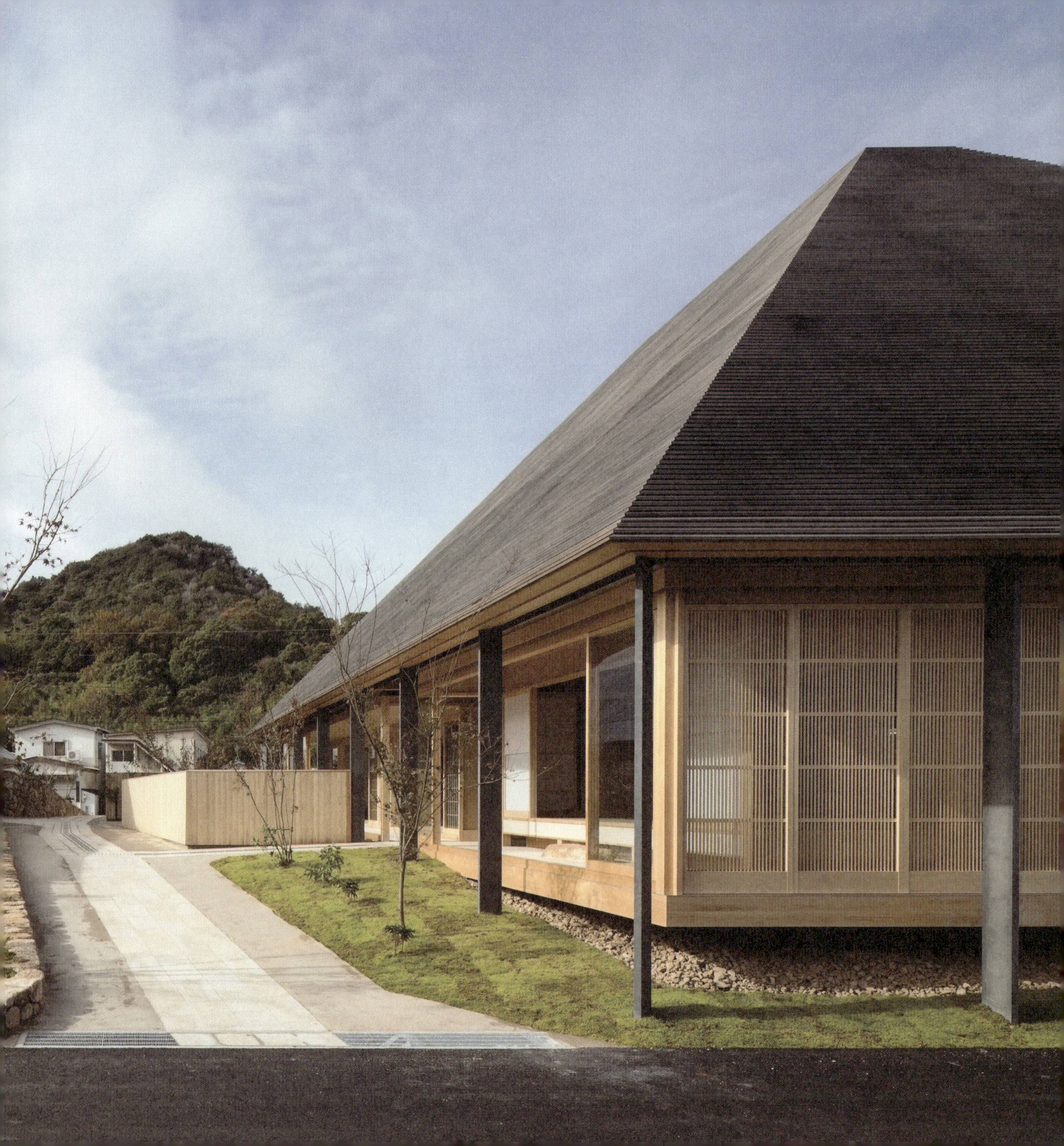

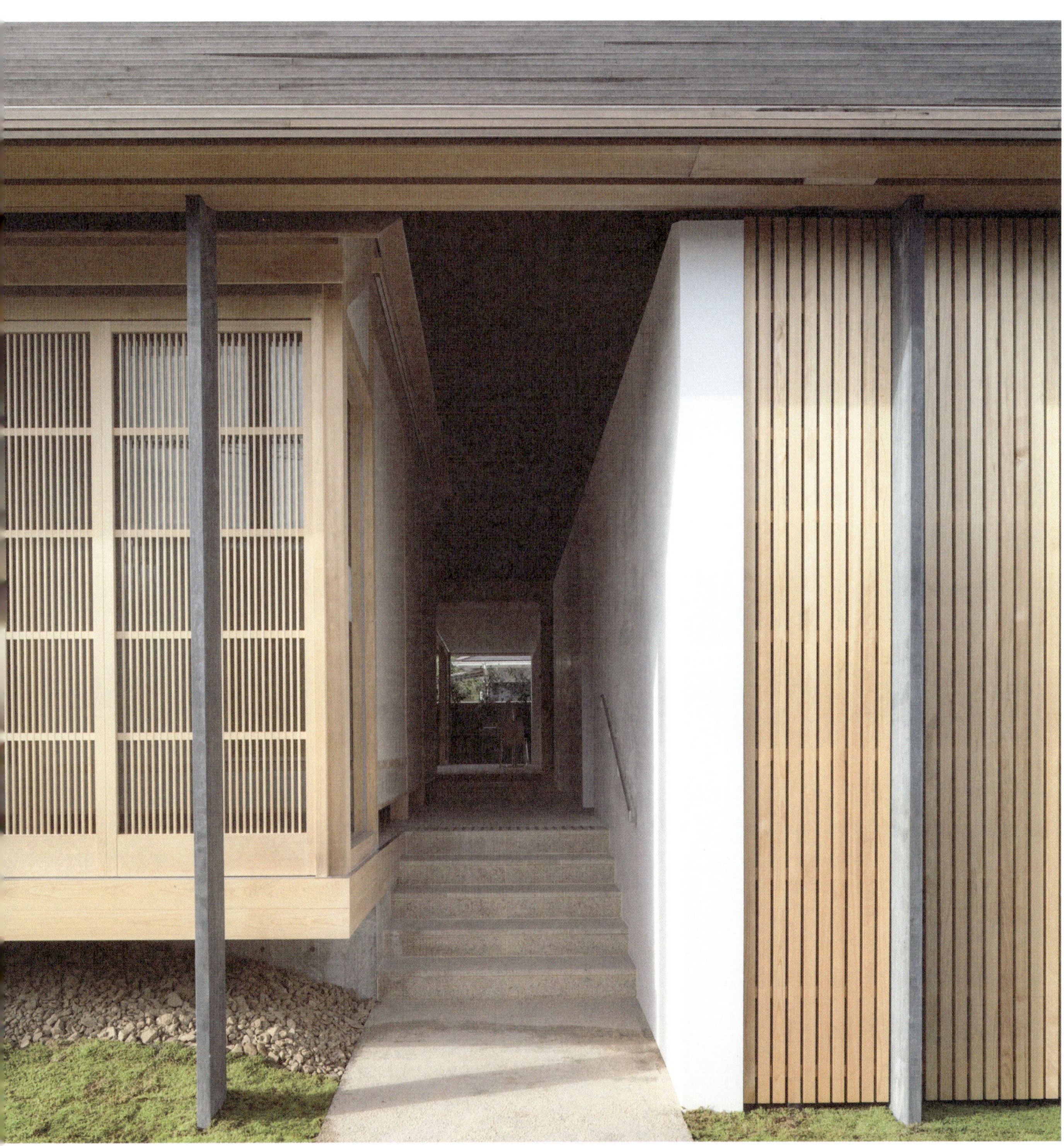

0 5 10M

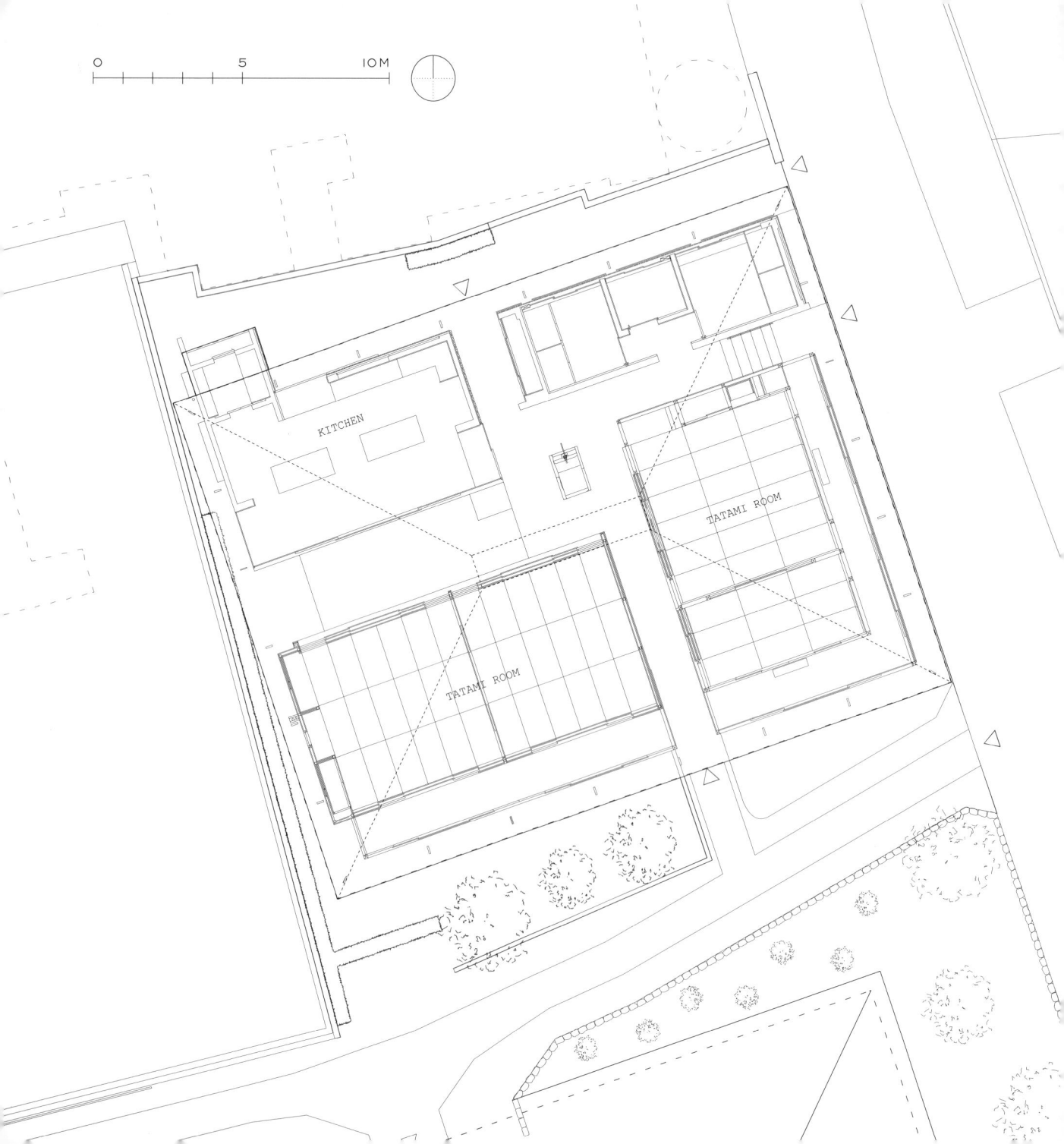

KITCHEN

TATAMI ROOM

TATAMI ROOM

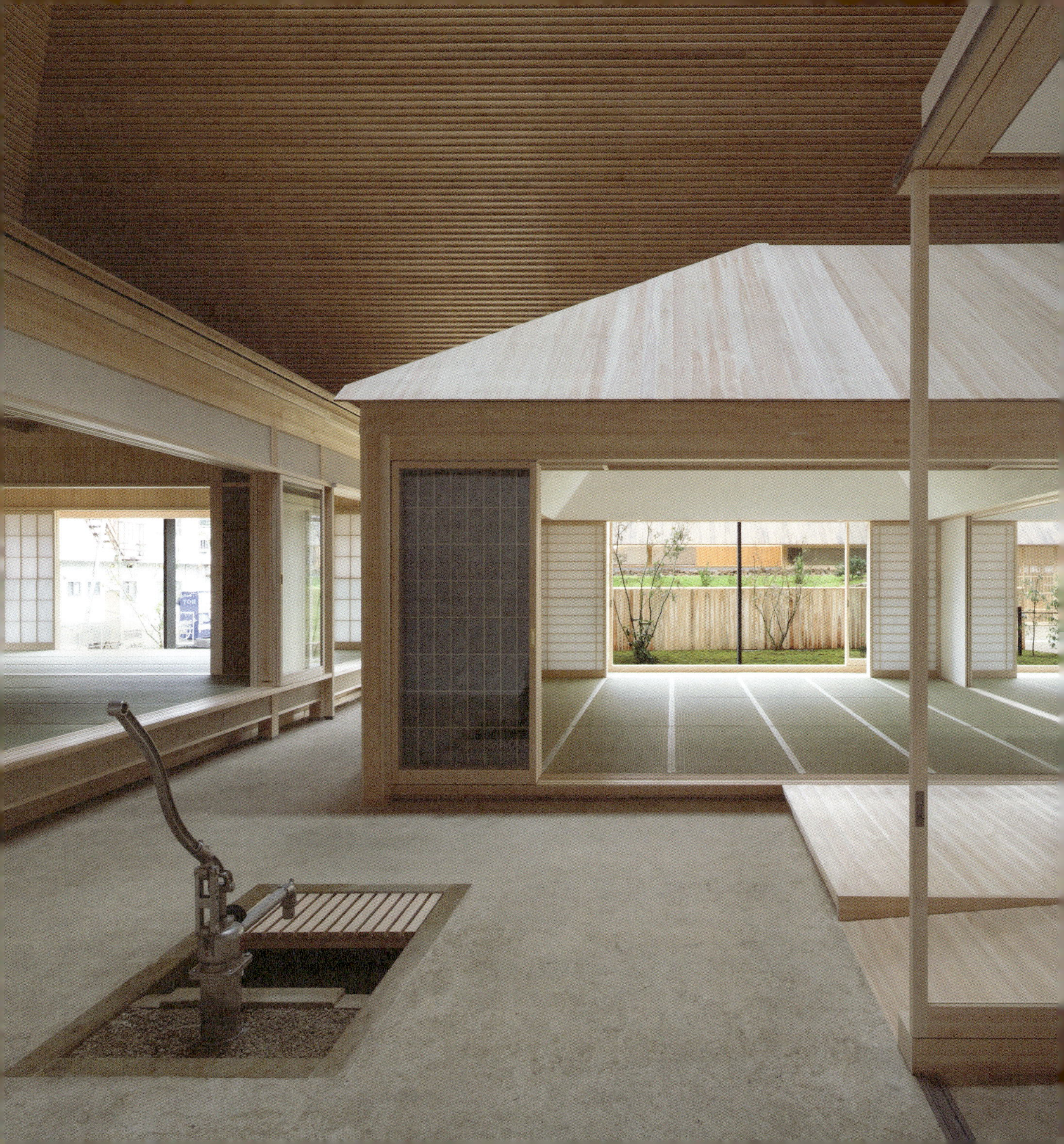

ルーバー受材

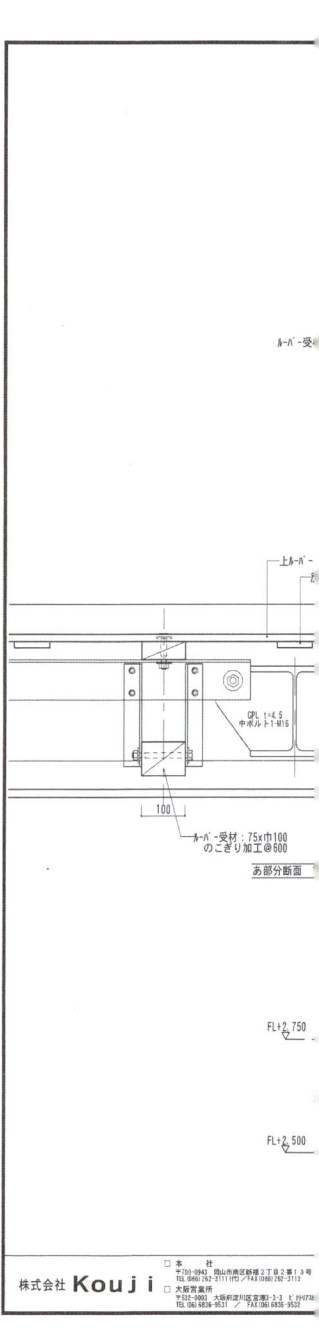

上ルーバー

CPL t=4.5
中ボルト1-M16

ルーバー受材：75×巾100
のこぎり加工@600

あ部分断面

FL+2,750

FL+2,500

株式会社 Kouji

□ 本　社
〒700-0942　岡山市南区新福2丁目2番13号
TEL (086) 262-3111代／FAX (086) 262-3113

□ 大阪営業所
〒532-0001　大阪府淀川区宮原3-3-31 PR972
TEL (06) 6836-9531／FAX (06) 6836-9532

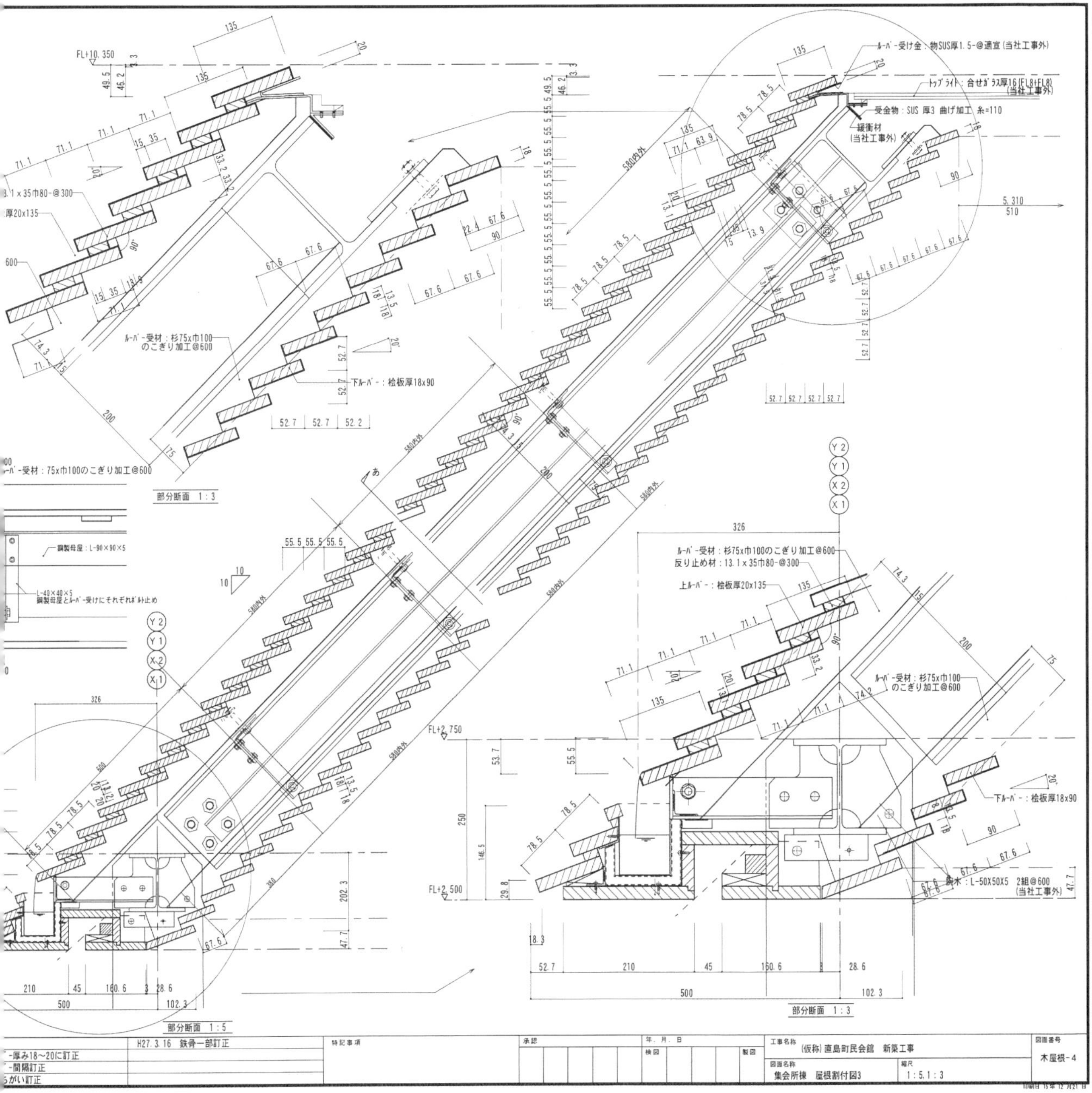

H27.3.16 鉄骨一部訂正	特記事項	承認	年.月.日	工事名称 (仮称)直島町民会館 新築工事	図面番号 木屋根-4
ー厚み18〜20に訂正			検図 / 製図	図面名称 集会所棟 屋根割付図3	縮尺 1:5, 1:3
ー間隔訂正					
らがい訂正					

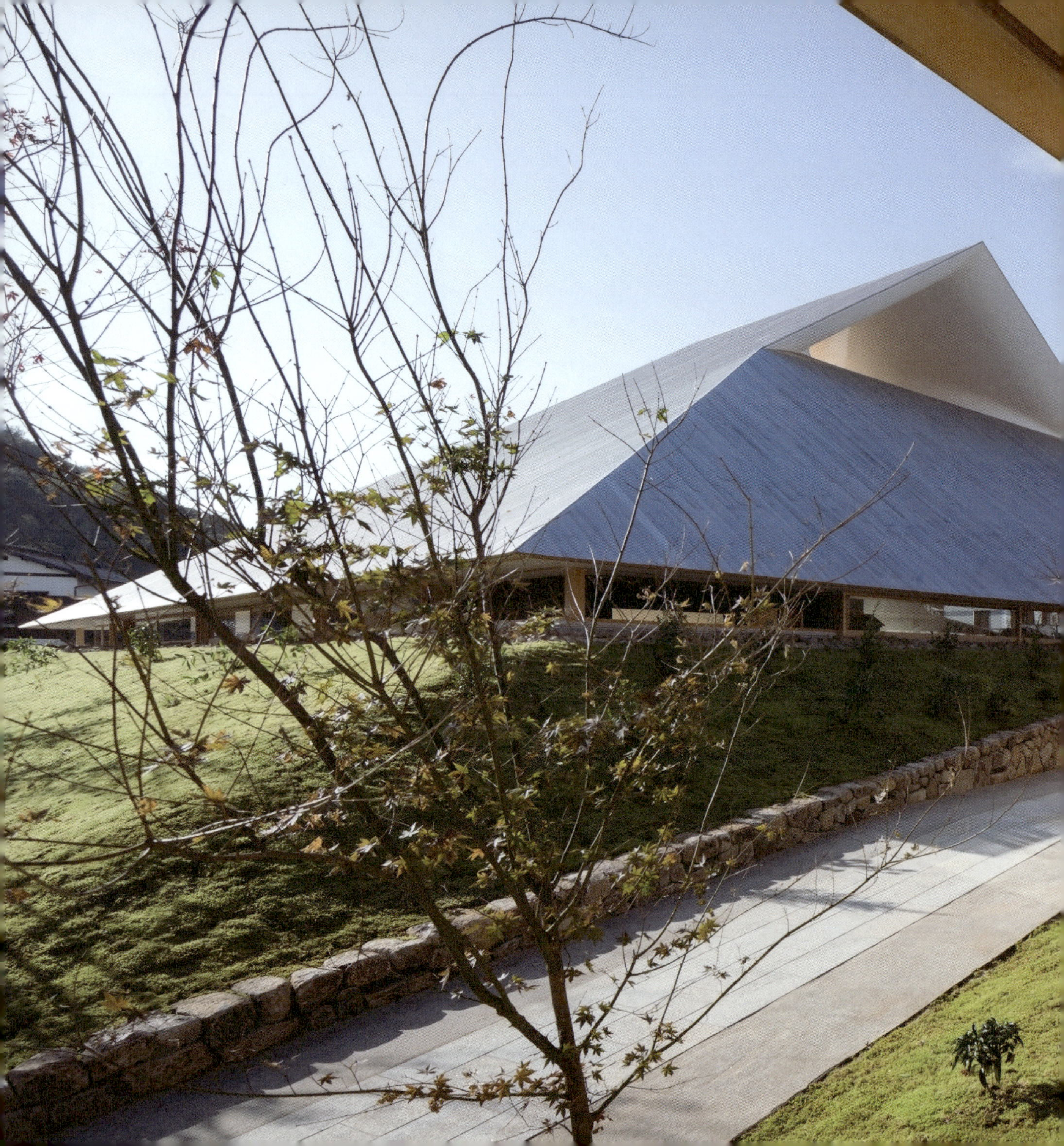

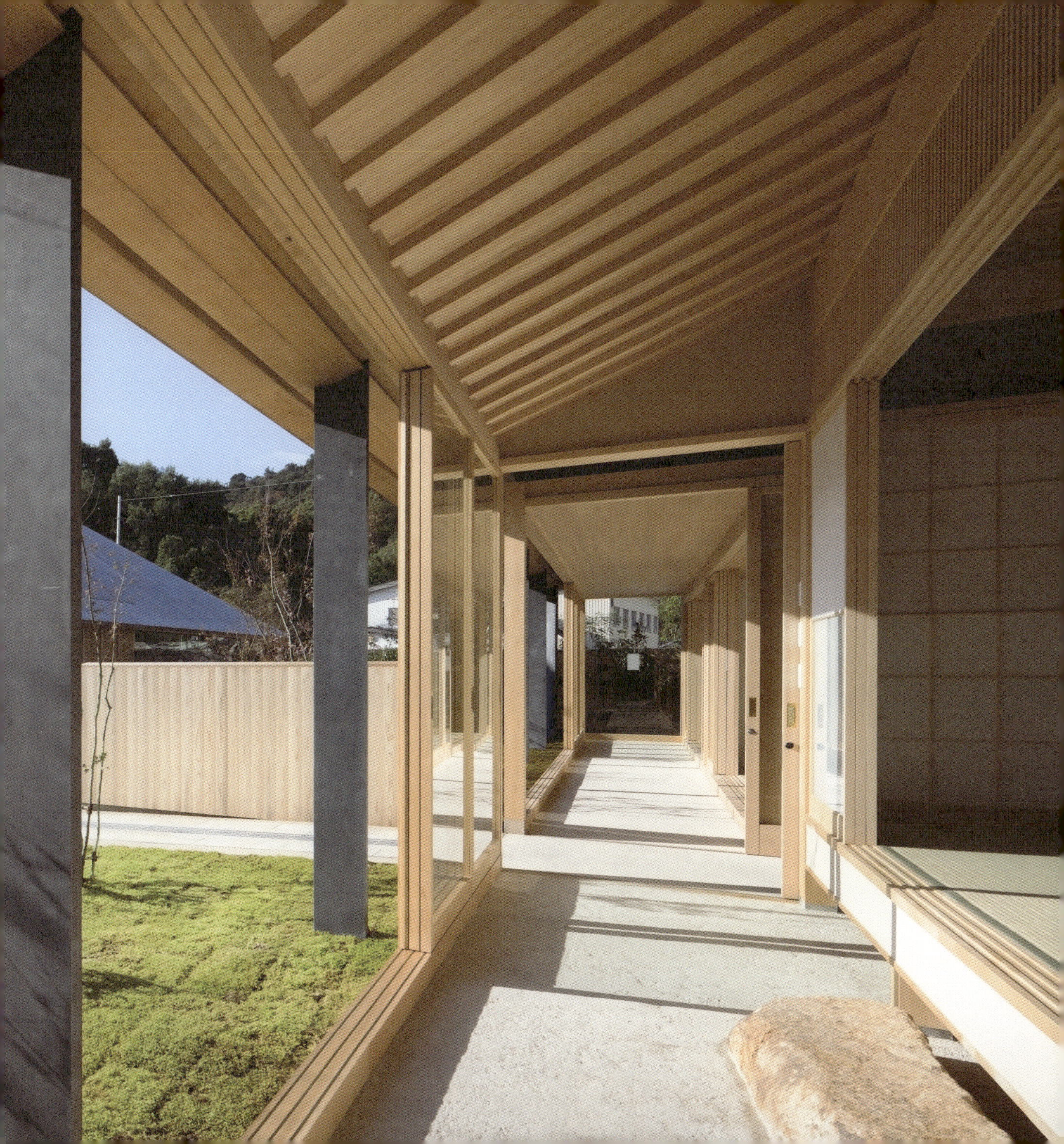

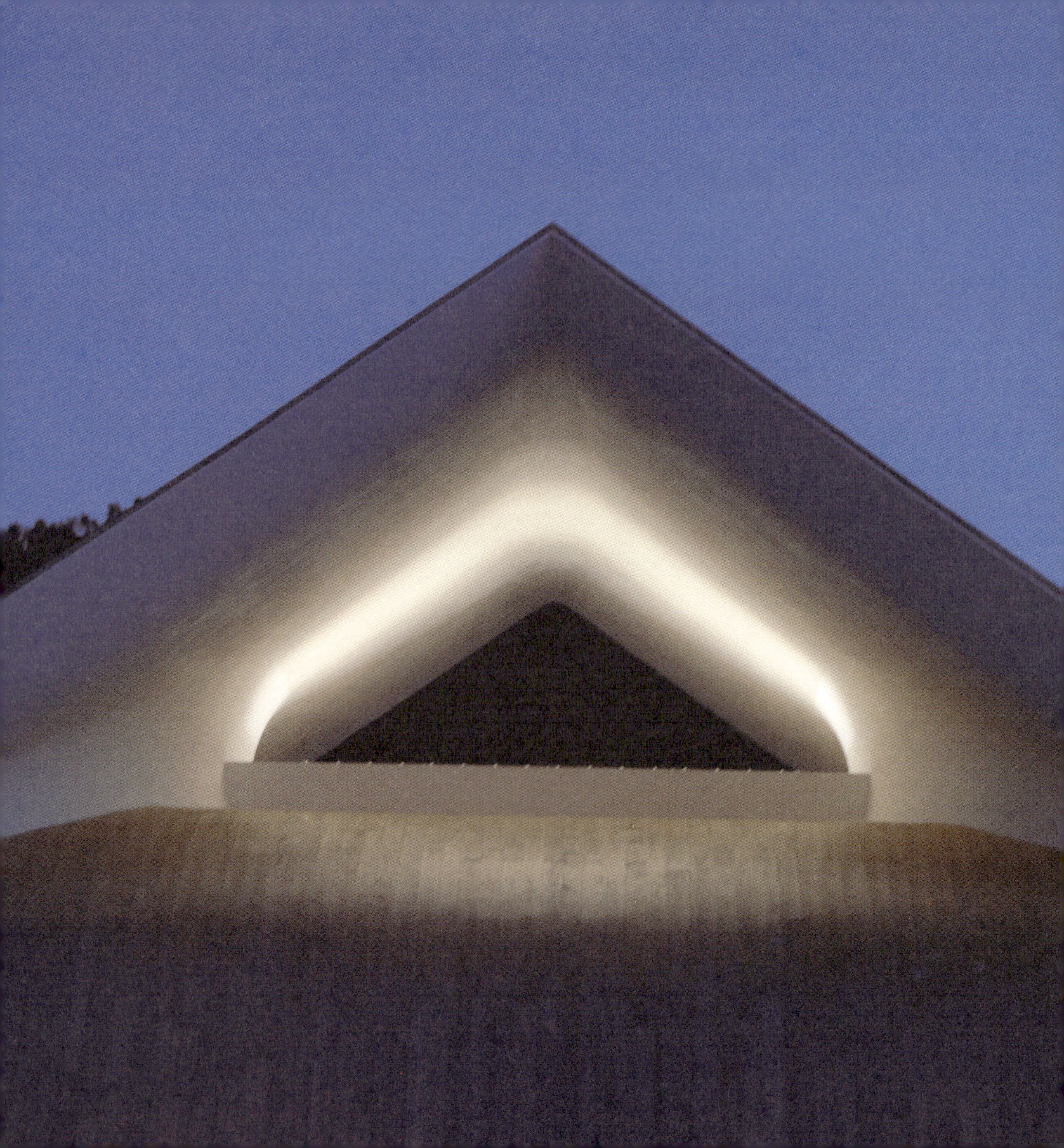

地球、あるいは瀬戸内海

千代章一郎／建築論

環境としての建築：「地球のディテール」

レイナー・バンハムが『環境としての建築』を著したのは、1969年である。「建築の解体」をもたらしたアーキグラムの提案が、「プラグイン」の都市から完全制御された衣服をまとう身体へと拡張していく時期である。言うまでもなく、それは（たとえ自虐的であるにしても）機械時代の進歩に対する盲目のなせる技である。その素朴な論理ゆえに、かえって庇護される空間をいかに制御し、快適に住むのかという原初的な動機を露わにしてもいる[1]。建築の空間は果てしなく高度に洗練され、もはや建築様式を無力化して環境としてどこまでも拡がっていくと同時に、また原初的な住まいへの問いに直面している[2]。環境制御技術の追求は、バックミンスター・フラーが「宇宙船地球号」[3]を、リチャード・ロジャースが「この小さな惑星」[4]を問題にしたように、巨視的な眼差しが求められると同時に、人間の身体の追求という微視的な眼差しが求められる。おそらく、アーキグラムの活動の軌跡はその最初の徴候である。

三分一が「地球のディテール」に言及する時、それはやはり「宇宙船地球号」や「惑星」と基本的には同義である。しかし、三分一の「地球」は「ディテール」を含んでいる。微視的なのである。よくよく考えてみれば、「地球のディテール」とは不思議な命名である。ディテールを見れば地球を見ることも感じることもできない。地球を俯瞰して見れば、ディテールはかすんでいく。

調停は、「リサーチ」と三分一が呼ぶ敷地周辺の環境調査である。三分一の建築を理解する上で最も大切なプロセスである。もちろん、現場に足を運ばない建築家はいないであろうし、そこからインスピレーションを受け、建築家自身の内在的思考が揺さぶられて新たな創造へと建築家は飛躍していく。一方で建築家は、感覚によらずとも、より科学的で実証的なデータを採取して体系的に空間に反映させることもできる。三分一は互いに矛盾するであろう両方をあたり前のように実践する。しかしそれ以前に、三分一自身が六甲の山頂で、弥山の山頂で、さまざまな現場においてカメラを携えて自らの身体を浸し、時には何日もかけて「リサーチ」する。得られたデータそのものにパラダイムの誤謬や暗黙の経験値が潜むことがあるかもしれない。それでも、「リサーチ」は、まるで神々を招聘する儀式のように、環境と人間が相即であることを自覚するために必要な行為である。この観点から『環境としての建築』を読むと、バンハムは（そして取り上げられている建築家たちは）徹頭徹尾、環境を対象化していることがわかる。対象化した上で、人間との関係を建築的に構築していく[5]。それに対して、三分一はまずもって環境と同化してしまうのである。

作為としての自然：「風・水・太陽」

「リサーチ」で三分一が最も注視し、あるいは自然を自然として体感していると自覚するのが、「風・水・太陽」である。しかし、それは要素還元主義的な論理ではない。空間的な感性の論理である。「もの」ではなく、あくまで「こと」、すなわち現象そのものが感性に触れる。自然現象と言ってしまえばそれまでであるが、三分一はそこに自然の作為を感

じ取る。ル・コルビュジエが「太陽・空間・緑」[6]と言う時、「24時間の太陽」の運動の軌跡がさまざまな人間的な空間を生み出し、自然と「調和」していく[7]。三分一がこの生動する空間を「風・水・太陽」という時、太陽はさまざまな空気の流れを生み出し、原初の環境を生み出し、自然が「自然」となっていく原動力そのものである。単に「光のもと」の建築のシンボル的光源ではない。「太陽のもと」で積み重なった歴史的環境はどこも唯一的であり、「風・水・太陽」という一般概念は地球上にはない。

そこには、すでに人間が含まれている。「風・水・太陽」という「動く素材」に育まれた環境は、それ自体作品である。作為と当為は相互反転する。リサーチと建築空間のためのシミュレーションとの境界は曖昧である。三分一は必ずと言ってよいほど作品を実現させる過程において(あるいは実現させてからも)シミュレーションを試みているが、それはシミュレーションという実験から定量的な解析結果を得てそれを形に反映させることだけを意味しない[8]。それ以上に、自然に身を浸すことのひとつの方法として、シミュレーションという行為そのものが重要である。ましてや、それがリサーチという儀式に支えられているのであれば、シミュレーションは作為の検証とは言い切れない。確かに、ル・コルビュジエはほとんど模型を製作してみせることはなかった。建築図面という2次元から3次元の空間を読み取ることを旨としていた。それもまた身を自然に近付けるひとつの方法論である。一方、三分一の事務所にはシミュレーションのためのオブジェ（模型）が散乱する。三分一の方法論の一端を示す象徴的な風景である[9]。

大地との邂逅

ル・コルビュジエはあくまで造形として建築を昇華させるために、あえて模型を用いることはなかった。建築図面を通じて、環境と響き合う造形を目指していた。この時、造形とその回りを取り囲む環境ははじめから別物である。一方、三分一はシミュレーションを通じて、その断片的な装置を通じて、「もの」ではなく「こと」を、端的に言えば空気を彫刻する（それゆえに、三分一の建築作品は「環境としての建築」にありがちなアンチ・モニュメンタリズムの立場[10]を取らない）。三分一は「リサーチ」によって環境と遭遇し、己が遭遇する他者を内面化する、しかしそれでも、内面化し得ぬものがあるがゆえに、他者を他者として自覚しつつシミュレーションを実践する。そこにはリサーチにおいて生じた目論見が否定されることもあるのかもしれない。それはいわば、大地との「邂逅の論理」[11]である。そのつねに一回的な行為、偶然性との遭遇の連鎖の中でこそ、三分一はディテールに「地球」を感じることができるのである。

丹下健三は、被爆地広島の土地を徹底的に造形として彫刻した。初めは否定していた慰霊の場を核とした都市のコアとして平和記念公園を彫刻した[12]。三分一は、瀬戸内という神々の遙かなる時間を内包した空気そのものを彫刻しようとしている[13]。歴史的に形成された伝統的技術をあからさまに現代の技術を使って解釈することはないにもかかわらず、三分一の建築作品に空間的な広がりと同時に歴史的な時間の広がりが感じられるゆえんである。大地との邂逅は、空間的な「同時的偶然」であると同時に、時間的な「経時的偶然」における所作でもある[14]。そこには、神社という形式によって一所にあらせられない神々の時間と場所を建立した先人[15]と同じ論理が横たわっているのかもしれない。確かに、三分一の建築は他にはない作品としての同一性を保有している。それゆえに、西洋の建築的伝統のさまざまな文脈で語ることもできる。そしてまた同時に、自らの建築作品としての同一性を否定して「地球のディテール」と邂逅していくがゆえに、西洋の建築的伝統から遠ざかっていくのである。

（1）身体への回帰は、空間における環境応答性への関心の本質的帰結である。たとえば、バーナード・ルドルフスキー、『建築家なしの建築』（1964）から『みっともない人体』（1971）への主題の推移。

（2）「建築家たちには、それにもう一つ先史時代について熟考すべきさらに深い理由がある。言語の構造と規範をまだ形骸化してしまう前に濫費する、熱病的言語の消費時代には、記号は熟することなく老化してその起源に逆戻りし、原始人の、言い換えればメトロポリスの岩塊の中で《原始的》状態に生きる人間の住居を思考することになる」（ブルーノ・ゼヴィ、鈴木美知訳、『建築の史的原型を探る』鹿島出版会、東京、1976、p.166）。「人間」「自然」への形而上学的問いを包含する近世の建築原初論とは異なって、今日の原型論はいくぶん即物的である（ジョゼフ・リクアート、黒石いずみ訳、『アダムの家』、鹿島出版会、東京、1995）。

（3）「われらの宇宙船のことで、わたしがおもしろく思うことがある。それが、ちょうど自動車と同じような、機械的な運搬器官だと言うことである。……この機械は、つねに円滑に動くためには、トータルなものとして理解し、手入れしなければならないのである」（R・バックミンスター・フラー、東野芳明訳、『宇宙船「地球号」』、ダイヤモンド社、東京、1972、pp.58-59）。おそらく、フラーの遺伝子を血肉化しない「エコロジカル・デザイン」はない。シム・ヴァンダーリン、スチュアート・コーワン、林昭男、渡和由訳、『エコロジカル・デザイン』、ビオシティ、東京、1997 を参照。

（4）「都市の必要性と、その必然としての都市の成長は、とどまるところを知らないのであるが、だからといって都市の生活が、文明の自壊を引き起こしてしまう性格をもつ必要はない。私は熱烈に信じる、建築と都市計画の技術が、私たちの未来を安全に守り、サステナブルで文明的な環境をもたらす都市を創造する手段に進化させることができるのだ」（リチャード・ロジャース、野城智也・和田淳・手塚貴晴訳、『都市 この小さな惑星の』、鹿島出版会、東京、2002、p.4）。

（5）「ランディの空気構造パヴィリオンと同じほど機械的に進歩したものにせよ、モーガンの学校と同じほど、最良の意味で、保守的なものにせよ、遠く離れた技術から借りた華奢な環境的指示に相応しい造形を発展させている、あるいは発展させはじめている、建築家たちを示しているのである。こういう相応しい造形が、一般に手近なものになったときにはじめて、調整環境が過去の一千年の建築と同じように得心のいくものとなるであろう」（レイナー・バンハム、堀江悟郎訳、『環境としての建築』、鹿島出版会、東京、1981、p.291）。『環境としての建築』終章。バンハムの著作の閉じ方は、取り上げる対象の新規性と比較して、著しく保守的である。

（6）「都市が拡張すればするほど、〈自然的条件〉は逆に軽視されるようになる。〈自然的条件〉とは、生物にとって欠くべからざる要素、太陽、空間、緑、が十分に存在するという意味である」。(Le Corbusier, La Charte d'Athènes, Plon, Paris, 1943, p.36 ; ル・コルビュジエ、吉阪隆正訳、『アテネ憲章』、鹿島出版会、東京、1976、p.65)。ル・コルビュジエの都市空間は何よりもまず、身体的健康、心理的快適性、精神的安寧のために存在する。どこまでも人間の身体に跳ね返ってくる環境としての「太陽・空間・緑」である。

（7）「自然は、混沌とした形－大空の丸天井、湖や海の断面、山々の輪郭－のもとに、われわれの目に現れる。われわれの目の前の風景は、ぼんやりと遠くに刻まれ、切り抜かれて、混乱でしかない。何一つとして、われわれが創り出した周囲の物と同じ輪郭をもつものはない。じかに見れば、自然は偶然的な混沌でしかない」。(Le Corbusier, Urbanisme, Flammarion, G. Crès et Cie, Paris, 1925, p.19 ; ル・コルビュジエ、樋口清訳、『ユルバニスム』、鹿島出版会、東京、1967、p.30)。「この混乱の時期にあっては［戦後復興期］、人間とその環境を形づくるこの根本原理にまでさかのぼらなければならない。人間とは一つの生物学として考えられたもの－心理的、生理的働きを有するものとしての人間である。環境とは、その永遠に変わらざる本質において新しく見直された環境のこと、すなわち、それは自然に他ならない……。自然の法則をもう一度見出すこと。そして人間とその環境－根本的な人間と深遠な自然を－を考察すること」(Le Corbusier, Manière de penser l'urbanisme, Éditions de L'Architecture d'Aujourd'hui, Paris, 1946, p.50 ; ル・コルビュジエ、坂倉準三訳、『輝く都市』、鹿島出版会、東京、1968、p.65)。自然に関するル・コルビュジエのふたつのテキストは、ル・コルビュジエの建築論の二面性を物語っている。すなわち、徹頭徹尾自然から自律した造形芸術としての建築作品、そして宿命的に一体となった自然の再発見としての人間的空間。その調和の様態は、両者が互いに関わり合いながら常に生動している状態のことである。

（8）「持続は、定義的に、シミュレートできない現象である。それは、つまり、シミュレーションは生命のような超合理的な現象に当てはめようとすると、全く確実に非合理的なものになるということである」（パオロ・ソレリ、工藤国雄訳、『生態建築論』、彰国社、東京、1977、p.129）。もちろん三分一は、ソレリのように、シミュレーション（あるいは実験）を排除して人間の精神的強度に依存するものではない。むしろ、持続している自然の中に人間が依存している諸要因を見いだす作業としてシミュレーションする。それはどこまでも仮説的である。

（9）しかし、三分一はクリエーションにおけるリサーチやシミュレーションの重要性を指摘しても、シミュレーションからクリエーションへの跳躍の論理については、語ることばをもっていない。あくまで身体的、感性的な事柄であるからである。

（10）アンチ・モニュメンタリズムにおける「記念碑的な構築物への再保証や心理的な指示の放棄」（バンハム、『前掲書』、p.267）は、やはりアーキグラムの系譜でもある。

（11）「「個物および個々の事象」の核心的意味は「一の系列と他の系列との邂逅」ということに存し、邂逅の核心的意味は可能にしないことも可能にあることをす、すなわち「無いことの可能」に存している。こうしてこれらすべてを根本的に規定している偶然性の根源的意味は、一者としての必然性に対する他者の措定ということである」（九鬼周造、『偶然性の問題』、岩波書店、2012（1935）、p.277）。三分一がリサーチという空間的な出会いを通じてシミュレーションという賽を振る時、それは偶然性との出会いの一形態である。予定調和の環境、一者としての建築空間を否定するものである。それゆえに、三分一の建築は「有機的建築」（フランク・ロイド・ライト）、あるいは「共生の思想」（黒川紀章）とは異質である。

（12）「私たちが考えた広島のコミュニティ・センターは、しかしきわめて特殊なものであった。それは広島市民生活再建の中核的な施設であるばかりではなく、さらに、あの広島の記憶を統一のある平和運動にまで展開させてゆくための実践的な機能をもった施設であって、それに加えて、記念塔のごときものの必要を認めなかったのである。

しかし、そのような判断にもかかわらず、私の心情は、迷わざるを得なかった。慰霊堂を含む記念塔は、広島の人びとが求めていることのなかに、意味があるように思えるのであった。無垢の犠牲者を、父や母や、妻や子にもつ広島の人びとの願いにたいして、何か慰霊し、祈念するための施設を、ささやかでも広島のためであるにしろ、もちたいと感じたのである。これが、私たちの答であった」（丹下健三、「廣島計畫（1946～1953）」、『新建築』、1954年1月）。そして丹下健三は、必ずしも慰霊の場は求められてはいなかった1949年の広島平和記念公園の設計競技において、「四つの記念的な施設－記念館－廣場－祈りの場所－原爆の遺蹟」を提案することになる（「廣島市平和記念公園及び記念館競技設計等選図案1等」、『建築雑誌』、第64輯、第756号、1949年、p.43。

（13）筆者：「ある時点で、かたちはこれで行こうと選択するわけですか」。三分一：「いやそうじゃなくて、徐々にまわりの環境を調整してボリュームが立ち上がっていくというか……。初めからモデルがあるわけじゃない」。（三分一建築設計事務所にて、2015年6月13日）。

（14）九鬼周造、『前掲書』、p.275。

（15）「本社ハ島の西北に在。故に、これを島の正面とし、佐伯郡の地方に相對して、其最近きは、鷄犬聞ふべし。東南のかたは地を去ること漸く遠く、正南ハ遙に伊豫に對し、西は周防の諸山を望む。嶋の地、清くして、樹木美しく、間ハずして、神ықの霊區たるを知しべ。弥山の嶺、高く聳え、大麓東北より、西南に亘りて、本社を擁す」（『安芸通史』巻十三、1825）。瀬戸内を巡行して安芸国厳島に鎮座した市杵島姫命（いちきしまひめのみこと）の社は、江戸時代にはすでに民衆の地であったが、詣での対象は、社と樹木が「間ハずして」渾然一体となった神聖な土地そのものであった。

THE EARTH, or THE SETO INLAND SEA
Shoichiro Sendai, architectural theoretician

Architecture as Environment: "Details of the Earth"

Reyner Banham wrote *The Architecture of the Well-Tempered Environment* in 1969. It covers the period of Archigram's proposals for the "dismantling of architecture," from the Plug-in City to their completely controllable clothing that envelops the body. Needless to say, they displayed a blindness (even assuming a degree of masochism) toward the progress of the machine age. As a consequence of this naive logic, rather than showing how protected spaces could be controlled, they revealed the primitive desire to create comfortable dwellings[1]. With a complete refinement of architectural space and neutralization of architectural style, they spread and connected throughout their environment while at the same time directly addressing the question of the primitive dwelling[2]. As problematized in Buckminster Fuller's *Operating Manual for Spaceship Earth*[3] and Richard Rogers' *Cities for a Small Planet*[4], the pursuit of technology for environmental control demands a macroscopic viewpoint, and simultaneously demands a microscopic view of the human body. Perhaps the earliest hints of this may be found in the activities of Archigram.

When Sambuichi speaks about the "details of the Earth," this is basically synonymous with the terms "Spaceship Earth" and "Small Planet." However, Sambuichi's "Earth" includes "details." These are microscopic. Thinking about it, "details of the Earth" is a mysterious term. If I observe the details, I cannot observe or feel the Earth. If I take an overall view of the Earth, the details are hidden.

Their reconciliation is achieved through studying the environment around the site, which Sambuichi calls "research." This process is very important in comprehending Sambuichi's architecture. Of course, most architects will visit the site and thereby receive inspiration, giving a jolt to their entrenched ways of thinking and inducing creative leaps. On the other hand, the architect does not have to depend on intuition, but may undertake a more scientific gathering of empirical data that will be systematically reflected in the architectural spaces. It is self-evidently true that Sambuichi practices both approaches, despite their apparent mutual exclusiveness. But beyond that, Sambuichi himself takes a camera and immerses his own body in various sites – the summit of Mount Rokko, the summit of Mount Misen – and sometimes does research for several days. Paradigmatic fallacies or implicitly subjective experiences may lie within the data so obtained. Nonetheless, just like a ceremony for summoning the gods, this research is necessary for gaining an awareness of the unity of the environment and human beings. From this viewpoint, when I read *The Architecture of the Well-Tempered Environment* I understand that Banham (and architects who follow him) thoroughly objectified the environment. According to this objectification, human beings and their relationships could be architecturally constructed[5]. By contrast, Sambuichi begins by assimilating the environment.

Nature as Artifice: "Wind, Water, Sun"

In doing research, Sambuichi makes close observations, or has a natural awareness through natural bodily sensations, of "wind, water, and sun." However, this is not the logic of elemental reduction. It is the logic of spatial intuition: an intuitive sensitivity not to "things" but always to "events," that is to say, to the phenomena themselves. Having described them as natural phenomena, Sambuichi can perceive the artifice of nature. When Le Corbusier proposed "sun, space, and verdure"[6] he used the centrifugal track of a "24-hour sun" to create various human spaces in "harmony" with nature[7]. When Sambuichi proposes "wind, water, and sun" for these spaces of vitality, the sun produces various air flows and an original environment, and is itself the motivating force for nature to become "nature." It is not merely the symbolic source of illumination for an architecture of the "essence of light." The historical environments that have accumulated under the "essence of sunlight" are everywhere unique, and generalized concepts of "wind," "water," and "sun" exist nowhere on Earth.

This already includes human beings. An environment nurtured by the "dynamic elements" of "wind, water, and sun" is itself a created work. Artifice and necessity are reciprocally inverted. The boundaries between research and simulations of architectural space are vague. Sambuichi, out of necessity we might say, tests simulations in the process of implementing a work (or even after it has been implemented), but having obtaining quantitative analytical results from these simulation experiments, it would be meaningless just to manifest these in the architectural forms[8]. Furthermore, as a method for immersing the body in nature, the artifice of simulation is important. Nonetheless, these simulations cannot be claimed as verifications of artifice if they are used to support the rituals of research. Certainly, Le Corbusier produced almost no models. His aim was to interpret three-dimensional spaces from two-dimensional architectural drawings. This is also a methodology for bringing the body closer to nature. On the other hand, objects (models) for simulations are scattered throughout Sambuichi's office. This scene symbolically displays one part of Sambuichi's methodology[9].

Encounters with the Earth

In order to sublimate architecture in sculptural forms, Le Corbusier always avoided using models. Through architectural drawings, he aimed at creating sculptural forms that would resonate with their environment. Consequently, these sculptural forms and their surrounding environments were exceptional from the outset. On the other hand, through simulations, through these fragmentary devices, Sambuichi, to speak frankly, sculpts the air not as a "thing" but as an "event" (which is why the architectural works of Sambuichi do not take the standpoint of anti-monumentalism[10] that is so common among works labelled "architecture as environment"). By means of "research," Sambuichi internalizes his confrontations with the environment and with other people, yet nonetheless some things cannot be internalized, so he implements simulations with an awareness of other people as other people. Perhaps the schemes that emerge from research may be rejected. This is the "logic of the encounter"[11] with the Earth, so to speak. It is because of the link between contingency and confrontation within these always-singular acts that Sambuichi can sense the "Earth" in the details.

Kenzo Tange moulded the ground at the site of the nuclear bombing of Hiroshima in a thoroughly sculptural way. He moulded the Hiroshima Peace Memorial Park as the core of the city, with the initially rejected venue for memorial services as its nucleus[12]. Sambuichi attempts to mould the air itself for the first time in the Seto region, in which lies latent the distant era of the gods[13]. Though he does not reinterpret traditional techniques for making historical forms by using unabashedly modern techniques, the architectural works of Sambuichi nonetheless induce a sense of expansion in space and a simultaneous expansion in historical time. Contained within these chance encounters with the Earth are performances of a spatial "synchronic contingency" and simultaneously a temporal "diachronic contingency."[14] Perhaps the same logic is latent in the form of Shinto shrines collectively built by our ancestors in the times and places of the absent gods[15]. Certainly, the architecture of Sambuichi possesses an identity found in the works of no one else. Simultaneously, he negates the identity of his own architectural works, which thereby become even further removed from the Western architectural tradition.

1) A return to the body is an unavoidable consequence of the interest in the environmental responsiveness of space. An example is the transformation undergone by the subject between Bernard Rudofsky's books *Architecture without Architects* (1964) and *The Unfashionable Human Body* (1971).

2) "Architects have another, more profound, reason for consulting prehistory. In an epoch of hasty, feverish building activity, when linguistic codes age without maturing and submit to wanton abuse even before they have been formalized, they revert to the original sources, to the habitat of uncivilized man and the underprivileged who live like aborigines within the metropolitan magma." Bruno Zevi, *The Modern Language of Architecture* (Seattle: University of Washington Press, 1978), p.222. Unlike the early modernist theory of the origins of architecture, which comprised a metaphysical questioning of "human being" and "nature," the theory of origins today is somewhat practical. See Joseph Rykwert, *On Adam's House in Paradise* (Cambridge, MA: The MIT Press, 1981).

3) "One of the interesting things to me about our spaceship is that it is a mechanical vehicle, just as is an automobile. ... an integrally-designed machine which to be persistently successful must be comprehended and serviced in total." R. Buckminster Fuller, Operating Manual for Spaceship Earth (Carbondale: Southern Illinois University Press, 1969), p.16. Probably there are no examples of "ecological design" that do not incorporate the genetic inheritance of Fuller. I refer to Sim Van der Ryn and Stuart Cowan, *Ecological Design* (New York: Island Press, 1996).

250

4) "While the need for cities and the inevitability of their continued growth will not diminish, city living per se need not lead to civilisation's self-destruction. I passionately believe that the arts of architecture and city planning could be evolved to provide crucial tools for safeguarding our future, creating cities that provide sustainable and civilising environments." Richard Rogers, *Cities for a Small Planet* (London: Basic Books, 1998), p.4.

5) "But some, perhaps most, of the buildings discussed in this book show architects evolving, or beginning to evolve, forms which are not the borrowed finery of far-out technology, but forms proper to the environmental proposition being made, whether that proposition is as mechanically advanced as Lundy's inflatable pavilion, or as conservative, in the very best sense of the word, as Morgan's school. Only when such proper forms are commonly at hand will the architecture of the well-tempered environment become as convincing as the millennial architecture of the past." Reyner Banham, *The Architecture of the Well-Tempered Environment* (London: Architectural Press, 1969), p.289. This is from the last chapter of *The Architecture of the Well-Tempered Environment*. Banham's way of closing the book is remarkably more conservative than the novelty of the topic being addressed.

6) "The more the city expands, the less the 'conditions of nature' are respected within it. By 'conditions of nature' we mean the presence, in sufficient proportions, of certain elements that are indispensable to living beings: sun, space, and verdure." Le Corbusier, *The Athens Charter* (New York: Grossman, 1973), p.58. The urban spaces of Le Corbusier exist above all for physical health, psychological comfort, and mental tranquillity. The environment of "sun, space, and verdure" everywhere reverts back to the human body.

7) "Nature presents itself to us as a chaos; the vault of the heavens, the shapes of lakes and seas, the outlines of hills. The actual scene which lies before our eyes, with its kaleidoscopic fragments and its vague distances, is a confusion. There is nothing there that resembles the objects with which we surround ourselves, and which we have created. Seen by us without reference to any other thing, the aspects of Nature seem purely accidental." Le Corbusier, The City of To-morrow and Its Planning (New York: Payson & Clarke Ltd, 1929), p.24. "En cette heure de trouble [the postwar reconstruction period], on remonte aux principes mêmes qui constituent J'humain et son milieu. L'homme considéré comme une biologie, – valuer psycho-physiologique; le milieu exploré à nouveau dans son essence permanente: et ce sera la nature... Retrouver a loi de nature. Et considerer l'homme et son milieu, – l'homme fondamental et la nature profonde." Le Corbusier, *Manière de penser l'urbanisme* (Paris: Éditions de L'Architecture d'Aujourd'hui, 1946), p.50. These two texts on nature by Le Corbusier indicate the duality of his architectural theories. That is to say, from pure nature to architectural works as autonomous sculptures, and human spaces as the rediscovery of an inevitable unity with nature. This harmonious state becomes a vital condition when the two sides are engaged with each other.

8) "Duration is, by definition, a non-simulatable phenomenology. That is, simulation is strictly irrational when applied to the ultra-rational phenomenon that life is." Paolo Soleri, *The Bridge Between Matter and Spirit is Matter Becoming Spirit: The Arcology of Paolo Soleri* (New York: Anchor Books, 1973), p.109. Of course, Sambuichi excludes Soleri-like simulations (or tests) and does not depend on human mental strength. Rather, the task of simulations is to discover the factors on which human beings depend within the duration of nature. This is always hypothetical.

9) However, even if Sambuichi emphasizes the importance of research and simulation in the process of creation, he has no words to describe the logic of the leap from simulation to creation. That is because it is always a physiological and emotional matter.

10) The anti-monumentalism of the statement "Such willingness to abandon the reassurances and psychological supports of monumental structure" (Banham, op. cit., p.265) is also part of the genealogy of Archigram.

11) "The core meaning of 'individuality and individual phenomena' exists in the 'encounter of one system and another system,' and the core meaning of the chance encounter is that the chance encounter may not have occurred, that is to say, it exists in the 'possibility of non-existence.' In this way, the primordial meaning of the contingency that fundamentally prescribes all of this is that inevitability for one person is supposition for another person." Shuzo Kuki, *Guzensei no Mondai [The Problem of Contingency]* (Tokyo: Iwanami Shoten, 2012 [1935]), p.277. When Sambuichi shakes the dice of simulation throughout the spatial encounters of research, this is one form of encounter with contingency. It is an opportunity to deny the Prastabilierte Harmonie (pre-established harmony) of the environment and architectural space as one person. For that reason, the architecture of Sambuichi differs from "organic architecture" (Frank Lloyd Wright) and "the philosophy of symbiosis" (Kisho Kurokawa).

12) "Our idea for the Hiroshima Community Centre is something exceedingly special. Not only is it the core facility for the rebuilding of civic life in Hiroshima, it is also a facility with the practical function of allowing a unified peace movement to develop memories of Hiroshima, and furthermore it is unnecessary for it to be recognizable as a commemorative monument.
However, in spite of such judgments, my feelings were at a loss. I felt that there was meaning in the demands from the people of Hiroshima for a monument that included a memorial service temple. With regard to the wishes of the fathers and mothers and wives and children of the innocent victims of the people of Hiroshima, I felt there should be a modest facility for prayer and memorial services. This is our response." Kenzo Tange, *"Hiroshima Plan (1946–1953)"*, Shinkenchiku, January 1954. So in the 1949 design competition for the "Hiroshima Peace Memorial Park," in which a place for memorial services was not a requirement, Kenzo Tange proposed "four commemorative facilities: memorial hall, plaza, prayer room, atomic bomb ruins." Kenzo Tange, *"Hiroshima Peace Memorial Park and Memorial Design Competition, First Prize-Winning Proposal"*, Kenchiku Zasshi, vol. 64, no. 756, October–November 1949, p.43.

13) Sendai: "At a certain point in time, do you choose the form you will use?" Sambuichi: "No, it's not like that, rather the volume gradually takes shape through adjustments to the surrounding environment. There are no models at the beginning." (At the office of Sambuichi Architects, 13 June 2015).

14) Shuzo Kuki, op. cit., p.275.

15) "This shrine is located in the northwest of Yashima. Therefore, it serves as the front of the island, corresponding to the area of the Saeki district, and in the immediate vicinity one may hear chickens and dogs. The land extends to the southeast, Iyo lies in the distance due south, and the various mountains of Suo can be seen to the west. The land of the island is pure, the trees and shrubs are beautiful, and without exception all of this should be regarded as the divine area of the shrine precinct. The peak of Yayama soars high, and this shrine embraces its foothills spanning from the northeast to the southwest." *Aki Tsuji* [Complete History of Old Hiroshima], volume 13, 1825. At the shrine devoted to Ichikishimahimenomikoto on Akiguni Itsukushima in the Seto region, already a populated area in the Edo period, the object of pilgrimage, the shrine, and the trees were "without exception" unified as sacred land.

安藝國

能美

宮島 弥山

島 江波
俵仁

地御前

府中 廣島

広島

HIROSHIMA

地形
EARTH

瀬戸に浮かぶ厳島や広島を囲う山々、広島を流れる川、橋、美しい街。

Nestled between mountains and flowing into the Seto Inland Sea lies the beautiful city of Hiroshima.

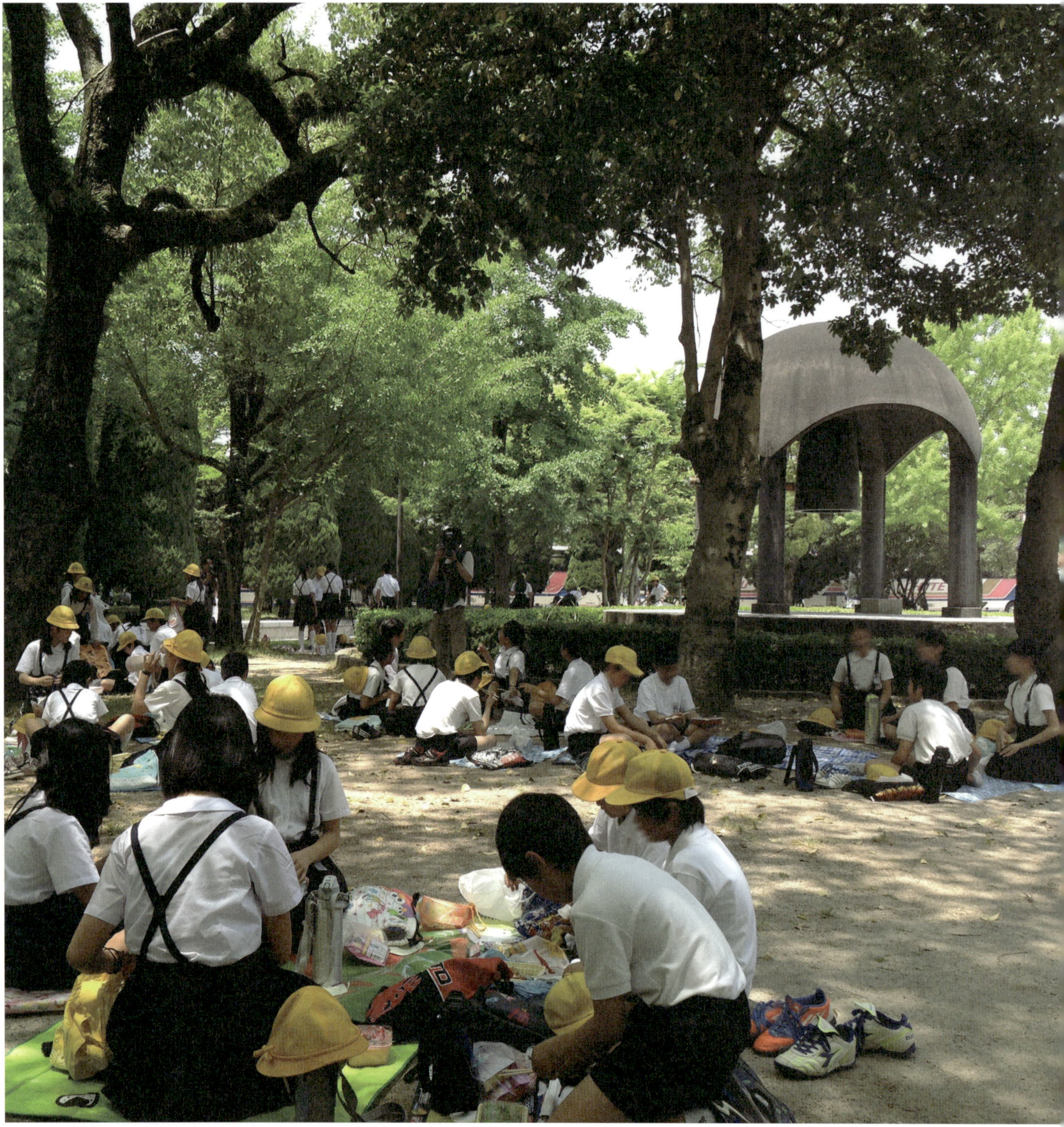

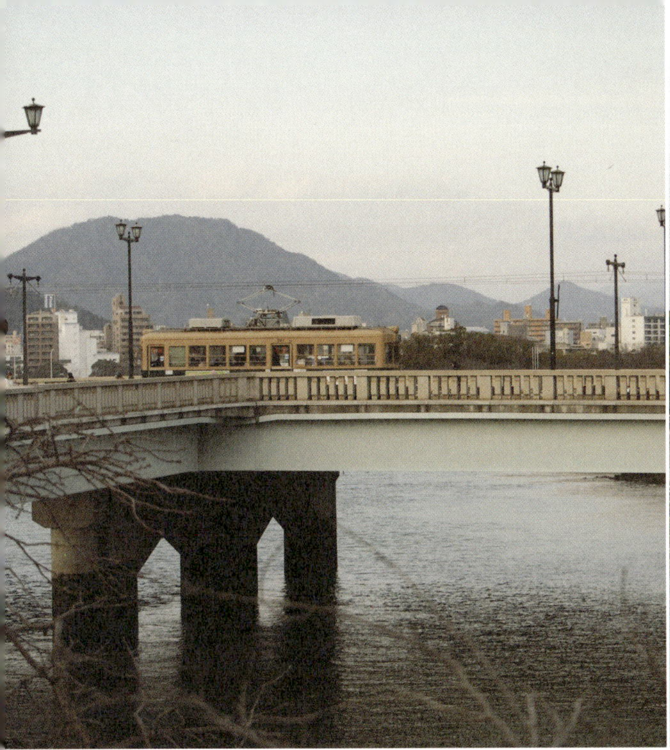

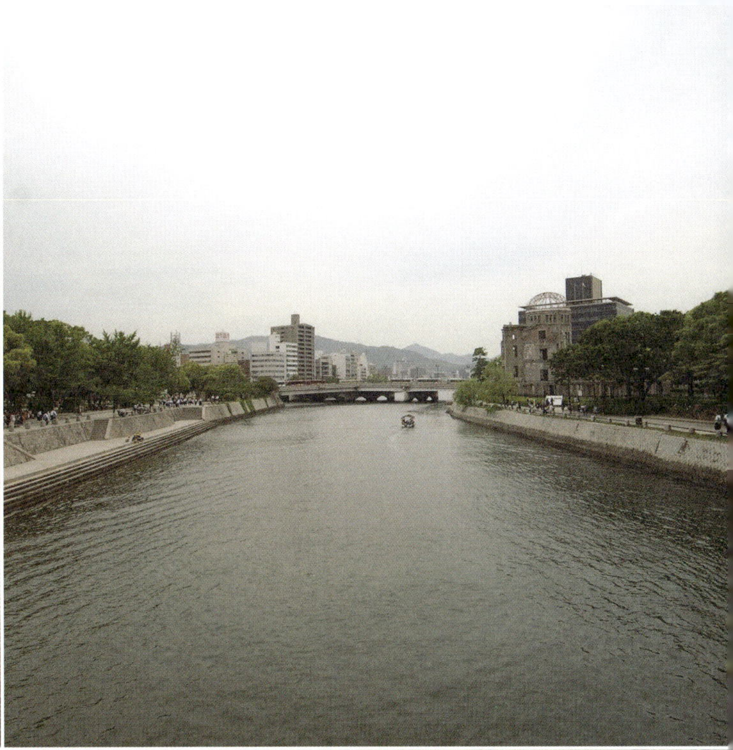

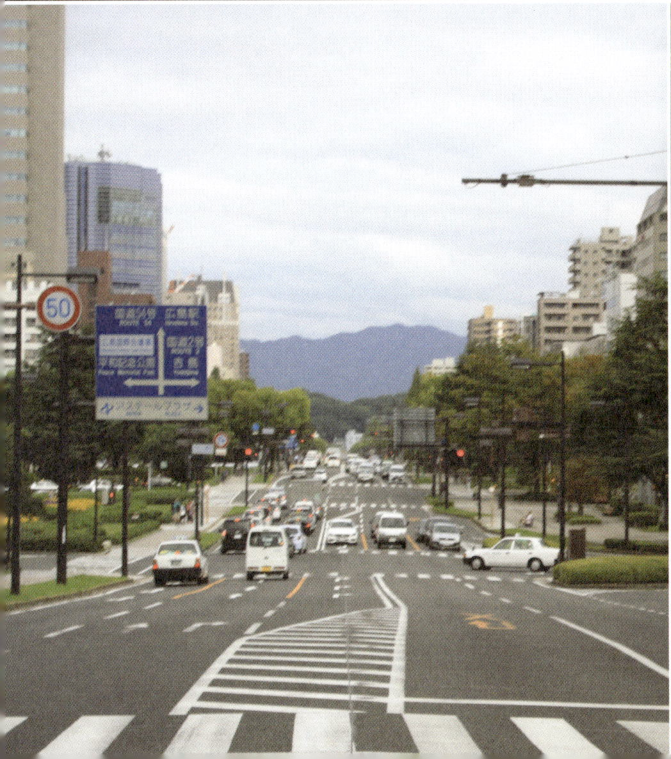
50

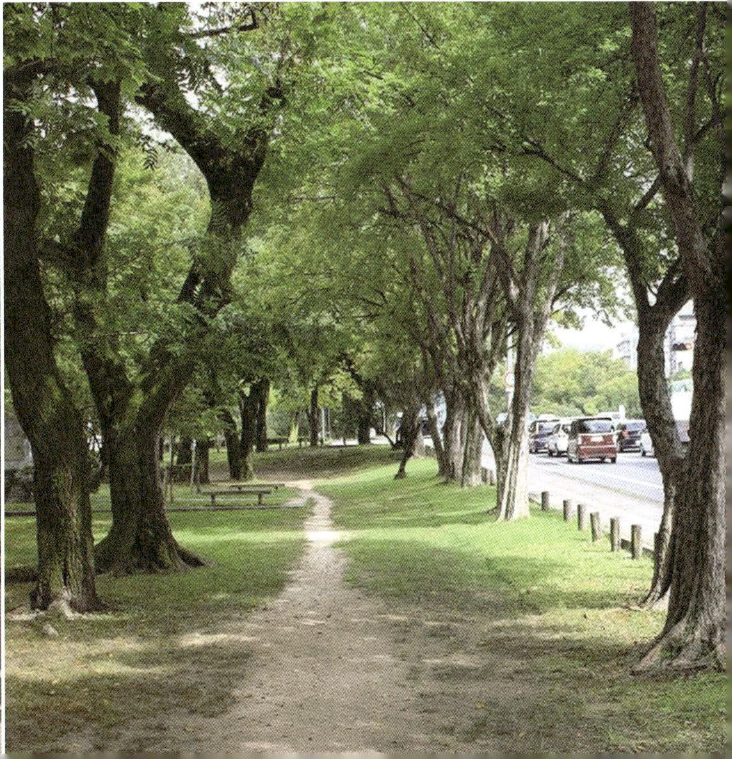

瀬戸の島々と広島の街は風・水を通して呼吸している。

The islands of the Inland Sea and the city of Hiroshima. Breathing wind and water.

広島の街と山の水は同じ水系でつながっている。清らかな水は常に人びとに豊かさを与えている。

The rivers of the city and the mountains are connected by the same water system.

すなわち広島の建物も地形であり、私にとっては水源の谷の地形と同じだ。風も同じように水源の谷にも都市の谷にも流れる。

The buildings of Hiroshima are also part of the terrain like the cliffs at the water source. The air flows similarly in the gorge as it does in the city.

rice field
水田

広島城　←　　　　→　seto inland sea　Miyajima
　　　　　peace

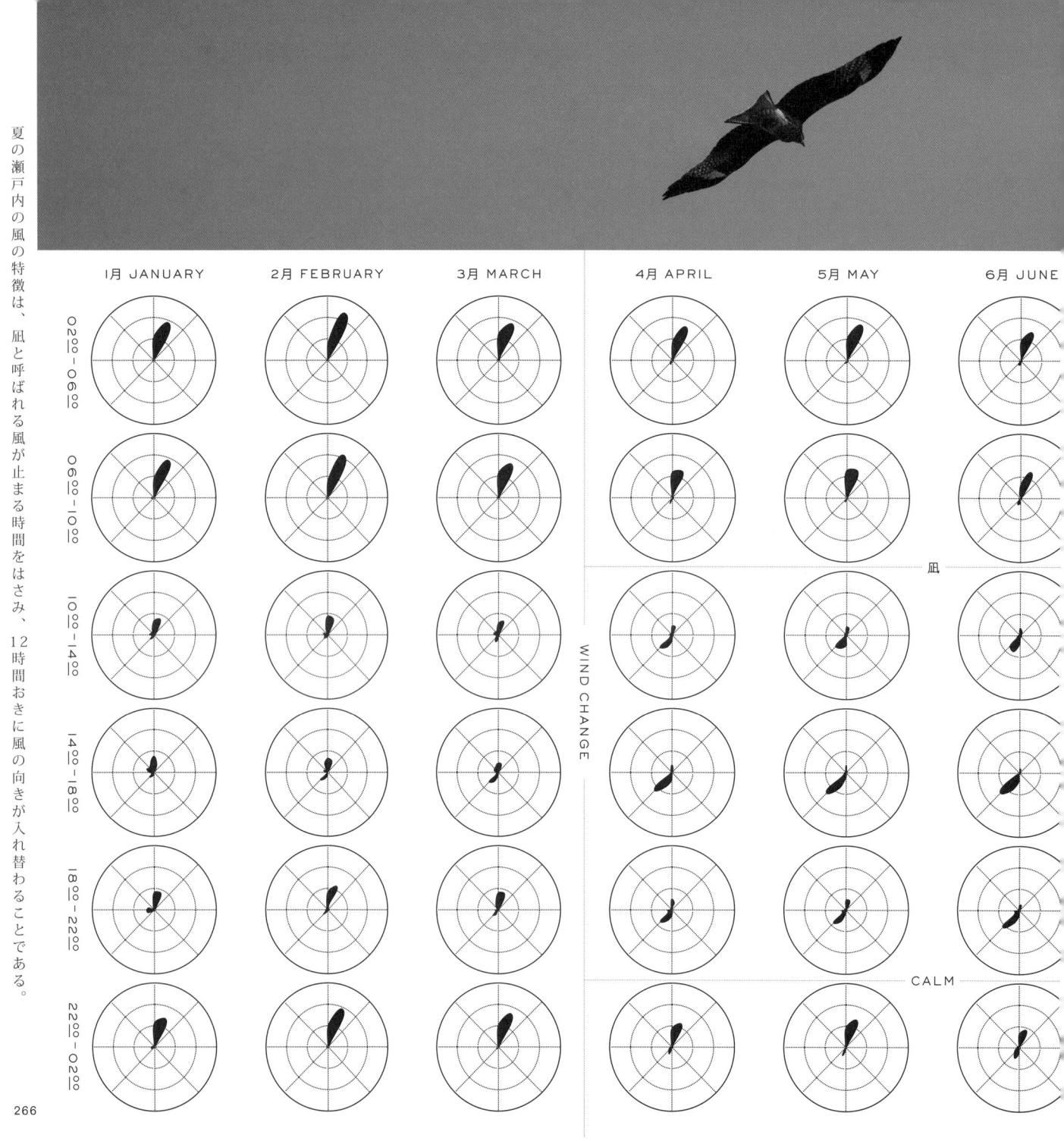

夏の瀬戸内の風の特徴は、凪と呼ばれる風が止まる時間をはさみ、12時間おきに風の向きが入れ替わることである。

1月 JANUARY　2月 FEBRUARY　3月 MARCH　4月 APRIL　5月 MAY　6月 JUNE

02:00–06:00
06:00–10:00
10:00–14:00
14:00–18:00
18:00–22:00
22:00–02:00

WIND CHANGE

凪

CALM

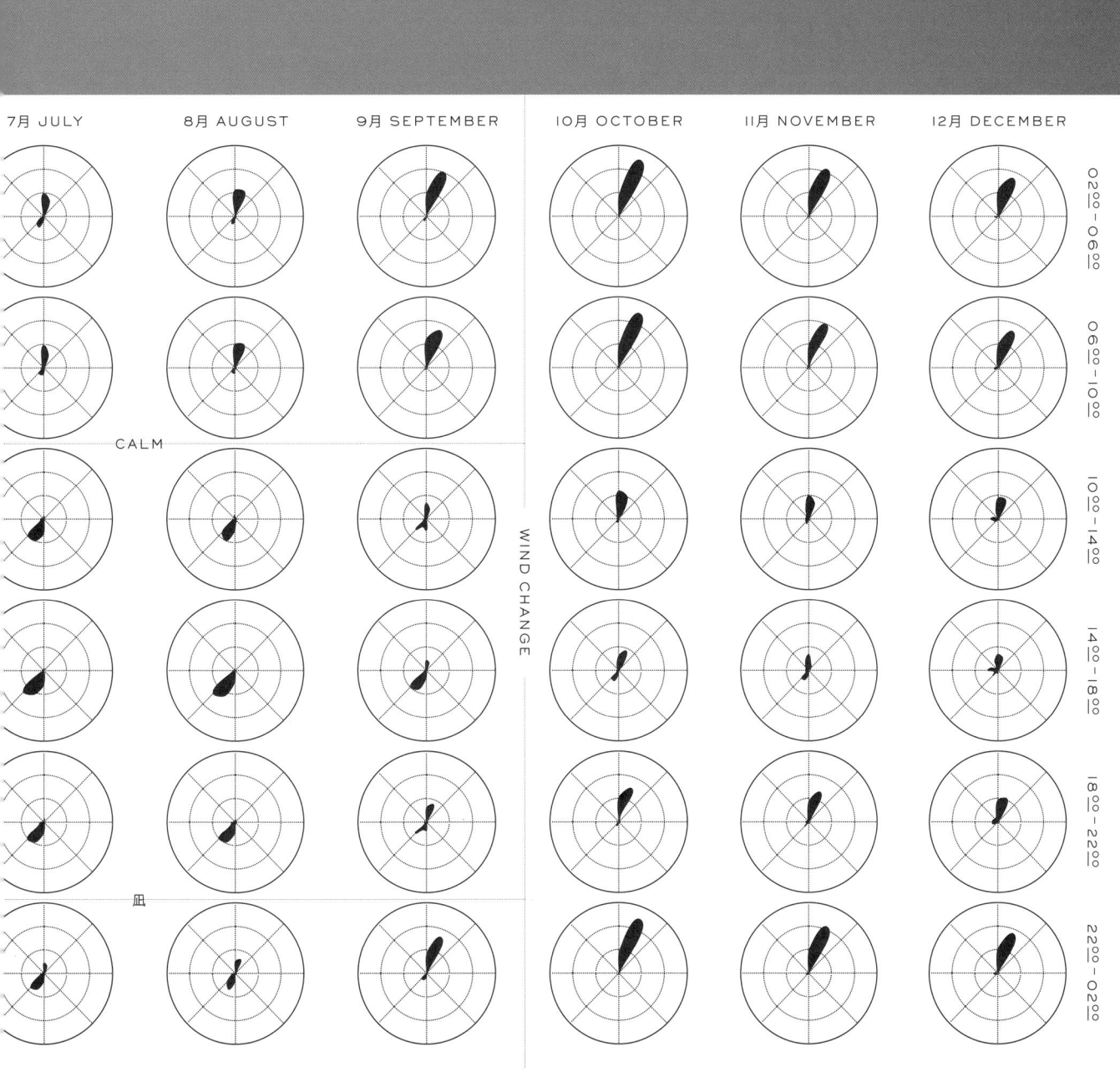

In the Inland Sea the wind changes direction every 12 hours, its particular characteristic being the intersecting periods of calm wind known as *nagi*.

	7月 JULY	8月 AUGUST	9月 SEPTEMBER	10月 OCTOBER	11月 NOVEMBER	12月 DECEMBER	
							02:00 – 06:00
							06:00 – 10:00
	CALM						10:00 – 14:00
			WIND CHANGE				14:00 – 18:00
							18:00 – 22:00
		凪					22:00 – 02:00

267

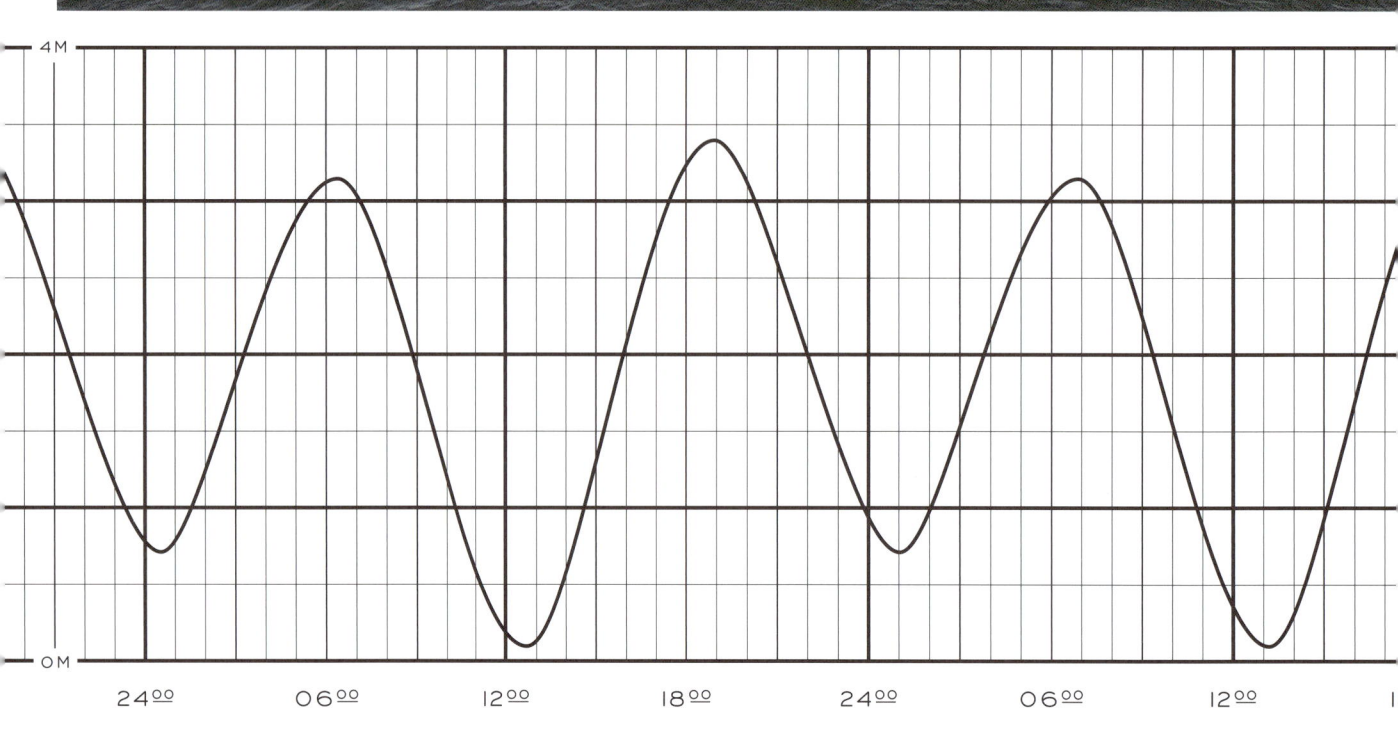

およそ６時間ごとに上下する潮の満ち引き。

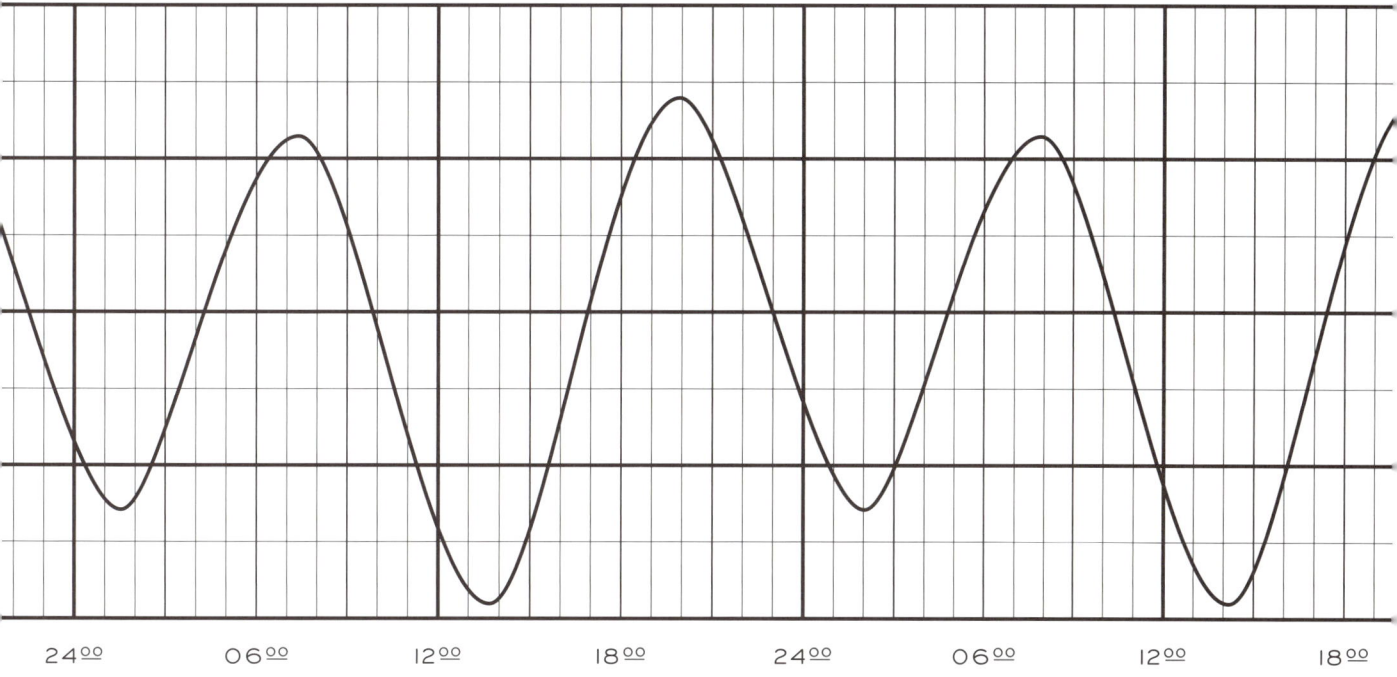

Hiroshima's steady ebb and flow, alternating approximately every six hours.

ひとつの建物も都市全体も地球の一部だと考えることができる。

One may consider a building not only as part of a city but as part of Earth.

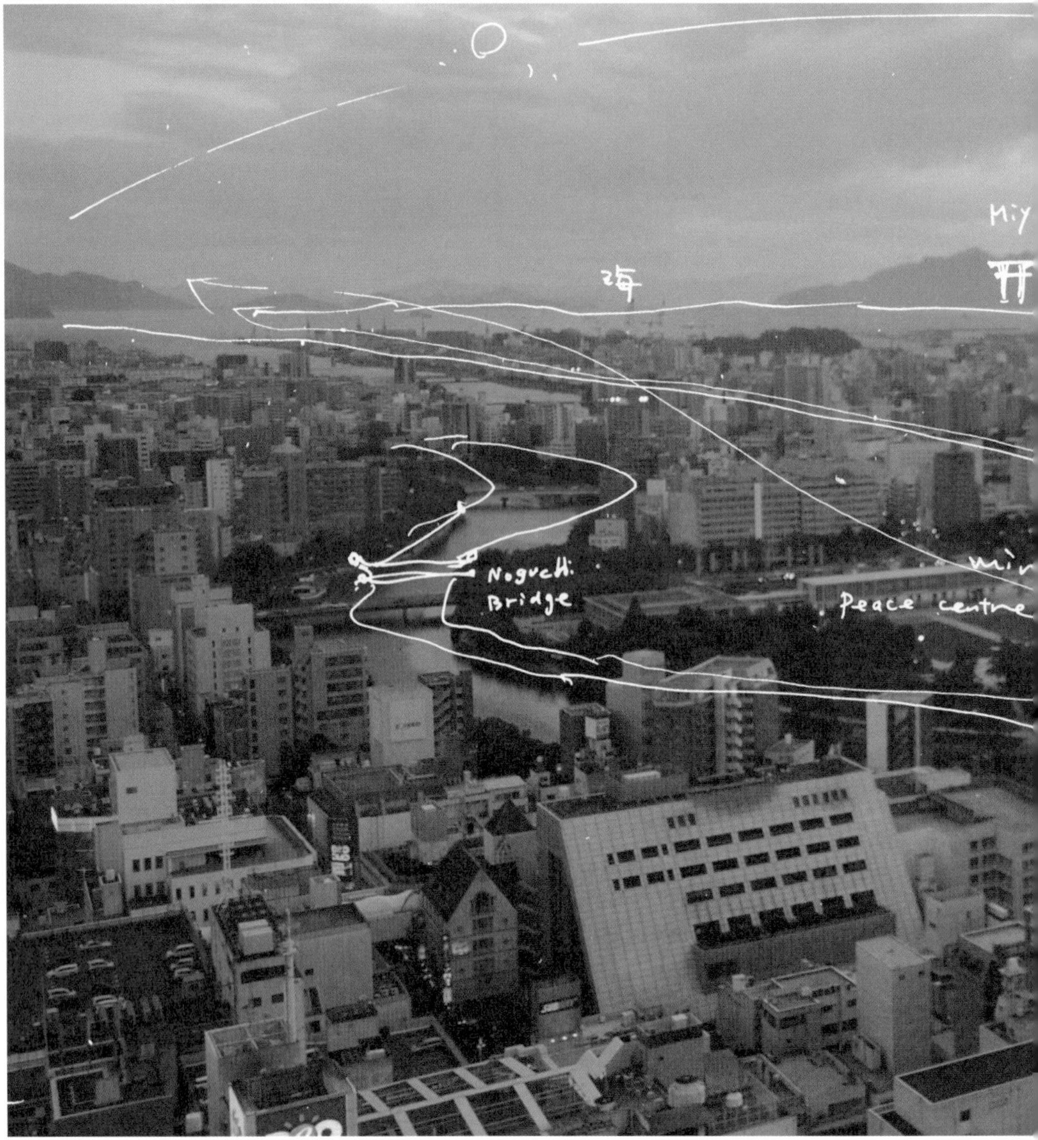

Miy
海
Noguchi
Bridge
Peace centre

Noguchi bridge

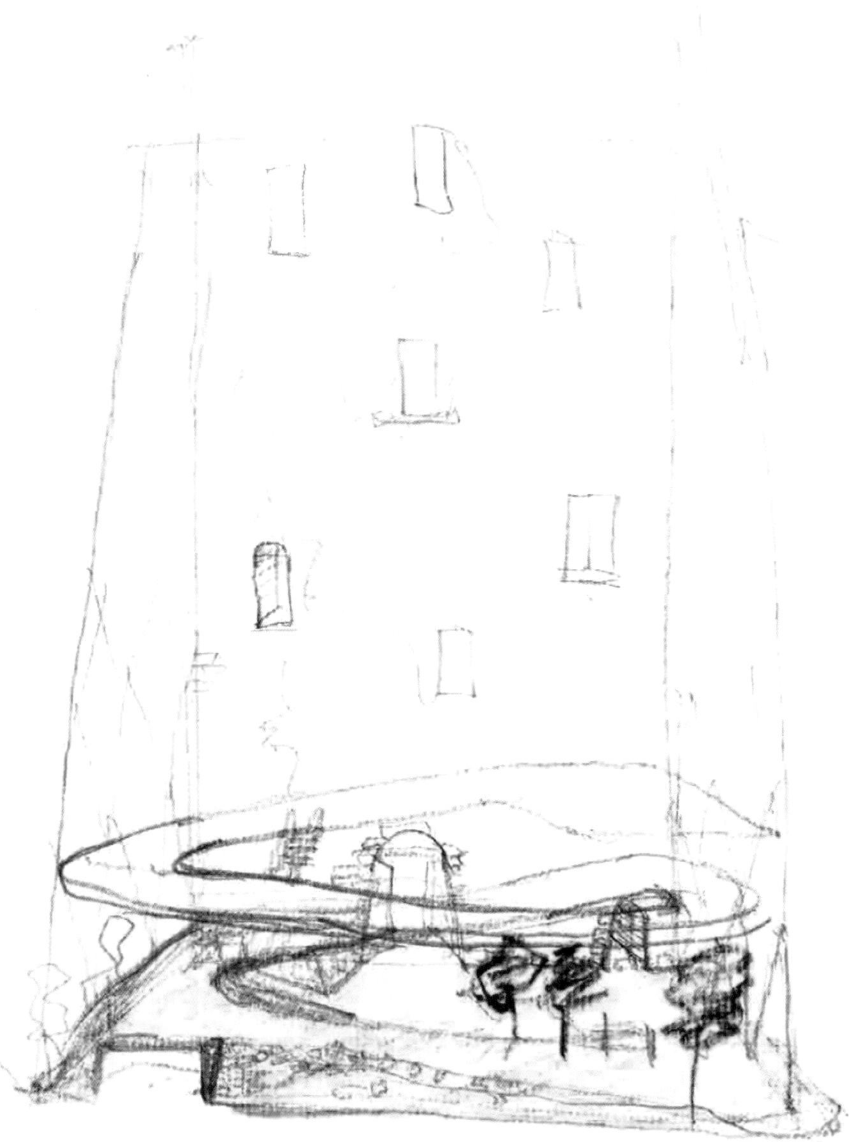

おりづるタワー

広島を訪れる人びとに最も感じてもらいたいのが、この地形から生まれる川の水と風の流れである。なぜなら、それらが広島の街そのものであり、復興を支えてくれたと考えているからである。平和が自然を育み、自然が人びとに平和な暮らしをもたらす。その両方の関係を伝えることが、このプロジェクトの大切なテーマとなった。

広島の水源は数十キロ離れた山々にあり、標高は1,000 mを超える。雪解け水などからなる清らかな流れは中流では棚田を潤し、広島の街に注ぎ込み、やがて宮島などの島々が浮かぶ瀬戸の海へと注がれる。その海や河口付近ではおよそ6時間ごとに潮の干満を繰り返し、常に水が入れ替わる。その水位はおよそ3m上下し、中世からの城下町の暮らしは雁木(がんぎ)を通して潮の満ち引きなど、常に水の動きと共にあった。また、広島の風は、夏には昼の海風、夜の山風と凪を挟みながら12時間おきに南北の風向きが変化し、常に空気が入れ替わる。この太古より今も変わらぬ自然の営み、水や空気が常に入れ替わる広島は、まさに呼吸する街である。

あの日、人類はかけがえのないこの宝を汚してしまった。しかし広島の街は呼吸を止めることはなかった。山々から三角州、海へと続く地形は残っていた。広島の復興を手助けしてくれたのも、その地形から生まれる風や水などの動く素材だった。太古より変わらぬ自然の営みが街を浄化し続けたと私は考えている。この水と空気こそ、広島の街の基本であり、それらを生むのは地形であり、育むのは平和である。

私はそれらを見て、感じてもらう場所が必要だと思った。

高さ約50 mの既存ビルも都市の小さな地形と見立て、あるものを活かし再生しようと考えた。その地形に緩やかに歩いて登ることができるスロープを計画し、その上には風や地形、川の流れ、干満、加えて平和の大切さを見て感じてもらう丘を設けたいと考えた。

70年草木も生えないと言われた広島。その70年が過ぎた現在、この丘に腰を下ろすと広島がいかに美しく世界に類を見ない復興を遂げた街であることが理解できると思う。そして人類は改めて何が大切か認識する必要がある。この場所は世界でもっとも自然の偉大さを感じることができる所である。

私は文化・個性の始まりとなるのは地形から生まれる動く素材だと考えている。それぞれの地域の動く素材を理解し、それに適したかたちを与えていくことで街や集落の文化・個性が育まれる。やがてそれが地球規模で結び付き、その文化を尊重した交流が平和な地球を創り出す。

どんな国にも故郷の動く素材がある。故郷の風、水、太陽、月、地形がいかに大切かということに気付いていただき、その思いをもち帰っていただければと考えている。

HIROSHIMA ORIZURU TOWER

Above all, I want people visiting Hiroshima to feel the flows of the rivers and winds that arise from its terrain. That is because I think these things are aspects of Hiroshima that will support its revival. Peacefulness nurtures nature, and nature provides people with a peaceful way of life. Conveying both relationships is an important theme for this project.

The source of Hiroshima's rivers lies in the mountains dozens of kilometres away, at an altitude that exceeds 1000 metres above sea level. Comprising water from snow thaw and so on, this pure flow irrigates the fields at midstream, pours into the town of Hiroshima, and before long flows into the Seto Inland Sea, in which Miyajima and other islands float. In the vicinity of the sea and the river mouth, the ebb and flow of the tide is repeated approximately every six hours, and the water is constantly being replaced. The change in water level is approximately three meters, and since medieval times, life in this castle town has followed the constant movement of the water, with stepped piers for the rise and fall of the tide. Moreover, in summer the winds of Hiroshima are constantly replacing the air, with the wind direction changing from north to south every twelve hours, in the lull between the daytime sea breezes and the night-time mountain winds. The workings of nature, unchanging from ancient times until today, constantly replace the water and air, making Hiroshima a town that breathes.

One day, people contaminated this irreplaceable treasure. However, Hiroshima did not stop breathing. The terrain of Hiroshima, from the mountains to the delta and sea, survived. Moving materials, such as the wind and water generated by the terrain, aided the revival of Hiroshima. I thought about continuing to purify the town by means of the workings of nature, which have not changed since ancient times. The water and air form the basis of the town of Hiroshima, generated by the terrain and nurtured by peacefulness.

I think it is necessary to have a place from where one may watch and feel these things.

Selecting an existing building about 50 metres in height from the small-scale terrain of the city, I thought about retaining and reviving what exists. I thought about planning on the terrain a gentle slope that could be climbed on foot, and above that establishing a hill from which the wind, terrain, river flows, and tides, as well as the importance of peacefulness, could be seen and felt.

It is said that trees and plants would not grow in Hiroshima for 70 years since that day. In the present day, after those 70 years elapsed, I sat on this hill and wondered how to make the world understand the beauty of Hiroshima, a town that accomplished an unprecedented revival, and the necessity for the human race to once again recognize what is important. It is here, more than anywhere else in the world, that the greatness of nature can be felt.

I think that culture and individuality originate in the moving materials that emerge from the terrain. With an awareness of the moving materials of each region, the culture and individuality of a town or village may be nurtured, and a suitable form thereby bestowed. Before long, these will become linked to the global scale, and interchanges respectful of other cultures will lead to the creation of peace on Earth.

Every country has moving materials in its old hometowns. I want to draw attention to the importance of the wind, water, sunlight, moonlight, and terrain of these hometowns, and have people take these ideas home with them.

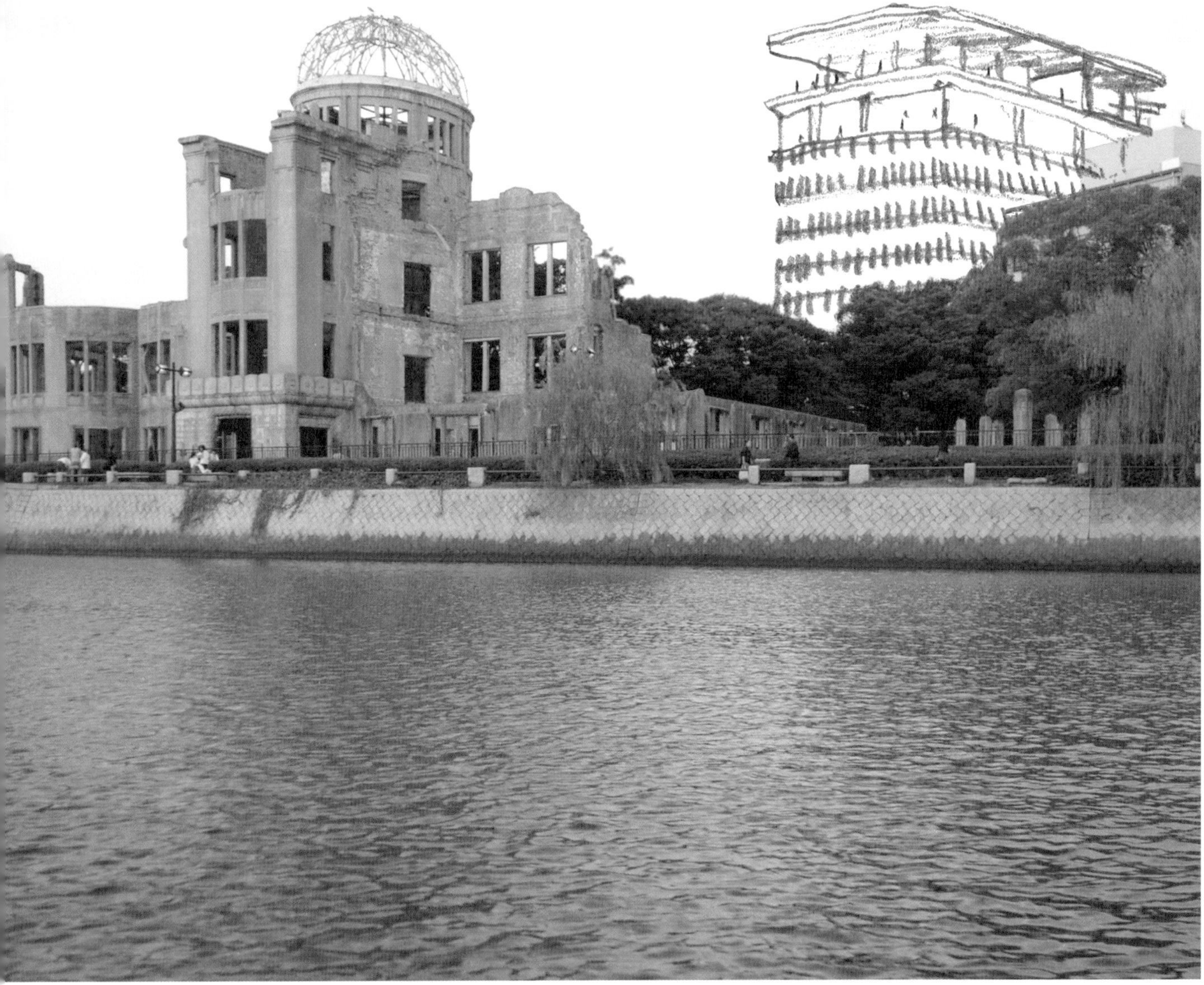

都市の丘を登る。

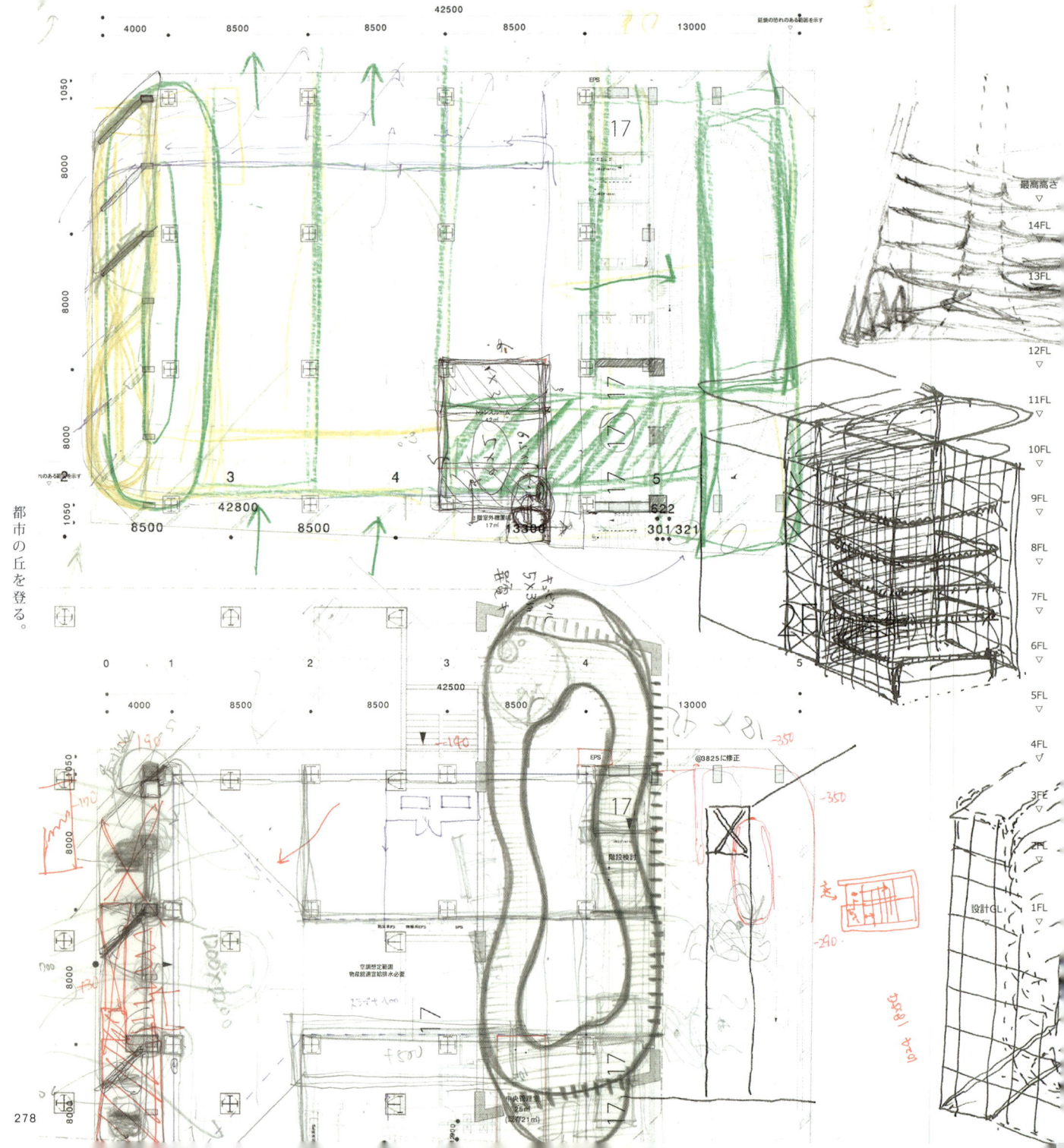

基準階3~12階平面図 1/150

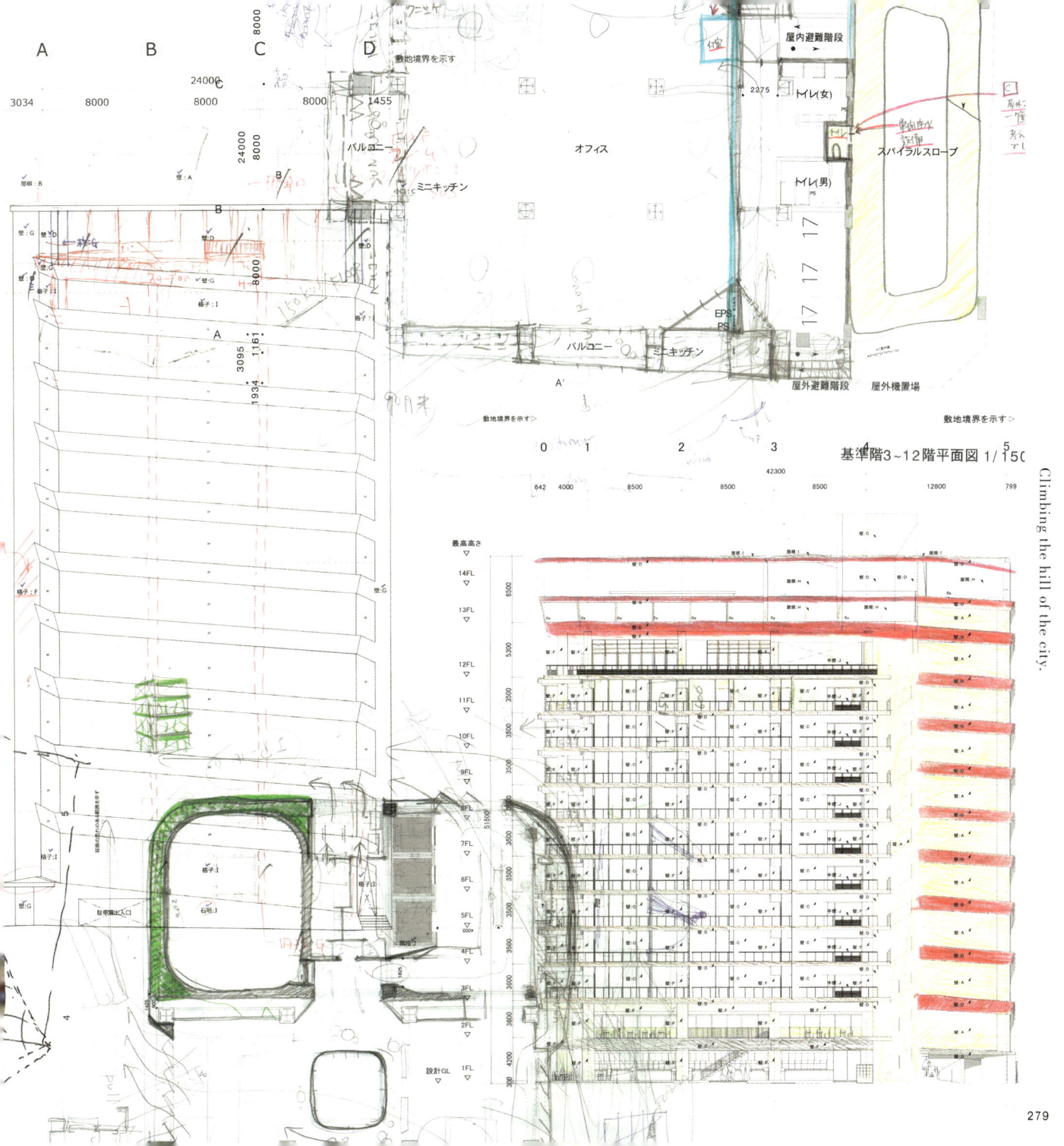

Climbing the hill of the city.

279

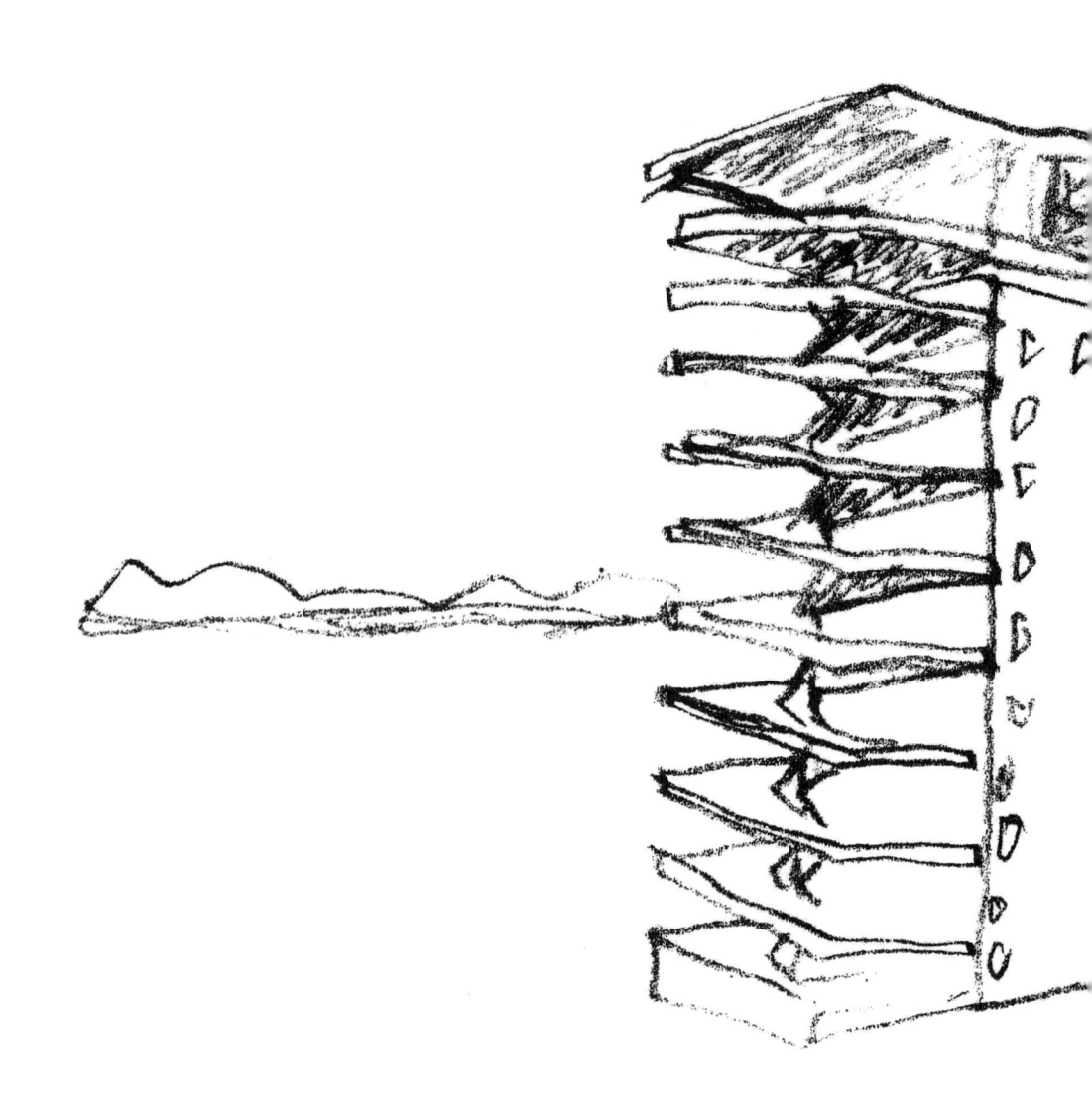

都市の丘を登り広島の風や水、
動く素材を見て、
感じてもらいたいと思った。

*"A hill in the city to climb
to feel the wind, water
and moving materials of Hiroshima."*

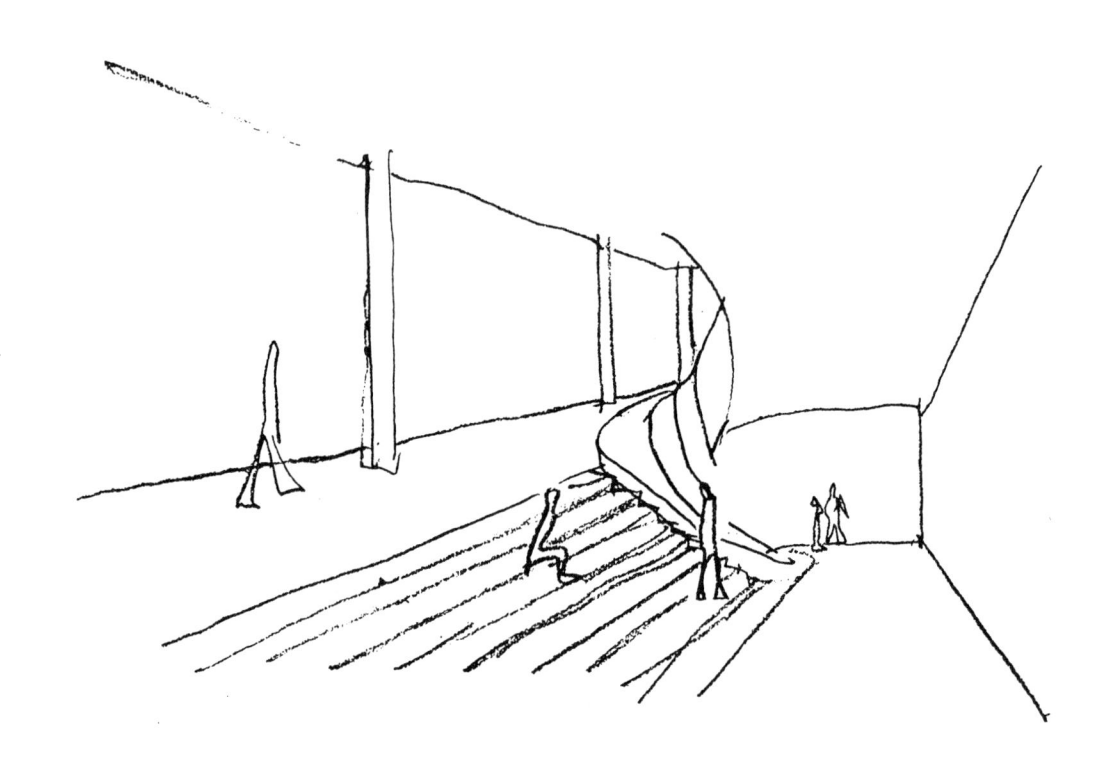

私は広島が復興を遂げた要因を呼吸する街にあると考えている。求めたのは広島の街にふさわしい呼吸する建築への再生であった。

まずビルの息苦しい外壁をすべて取り払い、骨組みのみを残すことで風を採り入れる力を最大限に引き出そうとした。軽くなることで既存躯体の構造的性能は、より健全なものへと繋がっていく。新たに付加するものは、この場所の風と水、太陽への適応と構造補強を同時に満たしながら、建物にさらなる魅力を与えるものでなければならなかった。

東のスロープと西のバルコニーは構造補強である。同時に屋上展望台まで登るスロープは開放的な半屋外空間とし、風が流れ夏場の直接光を遮る。世界中からここを訪れる人びとは、広島の風を感じながらゆっくりと登っていくことができる。各方位のバルコニーには夏の風向に合わせた角度のルーバーと緑のウィンドキャッチャーを設け、同時に夏場の直射日光や西日や防ぐ角度にもなっている。すべての窓が開放でき、どの階のオフィス空間にも風が通り抜ける。日々オフィスを利用する人たちは自然の光と風の中にある。屋上の展望台には丘を設け、大きな庇をかけた。丘に腰をおろす人びとと既存の建物を雨や強い日差しから守る。マウンドした丘と庇の効果で風を縮流し強めることで、広島の風・呼吸する街をより実感していただけるように配慮している。

大切なのは「風のリレー」。自然界や森と同じように。

この建物は風を止めることはない。吸っては吐き、また次の建物へ、そして街へ流れて行く。その建物の環境だけが良ければいいという考えを改めなければならない。

「呼吸する」とはそういうことである。

I think Hiroshima has been able to accomplish its revival due to the fact that it is a town that breathes. What was needed was a revival of architecture that breathes, appropriate to the town of Hiroshima.

First, by entirely removing the oppressive outer walls of the building, leaving only the structural frame, the maximum power of the wind could be drawn in. In becoming lighter, the structural performance of the existing frame is connected to something more stable. The newly added elements must enhance the charm of the building while simultaneously satisfying requirements for wind, water, sun, and structural reinforcement.

The eastern ramps and the western balconies provide structural reinforcement.

Simultaneously, the ramp that ascends to the viewing platform on the rooftop, an open half-outdoor space, blocks the flow of wind and direct light in summertime. People visiting here from all over the world can slowly climb upward while feeling the winds of Hiroshima. Angled louvres oriented to the summer wind direction and green wind catchers are installed in the balcony facing in each direction, which are simultaneously angled to protect against the summertime direct sunlight and late afternoon sun. All the windows can be left open, and breezes will pass through the office spaces on each floor. People use the offices every day amid natural light and air. A hill had been established in the viewing platform on the rooftop, with large eaves overhead. The existing building and the people sitting on the hill are protected from rain and strong sunlight. The effect of the mound of the hill and the eaves constricts and strengthens the wind, with the intention of enhancing the feeling of Hiroshima as a town that breathes.

What is important is the "wind relay," similar to the natural world or a forest.

This building does not block the wind. It inhales, then exhales, and the flow continues to the next building and onward through the town. We must change the idea that it is sufficient for just the environment of the building to be good.

This is what I mean by "breathing."

東西断面図　S:1/300

風の立面。

284

Elevations of the wind.

1/200 12F平面図

1/200 6F平面図

11F平面図

1/200 5F平面図

オフィスの中を森のように風が抜けて、次の建物へと風をリレーしていく。
The wind flows through the office as in a forest, continuing on to the next buildings.

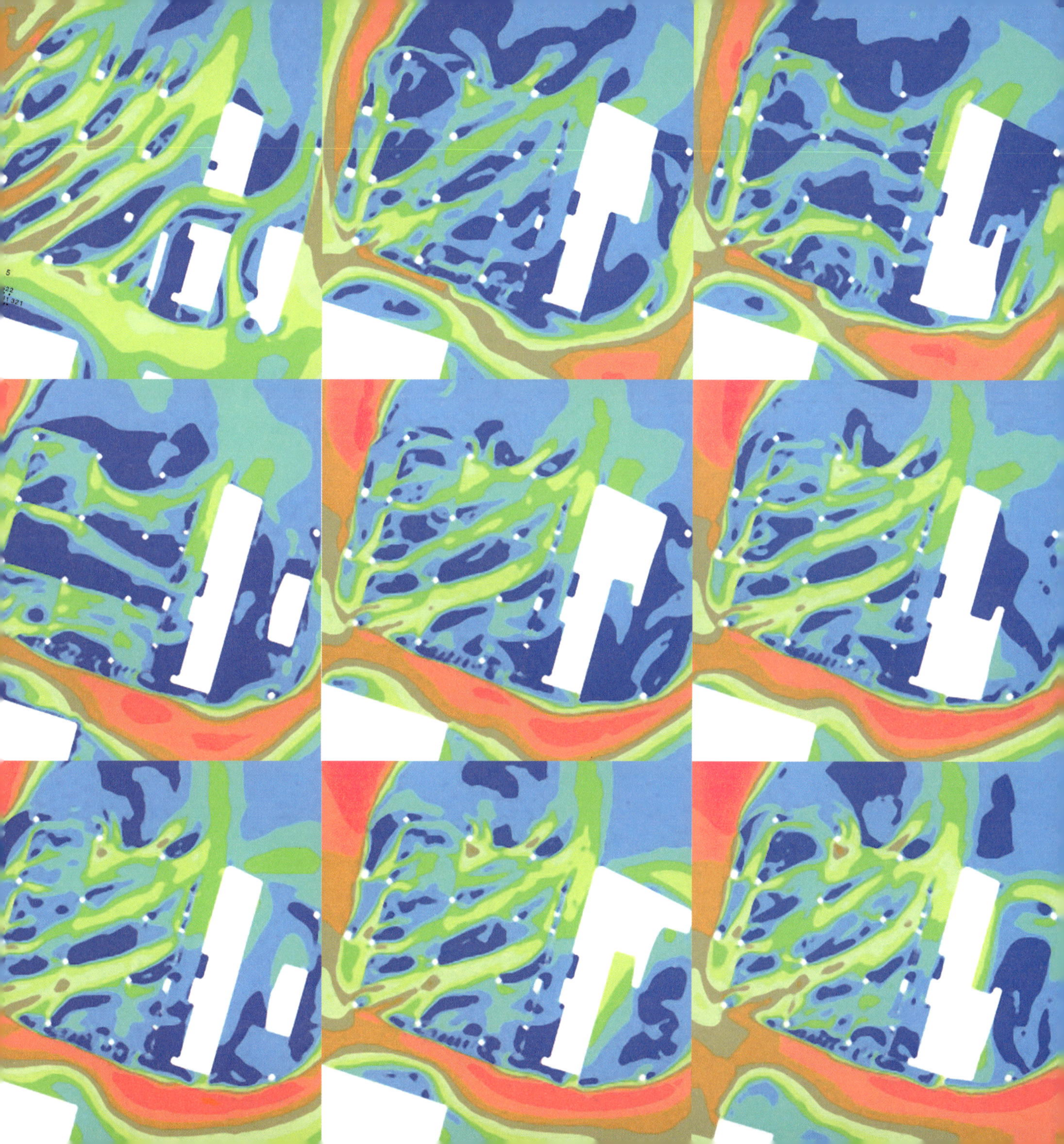

平和の丘、風の丘。

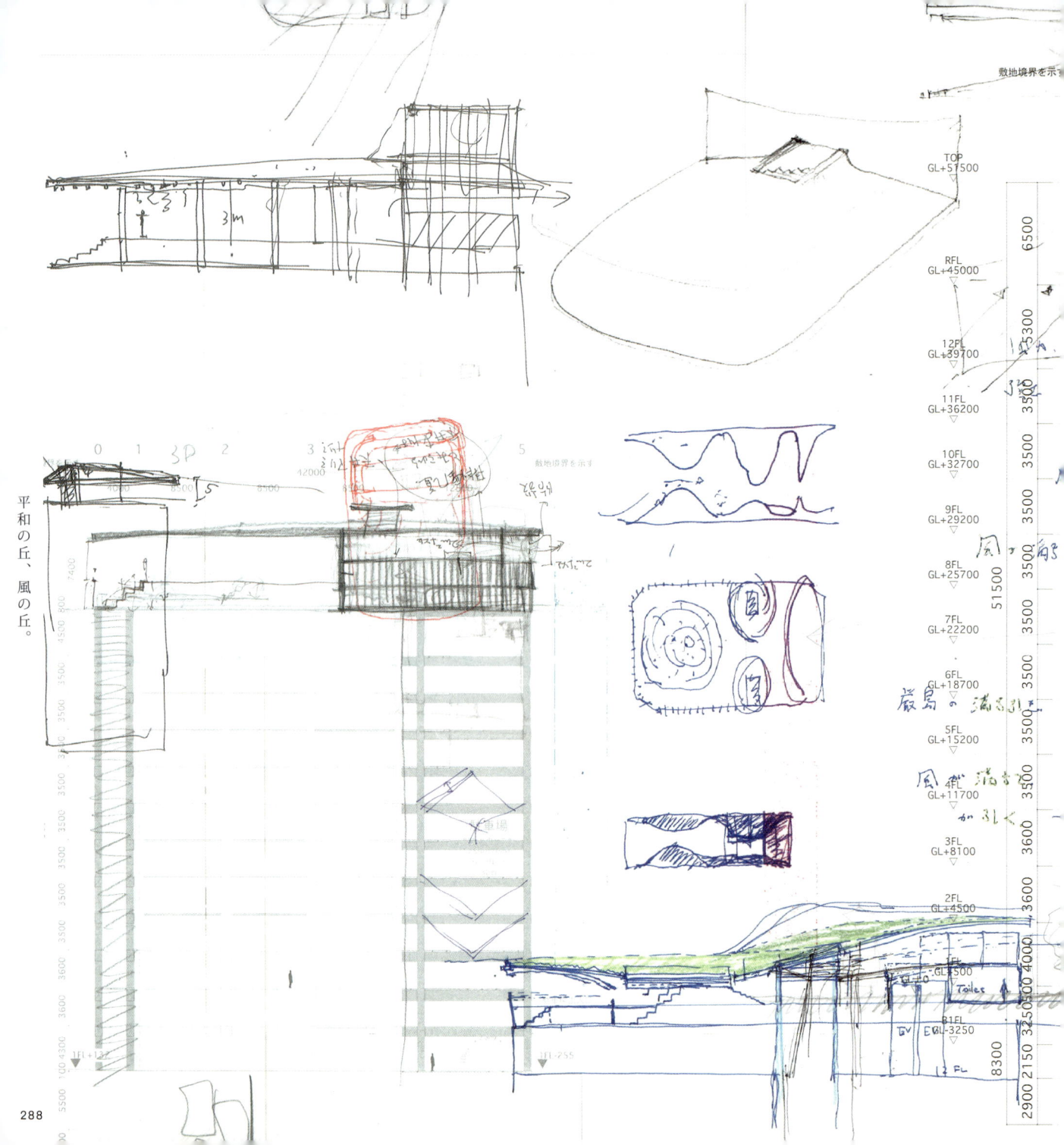

C B A ◁敷地境界を示す

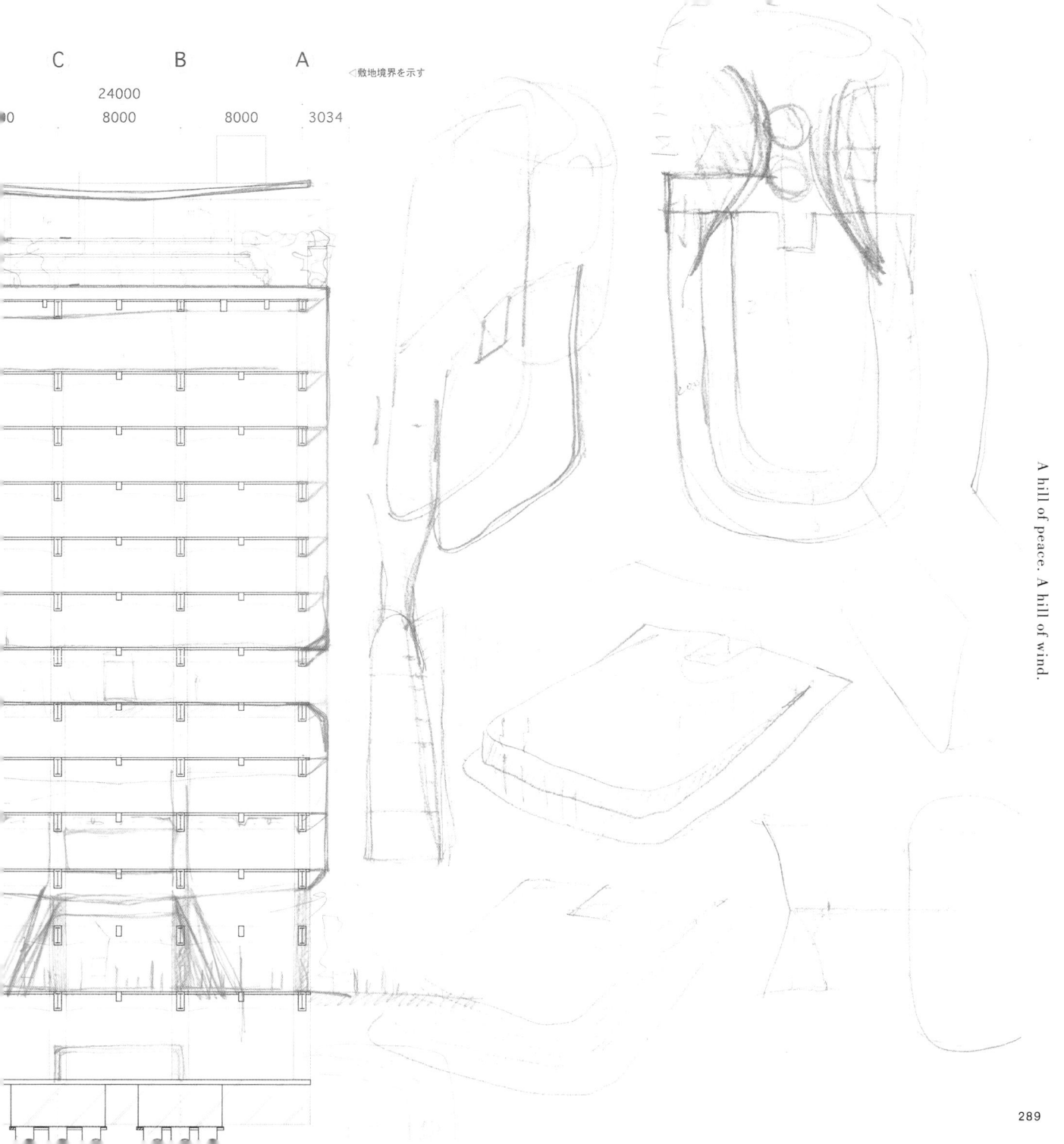

24000
8000　　　8000　　3034

A hill of peace. A hill of wind.

city

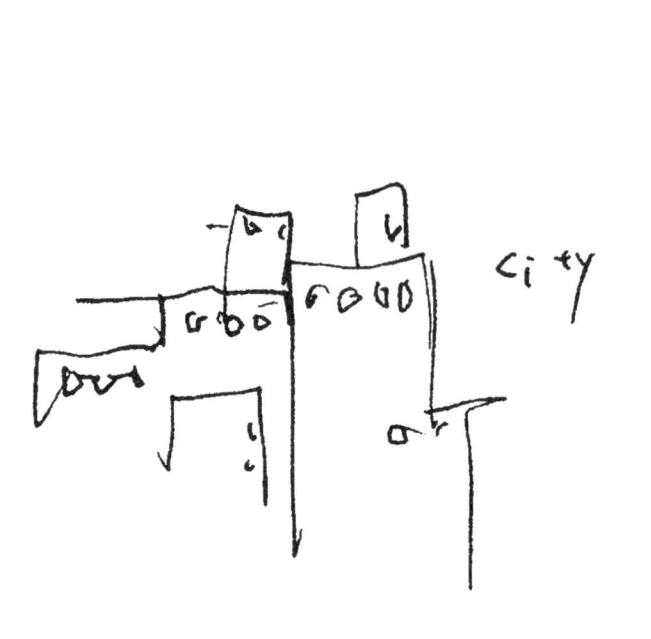

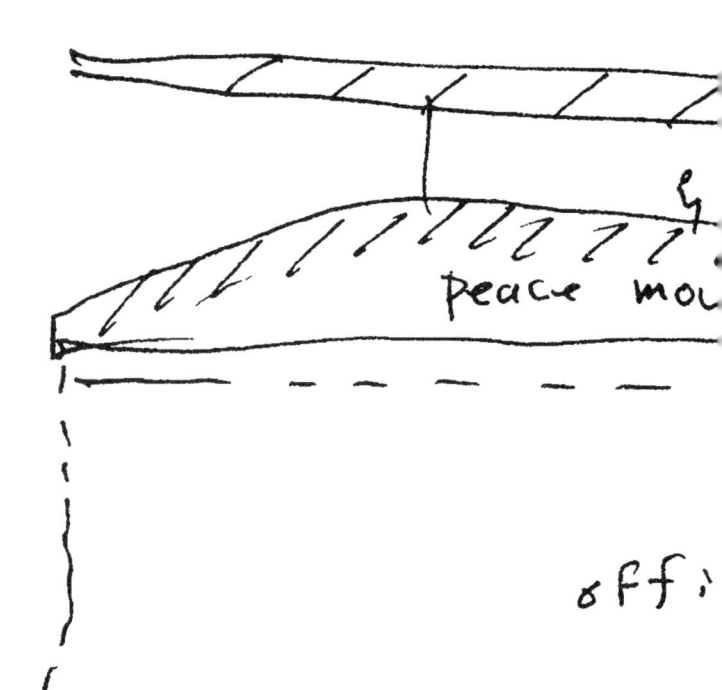

peace mo[

offi[

nature

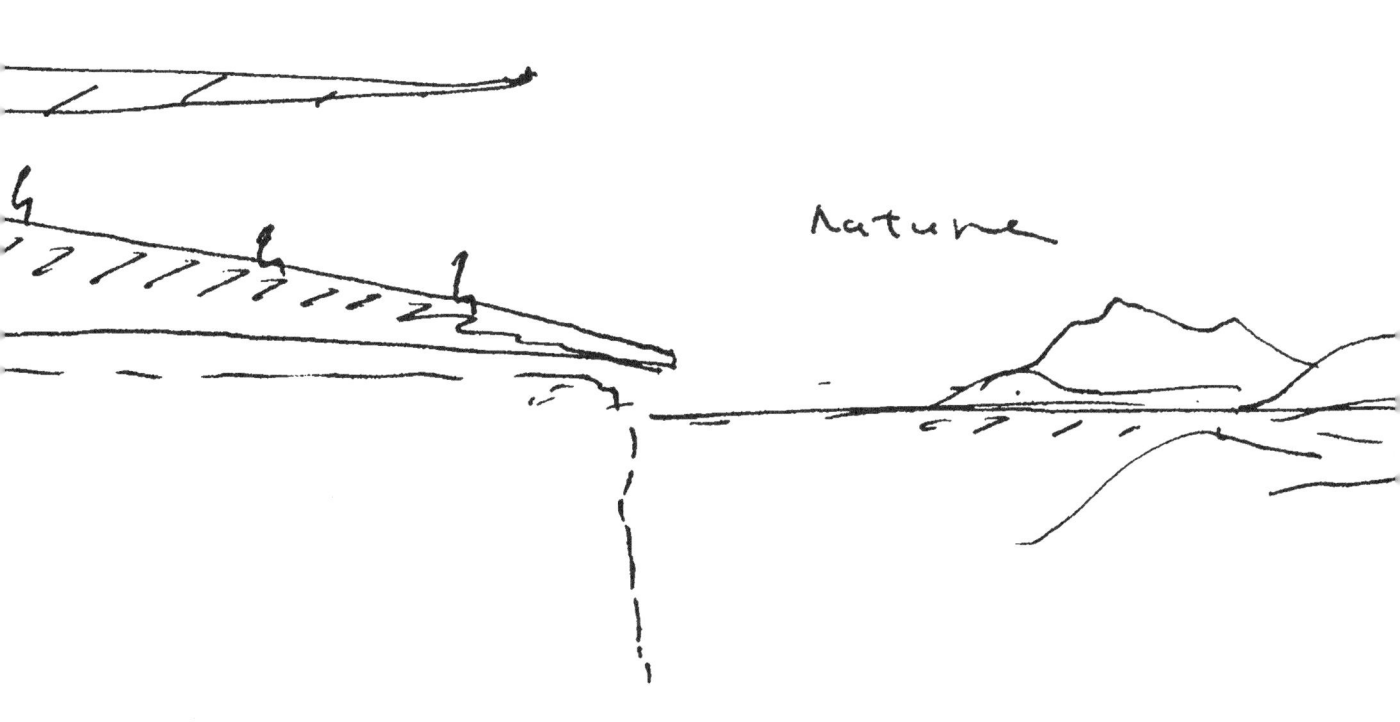

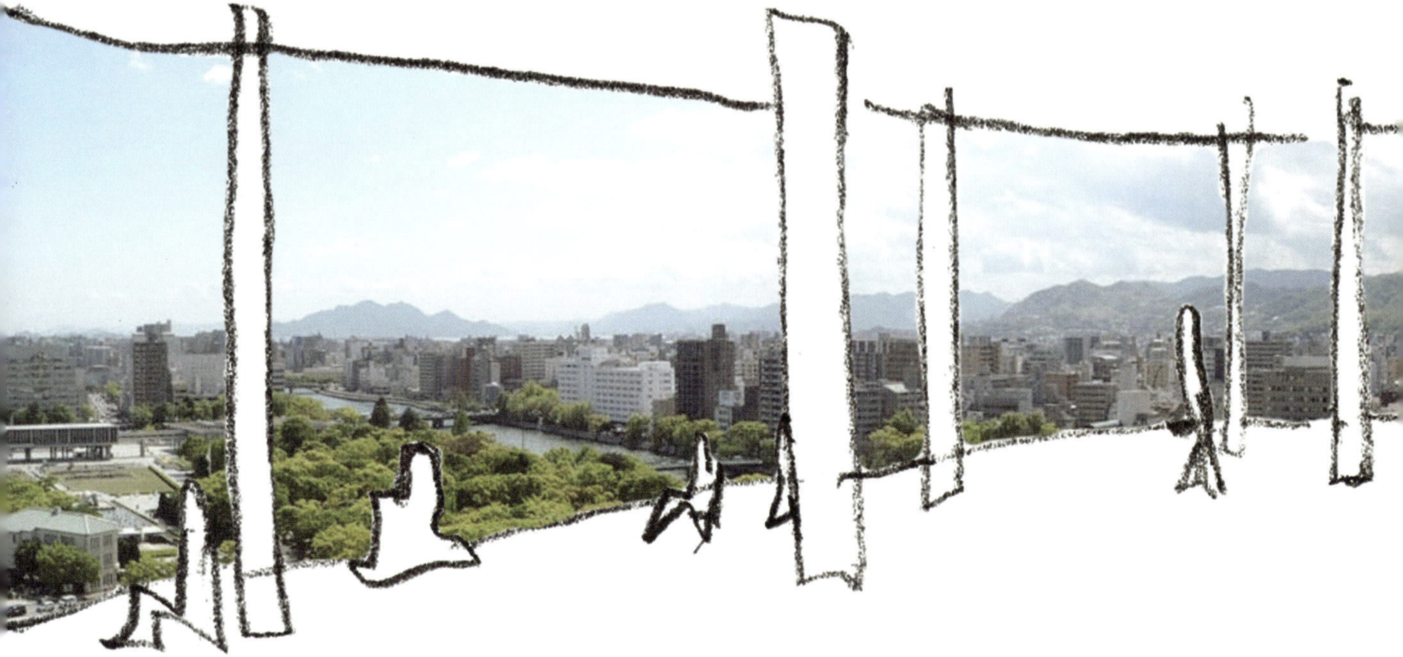

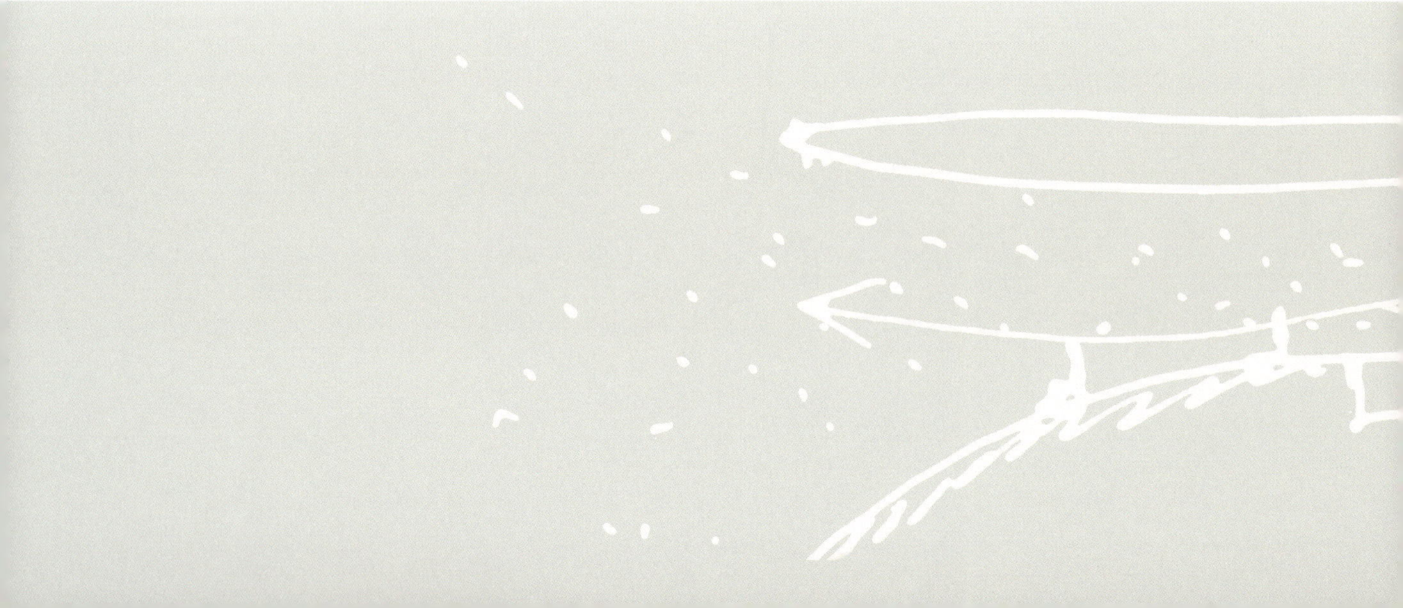

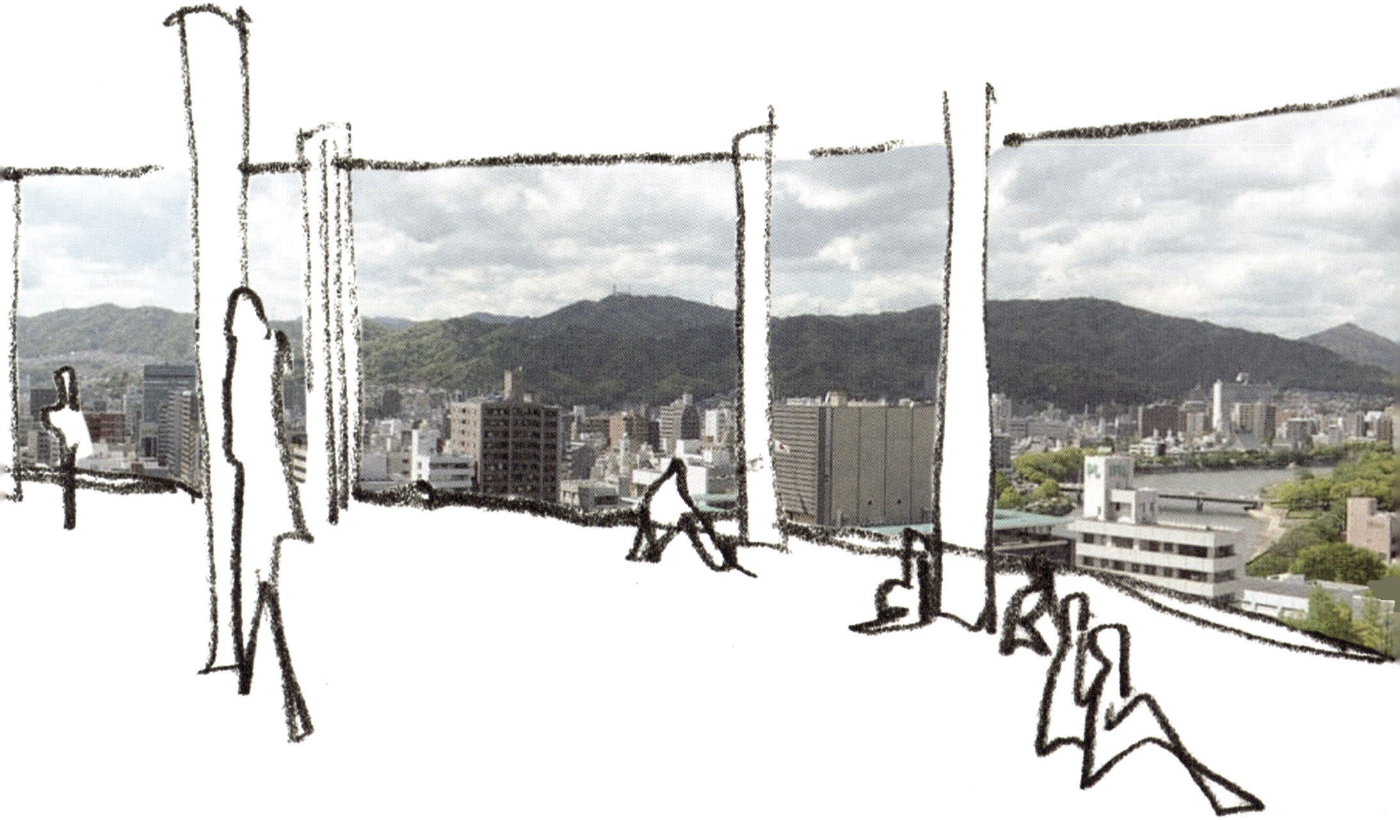

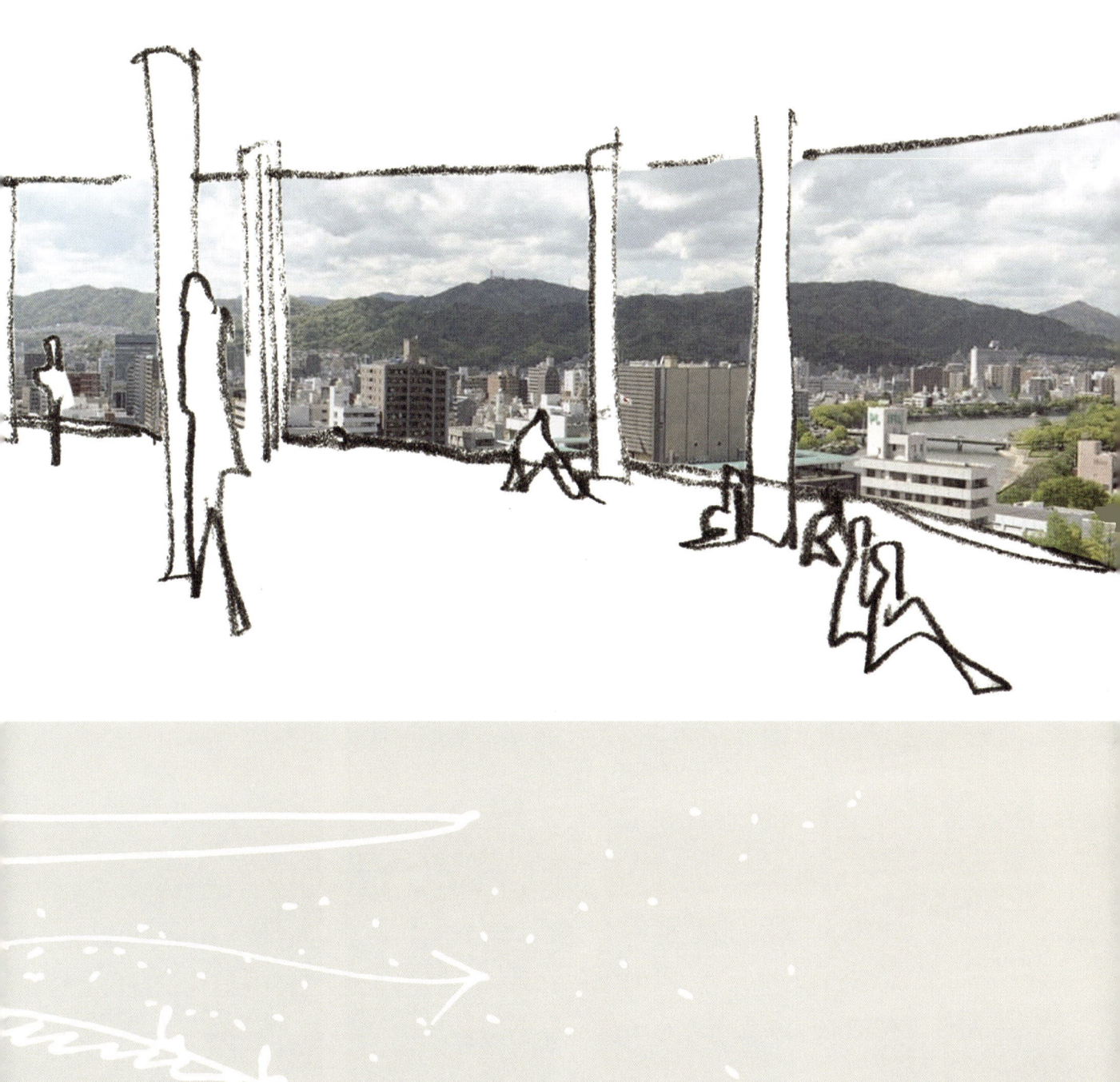

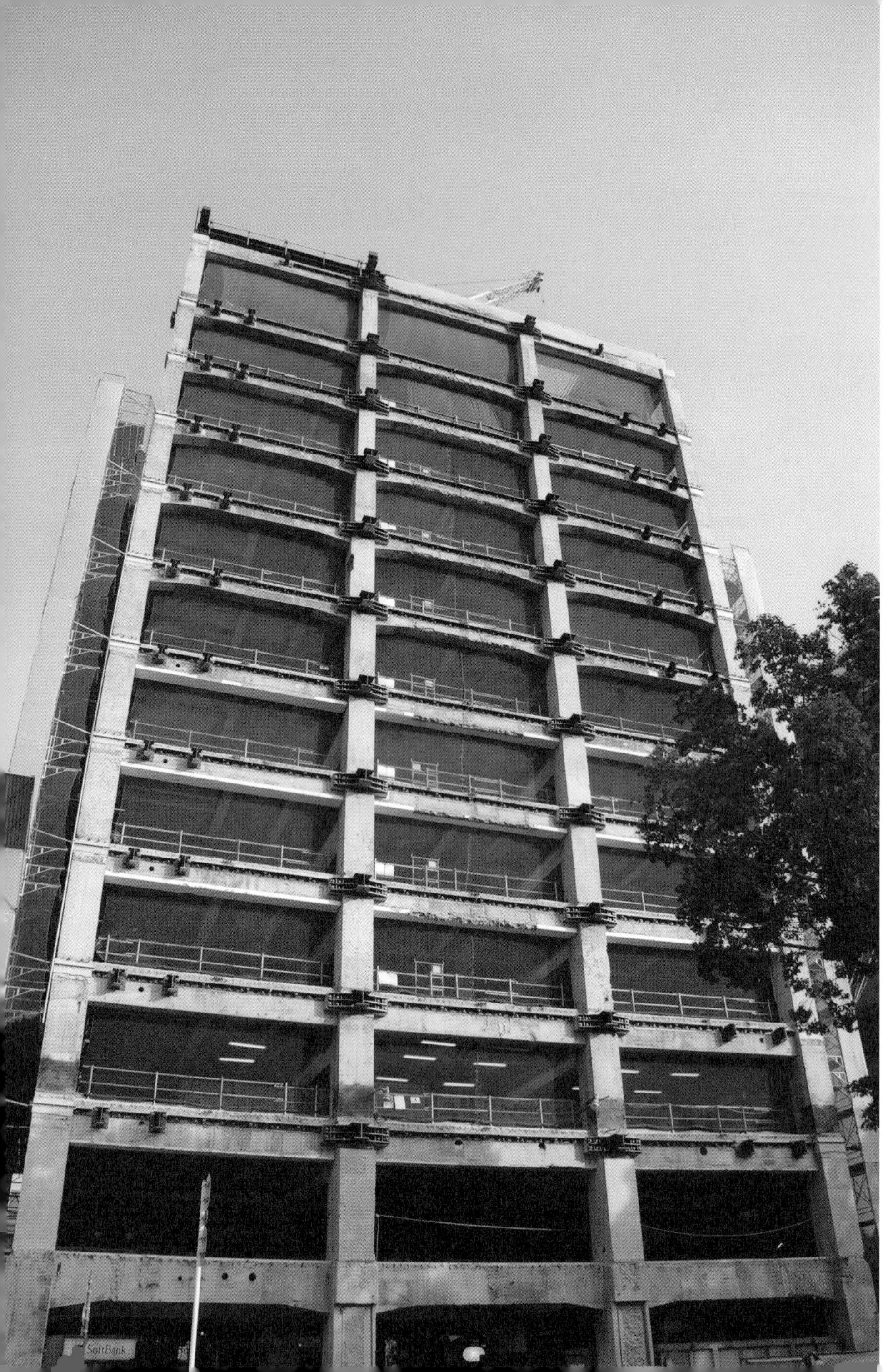
SoftBank

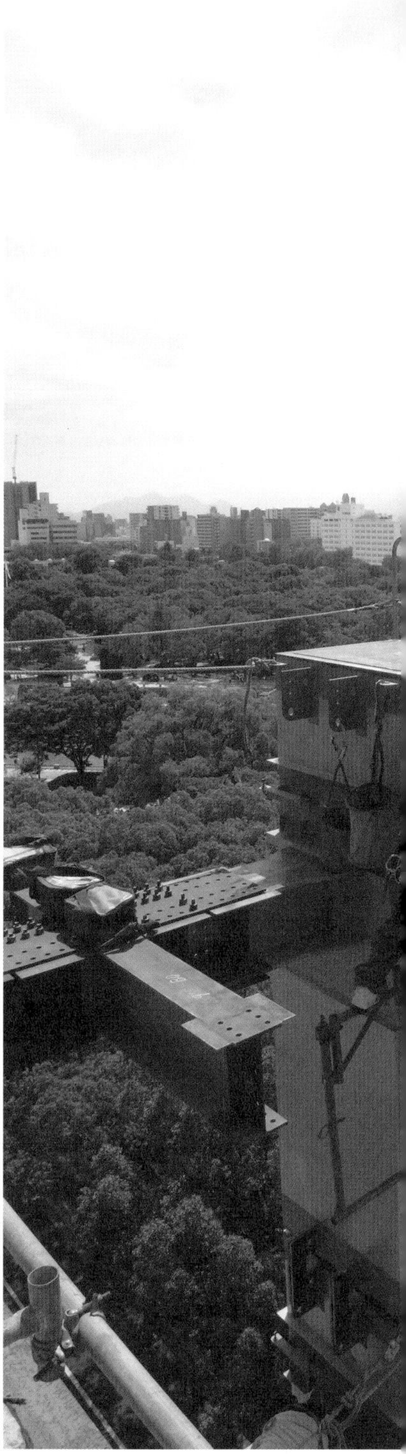

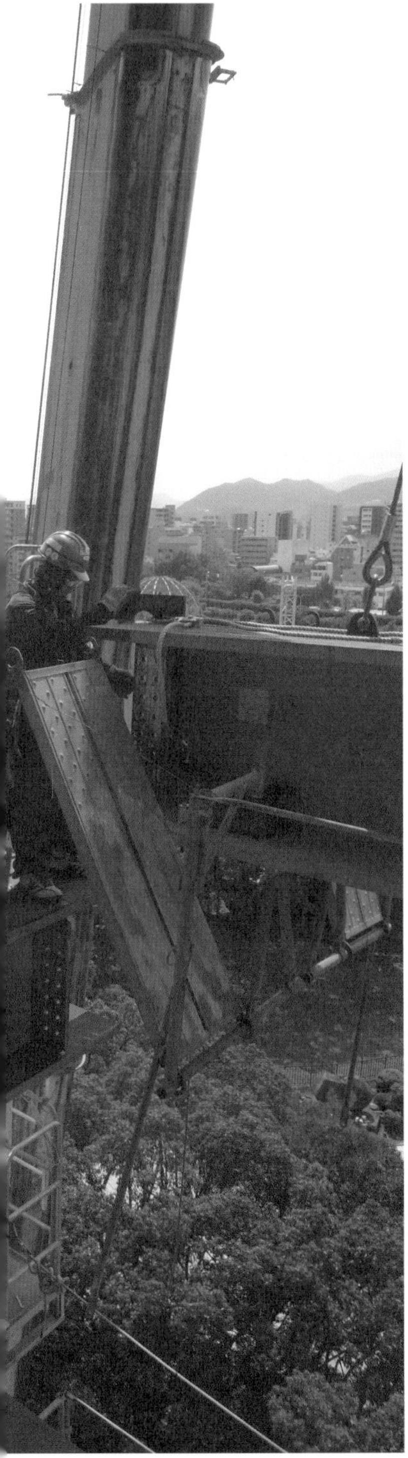
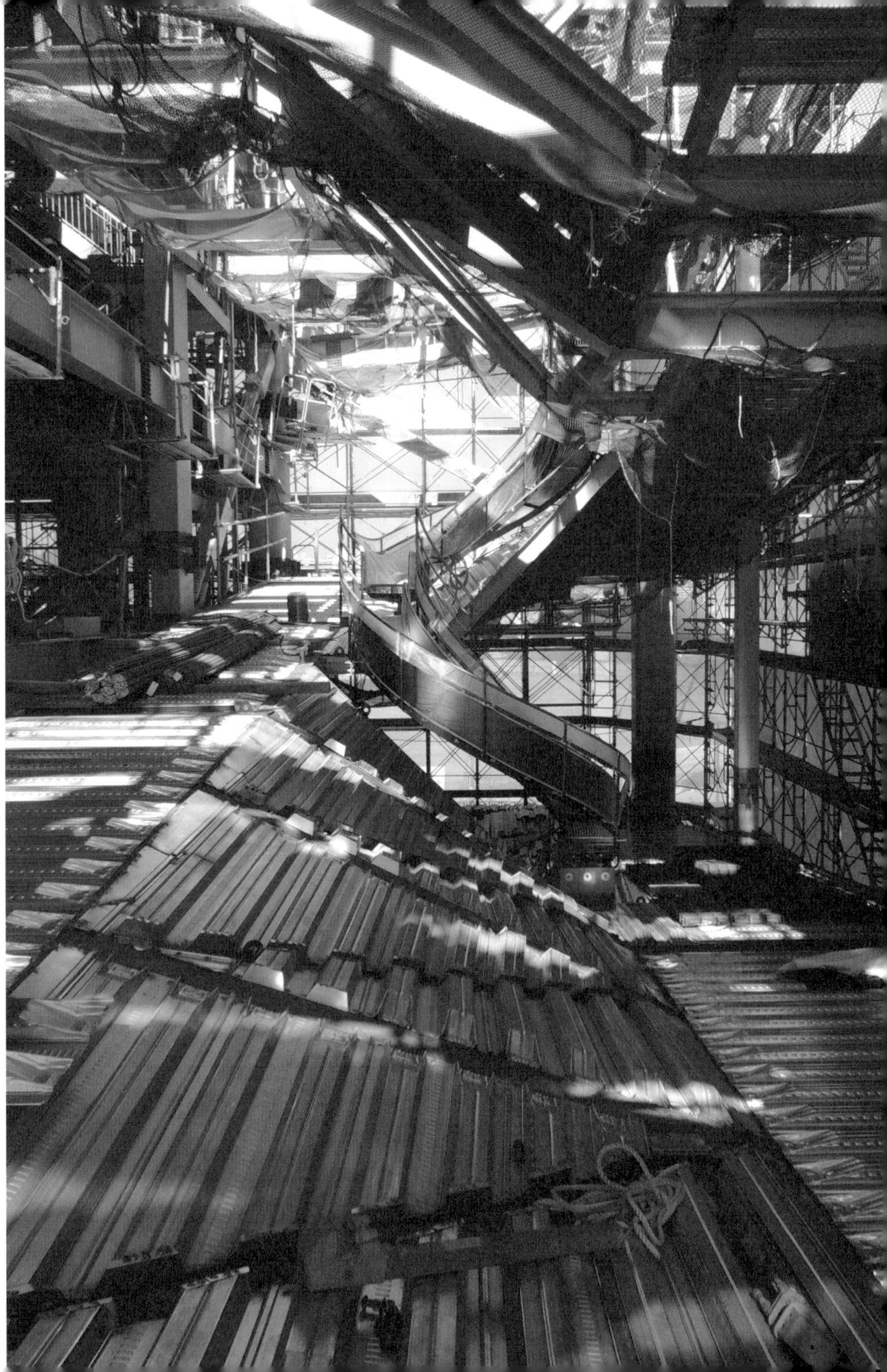

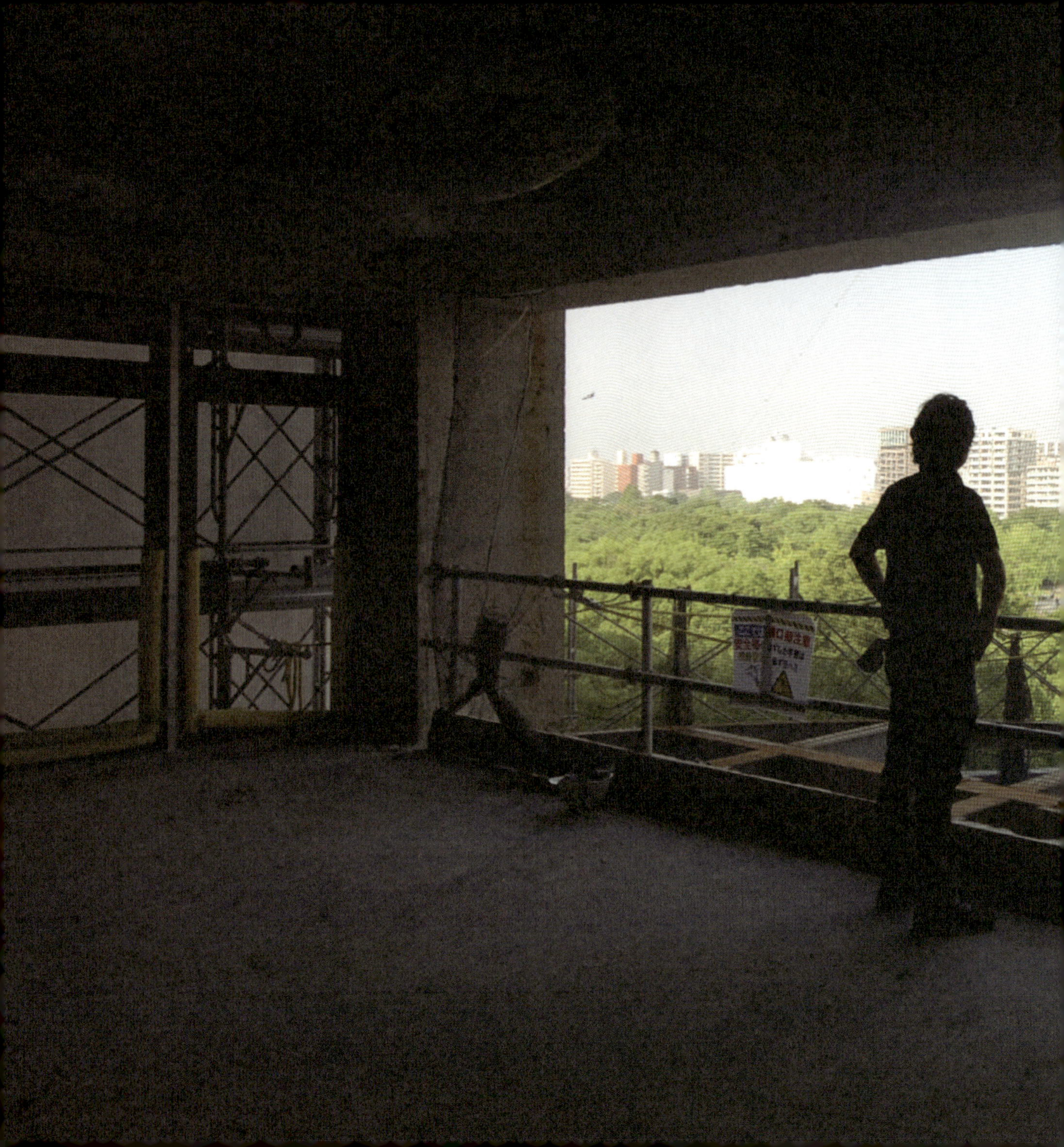

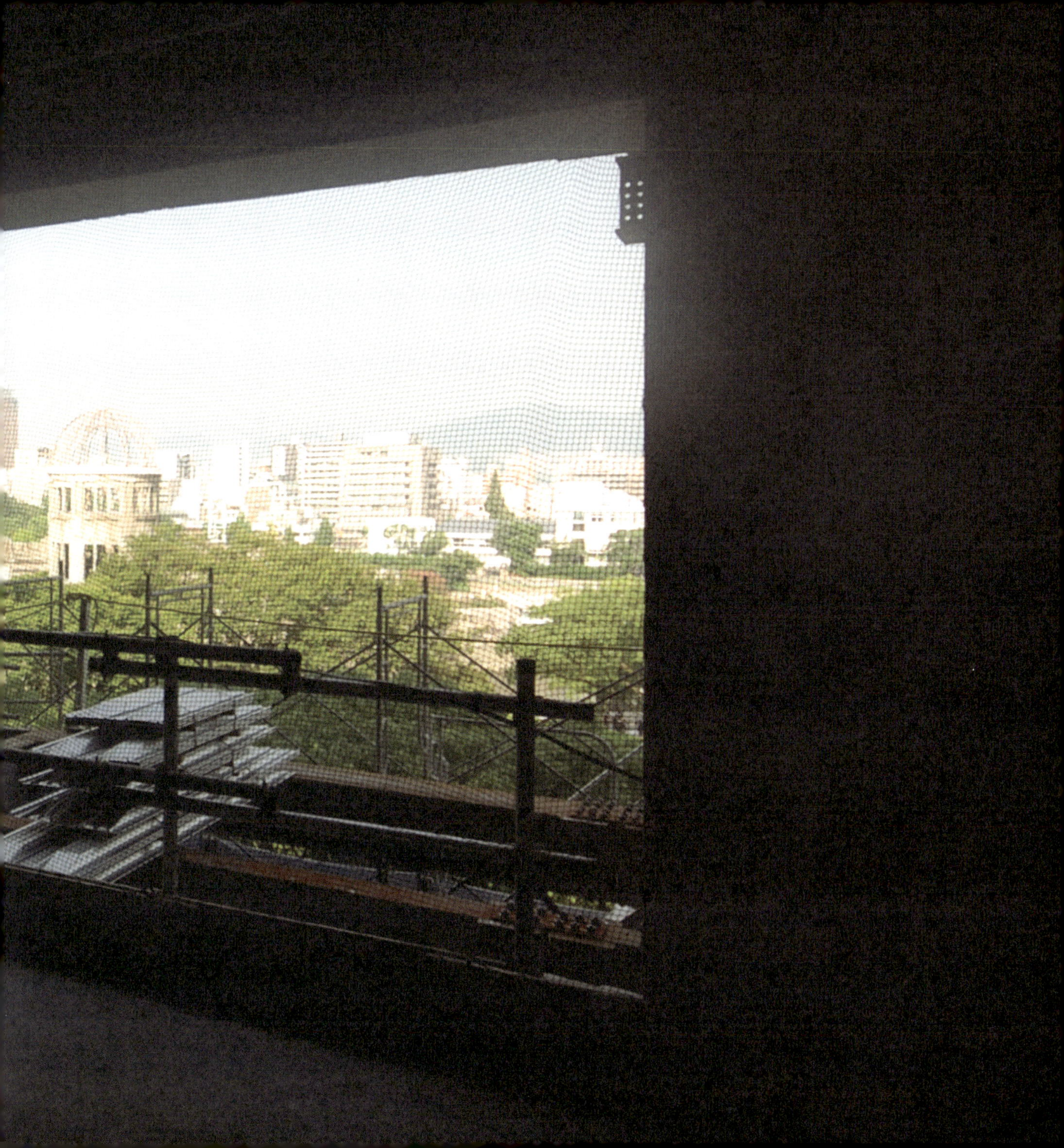

私が知って欲しい、見て、感じて欲しい
風や水、太陽などの動く素材は、
地形と共に住まう集落単位の
文化や歴史、習慣そのものである。
つまりは地球と人の営みのもっとも知的な
関係の基本的要素なのです。

三分一博志

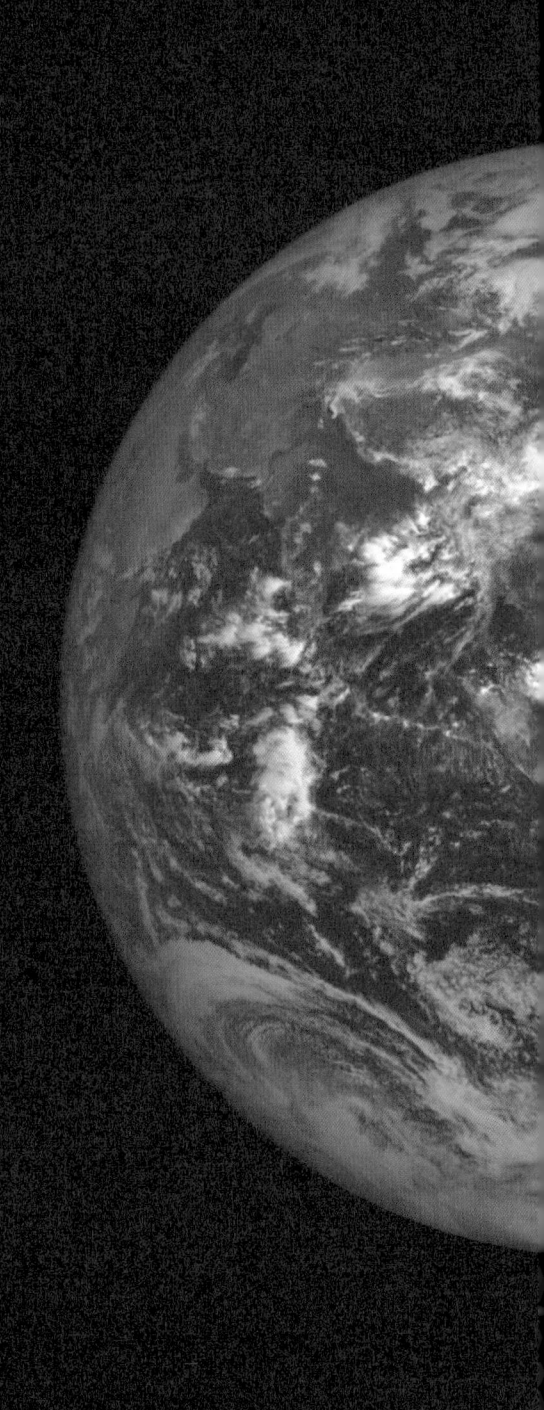

"I want you to understand, I want you to see and feel that moving materials such as wind, water, and sun are themselves aspects of the culture, history, and customs of the villages that coexist with the terrain. In other words, they are the basic elements of the wisest relationship between the activities of people and the Earth."

Hiroshi Sambuichi

三分一博志

1968年生まれ。三分一博志建築設計事務所を広島に設立し、現在デンマーク王立芸術アカデミー教授（非常勤）。主な受賞歴に、2003年吉岡賞、2010年日本建築大賞2011年日本建築学会賞作品賞など。

作品

おりづるタワー（広島県／展望台、物産館、飲食店舗、オフィス／2016年）；直島ホール（香川県／体育館、集会所／2015年）；直島の家またべえ（民家、ゲストハウス／2015年）；宮島弥山展望台（広島県／展望台／2013年）；白島オフィス（広島県／オフィス／2011年）；速度の家（専用住宅／2010年）；三輪窯Ⅱ（不走庵）（山口県／ゲストハウス、ギャラリー、保管庫／2010年）；六甲枝垂れ（兵庫県／展望施設／2010年）；Miyajima Office 船倉税理士事務所（広島県／事務所／2008年）；オタフクソース Wood Egg お好み焼館（広島県／事務所、展示場／2008年）；Energy Penthouse（専用住宅／2008年）；犬島精錬所美術館（岡山県／美術館／2008年）；プロジェクトウエスト（専用住宅／2007年）；Base Valley（専用住宅／2007年）；太陽の家（専用住宅／2007年）；ののやま矯正歯科医院（広島県／歯科診療所／2006年）；ストーン・ハウス（専用住宅／2005年）；民家再生計画（専用住宅／2005年）；brood（店舗、レストラン／2005年）；角田歯科医院（広島県／歯科診療所／2004年）；北向傾斜住宅（専用住宅／2003年）；ancora（山口県／工場、飲食店／2003年）；クリニック（広島県／歯科診療所／2003年）；テラス・ハウス（専用住宅／2002年）；三輪窯（山口県／保管庫／2002年）；エアー・ハウス（専用住宅／2001年）；Running Green Project（山口県／海浜公園施設／2001年）；Less（専用住宅／2001年）；ケース・スタディ・ハウス（専用住宅／2000年）

HIROSHI SAMBUICHI

Born in 1968. Established Sambuichi Architects in Hiroshima and since 2011 an adjunct professor at the Royal Danish Academy of Fine Arts, School of Architecture. Main awards received include 2003 Yoshioka Prize, 2010 Japan Institute of Architecture Grand Prix, 2011 Architectural Institute of Japan Prize.

WORKS

Hiroshima Orizuru Tower *(2016 / Hiroshima / Office building, product promotion centre, restaurant and observatory)* ; Naoshima Hall *(2015 / Kagawa / Multi-purpose hall and community centre)* ; House in Naoshima - Matabe *(2015 / Private residence and guesthouse)* ; Miyajima Misen Observatory *(2013 / Hiroshima / Observatory)* / Hakushima Office *(2011 / Hiroshima / Office)* ; House of Velocities *(2010 / Private residence)* ; Miwagama II *(2010 / Yamaguchi / Guesthouse, gallery and warehouse)* ; Rokko Observatory *(2010 / Hyogo / Observatory)* ; Miyajima Office *(2008 / Hiroshima / Office)* ; Wood Egg Okonomiyaki museum *(2008 / Hiroshima / Gallery)* ; Energy Penthouse *(2008 / Private residence)* ; Inujima Seirensho Art Museum *(2008 / Okayama / Museum)* ; Project West *(2007 / Private residence)* ; Base Valley *(2007 / Private residence)* ; Sun House *(2007 / Private residence)* ; Nonoyama Orthodontic Clinic *(2006 / Hiroshima / Dentist)* ; Stone House *(2005 / Private residence)* ; Farmer's House *(2005 / Private residence)* ; brood *(2005 / Shop and restaurant)* ; Kakuda Dental Clinic *(2004 / Hiroshima / Dentist)* ; Sloping North House *(2003 / Private residence)* ; ancora *(2003 / Yamaguchi / Bakery and restaurant)* ; Clinic *(2003 / Hiroshima / Dentist)* ; Terrace House *(2002 / Private residence)* ; Miwagawa *(2002 / Yamaguchi / Warehouse)* ; Air House *(2001 / Private residence)* ; Running Green Project *(2001 / Yamaguchi / Seaside park)* ; Less *(2001 / Private residence)* ; Case Study House *(2000 / Private residence)*

ストーン・ハウス Stone House 2005	北向傾斜住宅 Sloping North House 2002	Running Green Project Running Green Project 2001
三輪窯 Miwagama 2002	Base Valley Base Valley 2007	角田歯科医院 Kakuda Dental Clinic 2004
Miyajima Office 船倉税理士事務所 Miyajima Office 2008	エアー・ハウス Air House 2001	オタフクソース Wood Egg お好み焼館 Wood Egg Okonomiyaki museum 2008

作品情報

宮島弥山展望台
宮島の弥山山頂にある、環境省が設置する展望休憩施設。麓に位置する嚴島神社から1時間半ほど登った山頂付近は、大聖院弥山本堂、霊火堂をはじめとした神社仏閣の信仰の場でもある。嚴島神社と共に、弥山原始林(国の天然記念物)は世界遺産に指定されている。自然を体感できる登山道は、お勧め。紅葉谷から広電グループの運営するロープウェイも利用できる。本書掲載の建築写真は特別な許可を取って撮影したものであり現在の状況とは異なる。
(広島県廿日市市宮島町弥山)
www.miyajima.or.jp/sightseeing/ss_misen

六甲枝垂れ
神戸市六甲山系にある阪急阪神東宝グループ六甲山観光株式会社が運営する展望施設。毎年冬には周囲の氷棚より氷の切り出しが行われ、氷室に保存される。夏のはじめには氷室開きをし、夏には中央の風室にて冷風体験が楽しめる。秋には六甲ミーツ・アート 芸術散歩が開催される。
(兵庫県神戸市灘区六甲山町五介山1877-9)
www.rokkosan.com/gt

犬島精錬所美術館
犬島精錬所美術館は、犬島に残る銅製錬所の遺構を保存・再生した美術館。「在るものを活かし、無いものを創る」というコンセプトのもとつくられた美術館は既存の煙突やカラミ煉瓦、太陽や地熱などの自然エネルギーを利用した環境に負荷を与えない三分一博志の建築と、日本の近代化に警鐘をならした三島由紀夫をモチーフにした柳幸典の作品、また植物の力を利用した高度な水質浄化システムを導入している。「遺産、建築、アート、環境」による循環型社会を意識したプロジェクト。
企画運営:公益財団法人福武財団
アート:柳 幸典
建築:三分一博志
(岡山県岡山市東区犬島327-4)
benesse-artsite.jp/art/seirensho.html

直島の家またべえ
民家/ゲストハウス。非公開。瀬戸内国際芸術祭2016に際して、特別内覧会を予定。
管理:公益財団法人福武財団
(香川県香川郡直島町)

直島ホール
直島町が運営する町民会館。町民のレクリエーション施設であり、直島女文楽の練習場としても使われる。10月に本村で行われる八幡神社秋祭りでは中心施設として賑わい、瀬戸内国際芸術祭2016の会場・作品のひとつに選ばれている。建築家石井和紘の直島町役場に隣接する。本村集落内には家プロジェクトや建築家安藤忠雄のANDO MUSEUMが点在する。
管理:直島町教育委員会
(香川県香川郡直島町696-1)

おりづるタワー
広島マツダによって運営される複合施設。展望台、物産館、飲食店舗、オフィスからなる。建築家丹下健三の広島平和記念資料館、イサム・ノグチの平和大橋、建築家ヤン・レッツェルの広島県産業奨励会館(現世界遺産原爆ドーム)に隣接する。北には建築家大高正人の市営基町高層アパートや広島城が見える。展望台南西からは広島の街並み、遠くは宮島までを臨め、ふたつの世界遺産を観ることができる。開業は2016年9月を予定。
(広島県広島市中区大手町1-2-1)
www.orizurutower.jp

*各施設の詳細や、イベント情報等は管理先へお問い合わせいただくか、ウェブサイトにてご確認ください。(2016年3月現在)

WORKS

Miyajima Misen Observatory
An observatory established by the Ministry of the Environment at the summit of Mount Misen, on Miyajima island. From Itsukushima Shrine, which is located at the foot of the mountain, it takes about one-and-a-half hours to ascend to the summit, in the vicinity of which are the temples and shrines of various religious sects, including the temples and shrines of Misen Daisyoin temple and the Reikado (eternal fire hall). Together with Itsukushima Shrine, the Mount Misen Virgin Forest (a nationally protected natural monument) is designated as a UNESCO World Heritage site. If time allows, it is worth experiencing the natural environment along the mountain paths, but there is also a ropeway available part of the way. Special permission was obtained to take the architectural photographs published in this book, and they differ slightly from the present building.
(Mount Misen, Miyajima-cho, Hatsukaichi, Hiroshima)
www.miyajima.or.jp/english/index

Rokko Observatory
An observatory in Kobe's Rokko mountains, run by Hankyu Hanshin Toho Group Mt. Rokko Cable Car & Tourism Company. Every winter, ice is cut from the surrounding ice shelves then stored in ice rooms. At the beginning of summer the ice rooms are opened, and one can enjoy the experience of cool breezes in the centrally located wind room. In autumn, "Rokko Meets Art" walking tours are held.
(Gosukeyama 1877-9, Rokkosan-cho, Nada-ku, Kobe-shi, Hyogo)
www.rokkosan.com/gt

Inujima Seirensho Art Museum
Breathing new life into the ruins of a former copper refinery, Inujima Seirensho Art Museum was built around the idea of "using what exists to create what is to be". Exhibited here are works created by Yukinori Yanagi who used Yukio Mishima as a motif, a vocal critique of Japan's modernization, together with the remodeled architecture designed by Hiroshi Sambuichi. By using the existing smokestacks and karami bricks from the refinery as well as solar, geothermal, and other natural energies, the architectural design minimizes the construction's environmental impact. The building also employs a sophisticated water purification system that makes use of the power of plants. The project truly embraces the concept of a recycling-based society through its focus on industrial heritage, architecture, art, and the environment.
Administration: Fukutake Foundation / Art: Yukinori Yanagi / Architects: Sambuihi Architects
(327-4 Inujima, Higashi-ku, Okayama-shi, Okayama)
benesse-artsite.jp/en/art/seirensho.html

House in Naoshima - Matabe
Private residence / guesthouse. Not open to the public. A special preview has been planned for the occasion of Setouchi International Art Festival 2016.
Administration: Fukutake Foundation
(Naoshima-cho, Kagawa-gun, Kagawa)

Naoshima Hall
A public hall managed by Naoshima-cho. It is a facility for citizens' recreation, and also used for practicing Naoshima Onna Bunraku. Each October it is the central facility of the Hachiman Autumn Festival held in Honmura, and has been chosen as one of the venues and works of the 2016 Setouchi International Art festival. It is next to the Naoshima Town Hall, designed by architect Kazuhiro Ishii. Honmura village is also dotted with Art House Projects and the Ando Museum about and designed by architect Tadao Ando.
Administration: Naoshima-cho Board of Education
(Honmura 696-1, Naoshima-cho, Kagawa-gun, Kagawa)

Hiroshima Orizuru Tower
A multifunctional facility managed by Hiroshima Mazda. Consisting of an observatory, product promotion centre, restaurant, and office, it is near to the Hiroshima Peace Memorial Museum designed by architect Kenzo Tange, the Peace Bridge by Isamu Noguchi, and the Hiroshima Industrial Promotion Hall (currently the World Heritage–designated A-Bomb Dome) by architect Jan Letzel. Hiroshima Castle and the municipally managed Motomachi Apartments, designed by architect Masato Otaka, are visible to the north. From the southwest of the observatory there is a view of two World Heritage sites, as one can see the cityscape of Hiroshima as well as Miyajima in the distance. The opening is planned for September 2016.
(1-2 Naka-ku, Hiroshima-shi, Hiroshima)
www.orizurutower.jp

*For the details of each facility or information about events, please contact the respective administrators or check the listed websites. (Current as of March 2016)

寄稿者ほか

アレックス・ホメル・リー デンマークの建築家。アトリエ a.lee 主宰。コペンハーゲンを拠点として活動。デンマーク王立美術アカデミーにて博士研究員として「風土に根ざした建築の研究」を行なう。ルンゴー&トランベアの事務所勤務後、2006年以来さまざまな三分一のプロジェクトに参画。

モーエンス・プリップ=ブース デンマークの建築家。ヴィルヘルム・ヴォラートの下でルイジアナ現代美術館（コペンハーゲン）やニールス・ボーアのサマーハウスを設計。ヨーン・ウッツォンの下でシドニー・オペラハウスなどを手掛けた。アメリカ・イリノイ大学で准教授として教鞭を執った。ヨーン・ウッツォンに関する4冊の本の著作がある。

ミニック・ロージング デンマークの地質学者。コペンハーゲン大学付属デンマーク自然史博物館（地質学博物館）の教授。地球の生命の起源と、地球の地質学的進化への生命の影響を研究。2012年ヴェネツィア・ビエンナーレのデンマーク主任学芸員を務める。グリーンランド社会の調和のとれた発展にも尽力。

福武總一郎 公益財団法人福武財団理事長／株式会社ベネッセホールディングス最高顧問。岡山県出身。早稲田大学理工学部卒業。1973年福武書店（現ベネッセホールディングス）入社。1986年代表取締役社長。2007年代表取締役会長兼CEO。2014年同社最高顧問に就任。直島・豊島・犬島など瀬戸内海の島々を自然・アート・建築で活性化する活動（ベネッセアートサイト直島）を25年以上にわたって指揮。

千代章一郎 建築論。広島大学大学院工学研究院准教授。京都大学大学院工学研究科博士後期課程修了。博士（工学）。主著に『ル・コルビュジエの宗教建築と「建築的景観」』の生成』（単著、中央公論美術出版）、『技術と身体』（共著、ミネルヴァ書房）、『都市の風土学』（共著、ミネルヴァ書房）、Vocabulaire de la spatialité japonaise（共著、CNRS Éditions）、『歩くこどもの感性空間』（単著、鹿島出版会）ほか。

CONTRIBUTORS

Alex Hummel Lee is a Danish architect and founder of atelier a.lee. He is currently based in Copenhagen as a ph.D. fellow at the Royal Danish Academy of Fine Arts researching endemic architecture. After having worked for Lundgaard & Tranberg he became apprentice for Hiroshi Sambuichi in 2006 and has collaborated with him on various projects since.

Mogens Prip-Buus is a Danish architect. He worked for Vilhelm Wohlert on the Louisiana Museum and the summerhouse for Niels Bohr, and 9 years for Jørn Utzon on the Sydney Opera House and other projects. He was for a time Associate Professor at University of Illinois, U.S.A. Has written four books about Jørn Utzon.

Minik Rosing is a professor of Geology at the Natural History Museum of Denmark, University of Copenhagen. He studies the origins of life on Earth and the influence of life on the geologic evolution of Earth. He was Chief Curator for the Danish contribution to the Architecture Biennale in Venice in 2012, and is strongly engaged in harmonious development of the Greenland society.

Soichiro Fukutake is Chairman of the Board of the Fukutake Foundation and Executive Adviser of Benesse Holdings, Inc. Concomitantly to leading Benesse Holdings since 1986 and developing the activities of the group to include education, language/global leadership training, lifestyles, and senior/nursing care, he has spearheaded the Inland Sea renaissance around Naoshima, Teshima and Inujima focused on art, nature and architecture for the past 30 years through the development of Benesse Art Site Naoshima.

Shoichiro Sendai is an architectural theoretician currently living in Hiroshima where he works as an associate professor, Doctor Eng., at the Graduate School of Engineering at Hiroshima University. Major Publications include "Fudo in City" (*Minerva*), "Technique and Body" (*Minerva*), "The Creation and "the Architectural landscape": the religious architecture of Le Corbusier" (*Chuokouronbijutsu*), "Vocabulaire de la spatialité japonaise" (*CNRS Éditions*), "Kansei Space of the Children" (*Kajima Institue Publishing Co., Ltd.*).

クレジット / CREDITS

写真・図版
PHOTOGRAPHS & DRAWINGS

新建築社 / Shinkenchiku-sha p.55
中国新聞社、2014年11月6日朝刊 / The Chugoku Shimbun, 2014/11/6 (Morning edition) p. 58
阿野太一 / Daici Ano pp. 148-151
Arup & Sambuichi Architects pp. 220-221
小川重雄 / Shigeo Ogawa pp. 225-227, p .229, p. 232 (top), pp. 233-237, pp. 239-240, pp. 242-243
Arup p. 287
Image courtesy of NASA pp.298-299

資料提供
MATERIALS PROVIDED BY

岡 哲郎 / Tetsuro Oka p. 130 (top left)
在本桂子 / Keiko Arimoto p. 130 (top right, bottom left)
おかやま古写真DB委員会 / Okayama old photographs DB Committee p.130 (bottom right)
国土地理院 / Geospatial Information Authority of Japan p. 185
瀬戸内海歴史民俗資料館 / Seto Inland Sea Folk History Museum p. 186
広島観光コンベンションビューロー / Hiroshima Convention & Visitors Bureau pp. 258-259 middle

出典
IMAGE SOURCE

『岡山県名鑑』岡山県名鑑編纂所、1911年
Okayama-ken meikan, *Okayama-ken Meikan Hensanjo*, 1991 p. 130 (middle right)

上記以外は三分一博志建築設計事務所
All other photographs and drawings provided by Sambuichi Architects.

＊数点に限り著作権が完全に判明しないものがありました。お心当たりの方は編集部までご連絡ください。
*The copyright holders could not be fully identified for several items. To provide this information, please contact our editorial department.

アート
ART

柳 幸典 Yukinori Yanagi:
「ヒーロー乾電池／ソーラー・ロック」2008
"Hero Dry Cell/Solar Rock" (2008) p. 150
「ヒーロー乾電池／イカロス・タワー」2008
"Hero Dry Cell/Icarus Tower" (2008) pp. 150-151

翻訳
TRANSLATIONS

トーマス・ダニエル Thomas Daniell:
p. 4, p. 9, p. 42, p. 47, p. 88, p. 99, p. 138, p. 153, pp. 159-161, p. 183, p. 196, p. 224, pp. 248-251, p. 276, p. 283, p. 299, p. 302
鈴木圭介 Keisuke Suzuki:
pp. 11-13, pp. 59-61, pp. 107- 109

英語キャプション執筆
ENGLISH CAPTIONS

アレックス・ホメル・リー / Alex Hummel Lee

編集協力
EDITORIAL COOPERATION

南風舎 / Nampoosha

三分一博志　瀬戸内の建築

2016年3月18日　初版第1刷発行
2022年4月20日　初版第4刷発行

著者：　　　三分一博志
発行者：　　伊藤剛士
発行所：　　TOTO出版（TOTO株式会社）
　　　　　　〒107-0062 東京都港区南青山1-24-3
　　　　　　TOTO乃木坂ビル2F
　　　　　[営業] TEL: 03-3402-7138
　　　　　　　　 FAX: 03-3402-7187
　　　　　[編集] TEL: 03-3497-1010
　　　　　　URL: https://jp.toto.com/publishing

ストーリー・レイアウト：　アレックス・ホメル・リー
編集：　　　イェンス・H・イェンセン
印刷・製本：大日本印刷株式会社

落丁本・乱丁本はお取り替えいたします。
本書の全部又は一部に対するコピー・スキャン・デジタル化等の無断複製行為は、著作権法上での例外を除き禁じます。本書を代行業者等の第三者に依頼してスキャンやデジタル化することは、たとえ個人や家庭内での利用であっても著作権上認められておりません。
定価はカバーに表示してあります。

© 2016 Hiroshi Sambuichi

Printed in Japan
ISBN978-4-88706-357-0